Mike Mansfield

Majority Leader

Mike Mansfield

Majority Leader

A Different Kind of Senate
1961–1976

Francis R. Valeo

M.E. Sharpe

Armonk, New York
London, England

Library of Congress Cataloging-in-Publication Data

Valeo, Francis Ralph, 1916–
Mike Mansfield, majority leader: a different kind of Senate,
1961–1976 / Francis R. Valeo.
p. cm.
Includes index.
ISBN 07656–0450–7 (hardcover : alk. paper)
1. Mansfield, Mike, 1903– . 2. Legislators—United States—Biography.
3. United States. Congress. Senate—Biography
4. United States—Politics and government—1945–1989. I. Title.
E840.8.M25V35 1999
973.92′092—dc21
[B]   98–55373
CIP

Printed in the United States of America

The publisher gratefully acknowledges the financial assistance of
The Maureen and Mike Mansfield Foundation.

The paper used in this publication meets the minimum requirements of
American National Standard for Information Sciences—
Permanence of Paper for Printed Library Materials,
ANSI Z 39.48-1984.

BM (c)   10   9   8   7   6   5   4   3   2   1

To my Wife

Beth

Whose assistance and confidence were the indispensable ingredients.

Contents

Introduction

Mike Mansfield of Montana led the Senate from 1961 until 1977. It was an unbroken tenure unequalled in the annals of the Senate. It extended through the administrations of four Presidents—John F. Kennedy, Lyndon B. Johnson, Richard M. Nixon, and Gerald R. Ford.

The Mansfield leadership witnessed some of the most tumultuous events in the history of the Republic. They were years when the vestiges of legal racial segregation that had survived almost a century after the Civil War were finally laid to rest. The Senate at last broke through the barrier of its own rules and legislated the colorblind treatment of all Americans. The Civil Rights Act of 1964 determined that segregation should end, thereby opening the way for the races to grow together as one nation.

The period of Mansfield's leadership also coincided with the conversion of the limited U.S. intrusion in Indochina into an ill-fated American war and then, thanks in part to the Senate's efforts, to a complete U.S. withdrawal. Before the Vietnam War was brought to a close, however, more than 50,000 American lives were forfeited in a futile pursuit of the "communist menace" in Southeast Asia.

The Mansfield years were also the years when political assassination extinguished the lives of three prominent national leaders—John F. Kennedy, Robert F. Kennedy, and Martin Luther King Jr. In the same period,

President Richard Nixon and Vice-President Spiro Agnew were forced to resign from office.

Notwithstanding these and other massive shocks, such as the torching and looting of many American cities by mobs, a major constructive transformation took place in the nation. It was precipitated by an outpouring of social legislation unmatched since the early years of Roosevelt's New Deal. Whether derived from Kennedy's New Frontier or Johnson's Great Society, for the most part, this legislation helped American society not only to hold together but to stay abreast of a rapidly changing world.

The book provides an account of majority leader Mansfield's stewardship of the Senate during this troubled period. In replacing Lyndon Johnson as leader, Mansfield brought a different style to the role. His was a quiet and understated approach, as contrasted with Johnson's, but it exercised profound influence on how the Senate reordered itself to meet the challenges of a new day.

Author and Sources

The author brought to the preparation of the book a quarter of a century of participation in the federal service, spent mostly in the legislative branch of the government and primarily in the Senate. In succession, he served as chief of the Foreign Affairs Division and Senior Specialist in International Relations at the Congressional Research Service of the Library of Congress, Staff Associate of the Senate Foreign Relations Committee, Assistant to the Majority Whip (Mansfield), Assistant to the Majority Leader (Mansfield), Secretary for the Senate Majority (Democratic), and elected Secretary of the Senate.

In preparing the book, the author relied heavily on these personal experiences. They provided opportunities for close-up observation of the Majority Leader and the changing practices of the Senate. In addition the author depended on a journal that he maintained through the years, supplemented by a volume in the oral history series of the Senate Historical Office. This volume resulted from recorded interviews of the author with Donald Ritchie, Associate Historian of the Senate.

The following publications were also consulted and were especially helpful in the preparation of the manuscript:

Charles and Barbara Whalen, *The Longest Debate: A Legislative History of the 1964 Civil Rights Act* (Cabin John, Maryland: Seven Locks Press, 1985).
Gregory A. Olson, *Mansfield and Vietnam, a Study in Rhetorical Adaptation* (East Lansing, Michigan State University Press, 1995).

Louis Baldwin, *Hon. Politician, Mike Mansfield of Montana* (Missoula, Montana, Mountain Press Publishing Company, 1979).

William Conrad Gibbons, *The U.S. Government and the Vietnam War.* Three Volumes prepared for the Committee on Foreign Relations, Washington, D.C., Congressional Research Service, Library of Congress, 1988.

Acknowledgments

I wish to express my gratitude, especially to the Historian of the Senate, Richard A. Baker, and to his Associate, Donald A. Ritchie, for their unfailing assistance. Thanks also are due to the Maureen and Mike Mansfield Foundation at the University of Montana and its Chairman, Charles D. Ferris, and Director, Philip West, for their interest and help. I owe a special debt to my son James A. Valeo and his wife Leslie and to Robert Luken; Mrs. Harry Holthusen; D. George Trotter; Hon. Eugene Zuckert, former Secretary of the Air Force; and Dr. William P. Smith, Vice President Emeritus of George Washington University. Their encouragement and assistance contributed greatly to the emergence of this book.

Frank Valeo
Chevy Chase, Md.
March 1999

Mike Mansfield

Majority Leader

Prelude

A Snowy Day in Washington

On Capitol Hill that morning in January 1961, the stage was set for a presidential inauguration. After weeks of hammering and sawing, a roofed platform had been added to the East Front of the Capitol. Beneath the towering dome, rows of seats were reserved for members of the House of Representatives and the Senate. In between were places for the Supreme Court justices, the diplomatic corps, and other principal participants. Facing the elevated platform, concentric arcs of benches filled the plaza, waiting to freeze the bottoms of the invited.

As night closed on the preinaugural day, searchlights shafted beams skyward through the curtain of falling snow, picking out the statue of freedom, shivering atop the great dome. Far below, the plaza was wrapped in white shrouds, with seats poking out of the snow, like scattered tombstones in a forlorn graveyard. In their midst, on a crisscrossed wooden scaffold, the press box lifted high into the air. The box stared across the plaza at the inaugural platform, poised to pour out an endless flow of words and electronic images. After midnight, the silence of the plaza was broken by the sound of tractors, scraping shovels, and groaning trucks, as laborers and soldiers worked through the night to make possible the ceremony scheduled for the next day. Soon the benches facing the platform emerged from the drifts in which they had been buried by seven inches of snow. Along the mile and a half inaugural route from the Capitol to the White House, the viewing stands were brushed clean. Abandoned cars were pushed up onto sidewalks. The plowed snow was piled high in order to open a passage for the parade of an expected 30,000 to 40,000 marchers.

Although the storm had ended, the biting cold continued to ride into the city on high winds said to be coming from Siberia. Such was the state of Soviet Russian–U.S. relations at the time that the fierce weather was interpreted by some as Russian scientific meddling with the atmosphere designed to spoil the occasion. Notwithstanding, Inaugural Day loomed bright with sunlight and cloudless blue skies. That was taken to be a good omen that counteracted the twenty-degree cold and the cutting wind.

Shortly before noon, a bubble-top limousine arrived at the White House. President Eisenhower entered the car to join President-elect Kennedy on the rear seat. Vice President-elect Lyndon Johnson and the Speaker of the House, Sam Rayburn, rode the jumpseats. The two principles, both in top hats, waved to the assembled crowds as the limousine made its way to the Capitol.

The swearing in by Chief Justice Earl Warren converted John F. Kennedy into the thirty-fifth president of the United States. At forty-three years of age, he was the youngest person ever to be elected to the office and the first Roman Catholic. Kennedy's Inaugural Address sounded a thrilling call for youthful boldness, the high-pitched resonance of Bostonian diction and the cadence of an Irish ancestry obscuring the underlying note of political conservatism that ran throughout his address. His words were augmented by the speakers who proceeded him. There was Robert Frost, who at eighty-six had composed a poem for the occasion and then abandoned the attempt to read it when a blinding sun made it impossible for him to see the words he had written. He had resorted instead to memory and given a moving rendition of an earlier work, "The Gift Outright." There were deep surges from the throat of Marian Anderson singing a new black dimension into the "Star Spangled Banner." This was the same Marian Anderson who only a few years before had been denied use of Constitution Hall down the street from the White House because of her color.

The ceremony over, the new president and the inaugural principals stayed on Capital Hill long enough to have the traditional lunch in the Senate. After lunch, joined by his young wife, Jackie, the president rejected his top hat and took his place at the head of the inaugural parade. Then came forty bands blaring out marching cadences under the direction of drum majorettes, bare legs blue from the cold, pirouetting and twirling batons with extra vigor to counteract the chill. A million spectators along the route cheered and stomped themselves warm.

Like pilgrims to Mecca, most of the viewers had streamed into the Capital to bear witness not only to a change in administrations but a change in generations. Kennedy had given meaning to their pilgrimage with his imperative to the young: "Ask not what your country can do for you but what you can do for your country." The words were stirring, but they did not clarify the direction of Kennedy's leadership. Would he pick up the threads of Roosevelt's New Deal, the interrupted social revolution diluted by the demands of World War II and almost lost in the strange brew of postwar prosperity, technological progress and anticommunist anxieties? Or would the accent of his presidency fall on extending the leading role of the United States in the world? Towering during World War II, that leadership was already stretched taut by the end of nuclear exclusivity, the indecisive war in Korea, the collapse of the U.S.-supported government on the Chinese mainland and the impact of the McCarthy witch hunts. Would the young president seek to reaffirm the promise of a stalwart, steadfast, and compassionate America that had provided purposeful leadership in war as well as the vision of a United Nations in a world free of war?

More than anything else, the victory being celebrated on that Inaugural Day was a victory not for specific changes but for change itself. In the exhilaration of the hour, few thought of the climactic struggle against racial segregation that lay three years ahead. Ahead, too, was the vast federal effort to populate the New Frontier and build a Great Society with federal action designed to soften the inequities produced by the fortuities of birth and the indifference of affluence to poverty. Ahead, too, was an orgy of political assassination, the catastrophe of Vietnam, Watergate, and a disenthrallment of Americans with their government.

All this lay in wait for the nation, for the president, and for the two houses of Congress whose members were gathered on the inaugural platform. Especially did it await the Senate, already undergoing inner changes that would profoundly affect the way it played its constitutional role in the years ahead. For eight years, Lyndon Johnson of Texas (Democratic majority leader), had driven the Senate. Then his election as vice president had positioned him only "a heartbeat" from the presidency and left him hanging there until an assassin's bullets cut down the president.

The new majority leader of the Senate was Mike Mansfield of Montana. Elected unanimously, he was known to his colleagues for his decency and dedication. But as a legislative leader, he was an unknown. What kind of Senate would it be without Johnson? What kind of Senate with Mansfield? What kind of Senate where, for too long, too much had gone undone, too many of the nation's needs had gone unmet?

1

Capitol Hill Transition, 1961

Long-time residents of the city watched with an amused tolerance as the Kennedy team began to arrive in Washington during the closing weeks of 1960. The players quickly broke out of postelection huddles, exuding a promise of volleyball action as they moved into key positions in the government. Indeed, volleyball vied with touch football as the Kennedy appointees' sport of choice, and they pursued both vigorously in any available space at any free moment. The hallmarks of the Kennedy men were turtleneck shirts and square-toed, high-rise shoes. They arrived at the office early and, with jackets slung over chair backs, worked and talked well past closing time. The younger members soon initiated the bizarre game of pushing each other and anyone else within reach into swimming pools. Before long, dozens of aspiring New Frontiersmen were coming home dripping wet.

As it settled into a routine, the Kennedy administration was depicted by the media as young, upbeat, and competitive. It was competent as well as calisthenic. It was serious without being insufferable. Most of all, it was seen as oriented toward service, rather than self-serving. The description fit the new president. John F. Kennedy was a known quantity, having been a member of both the House of Representatives and the Senate prior to his bold reach for the presidency. He was a vigorous, handsome, self-confident, and sharply intelligent young man. He flashed a quick smile that, if not as broad as Eisenhower's, was at least as winning. As for his wife, Jackie, the new first lady was scintillating, charming, sophisticated, but still adequately domesticated for the times. While her penchant for moving with the international jet set did cause some eyebrows to go up, they were lowered again at the sight of her two all-American children. Pretty Caroline and her brother, John John, playing uninhibitedly on the White House lawn, were a delight, especially to the grandparents of the nation.

Change was written all over the new administration. The Kennedys and their associates displayed a degree of intellectual openness, a receptivity to new ideas, and a fresh idiom, the likes of which had not been seen in Washington since before the Joe McCarthy era of the early 1950s, indeed, not since the New Deal days of the Roosevelt administration. For all the openness, however, it quickly became apparent to members of the Senate and House that the new president would not permit the administration to be carried away by its inner exuberance. Kookiness was not acceptable. Before long, a frown from the president subdued the pool pushers. And notwithstanding an enlarged degree of intellectual tolerance, the politically correct remained quite circumscribed.

As if to underscore the steadiness of his course, Kennedy designated to his cabinet an orthodox mix of appointees drawn from business, politics, the universities, conservative labor circles, and Washington fixtures. For secretary of state, Kennedy reached into the permanent bureaucracy of the department and pulled out Dean Rusk of Georgia. As had Eisenhower, Kennedy went to the auto industry in Detroit and coopted Robert McNamara from the Ford Motor Company for secretary of defense. This appointment, in particular, provided a foot in the door of the federal government for the "whiz kids" of the emerging computer era. As it often did, Wall Street contributed the secretary of the treasury in the person of C. Douglas Dillon, an investment banker. A Republican patrician, Dillon had just completed a tour of service as Eisenhower's ambassador to France. Choosing him for participation in a Democratic administration appears to have been rationalized both by noting his reputation for progressivism, at least as defined by investment bankers, and by the need to reassure the public of the administration's fiscal conservatism.

The Search for a New Leader

Even though immersed in its own restructuring after the election, the Senate lost no time in confirming Kennedy's initial appointments. As in the House of Representatives, Democrats remained in control of the Senate but with the need to select a new majority leader to replace Lyndon Johnson. A number of senators were ready and willing to succeed Johnson, but in due course the choice narrowed down to three. Pushed forward by leading liberals was the name of Hubert H. Humphrey of Minnesota. In the earlier days of his career in Washington, the quixotic Humphrey, driven by his unique mix of inner demons and angels, seemed always in pursuit of an office just beyond the reach of his outstretched fingers. No sooner had he settled into one niche of the political hierarchy than he was off in pursuit of another. He had sought and lost the Democratic vice presidential nomination in 1956 to Estes Kefauver of Tennessee. In 1960, his defeat by Kennedy in the West Virginia primary ended his bid for the presidential nomination. When the irrepressible Humphrey cast his eye next on the vice presidential candidacy, that, too, was blocked by the formidable frame of Lyndon Johnson. Where to turn next?

The majority leadership of the Senate loomed into view, momentarily, as Humphrey's Holy Grail. In the mysterious ways of Senate communication, before the mass introduction of computers, word went from one corridor to the next that Hubert Humphrey was President Kennedy's selection for Senate majority leader. As evidence, it was pointed out that Humphrey was clearly closest to the president in ideological affinity. There were confirming nods and leaks to the press from obscure staff personnel in the White House, friendly Senate colleagues, and Humphrey's own staff.

Contrary to the rumors, Kennedy was not drawn toward Humphrey but shied away from him as a choice for the Senate leadership. At that point, Humphrey's aggressive liberalism, particularly on civil rights, had placed him beyond the pale in the eyes of southern Democrats. Among them were several chairmen of congressional committees who held the keys to Kennedy's legislative program. For the president to have favored Humphrey at this point would have been to wave a red flag before those powerful figures on Capitol Hill without whose acquiescence the New Frontier was unlikely to have been pushed forward at all.

As the brash young mayor of Minneapolis, Humphrey had sparked the successful drive to include a strong civil rights plank in the Democratic Party's platform for the 1948 presidential campaign. One of the political results was a formal split in the solid Democratic South. Senator Strom Thurmond of South Carolina moved his seat to the Republican side of the aisle on the Senate floor. The Democratic solons in the Senate, mostly from below the Mason-Dixon Line, had neither forgotten nor forgiven Humphrey for being in the vanguard of an issue that was to recast the politics of the South.

On those grounds alone, Kennedy would have steered away from Humphrey as Senate majority leader. The president was also familiar with the

Minnesotan's irresistible urge to grab the spotlight. Having first claim himself, as president, Kennedy had no desire to relinquish it to an ambitious majority leader of the Senate. He wanted no ambiguity as to the source of the Democratic Party's program; it would be the White House, not Capitol Hill. Finally, the president's memory was long and, notwithstanding his ready smile, his was not a forgiving nature. He had not appreciated Humphrey's tenacity in the campaign for the Democratic presidential nomination. In particular, he remembered being confronted repeatedly by Humphrey's moonlike smile during the vicious West Virginia primary where Kennedy's Roman Catholicism had been injected into the contest by a whispering campaign. It was never clear whether the origins of this use of bigotry to derail Kennedy's drive to the nomination came from Humphrey's camp or Johnson's or neither. In any event, since politics thrives on the conspiratorial, it was not difficult for the Kennedy people to assume that Humphrey had been part of a plot to pull the rug from under Kennedy in West Virginia.

The release of the trial balloon for Humphrey as Senate majority leader, however, was sufficient to raise anxiety levels in conservative Democratic circles. Without delay, the name of George Smathers was sent aloft like a Chinese fighting kite to puncture it. A new flood of rumors suddenly rushed through the Senate corridors. Not Humphrey but the handsome young senator from Florida was said to be President Kennedy's real choice for the Senate leadership. Smathers was recalled as having been the president's regular companion in a merry pursuit of women during their bachelor days in Congress. The rumors stopped short, but only barely, of allegations that they were still engaged jointly in the same nocturnal pursuits.

While they did not mind a Smathers boomlet as a counter to Humphrey, southern leaders did not want it pushed to the point of an irrevocable break in the party ranks. Their continued dominance of the legislative process depended on a Democratic majority in the Senate. That, in turn, required a semblance of unity among the Democrats, at least enough to ensure their own chairmanships of the legislative committees.

As the time drew near for the party caucus to elect the new Senate majority leader, attention shifted to a search for a realistic alternative to both Humphrey and Smathers. One was discovered under everyone's nose in the person of Mike Mansfield of Montana. After his first term in the Senate, Mansfield had served as majority whip or assistant leader of the Senate Democrats. He had been selected for that post by Lyndon Johnson.

Shortly after Mansfield had been hand-picked as party whip by Lyndon Johnson, the latter had suffered a serious heart attack in June 1955 that forced him to curtail his activities. This enabled Mansfield to obtain a considerable exposure on the Senate floor. He performed without a hitch as Johnson's faithful understudy. Conducting the Senate's business with modesty, he created an unpretentious but vivid impression by his unassuming and nonconfrontational style of leadership, which stood in sharp contrast to Johnson's flamboyance.

Mansfield was on hand in Washington during the weeks prior to the opening of the new Congress in January 1961. He stayed close to his whip's office on the gallery floor of the Capitol, making no effort to seek votes for his election as majority leader. To all outward appearances, he was a noncandidate. When pressed on his intentions, he assured his questioners that he had achieved his highest political ambition in being elected a senator from Montana. He also reminded them that elevation from majority whip to majority leader was not automatic, that each office was filled by a separate election in the Democratic caucus. He went even further in dissociating himself from pursuit of the office by volunteering the thought that either of the two frequently mentioned candidates—Humphrey of Minnesota or Smathers of Florida—would make an excellent leader. Mansfield's comments were eagerly interpreted in the Humphrey and Smathers camps as an expression of disinterest on Mansfield's part, and they beat the drums even louder for their respective candidates.

Before long, the rumblings were heard at the other end of Pennsylvania Avenue. Both the president and vice president recognized the danger of a disastrous split among the Democrats in the Senate if the choice were to be either Humphrey or Smathers. Both turned to Mansfield, Johnson telephoning first to express the view that as whip, he had a responsibility to the party and the Senate to assume the leadership. Mansfield's response was noncommittal as he continued to extol the virtues of the two ostensible candidates. Johnson brushed off his comments, insisting that neither Humphrey nor Smathers would be suitable for the situation. After some hesitancy, Mansfield asserted that he would not even consider the matter unless the president were in agreement with Johnson.

A call from the White House was not long in coming. In response to Kennedy's question: "What's this I hear about your not taking the Senate leadership?" Mansfield acknowledged his hesitancies. He ascribed them in part to his Roman Catholic and Irish origins, pointing out that if he were chosen, the three highest elected offices of the federal government, that of president, Speaker of the House, and majority leader of the Senate, would be occupied by men with the same religious and cultural roots. This coincidence, he thought, might not sit well with the public, especially since Kennedy was the first president of Roman Catholic faith. Kennedy reacted to these hesitancies with irritation, pointing out that he had already suffered that anachronism and was under the impression that he had disposed of it once and for all during the presidential campaign. With some impatience, he expressed the hope that he would not have to go over the same ground with the senator from Montana. Mansfield then agreed to take the Senate leadership provided, of course, that the Senate Democratic caucus chose him. The two phone calls cleared the way for his formal election as majority leader.

Word of his endorsement by the president and vice president quickly spread through the Senate, immediately deflating the Humphrey and Smathers balloons but causing little pain and no damage to the party. The liberals who had supported Humphrey found in Mansfield an acceptable alternative. If Mansfield was not exactly one of them, he was at least a westerner with a reputation as a progressive. Nor could they find much to quarrel with in his voting record either in the House or Senate.

To the southerners, Mansfield was a complex man, not nearly as raw-boned as he appeared. What they did understood of him was sufficient to predispose them to acceptance. They were satisfied that Mansfield was a cautious, conscientious, fair-minded senator who offered the best prospect for preserving sufficient unity to continue Democratic control of the Senate and hence their dominance of key committees. They also were aware that Mansfield was knowledgeable in international affairs, a skill still in very short supply on Capitol Hill. He had been strongly endorsed by the former chairman of the Foreign Relations Committee, Senator Walter George of Georgia, an endorsement that carried great weight with them.

Perhaps most important, southerners saw Mansfield as highly respectful of Senate traditions. His fondness for saying that he had achieved his "highest ambition" when he became a United States senator fell on receptive ears because, as southern legislative professionals, they themselves had arrived at the same point. In short, as they saw him, Mansfield had the makings of a solid Senate institutionalist, regardless of how he might vote on specific issues.

With the endorsement of both Kennedy and Johnson, his acceptability to both liberal and conservative Democratic colleagues, and an anchor in the articulate support of western Democrats, the senator from Montana was well positioned to appeal to the caucus as the logical selection. Mansfield was chosen majority leader by unanimous vote. In winning the leadership, Mansfield had made no promises and entailed no debts.

Late in December 1960, the Senate Democrats gathered in caucus, preliminary to the formal opening of the new Congress.

The primary purpose of the caucus of this initial Democratic conference was to welcome the newly elected Democratic senators and to make the formal choice of a new Senate majority leader. Lyndon Johnson, the carry-over majority leader, presided as chairman of the caucus.

Mansfield's name was quickly endorsed by Spessard Holland of Florida, a very articulate member of the southern contingent. Although not known for succinctness, Holland was the soul of brevity on this occasion, as if to discourage a prolonged reaching for what was a foregone conclusion. Brief secondings of the nomination came from representatives of all regional and ideological segments of the party. As expected, there were no other nominations, and Mansfield was elected by acclamation. Amid a standing ovation, Mansfield accepted the gavel proffered by Johnson, and the latter took a seat at the rear of the rostrum.

In his first acts as leader of the Democrats, Mansfield proposed that Hubert Humphrey be named assistant leader and George Smathers secretary of the Democratic conference. The nominations came as no surprise. Prior to the caucus, Johnson had suggested to Mansfield that the two men be included in the leadership but in reverse order. Mansfield demurred, insisting on Humphrey as assistant leader, and Johnson had not pressed his preference for Smathers. At the time, this did not seem to be a matter of great significance. As majority leader, Johnson had created the impression that the other two party leaders were essentially appendages of the majority leader, subject only to the most routine confirmation by the caucus. This impression had been accepted by Democrats themselves, as well as by the media. Mansfield seemed to be operating under the same prerogative when he proposed Humphrey and Smathers as second and third, respectively, in the party hierarchy. There were no challenges, and both men were elected unanimously.

The Legacy of LBJ

Mansfield's next proposal also brought what appeared to be a unanimous reaction, but of another kind. The new majority leader asked the caucus to name Vice President Lyndon Johnson as permanent presiding officer of the Democratic caucus. The immediate reaction to the proposal was one of shocked silence. It was as though a newly arrived mother superior had begun her tenure in a convent by naming the devil as the CEO. Mansfield's proposal was objectionable not only to those Democratic senators who were angry with Johnson for what they regarded as personal wrongs suffered under his leadership; it was also a kind of heresy. From early times, Senate traditionalists have sought to curb the influence of vice presidents in Senate affairs. The effort had long since succeeded in reducing the vice president's role to its bare constitutional bones, that of presiding over the Senate and casting a tie-breaking vote.

To be sure, what Mansfield had proposed was not related to the vice president's official functions. Instead, it involved the leadership structure of the Democratic Party in the Senate. The speechless Democrats, however, drew no such distinction. What they chose to hear was the continuation of Johnson's domination of the Senate by other means, and that they did not wish to hear.

Mansfield's election had drawn a momentary mantle of amiability over the Senate Democrats. With this proposal, the mantle was snatched away like a magician's cloak, to expose a den of hissing furies. What had been until then about as disputatious as a Lion's Club luncheon gave way to a crescendo of denunciation, sarcasm, and indignation. Paul Douglas of Illinois, Joe Clark of Pennsylvania, and several others were on their feet with heads shaking negatively, groping for words. The voice of Albert Gore Sr. of Tennessee, a Senate moderate, rose above the sputtering to express in his deliberate and erudite style what was obviously a widely shared sentiment. His face was flushed with indignation beneath the neat and orderly waves of gray hair, and his speech was slow and deliberate as he released his words in a prolonged drawl, intensifying the agony that they seemed intended to inflict on Lyndon Johnson. Gore expressed amazement at the unprecedented suggestion of the new majority leader, namely, that a vice president should be intruded into the affairs of the Senate. He warned of insidious consequences to the Senate's independence. Then he went to the heart of his complaint. He ran off a checklist of grievances, both real and imagined, that senators had suffered for eight years under the leadership of the towering Texan. There were those who suspected that Gore's anger was fed, at least, as much by Johnson's frustration of the Tennessean's personal aspiration to the presidency. Whatever the reasons, Gore laid out the sore points felt by many senators.

It is difficult to believe that Mansfield did not realize the kind of response that his proposal would evoke. He had stood quietly with a look of almost quizzical amusement on his face as the accumulated complaints of the prior eight years poured forth, flowed by him, and came to rest on Johnson, whose face grew redder with each new blast from the assemblage. Mansfield finally interrupted. He had advanced the suggestion, he explained, because he felt that Johnson could continue to make a major contribution to the Senate Democrats. He went to great pains to assure his colleagues that the idea of designating the vice president as presiding officer had been his alone, that he had discussed it with no one. It was, he repeated several times, entirely his own idea. With each repetition, fewer members believed that to be true. Instead, the murmurs of disbelief indicated that they were beginning to suspect that Mansfield had been had by

Johnson. In turn, they had no wish to be had by a Mansfield who, as majority leader, would not be much more than Johnson's surrogate.

Dick Russell interrupted the effusive defense of Johnson in which Mansfield seemed determined to smother himself. The Georgian pointed out in a fraternal but firm manner that the caucus had been unanimous in its selection of Mansfield to serve as majority leader, and the Senate Democrats wanted him to function fully in that role. Presiding over the caucus was a responsibility that precedent assigned to the majority leader. Besides, he noted, the vice president would have many new responsibilities in the executive branch and therefore would have little time to spare for Capitol Hill. He was supported by grunts and hurrumphs from all parts of the room.

As noted earlier, one of those who had joined in the denunciation of the proposal was Joe Clark of Pennsylvania. As the quintessential scold of the period, Clark took sadistic pleasure in lecturing the Senate periodically on one or another of its shortcomings. Now, face to face with a large captive audience, he decided to air his complaints once again and to try to sell his particular bag of reforms to the Democratic caucus. The main thrust of Clark's proposals was aimed at breaking up the concentration of power that rested in the hands of the southerners as a result of the seniority system and group cohesiveness. One of the changes Clark proposed was a reshuffling of the membership on the two principal party leadership committees: the Majority Policy Committee and the Steering Committee. Southerners were preeminent on both committees, and northern liberals had come to feel themselves all but excluded from the direction of the party's affairs. It should be noted that southern domination of the two committees was not attributable to Johnson. It was derived from a slavish adherence to the seniority system. Because of their seniority, southern Democrats were disproportionately more numerous on the two party committees, as they were on key Senate committees.

Russell seized on Clark's complaints as a way of reaching a compromise with the liberals. He offered his own resignation from the party committees in order to open places for the new majority leader to fill so as to meet Clark's criticism. Following his lead, other southern senators indicated that they might be willing to do the same. Mansfield rejected Russell's offer, proposing instead to increase the overall membership on both committees in order to accommodate the complaining liberals. He assured the supporters of the Clark proposal that his appointments henceforth would reflect their concerns. To that end, he called on the caucus to adopt a resolution directing the majority leader to constitute the memberships of the two committees so as to reflect the geographic and ideological spread of the party's makeup in the Senate and to subject his appointments to confirmation by the caucus.

With this proposal, Mansfield began disassembling the power that Johnson had accumulated during his eight years as Democratic leader. Although Mansfield was heir to this accumulation, the Montanan consciously chose not to keep it. This first divestiture set a pattern that Mansfield was to follow again and again as he sought to respond to what he took to be the basic complaint against Johnson's dictatorial rule.

It is not clear whether the caucus ever bothered to act formally on Mansfield's proposal to empower Johnson to preside over future caucuses. A formal vote was lost in the general satisfaction with Mansfield's resolution of the problem. Nevertheless, the pent-up fury that had been released in his presence was not lost on Johnson. He left the room as soon as he could, not to return to a Democratic caucus for a long time. When he did come back, it was as a guest of the majority leader.

The outburst of anger had served as a reminder to Johnson that he could expect his role as vice president to be as circumscribed as his predecessors. It was true that the vice president was not only the constitutional understudy to the president but was also the constitutional "President of the Senate." In the latter role, Johnson would be confined to a small anteroom and a ceremonial office off the Senate Chamber to await a tie vote. Then he would be permitted to cast a decisive vote to break the tie. Or, if he desired, he could spend his time sitting in the presiding officer's chair on the Senate floor, listening to his former colleagues propound the issues of the day. As for the vice president's role as understudy to the president, he could remain under wraps, like a benched football star, with little to do but wait for an untimely demise or other removal of the president from the White House. In short, as vice president, Lyndon Johnson found himself without significant power in his own right unless the unexpected were to take place.

Nor was there likely to be a payoff later for patience in the political purgatory in which he found himself. The need for another Democrat to succeed Kennedy in less than eight years was very remote. If Johnson himself were still around in eight years, he would be regarded in all likelihood as too old to serve as the Democratic candidate for president. Even if that were not the case, an orderly succession to the presidency from the vice presidency depended on the exercise of a high degree of deference to the sitting president, a requirement that, try as he might, did not set well with Johnson's impatient and imperious personality.

Some of Kennedy's less experienced advisors assumed that the best place to use Johnson was on Capitol Hill, especially in the Senate. They were awed by his reputation as a legislative operator. He was, it was said, the greatest majority leader in Senate history. Why not have him continue to exercise his legislative legerdemain in the Senate on behalf of the new administration? It was a naive expectation showing little perception of the Senate and even less of Johnson's nature. Johnson was indisposed to play the role of advocate for anyone or anything if it did not serve, at the same time, his own purposes. There was, to be sure, some of the rural populist in his ideological makeup and the social measures of Kennedy's New Frontier; especially those things having to do with the welfare of the old or education of the young had a personal appeal for him. His social conscience was well diluted, however, by what had become at that point his realistic appreciation of money as a principal mover in politics. As for supporting the president, both Kennedy and Johnson understood that their marriage in the 1960 election was one of political convenience. Johnson brought to it a dowry of the critical Texas electoral votes and, perhaps, the margin of victory in other southern states. He received, in return, the vice presidency and with it an outside chance of becoming president at some time in the future.

Even if Johnson had been prepared to run interference for the administration on Capitol Hill, it would have been an exercise in futility. Attempts to use the vice presidency to advance a president's program are scattered through Senate history. Invariably, the attempts have run into the rigid parameters of the office of "President of the Senate." By long-established tradition, vice presidents have been regarded not as of the Senate but merely out to pasture in the Senate. As for the constitutional power to cast a significant tie-breaking vote, that was an event that occurred two or three times, if that often. Otherwise, if a vice president insisted on remaining on Capitol Hill, he was confined to presiding over the Senate. In that role, he could repeat, in rote fashion, the opinions and procedural rulings whispered to him by the professional parliamentarian. Few occupants of the vice presidency chose to waste time in that fashion, yielding the gavel instead to the Senate's other constitutional presiding officer, the President Pro Tempore, elected by the Senate itself, who was by custom the senior senator of the majority party. The President Pro Tempore, in turn, usually designated the chore of presiding to others, more often than not to first-term members of their party.

Traditionally, Senate leadership has not rested in the hands of the vice president or even the majority leader. It was collective, rather than concentrated, divided among the chairmen of the legislative committees, the party committees, the floor leader, whip or assistant leader, the secretary of the party caucus, and the President Pro Tempore. Technically, these leaders were elected every two years, with seniority and incumbency the major determinants.

As a senator, Lyndon Johnson had been elected minority floor leader by the Senate Democrats in 1953 and majority leader in 1955. Young and energetic and with a lust for power, Johnson proceeded to enlarge the functions of the majority leader into a concentrated power base, something closely akin to that of the Speaker of the House. By the time he left the Senate in 1961, Johnson's reach as majority leader included the chairmanship of the party's Steering Committee, the Majority Policy Committee, and the Campaign Committee. He also reserved for himself the authority to handpick the whip and secretary of the party. He stopped short, however, of challenging the seniority system as it applied to the chairmanships of the Senate legislative committees, seeking instead to gather the chairmen, mostly southerners and westerners, closely around himself.

In developing this concentration of power, Johnson had at first the indulgence of most of his Democratic colleagues. It was often obtained by a bold aggressiveness that smothered objections even before they had a chance to be expressed. Physically, Johnson was well equipped for this approach. His nasal-twanged voice carried well not only within the Senate Chamber but through the swinging doors of the cloakrooms at the rear, where members sometimes repaired to get away from it. He could play it loud and rasping or soft but still piercing in a whispered *tête-a-tête*. He could project it hot with deeply felt anger or cold with furious sarcasm. He knew when to pray and when to curse, and he shifted with ease from one to the other. In short, he handled his tongue and larynx, those most useful tools of politics, with a crude but considerable skill. His towering height was an additional asset, permitting him to slant his eyes downward in addressing most of his colleagues and upward toward the ceiling in invoking God's assistance against a recalcitrant colleague. For the few who equaled him in height, he could maintain eye contact whether lifting himself on his toes or rocking backward on his heels. He used his edge in height often in face-to-face encounters, grasping jacket lapels or applying a kind of half-Nelson to prevent evasive action on the part of his prey.

As majority leader, Johnson had the support of the southern wing of the party, except on the issue of civil rights. He also enjoyed considerable backing from western Democrats. The northern liberals were the most difficult to bring around. To them, he offered choice committee assignments. He burnished already inflated egos. He soothed real or imagined slights. He probed for individual weaknesses, needs, and divisions and exploited them unashamedly. He passed out senatorial goodies, mostly trivial, yet so dear to some—a hideaway office in the Capitol, an honorarium at a petroleum producers' conference or independent grocers' association meeting. He saw to their presence at a ceremonial bill signing by the president in the presence of the press. He flattered members' wives and paid homage to their families. He saw to it that legislative favors were granted to converts and denied to recalcitrants, using his influence to release a pet bill from committee captivity or moving another up or down in time on the calendar for consideration by the Senate. He postponed debate to accommodate a member off on a speaking engagement. Most important, he steered campaign funds to which he had access in accord with the political dictum that "a friend in need is a friend indeed," and then had no hesitancy in calling on that friendship when he needed it.

Johnson wore a liberal stripe one day, a conservative the next. When the stakes were high, however, he seemed most often to come down on the side of decisive power, on the side of selected committee chairmen and those members with ready access to political money. It was not so much a matter of personal conviction but an obsession with what worked, with what served to strengthen his hold on the Senate, especially on the Democratic members of the Senate.

Johnson's tactics as majority leader performed wonders at the outset. For the first time in many years, Senate Democrats gave the appearance of belonging to the same party. Such effective opposition as there was to the Eisenhower administration was seen by the press as centering in the Senate and in the person of Lyndon Johnson.

The longer Johnson persisted in these tactics, however, the less effective they proved to be. As time went on, they made fewer and fewer friends and more and more enemies. Pockets of irritated opposition began to form, especially among liberals and others who felt themselves shortchanged and those with scarcely concealed aspirations for the presidency who saw Johnson's formidable frame blocking the way.

Although the rumblings among his colleagues reached his ears, he seemed almost unaware of the shifting tide against his leadership. As became tragically evident later in Vietnam, Johnson had a great capacity for self-delusion. The press, fascinated by Johnson's colorful style, had built him up into something larger than Senate life. It was his nature to wallow in this press attention. The more he received, the harder he worked to live up to the image of superpolitician. Mansfield was led to say at one point, "The trouble with Lyndon is that he believes his own press notices."

Johnson was hurt, but by no means crushed, by the outburst of hostility he had experienced at the party's first caucus under the new Mansfield leadership. As vice president, Johnson persisted for a time in attempting to keep alive the illusion of his relevance to inner Senate affairs. Bobby Baker, who remained as secretary for the majority, acted as a go-between, keeping open Johnson's lines of communication to selected members on the floor. In this connection Johnson also sought to retain the office in the Capitol that he had occupied as majority leader. Offices in the Capitol were utilitarian in that they reduced the wear and tear on a member's legs in traveling repeatedly from the Senate floor to the Senate office buildings. They were also prized as status symbols, their value as such being calculated on the basis of proximity to the Senate floor and square footage.

As majority leader, Johnson had occupied the Brumidi Room. Located immediately off the Senate floor, the room was opulent in size and decor. It dated back to the construction of the Senate wing of the Capitol in the mid-nineteenth century. Its high, arched ceiling was lavished with the imposing frescoes of the Italian painter, Constantino Brumidi, whose work also adorns the Rotunda and other places in the Capitol. Despite the pleadings of the Capitol architect concerning the room's historic value, Johnson added trays of fluorescent lights to the ceiling and installed a bathroom and shower in one corner to accommodate himself as majority leader. The room was in constant use, serving as the setting for many long nights of whiskey drinking, wheeling and dealing, and other forms of camaraderie among senators of Johnson's inner circle. Reporters dubbed the room the "Taj Mahal."

Had Johnson been able to keep the "Taj Mahal," he would have fared far better than Richard Nixon as vice president. The latter, when he served as vice president under Eisenhower had been confined to a couple of small rooms in addition to the quasi-public ceremonial room traditionally reserved for the president of the Senate. When he became vice president, Johnson sought to retain the Brumidi Room, a request Mansfield firmly denied. Instead, the room was placed under the personal protection of the majority leader, and the Capitol architect was directed to restore it. The fluorescent lights were removed from the ceiling. The blinds were drawn, and the lights that once had burned long into the night to accommodate Johnson's insomnia and his penchant for strategy sessions in the early morning hours were no longer lit. For several years thereafter, the room remained in darkness, except for an occasional ceremonial usage. After a while the "Taj Mahal" was forgotten, and, lest its most famous occupant suffer the same fate, Mansfield had fastened to the entrance a small brass plaque to commemorate Johnson's occupancy of the room. Confined in space as he was restricted in function, Vice President Johnson, in time, accepted the reality of his exclusion from Senate affairs.

The Style of a New Leader

The office that Mansfield occupied as the new majority leader was adjacent to the Brumidi Room. Mansfield affixed a similar plaque to these rooms to commemorate Kennedy's brief use of them as president-elect prior to his moving into the White House.

Previously occupied by the sergeant-at-arms, Mansfield's office had a subdued and utilitarian look, that is, utilitarian in the late-nineteenth-century sense of the word, and was appropriately convenient to the Senate floor. The suite consisted of a small working office sandwiched between a large conference room and an outer reception room. On taking over the quarters, Mansfield made few changes. He retained the well-worn desks and tables and leather upholstered chairs, adding one chair brought with him from his previous office as Senate whip. It was a Victorian piece, barrel shaped, with the seat set too low to the floor for current human proportions. It had been designated the "Churchill Chair" because it was said that the British prime minister, on a visit to the Capitol during World War II, had sat in it and pronounced it the only comfortable chair in the city of Washington.

The drab green walls and the immense mahogany doors gave the rooms an aura of an older Senate, an impression reinforced by the dimly lit paintings that hung in the gloom of the inner rooms, a Rembrandt Peale portrait of George Washington, another of Thomas Jefferson, and others of legislative figures out of a faded time.

Lest the suite be mistaken for an anachronism, Mansfield added a few contemporary touches. He found it both nostalgic and esthetically satisfying to have around him several paintings of cowboys and Indians as depicted by such Montana artists as Charlie Russell and Ace Powell. He also found space for some carefully selected photographs in the inner rooms. One was a framed clipping from a magazine. It was a view of the backs of a little boy and a little girl dressed in nondescript clothing of the 1920s. They were holding hands and gazing into the distance. The picture was a sentimental one, filled with an inexpressible affection and a wisp of hope.

Another was a photograph of President Kennedy, surrounded by officials and Secret Service personnel at Griffith Stadium, the original home of the National League's Washington baseball team. Bent back, arm raised, the president is pictured as preparing to throw out the traditional first ball for what was the opening game of the season in 1961. In the photo, Mansfield is positioned directly behind Kennedy with arms stretched wide. "It looks as if I'm holding him up," Mansfield once said in showing the picture. "That's what I'm trying to do."

The majority leader began a normal working day at about 5:30 A.M. in his Montana State office in the original Senate Office Building, and ended it in the same place usually around 7:00 P.M. Of the time in between, six to eight hours would have been spent in the majority leader's office, in committee meetings, on the Senate floor, or elsewhere in the Capitol.

Lobbyists and other favor seekers, unless they were from Montana, found no welcome mat outside the door of the majority leader's office. Inside the office, Mansfield had the couch in the outer reception office removed so that the uninvited could not lounge but would have to sit in rather uncomfortable upright chairs if they insisted on seeing him. Unlike the Johnson period, rarely did representatives of the executive branch in search of a direct line to the Senate find it in Mansfield's office. They would be greeted courteously and might receive a cup of coffee and a suggestion that they see particular members of the committee relevant to their respective departments, but that would be all. If they were cabinet members, Mansfield would go so far as to make the arrangements for a meeting with the committee chairman, at the same time stressing the noninterventionist nature of his role. The majority leadership, which had been the master gear for everything of consequence that transpired between the Senate and the executive branch under Johnson's leadership, turned ever more slowly. And Mansfield wanted it that way. He was not only not reaching for ever-increasing power and influence but deliberately shunting off much that he had inherited from Johnson.

Mansfield's Capitol office saw fewer and fewer callers. Unfailingly, he continued to receive the relatively few Montana constituents who found their way to the Capitol. He also welcomed students in groups from anywhere and gave them a talk on civics, government, and the Senate. When a group of fifty high school students came from American Samoa, a territory he had visited previously, he threw a luau for them in his conference room and, for the first time in living memory, a hula of thanks was danced in the Capitol.

Mansfield was readily available to the press either in his office, in the corridors, or wherever reporters managed to find him. When the Senate was in session, he made it a practice to arrive on the floor a few minutes before the opening bells to accommodate the news reporters. In these presession press conferences, he volunteered little except the Senate program. He rarely read a prepared statement but held himself out to questions. His answers were matter of fact, laconically pertinent, sometimes humorous, and only rarely newsworthy. On Saturday mornings, reporters could generally find him in his office. The regulars who covered the Senate for the Associated Press and other news services, as well as an occasional independent who happened to be in the press gallery on a weekend, could come in for a cup of coffee, often poured by Mansfield himself. More often than not, they would receive enough commentary from the majority leader for a weekend story.

In all his years in Congress, Mansfield never engaged a press officer and never complained of his treatment by reporters who, in his words, "always have the last word." If anything, reporters felt disadvantaged by Mansfield's proclivity for answering questions with a yes, no, or an occasional maybe and by his refusal to be drawn into conflicts with them or anyone else. His brevity often left media people speechless. This was particularly true on television news shows such as *Meet the Press* or *Face the Nation*. After he began to appear with some regularity on these programs, interrogators learned that it was necessary in interviewing Mansfield to have on hand two or three times the usual number of prepared questions or risk running out of profundity before running out of time.

In due course, the stampede of reporters who had beaten a path to Lyndon Johnson's Senate fell off drastically. Gone were the well-planned confrontations with the Eisenhower administration, mostly over which party was responsible for failing to balance the budget; the frequent hints of looming battles between Senate titans; the legislative circus, the midnight in-house comedies; and the well-planted leaks.

With Mansfield as majority leader, if the reporters any longer came in droves to the Senate, it was most often to attend the weekly "Ev and Charlie" shows. These were joint press conferences of the Republican leaders of the Senate and House. Held in the Senate press gallery, they featured Senate minority leader Everett Dirksen and Charles Halleck of Indiana, his House counterpart, with the former the star and the latter the straight man. In view of Kennedy's obvious appeal to voters throughout the nation, there were no frontal assaults launched on the White House. During the so-called honeymoon period, the new administration was subject only to pinpricks. Sitting cross-legged on a desk, Dirksen would feed to an enthusiastic if somewhat skeptical audience his own brand of bunkum, composed of one part fact, one part hyperbole, and several parts wit and humor. With Halleck nodding in assent, it was Dirksen's way of providing an authoritative Republican answer to the Democratic administration in the White House.

Despite Dirksen's valiant performances, the new center of action for the Washington press corps was no longer to be found in the Senate or the House. It had relocated in the White House. It was to the new faces in the Kennedy administration and especially to the president himself that the reporters beat a path. A press hiatus of this kind from the Senate would have brought forth lamentation and hand-wringing from Johnson or, for that matter, most other major political figures on Capitol Hill. Mansfield seemed to be bothered not at all by the loss of press interest in the Senate. On the contrary, he wanted it that way. He had known from the first that the Democratic Party's image would best be formed by the president and that while the Senate Democrats could supplement Kennedy's leadership in the process, they would be ill advised to contest it.

Others were not so content to watch the Senate settle deeper and deeper into what was beginning to resemble the cloistered quiet of a monastery.

Democrats who had first applauded Mansfield's election as majority leader began to have second thoughts. As time went on, they became increasingly concerned by press stories calling attention to the majority leader's "saintly" qualities even while comparing him in unflattering terms with his predecessor, Lyndon Johnson.

On a personal level, Mansfield did register in sharp contrast to Johnson. In the lampoons of the times, Johnson was sometimes portrayed as a tall-in-the-saddle cowboy in a Stetson hat riding out of the West, that is, west Texas. By contrast, the Mansfield caricature was authentic western to be sure, but hardly that of a cowboy. His prototype was the itinerant preacher riding from one frontier town to another, not on a horse but a mule and not cradling a Winchester but carrying a Bible under his arm.

In time, it dawned on many Democrats that they really knew very little about the leader they had elected. As assistant party leader, Mansfield had been obscured by the towering figure of Lyndon Johnson, but he had never complained about his place in the shadows. Nor did Mansfield appear to be living for the day when he would succeed the majority leader and was seeking to hasten its arrival in the devious but not uncommon ways of inner legislative politics. Instead, Mansfield seemed really content to puff on his pipe, say little, and perform the routine chores of the Senate floor adequately if unspectacularly in Johnson's absence. His support of the Texan in the Senate had been unwavering. He endorsed Johnson's candidacy for the presidential nomination and the votes of Montana's delegation had gone to the Texan at the San Francisco convention. The Kennedys had understood his position and never held it against him.

While assistant leader, Mansfield had remained meticulous in pursuit of his state's interests. Indeed, these interests never left the front burner of his concerns throughout his entire career in Congress. He understood fully that in the matter of political survival, constituency acceptance came before national leadership or international statesmanship. Even after his elevation to the majority leadership, Mansfield continued to speak of himself as the senator from Montana. Only letters addressed to him by Montanans were guaranteed an answer and, more often than not, a personal one. Letters from other states or other countries sent to him as majority leader were read but then discarded without answer unless by chance they contained some uniqueness that established a special claim on his attention. By the same token, the only visitors from the public sure of a personal reception were from his state. He was able to make time to see them in person because Montana was a long way from Washington and home-state visitors were few. This was an advantage enjoyed by all senators whose states contain small populations and are far removed from the Capitol.

It was not that Mansfield saw himself only as a senator from Montana. He coupled his deep sense of obligation to his state constituency with a sustained concern for overall national issues, in particular the nation's foreign relations. It was a difficult juggling act, especially with regard to international issues. Before World War II, Montana had been one of the great strongholds of American isolationism. As a senator, Mansfield's public statements on foreign policy were often as much an attempt to educate Montanans on international issues and their importance to the state as they were polemics designed to shake up the thinking of his Senate colleagues and the executive branch. Montanans trusted his leadership in foreign relations and its importance to the state. His success in that respect permitted him to enlarge his pursuit of international affairs without fear of losing his support at home.

The majority leader made a point of stressing that his main source of information on international matters was the press. Indeed, he was a voracious reader of foreign news that came to him via the press tickers in the Senate lobby and great metropolitan newspapers, such as the *New York Times,* the *Baltimore Sun,* and the *Washington Post.* Another source of information was provided to him by hearings of the Senate Foreign Relations Committee. Prior to becoming leader, Mansfield rarely missed a public session of the committee. But he was reserved in his acceptance of information provided in executive session or secret information communicated directly to him. Some senators delighted in the aura of drama and intrigue that surrounded sessions of the Foreign Relations Committee behind closed doors with high officials of the executive branch or other countries, with the ever-alert reporters waiting in the corridor outside for a filtered tidbit of news. Mansfield was not one of them. Indeed he often stayed away from such sessions, complaining that "you don't learn anything from these secret briefings that isn't in the *New York Times* usually sooner rather than later. If you attend an executive session or listen in private you're stopped from talking in public about what you already knew before the briefing."

Soon after his election to the Senate in 1952, Mansfield began to speak on foreign relations from the Senate floor. He made short informal comments from time to time, prompted by foreign news in the headlines. At intervals, he launched a long-running series of integrated speeches, usually read in a dispassionate voice to a near empty chamber but clearly establishing his position for the record. Such statements amounted to periodic reexaminations of existing policy, designed to focus Senate attention on aspects that he felt needed revision. Often, his statements had that effect, prompting concurrence or disagreement from a growing number of senators, such as

Javits of New York and Cooper of Kentucky, who shared his interest in international relations. Mansfield's statements were well covered by the press, and he was soon recognized as a new Senate voice in foreign relations. His readiness to speak out brought him attention not only in the nation's capital and Montana but increasingly throughout the nation and in other countries. His statements served to introduce in a cautious, circumspect manner a new point of view into what had tended to atrophy in public policy discussion as a struggle between "internationalism" and "isolationism." Many of his proposals fell by the wayside. A few were adopted. Others were dismissed, sometimes with ridicule, by the executive branch or by editorial writers.

Mansfield's "third man theme," as it was dubbed by a *Baltimore Sun* cartoonist, was invariably expressed by him in the context of "bipartisanship." This shibboleth had emerged during the Truman administration, with Republicans in control of Congress for the first time in many years. It was fostered by then Secretary of State Dean Acheson and by the Republican chairman of the Senate Foreign Relations Committee, Arthur Vandenberg of Michigan, as an essential for continued leadership by the United States in world affairs. Whatever its benefits, bipartisanship also had drawbacks. Among them, it could result in an insufficient congressional audit of the role the executive branch chose to play in dealing with the postwar world. It could also act to shut out the advice of responsible elements in Congress who feared to be branded isolationist if they chose to raise questions about prevailing policy.

Nevertheless bipartisanship had helped bring the nation through World War II, and the concept of the same kind of national unity operating in postwar foreign affairs commanded a large measure of public support. Most politicians felt it incumbent to do obeisance to the word, whatever reservations they may have had about its practice. Mansfield was no exception. Nevertheless, he was dubious of the concept, which he suspected was designed in the postwar years not so much to promote national unity as to coerce uncritical support for the executive branch in international affairs. He did not accept the contention then very much in vogue among political scientists that the constitutional writ of the president in foreign policy was absolute. Instead, he believed strongly that an independent input from the Congress, and particularly from the Senate, was a constitutional imperative that could serve the national interest.

In his view of the Senate role, Mansfield drew a distinction between the formulation of foreign policy and its execution. In the latter case, he readily conceded that the president's role, if not absolute, was certainly paramount. Even when in personal disagreement with a policy, he upheld the sole authority of the president or his designee (i.e., the secretary of state) to speak officially for the United States in its relations with other nations. In meetings with foreign dignitaries while traveling abroad, Mansfield deferred to the president's representative, that is, the U.S. ambassador, as the official spokesmen for the United States.

He also declined to issue statements on U.S. policy while in other nations that were at variance with announced positions of the president. Any differences he had were reserved for his return and sometimes expressed only privately to the president. Such was his respect for the presidential responsibility in the conduct of policy, moreover, that in the midst of international crises, he generally refrained from public expression of disagreement.

During the years of the Republican Eisenhower administration with John Foster Dulles as secretary of state, in periods that saw the Democrats in control of the Senate, Mansfield's style was in sharp contrast to that of other sources of opposition. Much of the latter came from the vestiges of prewar isolationist mentality and the anticommunist rantings of the followers of Senator Joe McCarthy. Although largely Republican by party label, these elements in American political life nurtured an inner fury that from time to time even focused on President Eisenhower and Secretary Dulles, whom they regarded as betrayers of Republican beliefs. By contrast, although a Democrat, Mansfield praised both men personally and reserved his criticism for specific policies or what he regarded as misapplications of policies. Notwithstanding his growing prominence as a responsible voice of the opposition, Mansfield became a favorite Democrat of John Foster Dulles. Mansfield was aware of the risk of charges of sell-out from his political colleagues but persisted in treating the secretary with consideration. He was motivated by his conviction that the president's responsibility for the foreign policy was preeminent, although the Senate might play a supporting role in its formulation and fine tuning. Moreover, gentle treatment of both friend and foe was part of his political stock in trade. With Mansfield, it was more than an adherence to the political adage of "catching more flies with honey than vinegar." The avoidance of personal confrontation was ingrained in his personality. It was his way. Even when some outrageous act compelled him to draw a line, his reproaches were free of rancor and expressed more in sorrow than anger.

Mansfield's style during his initial years in the Senate was a continuum of his decade of service in the House of Representatives (1943–1952). His Montana constituency changed both in numbers and character when he entered the Senate. In the House, he represented the western or frontier region of the state, concerned in large part with mining and hydroelectric power, with unionized labor a significant element of the constituency. As senator, the reach of his representation extended to include Montanans in the eastern part of the vast state, with large-scale interests in dry wheat farming and cattle raising. His new constituents tended to be more Republican in outlook and more attuned to the nation's growing stake in international affairs, especially trade. As any durable member of Congress, he sought to protect and enhance the interests of all his constituents within the context of those of the nation.

Mansfield's Background and Early Life

Unlike his Montana predecessors in the Congress, Mansfield was a cautious supporter of the great national transition that occurred during World War II, from a prewar isolationism into what was to become a deep U.S. involvement in world affairs. It was not an easy transition for him personally, any more than it was for the inhabitants of Montana. Without direct outlet to the oceans and with little direct trade or other contact with foreign nations, Montanans at the time were little concerned with the rest of the world. This state of affairs changed rapidly after the United States entered the war. Montanans served in the armed forces throughout the world. Troop trains traversed the state, crossing the vast grasslands from the Dakotas to the Rockies, carrying countless servicemen from every state of the Union in transit to the fronts in the Aleutians, the Pacific, and beyond. Military planes put down on hastily constructed landing fields in Montana for fuel and supplies before flying on to distant destinations. After the war, Montana's agricultural production helped feed a hungry world, and the state became a major factor in U.S. calculations for defense against nuclear attack. Still, traditional patterns of isolationist thought gave way slowly. Although Montana was strong in support of the national effort in World War II, many of its citizens looked forward to a return to the old ways after the conflict was won. Mansfield was not among them; he was aware that the changes were permanent and that there would be no return to the world of his boyhood.

Mansfield's political career was launched by a schoolteacher wife, a few friends, and students at the University of Montana in Missoula to whom he taught Far Eastern and Latin American history. "They were my machine," he was fond of saying, although once he became the Democratic nominee, he had the full support of the regular Democratic Party in the state.

Before teaching college, Mansfield was a student at the Montana School of Mines, which he entered at the age of thirty with a high school equivalency that he had obtained by studying nights with his wife's help. By day, he worked as a mucker in the copper mines of Butte, a job that was as it sounds. Before that, Mansfield was a private first class in the post–World War I Marine Corps, a common seaman in the U.S. Navy, and a private in the U.S. Army. He was discharged from the army when it was learned that he was only fourteen years old at the time of his enlistment and not the seventeen he had claimed. As a member of Congress, he was fond of joking that he was more favorably disposed toward the marines because the corps, unlike the army or the navy, had recognized his capabilities and promoted him from private to private first class.

This unusual career in the lower depths of the nation's armed services gave him a worm's eye view that immunized him permanently against the glamorization of military life. It also made him resistant to inflated claims on the nation's resources in the name of national security. After becoming majority leader, he was not averse to casting a no vote, sometimes the only negative vote in the Senate, against a military appropriation he found outrageously padded. Defense industry lobbyists found no profit in seeking him out.

Mansfield's military experience had given him an opportunity to see what was transpiring on the other side of the Pacific. In the early 1920s, he witnessed close-up the shifting power and the changing relations between a dominant West and an awakening East. World War I brought an end to the imperial Russian and German positions in China. The British persisted in Hong Kong, Shanghai, and other coastal Chinese cities and in India. The French remained in Indochina. But all began to feel the rising pressure from Japan and the stirring of emergent nationalism throughout the region. Something comparable took place in the Philippines, which by the 1920s had already been an American colony for more than two decades. Yet there was a difference between the United States in the Philippines and other imperial powers in the Far East. The concept of holding sway over another people did not rest easily with a nation that within living memory had fought a terrible civil war to end slavery. To many Americans, moreover, colonialism in Asia seemed a repudiation of the nation's birthright, won in a more distant time in the liberation of the American colonies from England.

So, having first killed numbers of Filipinos who seemed to want nothing more than what Americans had sought in 1776, the United States did an about-face. Thanks in part to congressional insistence in redefining our purposes in the Philippines, the dominant theme of the American presence became the creation of a Philippine nation capable of making a transition to democratic self-government. Thousands of American schoolteachers, sanitation and health workers, bureaucrats and experts of every hue were dispatched to the islands at the expense of American taxpayers to join private U.S. missionaries in what became a great effort to put a new face on American purposes there, one more acceptable to the American conscience.

Mansfield's wanderlust, which had served to carry him into the midst of an awakening Asia, had roots stretching back to his father and mother, who had left Ireland as emigrants to find a new life in America. They were part of the massive wave of European migration that took place at the beginning of the twentieth century. Much of this vast movement of humanity poured through Ellis Island in New York City before spreading throughout the nation. Mansfield was born in the lower part of Manhattan Island, in what was then an immigrant slum and is now the fashionable Soho district. It was there, too, that his mother died, not very long after his birth. When he was scarcely four, he was relocated with relatives in Great Falls, Montana.

At the time, the state was little more than a series of stops on the railroad tracks for travelers headed for the rapidly developing Pacific Coast or the beckoning goldfields of Alaska. To settle in Montana was to live by hunting and fishing in the midst of some of the nation's greatest mountain ranges and vast open spaces. Or if that was too random an existence, one's livelihood could be found in farming, cattle raising, mining, or simple services.

The Mansfields settled in Great Falls. In the early 1900s, Great Falls was a microcosmopoly of miners, tradespeople, railroaders, gandy dancers, cowboys, ranchers, drifters, and Indians. It also contained an early version of American environmentalists, the Thoreau-inspired nature lovers and a handful of artists, such as Charles Russell, anxious to record the vanishing frontier. When Mansfield arrived in Great Falls, the town was already well on its way to settling down. The seeds of middle-class virtue were germinating rapidly between the disappearing bawdy houses and saloons. Stable families, the Mansfields among them, were multiplying, and they cherished their homes, flower gardens, churches, schools, law and order, and Fourth of July picnics.

Montana became a state in 1889. A half-century later, Mike Mansfield was elected to represent the western district of the state in the U.S. House of Representatives. Montana had sent a number of stubborn individualistic legislators to Washington in the intervening years. One of the more notable was Jeannette Rankin, whose bronze likeness now adorns Statuary Hall in the U.S. Capitol, as one of the two members each state is permitted to honor in this fashion.

A Republican, Rankin was the first woman elected to Congress, taking a seat in the House of Representatives in 1917. Throughout her life, Rankin was a social activist, a crusader for women's rights, and a militant pacifist. Her revulsion against war was so intense that it led her to cast one of a handful of votes against U.S. entry into World War I. This "unpatriotic" vote was a major factor in defeating her attempt to gain a Senate seat in the next election. Nevertheless, she was returned to Congress years later, in time to cast the only vote against entry into World War II! Again, her lonely protest against war resulted in a defeat for her bid for reelection to the House.

When Mansfield arrived in the Senate after the 1952 election, he found as the senior member from Montana James E. Murray, who in turn had succeeded Thomas Walsh. Both predecessors were Democrats. Both harbored, as did Jeanette Rankin, the same strain of populism that is deeply imbedded in the politics of the state. Over the decades, this populism has found expression in Congress in the vigorous advocacy of such causes as public power and labor's rights.

Before World War II, Montana was a citadel of American isolationism and, notably, with regard to Europe. To forestall what he correctly perceived as the drift toward involvement in World War I, Montana's senior senator, Tom Walsh, had led the fight against legislation to authorize President Wilson to arm U.S. merchant ships against the German submarine menace to shipping in the north Atlantic. It was a time when unlimited debate was permitted in the Senate, and Walsh and a handful of like-minded colleagues had filibustered for weeks. The measure was finally passed, but the experience led to the adoption of Rule 22, the Cloture Rule, the first effort to limit debate in the Senate.

Another predecessor of Mansfield in the Senate was Burton K. Wheeler, a Democrat with strong maverick tendencies. In 1922 Wheeler bolted the party to run as the vice-presidential candidate of the Progressive Party, newly organized by Robert M. La Follette, the Wisconsin progressive. After that defeat, Wheeler returned to the Democratic fold, giving strong support to the domestic programs of Roosevelt's New Deal but little to his international policies. When World War II descended on Europe, a gap opened between Wheeler and Roosevelt. The former became convinced that the president was following Wilson's path toward involvement in the war against Germany. Wheeler reacted in the same fashion as Senator Walsh had done before the U.S. entry into World War I. He became a leader, along with Senators Gerald P. Nye of North Dakota and William Borah of Idaho, in the political effort to maintain U.S. neutrality.

Wheeler opposed measure after measure proposed by Roosevelt to aid Britain and the Allies, and at first his stand enjoyed wide support in the nation. There was even serious talk of Wheller's running for the presidency. Unfortunately for Wheeler, his following expanded until it came to include not only the isolationists but the American Nazi movement. Nevertheless, Wheeler continued to draw public support until the ground was cut from under his position by the Japanese attack on Pearl Harbor. A shocked Wheeler voted for the declaration of war against both Japan and Germany, but it was too late. Admiration turned to derision and hostility. Although he remained in the Senate until the expiration of his term in 1946 and later shifted his allegiance to the Republican Party, his political career, for all practical purposes, had come to an end.

This Montana heritage accompanied Mansfield to Washington after he won a seat in the House of Representatives in the elections of 1942. Later, in a fit of exasperation with Mansfield during the Vietnam War, Lyndon Johnson would describe Mansfield as one-third Burton K. Wheeler, one-third Jim Murray, and one-third Jeannette Rankin. To be sure, the ghosts of these predecessors did hover over Mansfield's perception of national and international realities. They were overshadowed, however, by his background as a teacher of history and his growing experience with international affairs as a member of Congress. Still, Montana's political history remained an integral part of Mansfield's uniqueness and as such made it particularly difficult to categorize his approach as a legislator.

Mansfield: Forging of a Different Kind of Senate

As majority leader, Mansfield was not easily extolled or condemned in a sound byte. He provided journalists with very little that was neatly packaged. He was not a colorful personality; neither was he a dud. He was not a pragmatist, yet certainly not an ideologue. He was neither purely liberal nor conservative, isolationist nor internationalist. He did not correspond to any of the particular touchstones by which politicians of the period were pigeonholed by the press.

He was fond of describing himself as one senator among others, not necessarily any better or worse, but with his share of shortcomings as well as strengths. He believed in the American system of government, and he believed in the Senate and its role in the system. The Senate was not for him, as it was for many others, a way stop in the ascent to higher office. To be sure, the thought of what might come next in his political career may have passed through his mind more than once. But the urge of the next step toward the beckoning summit of the presidency was not strong. And if it did arise in Mansfield, it did not remain long enough to become an obsession, as it did with many of his colleagues. For Mansfield, the Senate was an end in itself. Indeed, when he was elected senator of Montana, he insisted that his highest political ambition had been achieved.

Under Mansfield's leadership, the Senate evolved into something different from what had proceeded it and different, too, from what was to follow. Any particular Senate, of course, is a reflection of many factors. The Senate's membership changes with each election as does, most of the time, the ratio of the parties. Public issues also change. The interests of the media shift along with the faces of the newspeople who cover Capitol Hill. Such factors and countless others affect the legislative environment and set the dimensions for the Senate's character and achievements, or lack of them, in any given period. When that has been said, however, the nature of the Senate's leadership remains a critical influence. It does affect the distribution of national political power that is shared under the Constitution with the president and the House of Representatives. In short, it affects the Senate's role in the political leadership of the nation. It does put a stamp on any given period of the nation's history.

From the outset, Mansfield drew a sharp distinction between his responsibilities as one Senator from Montana and as majority leader of the Senate. He maintained a careful separation between the two offices, not only in location but in staffing, choosing primarily Montanans for the one but not for the other. His personal priorities between the two were never in doubt. The state's interests were looked after first. Only then did he concern himself with the demands of the Senate leadership. In handling the state's business, he was aided by a relatively small but effective staff. Montana's sparse population and its distance from Washington made it easier for him to split his time between the two offices; as a senator of Montana, he shared with one other member of the Senate the representation of only half a million people. The demands of constituents on his attention were lighter than for most other senators. Visitors from home were few, and he could see most of them himself. He could and did read newspapers from home. The same was true of the mail from the state, and he personally signed the responses.

His effectiveness in finding adequate time for both the state and national offices grew out of the absence of pretentiousness that he imposed on both offices and on a high level of personal efficiency. He was prepared to work long hours (a practice that drove him to the Capitol before six in the morning and kept him there usually until seven at night). He also possessed a remarkable memory, which enabled him to develop fingertip fluency in all matters affecting Montana and the leadership without resort to computers.

Priorities that put Montana first and the Senate leadership second reflected Mansfield's political realism at least as much as any deep absorption in state affairs. As far as possible, he steered clear of inner Montana political struggles. Rarely did he join the Montana delegations to the Democratic presidential conventions. He did not maintain a house of his own in the state. Seldom did he return to Montana more than three or four times a year to check popular sentiment and keep up his ties. Excessive appearances at home, he believed, would raise questions about neglect of the job he had been elected to do in Washington. Election years were an exception, but even then he campaigned personally only for a short time preceding an election. His campaign budgets never equaled in modesty those of his friend Senator George Aiken of Vermont, who spent less than $100 on one of his Senate elections. Nevertheless, Mansfield's long-time campaign manager, Jim Rowe, a prominent Washington attorney from Montana, was never hard pressed to raise the small sums he required. In Mansfield's view, expensive political campaigns that ran on for months were damaging not only to the candidates but also to the political system and to the country. On one occasion, he introduced legislation designed to limit political campaigns to ninety days prior to an election. The legislation went nowhere, but it did express his sentiments.

The priority that Mansfield gave to Montana affairs reflected his concern for the public trust that had been reposed in him by Montanans. It also had a lot to do with the practical problem of getting reelected to office, not to mention serving in the Senate leadership. It is amazing how often such an obvious order of precedence is forgotten by now-forgotten politicians who become intoxicated with the elixir of power that is copiously served in Washington. Mansfield was not one to fail a simple sobriety test in this connection. That is not to say that Mansfield was unprepared to take risks for fear of losing his seat. Indeed, a basic risk was his decision to give up a relatively safe House seat to run for the Senate against a Republican incumbent. The year 1952 was obviously going to be a Republican year, with Dwight D. Eisenhower at the head of that party's ticket and McCarthyism at the height of its national influence.

Mansfield never took an election for granted. Despite usually lopsided majorities in Montana elections, he remained the epitome of caution, and caution is the watchword of political survivors. Indeed, he may have been overly prudent at times in calculating what compromises with conscience were necessary for reelection; it is a common failing among successful politicians. After his first election to the Senate in the face of a Republican landslide, he was never in serious danger of rejection by the voters. In three subsequent bids for reelection, he was elected by very wide margins. Indeed, during his tenure as majority leader in the Senate, not a single Republican was elected from Montana to either House of Congress, a situation that can be regarded in significant part as a spinoff of Mansfield's stature among Montanan voters.

Mansfield's approach to the majority leadership differed from that of any of his predecessors. Among those who had occupied the office before him, some had stressed floor functions and nothing more, that is facilitating or manipulating the flow of legislation after bills were reported out of committees for final Senate action. Others saw the leader as primarily a spokesman for the president in the Senate if the president was of the same party, or leader of the legislative opposition if the opposite were the case. Still others saw the leadership as a place to make a record either for personal or party aggrandizement. Mansfield absorbed aspects of these various approaches and then added another dimension to the majority leadership. To him, the responsibility included safeguarding the Senate's constitutional share of the national leadership and its institutional heritage, regardless of which party controlled the White House. In this aspect of the office, he made no distinction between Republicans and Democrats in the Senate. He spoke for the Senate as a continuing and unified entity, quite apart from its internal political and other divisions. Soon convinced of his sincerity on this score, the Republican leadership invariably supported him in matters in which the Senate found itself in confrontation with the other branches or wherever and whenever its institutional interests were at stake, as when vice presidents using their constitutional role as president of the Senate sought to advance the purposes of a particular presidential administration.

While holding out a generous hand to the Republican minority, Mansfield was never unmindful of his roots in the Democratic Party. The Senate is organized as a partisan body. A majority leader owes his office not to the Senate as a whole but to his party; he is elected for two-year terms, not by the Senate but by members of his own party's caucus, and serves at its pleasure. In that sense, the leader is accountable only to his party colleagues. Mansfield drew a distinction between Senate Democrats as a political grouping and the whole Senate as a constitutional institution. He also drew a distinction between the Senate Democratic caucus and the National Democratic Party organization, headquartered in Washington and concerned primarily with presidential elections. Following the example of Lyndon Johnson, he accommodated himself to the realities of Democratic Party politics.

As Senate majority leader, Johnson had often found himself in aggressive and sometimes public confrontations with the chairman of the party's national committee, each asserting the right to be the voice of Democrats during the incumbency of President Eisenhower. Mansfield avoided open breaks of that kind, in part by disclaiming any such all-party distinction for himself; he was even reluctant to assume the role of spokesman for the Democrats in the Senate. Nevertheless, he was as determined as Johnson to keep the National Democratic Committee out of the Senate's affairs. As chairman of the National Committee, Robert Strauss, a long-time Texas associate of Lyndon Johnson, sought to make such a penetration during Mansfield's tenure as Senate leader. But after several breakfasts with the leadership that yielded nothing more than coffee, bacon and eggs, and pleasantries, Strauss abandoned the attempt.

As Democratic leader in the Senate, Mansfield saw his role as harmonizing the various viewpoints held by Senate Democrats. When full orchestration was not feasible, as was often the case, he refused to choose from among the various positions to champion in the name of the leadership. The only exception was a position formally adopted by the Majority Policy Committee and the Democratic caucus. In dealing with the president, he held to this concept during both Democratic and Republican administrations, resisting efforts to prod him into assuming that his was the overriding voice of the Senate Democrats. So determined was he to avoid even the appearance of pressure on his colleagues to follow his lead that he often withheld his own vote on controversial issues until other members had voted; all the while his floor staff remained under orders not to state his personal position, even if requested to do so by one of his colleagues!

As leader, his insistence on being last rather than first, the servant and not the suzerain of the Senate, fitted his personality like a comfortable suit. He did not like being at the front of the line, not only in the Senate but elsewhere. Frequently, for example, in using commercial planes, well-meaning ground personnel would offer to board him first; invariably the offer was politely refused, and he took his place in the line. The reasons for his reluctance to "act like a leader," a charge often leveled at him, were not only well grounded in his character, they were also attuned to the Senate and the political situation in the institution at the time of his election to the leadership. As he saw it, the Democratic caucus, deeply divided on major issues, had given him no carte blanche to put forth a "Senate Democratic position." On the contrary, Democrats let it be known in no uncertain terms at the outset that they had a surfeit of Johnsonian presumption. Without specific authority from the caucus, Mansfield would not act as spokesman for the Democrats on contentious questions. Later, he would seek such authority from time to time from the Policy Committee and the caucus, notably in his efforts to end the Vietnam War. But throughout his leadership, he steadfastly refused to be the voice of the party unless it was a matter affecting the Senate as a constitutional body. Then, after consultation with the minority leader, he was prepared to speak for the institution as a whole.

Another consideration prompted him to downplay his party role. With Democrats in control of both the presidency and the Congress, there was room only for one party image maker. He was convinced that the public's impression of what the Democratic Party stood for had to come from President Kennedy, and he regarded Kennedy as fully capable of representing the best that the Democrats had to offer to the country. Mansfield believed that the most effective way to help the president would be by securing a full hearing for his program in the Senate and by bringing to a vote the numerous pieces of legislation that would be required to translate Kennedy's program into action. To that end, he sought to minimize the pursuit of issues that were seriously divisive of the party. For those that could not be avoided, he felt it best to try first to placate the relevant committee chairmen, in the hope that they would not throw a monkey wrench into the procedural machinery.

In the Senate of that time, it would have been illusory for him to presume to do more. In the first place, the stance of an aggressive leader would have been alien to his nature. Moreover, there were few acceptable sanctions for coercing a member into toeing the party line if, indeed, it were possible to delineate such a line. Mansfield's nonpresumptuous approach was undergirded by his patience. He could play the waiting game better, perhaps, than anyone else in the Senate. Once, for example, he managed to achieve a breakthrough on a very minor matter in the face of one of the Senate's periodic temper tantrums that frequently led to endless pontificating on procedural trivia. The breakthrough came, however, only after hours of waiting for the torrent of words on the Senate floor to dry up. Returning to his office, Mansfield slumped wearily into a chair and in a rare complaint informed no one in particular, "You can do anything in the Senate, provided you have the patience and provided you live long enough."

Mansfield's was not an ordinary patience. It was an awesome, monumental, fearsome, incredible patience. It enabled him to sit stiffly erect at his desk on the Senate floor, waiting imperturbably, hour after hour, and sometimes, day after day, for "one final word" from a Spessard Holland of Florida, a Sam Ervin of North Carolina, a Wayne Morse of Oregon, or some other of the more long-winded of the era. The "final word" often came at the end of a run-on sentence that reached a period, not with the speaker's but the Senate's exhaustion. Mansfield did indeed have the "patience of a saint," and it supported the tendency on the part of the press to portray him, inaccurately, as a kind of quasi-religious figure in politician's guise.

As time went on, he was not above losing his saintly patience, particularly when confronted with what he regarded as behavior unworthy of the Senate. In one instance, Mansfield learned that Jesse Helms, a newly arrived senator from North Carolina, had been overheard "conspiring" in the Senate corridor with James Allen, a senator from Alabama who was highly skilled in the rules. In accordance with the "plot," Helms was to offer to preside over the Senate in order to make a ruling that would further complicate and delay an already snagged procedural situation. The conspiracy in this case was little more than a college prank. But when Helms took the chair, ignored the parliamentarian's advice, and delivered the ruling, Mansfield was livid. He denounced the perpetrators in no uncertain terms, taking on, in the process, the characteristics of St. Patrick driving the snakes out of Ireland. In this rare outburst of righteous indignation, the majority leader won the sympathy and support of both Democratic and Republican colleagues, including a cease and desist from the two senators who had aroused his anger in the first place. Instances of articulated anger were uncommon on the part of the majority leader. When he gave vent to them, they were invariably accepted as justified by his colleagues, who were convinced of his integrity and increasingly supportive of his determination to lift the level of dignity in the Senate.

Mansfield's personal characteristics included a passion for egalitarianism, notably among senators. In a Senate that had grown accustomed to acting in accord with the Orwellian dictum that among the pigs of the Animal Farm, all are equal but "some are more equal than others," the majority leader insisted that "all Senators are equal"—period. He believed in the concept, he expressed it again and again, and he lived it. At first, Mansfield's constant reiteration of the truism went unnoticed; then the "one Senator one vote" theme began to raise eyebrows. What was Mansfield saying? More important, why was he saying it? The more privileged members looked over their shoulders to see who he might have in mind. The less privileged, for the most part the younger members, heard what he was saying but waited to see what it meant. In practice, the Senate that Mansfield inherited from Lyndon Johnson was shot through with inequities, some inherited by the Texan that he did little to correct and others added by the Texan. Nor were they minor inequities, such as might exist in any long-established institution. Instead, they were inequities of substance in that they had to do with sharing the constitutional power of the Senate and how it was to be wielded for the nation. In Johnson's Senate there was, first, the inequity of the majority leader and all the others. There was the inequity of the Majority and the Minority. There were Senators and there were committee chairmen. There was selection by seniority for membership on sought-after committees such as Appropriations, Armed Services, Foreign Relations, and Finance. For the junior members there were the leftovers— that is assignment to such committees as Post Office and Civil Service, Rules, and District of Columbia. Johnson made a dent in the seniority system by occasionally exercising arbitrarily the power of committee assignment when a vacancy existed. But unchallenged selection by seniority remained the overwhelming practice. Under Johnson, there were senators of the inner club who received a lion's share of the perquisites, large and small; other senators took the crumbs that fell from the table.

Inequities in power are inevitable in the inner workings of any legislative body. In the Senate of 1960, however, they approached intolerable levels. Many Democrats, as previously noted, had given vent to their anger at the first party caucus under Mansfield's leadership. Indeed, denunciations of his predecessor's high-handedness and demands for reform were still ringing in Mansfield's ears as he groped his way into his new responsibilities.

Johnson's use of the leadership had infuriated not only Democratic colleagues but also Republicans, who were especially disturbed by his manipulation of the calendar of legislation and other floor proceedings. Minority leader, Everett Dirksen had been quick to lash back whenever an opportunity presented itself. In short, each party leadership was constantly on the lookout for an opening to embarrass the other. At the same time, liberals were ever ready to fire verbal shots at conservatives, and the latter were ever ready to lash back. Senate sessions were called on Johnson's whims, and often they ran far into the night or overnight as he sought impatiently to ram through a bill over objections. Not only the parties but factions within each party mounted floor guards to prevent sneak attacks on their interests.

Mansfield bristled at evidence of domination of some by others. So, from the outset, he preached the doctrine of Senate equality. What was confusing, however, was that he seemed blind to the existence of vast inequities in the Senate. In any event, he refused to discuss them, preferring that his actions speak for him. He sought no special treatment for himself as majority leader, accepting instead only the time-honored practice of priority recognition, a practice easily upheld because the desk of the majority leader was located in the direct line of vision of the chair. Even then, Mansfield frequently yielded his leadership desk to the committee chairman or other designee when matters of particular interest to them were under consideration. He took up legislation in the regular order listed on the Senate calendar so that sponsors did not have to ask him to call up their bills as though it were a favor granted by the leadership.

At one point, Vice President Johnson advised all Kennedy cabinet members to seek out the majority leader when they had legislative problems in the Senate, valid advice at an earlier time. Mansfield, however, received cabinet officers courteously, but in turn referred them to the appropriate committee chairmen. In due course, cabinet members ceased bothering to check in with the majority leader except in unusual circumstances, and that was the way Mansfield wanted it.

In attending regular weekly breakfast meetings inaugurated by President Kennedy, Mansfield invariably arrived with other members of the majority leadership, notably the majority whip and the caucus secretary. When called to the White House by the president on some particular legislative matter,

Mansfield insisted that the relevant committee chairman and, where appropriate, ranking minority members and others accompany him.

In another gesture of divestiture, Mansfield refused the multi-room suite built into the then newly completed East Front extension of the Capitol. The suite of several rooms had been designed for use by the majority leader in accordance with Lyndon Johnson's specifications. Having rejected it for himself, Mansfield also turned down a suggestion from Johnson, as vice president, that it be assigned to him. Instead, Mansfield divided the suite into several smaller offices. Without asking any quid pro quo, he turned them over to senators on the basis of strict seniority. The recipients were not only Senate patriarchs, they also happened to be chairmen of major committees and mostly southerners, who then relinquished space elsewhere in the Capitol. Mansfield did make one exception to the seniority system in this instance. He reserved two offices with a connecting bathroom for the only women members of the Senate at the time. One was assigned to Margaret Chase Smith of Maine, a Republican, and the other to Maureen Neuberger of Oregon, a Democrat. While dismissed by some members of the "Gentlemen's Club" as an amusing gesture of gallantry, the assignments made clear that Mansfield's dictum of equal treatment of all senators embraced both sexes. Female senators found themselves without private toilet facilities in the Capitol, and Mansfield was determined to rectify this oversight at the first opportunity.

Mansfield continued the Johnson practice of meeting regularly with Democratic committee chairmen and with the Majority Policy Committee. The tone of the meetings, however, underwent a drastic change. Under Johnson, these luncheon sessions had been the setting for story swapping and a venue for the bargaining byplays of legislative politics. Johnson would also bluntly push chairmen at the meetings to take various committee actions. By contrast, Mansfield conducted the meetings with a minimum of small talk and with little or no indication of his own priorities or preferences. He never bargained apples for oranges to obtain a desired vote, and he also eschewed the use of pressure except as the president's announced legislative program might be involved. When that occurred, Mansfield would make discrete inquiries of committee chairmen from time to time as to the status of particular bills that were of interest to the White House. But he never demanded an explanation of delays. At most, he would ask committee chairmen to "see what you can do" to expedite a bill on the grounds that any measure in which the president had expressed concern deserved the respectful and priority attention of Congress, as a matter of courtesy and comity between the branches. By this approach, Mansfield simply underscored what was the reality; the movement of a president's program through the Senate was not primarily controllable by the majority leader but by the committees and especially their chairmen. He made it clear to the Kennedy emissaries on the Hill that he would be glad to take up the president's bills on the Senate floor expeditiously but that if they were impatient for a measure still in committee, it was their responsibility to persuade the chairman to move it. As leader, Mansfield did not see himself as some sort of *deus ex machina* who, by clever manipulation, deal making, or sheer force of personality could extract legislation from committees. He had been in the Senate long enough to know that it did not work that way. The Senate Rules made it clear that in the absence of a huge demand for action, a majority leader could not compel a committee chairman to report legislation. Such an overwhelming demand was nowhere in sight in 1961 for the more controversial items in Kennedy's program. Mansfield was not willing to try to move the program by cajolery, bluster, or various forms of parliamentary bullying, bribery, or blackmail. Such an approach was not only alien to his nature; it was, in his view, demeaning to the Senate. So while praising his predecessor effusively for achieving as much as he did, Mansfield worked to deflate the aura of omnipotence with which his predecessor had surrounded himself in the office of majority leader.

At the outset of his leadership, Mansfield gave tangible evidence of how he proposed to proceed. To achieve a higher degree of egalitarianism he undertook to revamp the Democratic Steering Committee on the basis of a directive that he extracted from the Democratic caucus. In the Senate, the Democratic Steering Committee has only one function. How it performs it, however, is of critical importance. The committee determines the assignment of Democratic senators to the various standing committees of the Senate. As the then majority leader, and therefore also chairman of the Democratic Steering Committee, Lyndon Johnson personally made the assignments, and these were then, invariably, rubber-stamped by the Steering Committee. Johnson was hailed for breaking through the ritual of seniority that had long governed such selections. He did not hesitate, for example, to appoint first-term senators to major committees. Mike Mansfield himself was a beneficiary of this innovation, being designated as a freshman to the Foreign Relations Committee. It soon became apparent, however, that whatever virtue attached to this achievement was tempered by Johnson's expectation that the new members would be properly grateful to the majority leader and, when necessary, show their gratitude in votes or other appropriate actions.

As chairman of the Steering Committee, Mansfield refused to select the Democratic designees to the Senate standing committees. Instead, he insisted that the Steering Committee make a collective decision on these assignments and that this be done by secret ballot. When senators came to him seeking his intercession for a prized committee assignment, Mansfield asked that their preferences be put in writing and promised only to bring all such requests to the attention of the Steering Committee. For himself, he stressed that he had only one vote on the committee. Following this procedure, Mansfield could claim no IOUs for favors done. Thanks to the use of the secret ballot, moreover, neither could any other member of the Steering Committee.

The change was a genuinely democratic reform, moving the Senate Democrats in the direction of a more equitable division of institutional power. Standing Committee membership, by its power to assign members to legislative committees, has much to do with defining the character of a party to the public, not to speak of its impact on shaping the specifics of emerging legislation. By abandoning what had been one of the key tools of his predecessor, Mansfield did much to restore democratic practice in this obscure corner of the legislative process.

The majority leader's eagerness to divest himself of intraparty power left his Democratic colleagues feeling perplexed. Despite protestations to the contrary, the aggrandizement of personal power is a constant in legislative bodies, and accumulations are usually disgorged by individual members or groups only with the greatest reluctance. Hence, other senators were at a loss to understand Mansfield's motives and, at first, looked for the hidden gimmick. They were also perplexed because his divestitures at first seemed only to enhance the powers of those already heavily endowed by Senate practice, that is, the committee chairmen. Enhancing the power of the already powerful seemed hardly to be headed in the direction of the "equality of all senators" that he continued to preach. Not readily apparent was that what was being disgorged was only what Johnson had accumulated and what Mansfield had inherited from him. In the process of restoring it, he highlighted those who really moved the Senate under the Rules. It was not the majority leader, not even the Senate as a whole but the senior members of the party ensconced in standing committees and, more specifically, in the chairmanships. Mansfield preached equality but only when authorized by vote of the caucus, the authentic voice of all the majority members, did he move to put flesh on the concept in party practices; indeed, that was the only time he could make such changes and make them stick.

He was determined that leadership in the Senate would not be a one-man performance. It was to be a party performance and, in due course, a Senate performance, because in addition to shuffling his party's practices, Mansfield leaned over backward in seeking to bring the Republicans into the show by being more than fair to the minority.

In the matter of standing committee assignments, for example, as between the parties, seats are divided in rough proportion to the total membership of the parties in the Senate. Since it is not possible to make fractional assignments, it is often necessary to set ratios in particular committees that slightly favor one party or the other. Which party is given the fractional seat on select committees had been a source of much haggling and charges of unfairness on the part of the minority party. Mansfield dealt directly with Everett Dirksen, the Republican leader, in determining committee size and ratio. In virtually every instance, he chose to accommodate the minority leader. Mansfield ignored mutterings from his own party ranks about giving away the store. It was, however, a small gesture, with little, if any, impact on committee function or legislative flow, but it was a gracious gesture, an act of deference that underscored Mansfield's determination to shift the demeanor of the Senate away from petty partisan confrontation. Its meaning was not lost on Everett Dirksen and the Republicans.

Mansfield treated the entire membership with great consideration, often at the expense of his own convenience. He asked no special favors and never demanded a quid pro quo for favors rendered. In conducting business on the floor of the Senate, Mansfield downgraded the role of the majority leader to that of servant of his party and, in some respects, of the Senate as a whole. He insisted that the chairmen themselves manage the bills emerging from their committees when they were being debated on the Senate floor. Moreover, the newest members of the Senate were urged by him not to hang back demurely, as tradition demanded, but to participate fully in the proceedings, all the while stressing their equality and their importance to the nation.

Under Mansfield's leadership, the daily sessions of the Senate were steady, plodding, and of minimal length. Such business as came before the Senate was conducted with little conflict and even a degree of genuine courtesy. Daily floor work was usually completed in time for members to go home at a respectable hour, a consideration of major importance, especially to younger members with growing families.

Gone was the circus atmosphere engendered by Johnson's presence and tactics. Gone was the political theater. As the melodrama faded, the tears, real and feigned, dried up. The great bursts of laughter were more muted. The flames of fury were dampened. The cliffhanger votes grew fewer and were rarely highlighted. The transcendent victories and the bitter defeats were no longer drowned in bourbon in the Capitol hideaways. Under Mansfield, the Senate became a less animated place, to some a boring place. Except for the conducted tours marching in and out at intervals, the public galleries were usually empty. When drama did arise, however, it was authentic, emerging from the substance of issues, as in the case of civil rights or the war in Vietnam, rather than contrived from the clashing of inflated egos.

Gradually, the stereotypes of senators as Claghorn and Kentucky Colonels disappeared from television and radio comic shows. So, too, did the depiction of the Senate as a circus ring, with the ringmaster, a tall Texan, snapping a whip to put the Senate lions through their paces.

The Senate under Mansfield came to be seen by the press as a rather dull place. The new leader certainly did nothing to halt the change; if anything, he appeared anxious to accelerate it. The quiet in the Senate corridors after dark did not set well with some senators. These members of the old "Inner Club" shook their heads and grumbled over early lights-out. With little life other than the Senate, many missed the camaraderie of a favorite watering spot in a hideaway off the Senate floor. Excessive drinking under the Capitol dome had been one of the not-very-well-hidden sins of the Senate. Mansfield sought discreetly to cut down the liberal flow of alcohol. Key staff personnel who doubled as saloonkeepers were instructed not to encourage the practice. He also set an example in his own office, offering coffee to visiting colleagues instead of bourbon and bottled water.

Wayne Morse of Oregon, the great dissenter of the era, was the most outspoken enemy of drinking in the Senate. At one point, he went public, denouncing liquor as a poisonous evil and its consumption in the Capitol as illegal. He approved of the majority leader's efforts to restrain the flow of alcohol, which was not only in accord with his principles but also suited Morse for another reason. Drinking and late sessions went together. By discouraging drinking, Mansfield reinforced his attempts to complete the Senate's regular daily business at a reasonable hour. That suited Morse fine because it left the floor free for him to indulge his penchant for making long and erudite speeches on the issues of the day. Morse knew that maximum useful press coverage on the West Coast could be obtained by beginning to speak very late in the afternoon, after his colleagues had departed. Such timing was too late for press deadlines on the East Coast. But it was early enough for deadlines on the West Coast, and it was there, especially in Oregon, that Morse wished to be heard.

Whenever Morse advised the majority leader of his intention to make a lengthy speech, Mansfield designated him to move the adjournment of the Senate on finishing his statement. By that time, most other members were home finishing supper. A brilliant speaker, Morse would deliver his long statements on an empty Senate floor. A colleague, serving as designated presiding officer for the closing of the session, would be waiting, poised to bring down the gavel of adjournment and head for home as others had done, sometimes hours before. The final moment was never certain because

Morse might begin with prepared remarks but then get carried away by his own words and extemporize with cogent but extended additions.

On one occasion, Senator Dan Brewster of Maryland, serving as presiding officer, brought down on his head Morse's undying wrath when he brought down the gavel prematurely. He had dozed briefly in the chair and was awakened by an unusual silence in the chamber. Assuming that Morse had finished his statement, he geveled the Senate into adjournment and rushed out of the chamber. Whereupon he learned that Morse had not finished but had merely paused to catch his breath and take a sip of water. Despite effusive apologies, Morse was unimpressed and regarded Brewster with a suspicious eye thereafter.

Mansfield's emphasis on early daily adjournments pleased new members, who had heard the tales of horror surrounding Johnson's penchant for late- and all-night sessions. Mansfield offered other changes in practices with this group especially in mind. He made it a practice, for example, to meet with all newly elected senators—Republicans and Democrats alike— at private luncheons in his office. There he urged them to speak out freely not only on issues but on grievances. With the caution common to most surviving politicians, few were prepared to go too far. At first, most avoided challenging such sacred cows as a stilted deference to senior members. None rushed to the floor to make a maiden speech in the first few weeks of the session. Nevertheless, Mansfield had planted another seed for his doctrine of egalitarianism, and it would grow with time. In due course there appeared in the Senate those who, like Joe Biden of Delaware and John Culver of Iowa, took him at his word.

The Leader of the Minority

The most significant reaction to Mansfield's new approach came from Everett McKinley Dirksen, the Republican minority leader. Dirksen had for years jousted with Mansfield's predecessor in parliamentary games. He was Johnson's superior in wit, if not in maneuver, and when challenged he could be an intensely partisan Republican. Dirksen knew all the tricks of the trade, and he played them without hesitancy, delighting in confounding or infuriating his Democratic adversaries. The senator from Illinois had been something of an actor before embarking on a political career. He not only had a great sense of humor but also a flair for the melodramatic. He delighted in drawing on both gifts whenever an opportunity presented itself. Once, for example, Hubert Humphrey, then the Democratic whip, and Dirksen were together on an otherwise empty Senate floor. The Senate had just convened and was in what is known as the Morning Hour, a period set aside at the beginning of each day for the delivery of short statements by any member. Dirksen made his comments. Then the Democratic whip began to read a prepared statement. It was innocuous enough, having to do with the sorry appearance of the Capitol grounds. The statement was the sort of tidbit that staff aides frequently put into senators' hands at the last moment. In this case, the architect of the Capitol was being urged to take better care of the flowers and shrubbery. The horticultural references, however, caused Dirksen, a renowned gardener, to perk up his ears and look up from the papers he was shuffling on his desk. He interrupted Humphrey and asked him to yield, a request to which the Minnesotan gladly acceded, expecting some sort of concurrence from the minority leader in his criticism of the groundskeeping. Dirksen did concur and then proceeded to deliver, without a moment's hesitancy, a profound and poetic dissertation on the beauties of the marigold and what this humble and much maligned flower would add to the beauty of the Capitol grounds if the architect would only see to its inclusion in the landscaping. In a straight-faced but extravagant delivery, he described in minute detail and with appropriate gestures this familiar flower, extolling its matchless beauty and perfume and detailing its other admirable qualities. His detailed commentary on the marigold left the usually voluble Humphrey speechless, quite possibly for the first time in his life.

Dirksen had been a controversial figure among his Republican colleagues prior to his election as minority leader. He was remembered for his passionate attempt to stop the Eisenhower nomination in the 1952 presidential convention and his hostility to the liberal Rockefeller wing of the party that was pushing it. He had mellowed with time and as Republican leader of the Senate had come to enjoy the affection and respect of his colleagues. Dirksen was warm, earthy, and gregarious—his Capitol office just down the corridor from the floor was a favorite place for Republican senators to stop by for a drink and chat, and it was later to become the main venue for the bipartisan effort to pass the landmark civil rights bill of 1964.

Unlike Mansfield, Dirksen could be ruthlessly partisan. It was a partisanship, however, tempered by his minority position and by an ear well attuned to shifting public attitudes. He had a good sense of what could be done and what could not be done by a political opposition and what the public would and would not tolerate in politics on serious national issues.

Dirksen was well aware that Mansfield was not a match for his parliamentary histrionics. He also knew that his adversary, if Mansfield could be called that, had little in common with Lyndon Johnson other than a party label. He heard what the new majority leader was saying about an egalitarian Senate. At first, he reacted with a bemused patience, waiting for the other shoe to drop. It was as though he had heard it all before, but if that was what Mansfield wanted for starters, he would indulge him. In time, he was impressed by Mansfield's apparent sincerity and dogged persistence in pursuing the theme, despite the evidence to the contrary that permeated the Senate. Nevertheless, he remained on guard, groping for the hidden stiletto under Mansfield's sober and self-effacing demeanor. Finding none, he was slowly persuaded that what the Montanan was concocting was not some bizarre political snake oil. Instead, he decided Mansfield's concern for the Senate as an institution was genuine and his repeated assertion that "all senators are equal" was not only his conviction but, more important, that it included Republicans.

The conclusion that Dirksen reached about the majority leader by no means applied to the other Senate Democrats. Dirksen did not think that the leopard would change all its spots. As for the link that existed between Republicans and southern Democrats, Dirksen had always understood its limits. He knew that Russell and the main body of his southern followers remained Democrats to whom Republicans could relate only in a kind of on-again, off-again common-law marriage. By the same token, Dirksen was aware that whatever new sweetness and light was reaching him from across the dividing aisle on the Senate floor came from Mansfield, not from the Democrats as a whole. They remained objects of his disdain, to be endured perhaps, but not to be trusted and certainly not to be embraced. This was especially true of the Democratic liberals.

In the eyes of the minority leader, Mansfield was a little naive, perhaps, but a man who could be counted on, a man whose word was ironclad, a man with genuine feeling for his fellow man and, above all, a senator's senator. With such a majority leader, Dirksen was open to cooperation. He could be reached by appeals to his patriotism, to his sense of the dramatic in which the great looming legislative issue of civil rights was steeped, and to his sentimental affection for the Senate, the last stage on which he was to tread in his lifetime. In short, he was ready to act in concert rather than confrontation with the majority leader on certain national issues. There was the proviso, however, that the issues had to be the right issues from his Republican point of view, and the right buttons of his psyche had to be pressed at the right moment. In the last years of life, Dirksen was ready to stake out his claim in history as a statesman, not a political buffoon.

Initially, the principal changes in the Mansfield Senate were in mood and atmosphere. The chamber grew quieter and more orderly. Harangues were fewer. The petty bickering diminished. The partisan need to be always on guard against the unexpected body blow declined and eventually disappeared. If the lions did not exactly lie down with the lambs, at least the jungle lost some of its terrors. There were still dark corners even as new light streamed into the chamber. But, overall, the pervasive suspicion and cynicism of the Johnson years was replaced by a degree of trust and good faith.

The majority leader seized every opportunity to encourage and intensify the transition. He drew back from the media spotlight, even as he thrust others of both parties, and especially younger senators, into it. He saw no faults in anyone, at least none that he would express publicly, and was untiring in his praise of others, notably the minority leader. Dirksen reciprocated in the perfumed oratory of which he was a master. In due course, the entire Senate joined as in a Greek chorus to sing the praises of both leaders, some choking on a note here and there, but virtually all trying to follow the score as written and directed by the new majority leader.

2

The Kennedy Years, 1961–1963

The first two years of the Kennedy administration indicated that the Senate had adapted to the change in atmosphere under Mansfield without difficulty. If not spectacular, the pace of legislative action was respectable. Undoubtedly, it was spurred by a readiness to accommodate a popular young president in the traditional honeymoon period with the Congress. But there was also a desire to adjust to Mansfield's self-effacing leadership and to support his efforts to free the Senate from the lingering ghosts of Johnson's once overbearing presence, not to speak of his stentorian voice. Johnson spent less and less time in his old haunts after having been rebuffed in his initial attempt to continue running the Senate from the graveyard of the vice presidency.

Under Mansfield's leadership, appropriations bills were steered through the Senate promptly on clearing the House, which by tradition acted on them first. In addition, prompt Senate approval was given to continuance of a number of federal programs having to do with labor, health, and education. The Senate also agreed to legislate several new features included in the Kennedy program. One, in particular, caught fire. Seizing on a proposal first advanced in the Senate by Hubert Humphrey, the president called for the establishment of an Overseas Peace Corps. The initial proposal involved sending young Americans abroad to live and work among people suffering from such ills of human neglect as malnutrition, preventable disease, and illiteracy. As presented by Kennedy, American volunteers would transmit basic techniques of modern enlightenment to the overlooked of the world— things that would permit them to make material improvement in their lives. The idea, of course, had its roots in American religious missionary activities in the "backward" places of the world. What was new in the Kennedy proposal was the absence of the religious element and the accent initially placed on youth in recruitment. In effect, young Americans would serve as secular missionaries to bring those living beyond the pale into the beginnings of a more or less American version of the modern world. A by-product of the enterprise would be a retouching of the image of a caring America, a beacon of hope to the downtrodden that had become somewhat blurred in the chauvinistic bombast of the Cold War.

The legislation was adopted with great fanfare, broad public approval, and little dissent in Congress. The president appointed his brother-in-law Sergeant Shriver as the first director of the Peace Corps. Shriver, in turn, chose Bill Moyers as his deputy. Moyers did much to project the new program to Congress as an expression of America's genuine concern for the poor and suffering of the world and as an example of our peaceful intentions toward the rest of humankind. The Peace Corps also offered, by inference, a genteel and effective way of fighting communism, giving it a strong appeal to idealistic young Americans. Finally, to such penny pinchers in Congress as Harry F. Byrd of Virginia, then chairman of the Senate Finance Committee, the Peace Corps appealed as foreign aid "on the cheap" because its projects involved very little in the way of costly equipment and supplies and would be carried out by youthful volunteers. Receiving only a modest stipend, the volunteers would live in circumstances not much better than those of the people they had come to help. With that sort of buildup and with the president's ringing leadership, Congress was easily persuaded to vote a comparatively modest appropriation for the new foreign aid enterprise.

What Moyers, Shriver, and others avoided mentioning was that the Peace Corps opened up a constructive outlet for the restless youth of the 1960s, the James Dean–Jack Kerouac generation. The Corps appealed especially to youngsters from middle- and upper-income American families seeking answers to age-old questions of identity and purpose. It provided an opportunity to get away from affluent, overprotective homes and to suffer some personal deprivation for a noble purpose. That may indeed have been its greatest virtue.

After rugged fitness training in Puerto Rico and elsewhere, the volunteers went on to teach basic English, simple farming techniques, and latrine-level sanitation in such exotic, if uncomfortable, settings as the frigid

Andean alti-plano, the mosquito-ridden klongs of Southeast Asia, and isolated tribal reserves in Africa. In this way, not a few Corpsmen and -women discovered an inner fortitude that would serve them well on their return to the states. Indeed, many of the early graduates of the corps moved on to careers of service in education, government, and industry that enabled them to inject an enriched element of human concern into the affairs of the nation.

Although scarcely a drop in the bucket of world need, the Peace Corps served, at least in its early years, to strengthen at home and abroad an awareness of that need. Moreover, since the corps was based on compassion for the less fortunate, it filled gaps in the awareness of the benevolent side of the United States, gaps left by dwindling missionary and educational efforts in out-of-the-way places in the world. As such, it was a factor in stimulating similar activity by other affluent nations and the United Nations.

The rest of the legislative record of the 87th Congress, the initial two years of the Kennedy administration, represented a promising start on the administration's New Frontier program. Under Mansfield's leadership, the Senate's share in this performance went largely unnoticed in the press; and the House of Representatives, under Speaker John McCormack, fared only slightly better. The White House provided the news focus in the nation's capital. What transpired there was the stuff of human interest and national drama. Kennedy quickly became a master of the presidential press conference. His erudite style and excellent command of the issues, as well as the language in which he discussed them, represented a marked change from Eisenhower's homely, if amiable, fumbling for words. Obviously, Kennedy relished what he was doing, and his wit, intelligence, and humor were effective foils against the probes of reporters.

The new lifestyle in the White House was also widely publicized and, on the whole, received national approval. Jackie Kennedy undertook to redo the White House in a fashion more suitable to the times. In the 1960s that meant something approaching its earlier aristocratic decor. Rich friends and renowned decorators eagerly came to her aid with money and advice. Scouts went far and wide in search of original furnishings and historic memorabilia. Among their finds was one that threatened the peace between the White House and Capitol Hill. Jackie Kennedy's decorators discovered a huge crystal chandelier hanging in a public corridor on the Senate side of the Capitol. It had been removed from the White House in a refurbishing during the Grant administration and consigned to a junk dealer. Rescued by the then far-sighted architect of the Capitol, the chandelier had hung contentedly for decades in its Capitol location. Day in and day out it showered a benign light on countless tourists trudging through the corridors. Once a year it was lowered in order to clean each of the hundreds of crystals of which it was composed, a task involving three workers for three days.

The chandelier, along with most of the historic furnishings in the Capitol, were in the custody of George Stewart, the architect of the Capitol. A former member of the House of Representatives and not a trained architect, Stewart became a frequent center of controversy largely because of his obsession with enlarging the Capitol. He had carried on a long struggle to persuade Congress to extend the East Front of the building by several feet and had finally succeeded in this endeavor when it was realized that the extension could supply space for convenient offices for selected members of both houses, including a large suite for Lyndon Johnson.

When the Kennedy administration came to town, Stewart was engaged in an attempt to repeat this feat with regard to the West Front. Here he was confronted with formidable opposition that came not only from Congress but from the press and the purists in the world of historical architecture and preservation, who had been outraged by Stewart's successful coup in regard to the East Front. But Stewart was a stubborn man, and his obsession gave him no peace. He lobbied day and night among members of Congress and their staffs, seeking support for his dream. On weekends, he prowled the grounds of the Capitol, picking up stones that he claimed had fallen from the disintegrating West Front of the building, proof that the wall had to be replaced. He caused huge wooden props to be placed between the sandstone columns to keep them, he said, from buckling. Immense reinforcement beams were placed against the base of the wall, he said, to stop the façade from collapsing. Nevertheless, he resisted all proposals to repair the façade, fearing that such repair would end his hope to extend it.

Preoccupied in this fashion, Stewart was impervious to Jackie Kennedy's repeated requests for the return of the crystal chandelier to its ancestral home in the President's House. Her determination rose with her ire at Stewart's indifference to her plans. Jackie Kennedy pleaded with Lyndon Johnson for help, promising dire consequences for Stewart if he persisted in ignoring her demand for the chandelier. Pleading that his writ as vice president no longer ran very far on Capitol Hill, Johnson dumped the problem on the Senate majority leader. The tempest in a teapot was on the verge of being upgraded to a hurricane when Mansfield agreed with the architect's office to turn the "goddam thing" over to the White House. Reluctant to surrender any part of the congressional patrimony, however, Mansfield insisted that the transfer be made on a formal loan basis and with no fanfare, thus avoiding the public storm that Jackie Kennedy had promised to launch if she did not obtain the chandelier. Early on a Sunday morning, with the

Capitol empty of visitors, the chandelier was removed and carted to its original home. Its disappearance went unnoticed by the press, the public, and, apparently, even by the preoccupied architect. Several years later, with the principal actors gone from the scene, the loan was called in. The glittering chandelier was reclaimed from the White House and rehung in the Senate corridor.

If there were such lighter moments in the early days of the Kennedy administration, there were also very serious ones. Kennedy had not been in office long when he found himself mired in the Bay of Pigs. Although the basic U.S. policy of unremitting hostility toward the Castro government was inherited from the Eisenhower administration, Kennedy and his closest advisors had only themselves to blame for what was to be an ill-fated attempt at a violent overthrow of Fidel Castro. During the election campaign of 1960, the Kennedy camp had all but attributed Castro's success to the Eisenhower-Nixon policy and had been severely critical of the Republican administration as "weak and vacillating." Such terms were politically inflammatory synonyms for the intelligent restraint that marked President Eisenhower's initial attempt to guide American relations with Cuba through the fierce revolutionary transition in that country. Unfortunately, in the later lexicography of foreign affairs, restraint and weakness were too often regarded as synonymous.

International Affairs: Cuba, Berlin, and the Soviet Union

While the Republican Party was being criticized by Democrats during the 1960 presidential campaign as being soft on communism and of other deficiencies in dealing with Castro, the Eisenhower administration had already abandoned the possibility of restraint in working out an accommodation with Castro. Instead, the administration initiated an alternative proposed by the CIA. At the time, the agency was headed by Allen Dulles, whose brother, John Foster Dulles, was secretary of state. Among other things, the plan involved a highly secret setup in Guatemala where U.S. operatives trained Cuban expatriates for a military expedition designed to recapture their homeland. Aided by U.S. military transportation, a secret landing by the expeditionary forces was to take place at the Bay of Pigs on Cuba's north coast. The invasion would be timed to coincide with an organized uprising of dissidents inside Cuba, also masterminded by CIA operatives. Any awareness of this plan in the Senate was informal and confined to a handful of CIA allies, a group that did not include the majority leader.

Once in office, President Kennedy had the power to cancel the Dulles plan. That he did not do so was in part the result of a gross overestimation of its prospects for success. Perhaps even more significant may have been the fear that cancellation would have been interpreted by the media as evidence of Kennedy's weakness in dealing with communism. Such a prospect would have frightened the most stalwart Democratic politician in that period. In any event, Kennedy's decision to go ahead with the plan in April 1961 resulted in a complete disaster and another exodus of Cuban political refugees to the United States, especially to Florida.

The positive public reaction to Kennedy's acceptance of responsibility cut off any inclination in the Senate to make political capital out of the disaster. And the Republicans would have been hard put to fault the president for trying to carry out a plot for getting rid of Castro concocted during a Republican administration. As for the Democrats, the Bay of Pigs provided the kind of militant anticommunist action against Cuba for which so many had seemed to be clamoring during the presidential campaign. The majority leader avoided mention of it, and the Senate quickly moved on to other matters.

The most serious aftershock of the disaster was the Cuban missile crisis. Emboldened by his success in stamping out the U.S.-sponsored coup and confronted only with hostility from the United States, Castro intensified his ties with the Soviet Union. Egged on by Moscow, he accepted Soviet assistance in secretly installing in Cuba medium-range missiles capable of carrying nuclear warheads to U.S. cities. With the installation came Soviet military technicians to train and assist the Cubans in their use. The emplacement of the missiles, however, was discovered by U.S. aerial reconnaissance in October 1962, prompting Kennedy to summon a high council of state. In asking for advice, it was quickly apparent that the president would reject any suggestion that did not assure the removal of the missile installations. He was prepared for a military confrontation with the Soviet Union, if necessary, to force the withdrawal. The majority leader and congressmen of both parties and houses were present at the meeting. None raised a dissent.

Kennedy's planned reaction involved a U.S. naval interdiction of Soviet ships carrying missiles for Cuba as they approached the island and a demand for the removal of the emplacements already on the island. For several hours after this ultimatum, it was as though a comet had suddenly locked onto a collision course with the Earth. The nation held its breath. Those who had built underground nuclear shelters in their backyards (one of the growth industries of the period) crawled into them. Some Americans congregated in churches and prayed. Others threw together doomsday parties and drank champagne while awaiting the end. Still others hugged one another and their children in silence. Few failed to recognize the seriousness of the situation. After what seemed interminable hours, Khrushchev ordered the Soviet supply ships to turn around and return home without attempting to unload their deadly cargo.

Although no shots were fired in the incident, the direct confrontation between the United States and the Soviet Union brought the world as close as it has ever been to the nuclear abyss. Interestingly, at that critical moment, the more strident voices were stilled on Capitol Hill.

Kennedy's popular acclaim for handling the Cuban problem could not be converted into pressure for action by the Congress on his domestic program. The needed legislation continued to face a long and tortuous journey through the House and Senate. Predictably, Speaker McCormack looked the other way when the administration's "must" list was sent to the Hill. It was left to the president's emissaries to find their own way to bring about committee acceptance of individual pieces of legislation. The same was true in the Senate. But the majority leader opened his office to the president's men, notably to Mike Manatos, a former Hill employee, who proved to be a fortuitous choice of the new administration. Manatos had spent years as administrative assistant to Senator Joe O'Mahoney of Wyoming, an outstanding progressive of the Roosevelt-Truman period. In his new role as the president's liaison with the Senate, Manatos's reputation, down-to-earth manner, and knowledge of Senate ways were keys that readily opened doors of members of both parties.

One item above all others concerned the president at the outset of his administration. It was a tax revision—mostly a tax cut for business—aimed at stimulating the economy out of a recession. Kennedy deemed the revision essential for "getting the country moving again." The measure was an early version of "supply side economics." In the House, the administration's effort to secure its passage was confounded time and again, all in good humor, by the fancy footwork of the eccentric chairmen of the Ways and Means Committee, Wilbur Mills of Arkansas. Mills delighted in the national publicity he received as he played fox to Kennedy's hounds on tax revision. After weeks of panting after the wily Mills, the hounds were finally brought to bay by the fox. Presidential concessions to Mills and other key legislators was the price of committee approval of the bill. Once having cleared the House, the tax measure encountered little resistance in the Senate.

Other than the tax cut, key items in the Kennedy program proved to be nonstarters during the first two years of the administration. Nevertheless, the tax cut and Kennedy's handling of the Cuban missile affair, plus a few innovative programs such as the Peace Corps and the Alliance for Progress, the latter designed to resuscitate hemispheric goodwill, were sufficient to hold off the Republicans. In the midterm elections of 1962, Democratic strength was enhanced in both houses. To all appearances, the country was satisfied with its Democratic leadership.

In the Senate, Mansfield was unopposed for a second term as majority leader. He continued in the same understated fashion stressing the right of all senators, the most recently elected no less than the most senior, to equal treatment from the leadership. His appointments to the Policy and Steering committees reflected the principle and, as chairman of the Steering Committee, he admonished his colleagues to see to it that newer members received a fair share of sought-after assignments to legislative committees. He pressed the newly elected members to abandon the "blushing-bride" posture to which Senate tradition had consigned them. Although his advice to get fully into the business of the Senate from the outset was still greeted gingerly by the new arrivals, the time lag from election to active participation in the Senate's affairs was shortened by his exhortations.

Minimizing his own role, Mansfield stressed that the Senate as a whole was to be credited with the respectable record achieved in the previous Congress. Republicans, led by Minority Leader Dirksen, joined Democrats in praising the majority leader for his evenhandedness. They glowed in the spotlight of Mansfield's praise for their dedication, while Mansfield made little of his own contribution. It was indeed a halcyon moment for the Senate.

Kennedy began the second half of his first term with strong popular approval at home, a popularity matched by his wide acceptance abroad, particularly in Western Europe. It was an acceptance gained by his handling of the overnight appearance of the Berlin Wall in August 1961. ?Suddenly, there it stood, impervious in the midst of an international uproar. It spelled out in concrete what Churchill had meant when he first spoke the words "Iron Curtain" to describe how the Russians had divided Europe. Kennedy withstood the demands of those who, in frustration or in an eagerness to have a go at communism, called on him to tear down the silent barrier. To placate this fury, Kennedy went so far as to travel to Germany to deliver a fist-shaking speech at the Wall and to promise that one day it would come down. He also mobilized military reservists at home. But he refused to be pressed into military or other provocations that could lead to war.

The Senate joined the president in the initial outburst of condemnation of the Wall. Members of both houses visited Berlin to shake fists at the abomination. Indeed, it became *de rigueur* for American political figures to be photographed peering over the barricade into East Berlin from a hastily built watchtower on the West side. Despite the fiery denunciations, however, few quarreled with Kennedy's decision to avoid pushing the crisis into outright conflict.

The Berlin Wall ended any immediate expectation of reunifying Germany, until then a cardinal principle of U.S.–European policy. While the principle was not abandoned, it was laid aside for some years and all but forgotten until German reunification was reborn out of the inner weaknesses of the Soviet Union and the initiatives of the Germans themselves on both sides of the barrier.

Before becoming majority leader, Mansfield had supported John Foster Dulles in the latter's pursuit of German unification, all the while groping for a way to end the dangerous military confrontation of the occupying forces in that city. At one point Mansfield had advocated a neutralized and unified Berlin under the United Nations. The idea received a respectable hearing in Germany and found echoes elsewhere in Western European, but drew a strong negative response from the executive branch in the United States. After the erection of the Wall, Mansfield rarely mentioned the subject. Instead, following Eisenhower's lead, he began to advocate a reduction of U.S. forces in Western Europe. He argued, as had Eisenhower, that a sharp drop in numbers would still leave enough to serve as a trip wire, at a substantial drop in costs. His quest went on unsuccessfully for years, not to bear fruit until after he had left the Senate.

Any improvement of relations with the Soviet Union was inhibited not only by the Wall but also by laws that had accumulated over the years before Mansfield became Senate leader. As often as not, such laws were designed by one member or another to upstage the president or the Department of State and force them to minimize contact with communist countries. Congressmen also used the tactic during the McCarthy period of vying with one another to prove the superiority of their anticommunist credentials. Although many of the authors of these measures had disappeared from Congress when Mansfield became leader of the Senate, their work lived on after them. Undoing what has already been done is one of the more difficult legislative maneuvers, but many of these laws had to be repealed or modified before the relationship with the Soviet Union could undergo a significant change for the better.

Throughout the years of Mansfield's leadership, Senator Henry ("Scoop") Jackson of the State of Washington was in the vanguard in opposing any easing of legislative impediments to contact with communist countries. Not only did Jackson resist removing existing impediments, he sought repeatedly to invent new ones. A leading Democrat, Jackson's personal aspirations regarding the presidency had been frustrated by Kennedy in 1960. As a consolation prize, Jackson was given, not the vice presidency or even a major cabinet post, but the political dead-end of chairman of the Democratic National Committee. Generally regarded as a liberal in domestic matters, Jackson received much support from labor in a state where labor was a powerful political factor. But Washington was also a state where the American Communist Party had made major political inroads during the Roosevelt administration, with some successful candidates for public office accepting its open support. The leftist politics of the state suffered a severe backlash during the McCarthy era. Orthodox Democratic politicians such as Jackson hastened to separate themselves from any association. For a sitting politician, one of the better ways to establish one's anticommunism was to demonstrate a willingness to make life, or at any rate relations, miserable for the Soviet Union through the offering of legislation that would hamstring any moves by the executive branch to make them better.

Another relevant element in Jackson's political background was the fact that Washington housed the Boeing Aircraft Company, a major contractor for the Defense Department, then as now. The department's purchases of expensive military hardware not only meant huge profits for the company but jobs, thousands of them, for residents of the state, many of whom had settled there during World War II and whose comfortable livelihood thereafter remained interwoven with the success of Boeing. That, in turn, was not unrelated to the continuance of the Cold War. Boeing was a principal source of employment for union labor, which on the one hand shared the company's interest in defense orders and on the other was a powerful element in the Democratic Party. Such factors played on Jackson as a senator of the state at a time when he was seeking to carve out a route to higher office. That road was blocked, first by Kennedy and then by Johnson. Thereafter, Jackson concentrated his attention on strengthening his power in the Senate. He sat on the Armed Services and the Commerce committees, and he chaired a special Committee on Human Rights. The assignment placed Jackson in an excellent position not only to represent his state's interest in defense contracts but also to oppose a rapprochement with the communist nations. Jackson was able to throw sand into the gears of presidential efforts to develop an opening to Eastern Europe. In time, Jackson found himself in a shrinking majority in his resistance to dismantling the legal basis for the Cold War, but he did not abandon his effort. Instead, he shifted tactics, linking legislative changes sought by various presidents to such disparate questions as Soviet willingness to grant exit visas so that Jews might emigrate or on the progress on human rights in the Soviet Union.

Domestic Problems and Legislation

Kennedy's handling of foreign affairs was generally supported on Capitol Hill. The same could not be said for his domestic legislative program. Not long into the first session of the 88th Congress, it became evident that the program would not have easy sailing. At that point, one problem was beginning to loom over all others, that of growing tensions among blacks over the inequities of racial segregation, a condition that was by law still the rule rather than the exception in the South. Nevertheless, the Kennedy administration seemed to be sitting on its haunches waiting for this problem to go away before proceeding to other legislative business of the New Frontier. But the problem would not go away. On the contrary, the tide of black anger was rising to flood stage. The president's position in the matter was clear. He was strongly opposed to segregation. Where he could legally do so, he came down firmly on the side of desegregation. A case in point was his insistence on carrying out the *Brown* decision on integration of the public schools. As was Eisenhower in the Little Rock confrontation, Kennedy was prepared to call up the National Guard in order to extend the scope of the law to state colleges and universities that barred their doors to blacks. A Democratic governor, George Wallace of Alabama, was the personification of white resistance to desegregation.

In dealing with Congress on the issue, Kennedy was not unaware of the complex procedural difficulties facing even the mildest civil rights legislation. Moreover, he understood fully the adverse political consequences of pitting Democrat against Democrat over this divisive issue in the Senate. Nevertheless, he was committed to advancing desegregation and was fearful that, unless the pace of progress was speeded, there would be serious danger of violent racial unrest. As 1963 began, Kennedy ordered the Justice Department to draw up a comprehensive civil rights bill. With draft legislation in hand, the president's emissaries, led by Attorney General Robert F. Kennedy, marched up Capitol Hill to explore the possibilities of proceeding.

They received a cordial welcome from the House Committee on the Judiciary, led by Emmanuel Celler, who had already served forty years in the House and who, with a largely black constituency in the Bedford-Stuyvesant sector of Brooklyn, New York, was a long-time advocate of an end to segregation. The response from the House indicated that the Judiciary Committee was primed to come to grips with the issue and that a clear majority of representatives were favorably disposed toward strong legislation. Kennedy's emissaries were advised, however, to check the waters in the Senate.

Chairman "Big Jim" Eastland of Mississippi was in firm control of the Senate Judiciary Committee. By nature, Eastland was the soul of courtesy and, provided the subject was not civil rights, was most obliging. Bobby Kennedy lingered only long enough to exchange pleasantries with the chairman, before moving on, empty-handed to the Senate majority leader's office. There, the advice from Mansfield was simple and blunt: back off for the time being. Mansfield's reluctance to give even a suggestion of encouragement to the administration did not set well with the Justice Department or civil rights advocates, and it led to a direct inquiry from the president. Mansfield insisted that any attempt to maneuver a civil rights bill through the Senate at that point was doomed to failure. The only result would be a decisive split in the Democratic ranks, which otherwise might remain cohesive enough to pass a number of measures in the president's program. Mansfield did agree to make a try at a civil rights measure sometime during the 88th Congress, although with what prospects he was not at all sure. The president had no choice but to acquiesce and he ceased pressing the Democratic-controlled Senate to act on the measure at that time.

Legislative Inaction and Reaction to Mansfield

Unfortunately, the postponement of the civil rights confrontation seemed to be an invitation to the Senate to relax on a whole range of questions. In view of Mansfield's tolerant leadership, that was easy enough. Not only was there no civil rights measure, there was very little of anything else moving in the Senate. As the third year of the Kennedy administration unfolded, fewer and fewer senators showed up for the daily sessions. When they did come, more often than not, it was not to legislate but to pontificate on all matters, national and international. The flow of legislation from the committees to the floor slowed to a trickle. When Mansfield inquired, always discreetly and with deference, of the committee chairmen as to the reasons, he heard complaints of the difficulties of rounding up enough committee members even to form a quorum. There was also reference to delays on the House side that had tied the hands of the Senate committees.

Mansfield took to the Senate floor repeatedly to remind all members of the need to be present to conduct business. He resorted to telegrams to urge Democratic senators to be on hand for specific votes. But that was as far as he would go. He refused to plead or to criticize, and he made no attempt to bullwhip senators into carrying out their prime responsibility. As for problems with the House, he declined to discuss them with the Speaker, limiting his contact with the irritable McCormack to ceremonial joint meetings. In short, he suffered the Senate slowdown in silence, blaming nobody in particular and attempting to put the best face possible on the situation.

Day after day, folder in hand, Mansfield strode the half-hundred paces from his office to the Senate floor. Before the official opening of the Senate, he talked briefly with the reporters gathered around his desk and shook hands with Everett Dirksen on the Republican side of the aisle. He shuffled papers impatiently while standing at his desk awaiting the end of the chaplain's prayer. Then he ran through the calendar of uncontested bills, passing them without objection in rapid succession. If an international development had caught his attention in the morning press, he might discuss it briefly. If a noteworthy event had occurred in Montana, he might ask permission to insert a press clipping in the *Record* to mark the occasion. These routine chores done, he left the chamber, usually making a brief stop to read the latest entries on the news tickers before returning to his office.

In the late afternoon he appeared again, in a near-empty chamber, to announce the program for the following day and to adjourn the Senate. The Senate clerks, grouped around the presiding officer's desk, would shake their heads in dismay at one more wasted day. Mansfield answered queries from newspeople on the embarrassing absence of progress with a thin smile and very few words, his head held high and his demeanor increasingly stiff.

The winter of 1963 melted into spring. The cherry trees burst into pink blossoms around the Tidal Basin and on the sloping Washington Monument grounds. A senator's daughter was crowned queen of the Cherry Blossom Festival as the fragile flowers withered in the heat of an approaching Washington summer. The long, hot days of July and August went by slowly. The weather cooled with the beckoning of autumn.

In the third year of the Kennedy administration, the Senate had settled into what had become an ordered pattern of aimlessness, seemingly sheltered by the thick walls of the Capitol into unawareness of the social thunderstorms closing in on its ramparts. In contrast to the respectable record of the 87th Congress, that of the 88th could already be dismissed as dismal. Not only was there no action on civil rights but most other measures sought by the Kennedy administration also seemed bogged down at various stages in the legislative process.

Although September had arrived and there was talk of adjournment in the corridors, even the regular appropriations bills were held up by a petulant dispute between Senator Carl Hayden, chairman of the Senate Appropriations Committee, and his House counterpart, Clarence Cannon of Missouri. The latter refused to lead his committee to the Senate side of the Capitol to meet the Hayden committee in conferences to iron out differences between the House and Senate versions of the bills. Cannon insisted that conferences between the two committees had to be held on the House side of the Capitol. To be sure, there was more to the dispute than an age-before-beauty confrontation of two old men. In fact, Cannon, an authority on parliamentary procedure, was convinced of the House's constitutional primacy in all matters pertaining to money. He was determined that the Senate concur in his interpretation by aping the emperors of ancient China, who expected periodic visits from rulers of lesser tribute states as evidence of subordination. Thus Cannon insisted that senators come to the House if they were so bold as to seek changes in the House version of an appropriation bill. It would be a symbolic gesture, to be sure, but in legislative bodies, where precedent counts for much, the Senate's submission in this fashion would serve to reinforce the House's preeminence in financial matters.

Carl Hayden, in his eighties at the time, based his adamancy on having to "walk so far" and left it to Dick Russell of Georgia, second in seniority on the committee, to resolve the dispute. Russell, also an authority on parliamentary procedure, countered Cannon's claim by pointing out that the Constitution granted the House initiatory power only in revenue-raising legislation, not in appropriations. Not only did Russell oppose Cannon's view of House superiority, he demanded that the House give back what it had usurped over the years and accept the Senate's right to initiate appropriations bills, or at least half of them. Neither side would give ground, and in 1963 the annual appropriations bills languished in legislative limbo.

The impasse had precedent in the struggle for dominance between the House of Commons and the House of Lords in British parliamentary practice, a dispute that lasted a century or more before ending in domination of the process by the Commons. Unfortunately, however, in the U.S. instance, the dispute resulted in weeks of inaction on basic money legislation for operation of federal departments, an essential of orderly government. The matter was finally resolved by finding a meeting room near the Rotunda of the Capitol, the Rotunda being situated midway between the House and Senate wings of the building. Claimed by the House (a claim disputed by the Senate), the Rotunda is a sort of no man's land under the custodial care of the architect of the Capitol, who is appointed by the president with the consent of the Senate and closely watched by the Speaker of the House.

By such posturing, rather than in acts of substance, were Congress's responsibilities receiving expression during the trying third year of the Kennedy administration.

The Nuclear Test Ban Treaty

The Senate did manage to record one major achievement in the period. By more than the required two-thirds vote, it approved for ratification a treaty with the Soviet Union and the United Kingdom that barred the testing of nuclear weapons in the atmosphere. The treaty marked a breakthrough in what until then had been a futile search for a start in imposing rational restraints on the race for nuclear supremacy. As such, it also heralded a resumption of serious diplomatic groping for a better way than mutual terror to assure civilized survival in a nuclear age. The search had been in abeyance for a decade after the general collapse of Soviet–U.S. cooperation at the end of World War II.

The basis for a ban on nuclear testing had existed for several years. From a U.S. point of view, it was apparent that the nation had far more to gain than to lose from such a ban. The United States had already done by far most of the testing of nuclear weapons and presumably knew more than the Russians about what could be learned from testing. In 1963, moreover, there was little doubt that the United States held a substantial advantage in both quantity and quality of existing nuclear weapons. Although the Soviet Union was presumed to be fast closing the gap, it was unlikely that further testing would have yielded any great advantage to either country. At the same time, concerned scientists in the United States and elsewhere, including the Soviet Union, were documenting the dangers of nuclear fallout and urging a cessation of testing. Carried by atmospheric winds, radioactive particles from such explosions were indifferent to national boundaries, and this perilous by-product of testing was coming to rest, among other places, in the United States and the Soviet Union. Scientific reports indicated an increasingly serious effect on human health in both countries and much of the rest of the world.

For example, when the fallout from Strontium 90, a particularly virulent radioactive element, came to rest in bovine pastures, it traveled from the soil to the grass to the cows' milk, for which it seemed to have an affinity, and its long-lived propensities were likely to outlive the shortened existence it caused involuntary recipients. This progression was of particular concern to the United States, a heavy consumer of milk and milk products.

Nevertheless, some engineers, physicists, military leaders, and government officials whose careers and sense of self-worth were intertwined with the perfection of nuclear devices refused at first to budge on the question of continuing tests. Such was the level of suspicion between the Soviet Union and the United States that both governments clung to similar individual positions on the grounds of national defense. At the same time, each blamed the other for the failure to bring the practice of testing to an end despite the obvious peril that it posed for the earth's livability.

The governments of the two countries downplayed the risk while continuing to test the devices. In time, mass protests against testing erupted throughout the world. They were particularly vehement in Japan, which alone had experienced the vast destruction and other consequences of nuclear explosions in warfare. Protests grew more vehement and widespread in the United States, finally compelling a serious search by the Eisenhower administration for ways to eliminate the danger.

Senator Humphrey, as chairman of a special Senate Disarmament Sub-committee, considered offering a proposal for a Treaty to Ban Nuclear Testing. Before he could do so, the Soviet Union seized the idea and set forth the same proposition at the United Nations. Caught by surprise, the Eisenhower administration at first dismissed the Soviet proposal as just another propaganda ploy. Public concern over nuclear testing, however, was not assuaged and demanded an exploration of the idea. The administration continued to stall, stressing the problems of verification in the Soviet Union, all the while continuing its own tests of nuclear devices.

Soon after his victory in the 1956 election, President Eisenhower let himself be persuaded to explore the possibilities of a test ban treaty. The Russians sought to force the issue by inaugurating unilateral test moratoriums conditioned on a response from the United States. When none was forthcoming, they gained worldwide acclaim while remaining in a position to continue testing in the periods between the moratoriums. Finally, the United States and the Soviet Union entered into on-again, off-again negotiations that stretched over months and into years. Each sought the maximum public relations advantage from this process by fixing blame on the other for the failure to stop testing. At the same time, both hastened to eke out the last possible technological advantage by accelerating testing activity for fear that a growing world outrage, including that of their own people, would finally compel a halt.

On assuming the presidency, Kennedy had no hesitancy in taking up negotiations with the Soviet Union at the point where the Eisenhower administration had left off. In doing so, he had the enthusiastic support of Hubert Humphrey and other Democrats in the Senate. Republicans were more cautious. Some senators emphasized the dangers of nuclear fallout. A few scoffed at it. Many avoided mentioning it at all, stressing instead the dangers of permitting the Russians to gain an edge in nuclear weapons.

Two years into the Kennedy administration, the United States and the Soviet Union signed a Nuclear Test Ban Treaty. By that time, the original concept of a total ban had been diluted. The draft treaty prohibited only tests in the atmosphere, in outer space, and in the seas. Left undisturbed was the right of each nation to continue its experimental explosions underground, where presumably they would not constitute a hazard to human health. The presumption was not entirely accurate, and decades later an international ban on all testing was finally achieved.

The treaty signed during the Kennedy administration was a breakthrough in the freeze in U.S.–Soviet relations. It was an act of international reason at a time when such acts were few and far between. Ratification by the Senate was an early milestone in Mansfield's leadership in the Senate. In the process of ratification, the treaty received the unanimous endorsement of the Foreign Relations Committee. Mansfield deferred not only to the chairman of the Foreign Relations Committee, Senator Fulbright, but also to Senator Humphrey, to the minority leader, and to anyone else who wished to be in the spotlight. Mansfield's concentration was on obtaining the Senate's approval, and he praised all effusively for the achievement, while claiming none of the credit for himself. After an initial hesitancy, Minority Leader Dirksen persuaded himself and then sought to persuade his skeptical Republican colleagues that the treaty was "an idea whose time had come." Dirksen frequently used this circumlocution to signify that he had changed his mind without acknowledging that he had done so.

In the final Senate vote on the Nuclear Test Ban Treaty, fifty-five Democrats and twenty-five Republicans supported ratification. Among the latter, almost the entire midwestern contingent, previously hesitant or negative, shifted on the issue. On the Democratic side, "Scoop" Jackson, who had initially resisted the idea of a treaty and counseled Humphrey to stay away from it, could not resist the groundswell for ending the tests and cast his vote with the majority. The negative votes came mostly from southern Democrats. They were joined by Texas Republican John Tower, who voted with them more often than not, despite differing party labels. Also joining the southerners were western Republicans, including the then most voluble defender of the Pentagon in the Senate, Barry Goldwater of Arizona.

Disruption of the Republican-southern coalition on this vote came as something of a surprise to many observers. The treaty was an issue on which the two groups might have been expected to be together, since they shared deep doubts as to the wisdom of any agreement with the Russians. Both also tended to equate a huge defense budget with patriotism, if not national prosperity. The key factor was the shift by Dirksen. The minority leader's decision not to lend his support to the southern-Republican coalition in this instance did not mark the end of his readiness to use this linkage to exploit the ideological split among the Senate Democrats on other issues. Nor did it mean that he had set aside his roguish delight in deflating the pomposity of some Democrats who were the treaty's most vehement supporters. He never lost the urge to stick a pin in the pretentious. In this instance, however, he restrained the urge in deference to the importance of the treaty to the nation.

Dirksen understood, too, the importance of a successful vote on ratification to the majority leader and his style of leadership. Unlike his predecessor, Mansfield required no deflating; he was the least pretentious of men. Nor had he shown any inclination whatsoever to play dirty pool with such ideological splits and divisions that existed in the Republican minority. In short, Dirksen was satisfied that Mansfield was running the Senate for Republicans as well as Democrats and as closely in accord with the Golden Rule as was ever likely to be found in a legislative body. Mansfield's approach was eminently agreeable to Dirksen and predisposed him to cooperate whenever possible. Dirksen's decision to support the Nuclear Test Ban Treaty was an early reflection of what was to be the statesmanship of his final years in the Senate.

The COMSAT Bill and Cloture

Without Dirksen's participation, a Republican–southern Democratic coalition did not emerge on the Nuclear Test Ban Treaty. This was a precursor of what was to come on the issue of civil rights, where Dirksen was to play an even more significant role. Actually, there had been an earlier and highly significant, if less noticed, breach in the alignment. In that case, the Republican leader was the pivot. The issue involved legislation regulating the use of outer space for telecommunications. A half decade after the launch of the first space satellite, it was widely recognized that a revolution in communications was in the offing, opening a potential not only for vastly expanded communications within and between nations but also an opportunity for huge profits for those who controlled the networks. Also evident from the outset were the prospects of a chaotic cacophony in the heavens in the absence of adequate regulatory mechanisms. In short, there existed a need for some sort of intervening authority, both national and international, if the full potential of the new medium were to be realized.

Nationally, the question of the kind of intervention, and to whose advantage, rested with Congress. In the Senate, the matter came within the purview of the Commerce Committee. Not unexpectedly, the chairman of the Committee, Robert Kerr of Oklahoma, came down on the side of less, rather than more, government participation in the development and more, rather than less, private enterprise in controlling this great new natural resource. His views predominated, and the bill that was drafted and sent to the Senate by the committee had the government sponsoring but not dominating a quasi-private monopolistic corporation to develop the communications potential of outer space.

Kerr had little trouble in committee in winning bipartisan endorsement for this approach. Even John O. Pastore of Rhode Island, Kerr's frequent nemesis, went along. With this support, plus a cooperative executive branch and the backing of the large communications corporations, no difficulty was anticipated in securing prompt passage of the Communications Satellite (COMSAT) bill by the full Senate. But the Senate contained a small contingent of vigorous antimonopolists and a few advocates of public ownership. This group was directly descendent from the New Deal and other populist movements that had fought for public or cooperative ownership of public utilities in an earlier day.

True to this heritage, Wayne Morse of Oregon became the principal spokesman in opposition to the Kerr bill. Supporting him was a scattering of liberals who were always ready to do battle with the dragons of private monopoly. Morse launched a prolonged educational discussion of the proposed Communications Satellite Act of 1962. The term "educational discussion" was coopted from the vocabularies of southern senators, who usually employed it to announce a filibuster against a civil rights measure.

To be sure, Morse was one of the more long-winded members of the Senate. But his speeches were invariably erudite. Even though he spoke at length on many issues, he had not used the filibuster as a tactic to try to prevent a vote on a measure. He was, in fact, an enemy of the filibuster and had declared himself "always ready to vote for cloture" to shut off debate. It is doubtful, therefore, that when Morse set out to oppose the Kerr bill, he expected to prolong the discussion of COMSAT for more than a day or two. In their impatience to nail down the measure, however, Kerr and others quickly raised the charge of filibustering. Goaded by the accusation, Morse then began to show resistance to bringing the debate to a close, specifically requesting the majority leader to protect his rights in his absence from the floor. He received such assurances from Mansfield, who was ever ready to accommodate any member fearful of being tricked while under siege.

Educational discussion or not, after several days even the seemingly inexhaustible Morse began to run out of words of relevance. It became apparent that he and the small band of liberals who had come to his aid were intent on talking COMSAT to death. In short, a filibuster was indeed in progress. A backlog of other business began to build up behind the stalled measure.

There were several ironies in the situation. In the first place, a filibuster was being sustained by liberals for the first time in living memory. This group had repeatedly denounced the archaic Senate rules under which it was possible for a minority to block the Senate from making a decision on a bill. From the liberals had come the strongest criticism of filibusters when used to stop civil rights legislation. Now, such senators as Douglas of Illinois found themselves engaged in this dubious practice, doing precisely what they had time and again denounced southerners for doing.

With the tables turned, the southern Democrats might have been expected to take sweet revenge in reciprocal denunciation of the liberals for holding up the Senate. Some were so inclined but not Russell of Georgia.

As the great advocate of unlimited debate, Russell insisted that this "right" of all senators was what set the Senate apart from all other legislative bodies. He insisted that any attempt to curtail this right was unworthy of the Senate. In dealing with COMSAT, Russell remained consistent. He eschewed the temptation to criticize the liberal filibuster. Although solidly behind the bill that was being held up, he did not question the method that the liberals were using in the effort to prevent a vote on it. Commanded to silence by Russell's example, the southern contingent almost to a man fell in line. Few words of criticism came from that quarter as Morse droned on. If the southerners now found themselves drowning in a flood of words, as they had deluged their colleagues repeatedly in the past, at least they had the decency to suffer in silence. Not so the Republicans. Led by Dirksen, they took delight in taunting Morse and his small band of liberals for seeking umbrage in the same filibuster they had so often denounced in the past. Dirksen saw an opportunity for the display of histrionics, and he used his full repertoire to highlight the hypocrisy of their position.

Except for the pleasure of taunting his adversaries, however, nothing else resulted from Dirksen's efforts. To be sure, the liberals were somewhat embarrassed by the inconsistency of their position. They could only protest the innocence of their intent, even as their credibility was fast drowning in their own words. Taunts notwithstanding, they had no difficulty in sustaining the talk day after day. All the while, the substantial majority of senators who favored the COMSAT bill was powerless to vote on the measure. After a while, the liberal filibusterers no longer seemed embarrassed by their performance. It was as though they had suddenly discovered a hidden pleasure that their scruples had prevented them from savoring in the past. The more they indulged themselves, the more they appeared to enjoy it. With the pressure of other business building up, they were even beginning to nourish some hope of forcing the leadership to lay aside the Kerr bill.

In his puckish delight at catching the liberals doing what they had always denounced as virtually an immoral act, Dirksen overlooked something that Russell had not. By deriding the liberals, Dirksen was also ridiculing the Senate dogma of "unlimited debate." Mocking the one opened the door to mockery of the other. To deride extended debate as a device to hold up the COMSAT legislation would undermine the filibuster in forestalling civil rights legislation. It would foreclose use of this procedural safety hatch by which Republicans had been able to escape moral responsibility for their unspoken assistance to the southerners on civil rights. No longer could they proclaim their fealty to Abraham Lincoln by expressing a readiness to vote for civil rights legislation if they had the chance to do so even as the southerners were sparing them the necessity for doing so by using the filibuster to talk such measures to death.

Frustrated by the continued tie-up in the Senate over the COMSAT filibuster, Dirksen was in a receptive mood when Senator Kerr, its sponsor, approached him for cooperation in seeking a way to break the filibuster. Together, they called on the majority leader. Until that moment, Mansfield had remained aloof from what was transpiring on the Senate floor. He listened to their summation of the situation. Kerr and Dirksen then asked Mansfield to intervene actively in an effort to cajole Morse into abandoning his filibuster. If that failed, they urged that Mansfield lengthen the Senate's workday to twenty-four hours in order to exhaust the filibusterers. The majority leader readily agreed with them that a filibuster was in progress. He pointed out, however, that he had no power as one senator to bring the filibuster to a close. Nor, as majority leader, would he beg or cajole any member of the Senate for his vote. Senators were grown-ups, and he assumed they would resent such treatment, as would he. Neither would he threaten Morse with dire consequences. That would be a fruitless course, in any event, as Dirksen knew, since Morse had left the Republican Party because of attempts to force him into line. Mansfield would not seek to isolate Morse.

Although he regarded it as futile, Mansfield did comply with their proposal to lengthen daily sessions. But there would be no late-night, much less all-night, sessions in an effort to wear out the filibusterers. As Kerr and Dirksen they should know from past experience, when pajama sessions had been attempted by Johnson, that course invariably led to just the opposite of what was intended; it wore out the majority, rather than the filibustering minority. In short, if the filibuster was to be ended, it would be up to the Senate as a whole, acting under the Rules, to bring the debate to a close. Otherwise, Mansfield would simply pass over the COMSAT bill at some point and take up the next item on the calendar. What Mansfield did not say was that, under the Rules, the only path open to ending the filibuster was the adoption of cloture under Rule 22, something that the Senate had failed to do time and again on civil rights legislation. Dirksen understood this without its being said, however, and he spoke the unspeakable, ungentlemanly word "cloture." Mansfield conceded that cloture would be within the Rules. Much as he disliked silencing any member who thought he had something to say, he would support cloture in this instance. But he went on to remind both Kerr and Dirksen that invoking Rule 22 required a two-thirds majority. There would be no possibility, therefore, of shutting off the debate unless the Republicans were prepared to exert every effort in concert with the Democrats to obtain the necessary votes.

Dirksen made a quick mental calculation and persuaded himself that the votes could be had. As for Kerr, he had strong ties to the southerners and had rejected cloture on civil rights bills in the past. If he shifted, he might also persuade some western Democrats, who had previously opposed cloture on principle, arguing that it would weaken the overall legislative power of their less-populous states. It would be a new course for Kerr, but in his determination to pass the COMSAT bill, he agreed.

With these assurances, Mansfield filed the required petition signed by sixteen senators calling for the closing of debate. Two days later, the Senate adopted cloture by a vote of 73 to 27. All but two Republicans, Barry Goldwater of Arizona and John Tower of Texas, voted with the majority. In losing, Morse received the support of his liberal allies and a number of westerners who held out against Kerr's blandishments, including Carl Hayden of Arizona, who had never voted for cloture and had vowed that he never would. In what must have been one of the more ironic experiences of his career, Morse also found himself supported in the vote against cloture by a solid phalanx of southern Democrats, led by Richard Russell. In voting with Morse, the southerners were proving their consistency as well as their astuteness. While they favored the bogged down COMSAT bill, they favored unlimited debate even more because it was the key to their rearguard resistance to civil rights legislation. Only after cloture had been invoked, in spite of their negative votes, did they wheel around as if on signal to vote on passage of the COMSAT bill itself.

There was jeering and cheering over the outcome, but neither came from the majority leader. As though to stress his insignificant role, Mansfield disappeared from the floor before the announcement of the vote, leaving it to others to enjoy the warmth of success. Indeed, the vote was interpreted as a victory for Kerr and Dirksen with a brilliant assist from Bobby Baker, the secretary for the majority, who had worked overtime to line up the cloture votes. Mansfield's role was scarcely noted.

Dirksen's Republicans celebrated the victory and not only because the COMSAT bill was in accord with Republican economic philosophy because it stressed the role of business in space communications while restraining the role of government. They celebrated, too, because of their role in the cloture vote. Their votes had been the decisive factor in defeating the despised liberals, especially Morse, who had been a thorn in their side as a Republican and proved to be no better after becoming a Democrat.

The liberals might have been able to find some solace in their defeat if they sought it. Until that moment, the filibuster had been regarded as virtually an exclusive device, patented by the southerners, and reserved for use in situations involving civil rights. For years, it had not occurred to any other group to tie up the Senate indefinitely by organized talk in order to prevent a major bill from coming to a vote. The Morse filibuster, crude though it was in comparison with those of the southerners, nevertheless had broken the latter's monopoly. It had underscored the ease with which the Senate could be brought to a halt by any determined minority. What had previously been used almost exclusively on one issue could also be used indiscreetly on any issue. In short, the Morse filibuster brought into focus a dangerous structural weakness in the Senate as an institution, a weakness that could render it impotent. It was in that sense an eye opener to senators who, under the mores of the Senate, felt squeamish about cutting off a colleague, even one carried away by the sound of his or her own voice. Now the filibuster could be seen more clearly for what it was: a subversive procedural instrument that eroded the Senate's constitutional responsibility to decide measures by a simple majority vote unless specifically provided for otherwise by the Constitution.

Another consequence of the Morse cloture vote was that the entire Senate had witnessed the successful operation of Rule 22 to end the filibuster. Previously, only Hayden of Arizona could claim that distinction. It was the first time in thirty-five years that the Senate had voted to shut off debate and only the fifth time in its history. Those who had previously been led to believe that Rule 22 was something abrupt and brutal or ungentlemanly found out differently. Even while it brought debate to a close, cloture was scarcely the ogre depicted by the southerners. It was far from a gag rule. On the contrary; built into Rule 22 was a scrupulous regard for the reasonable rights of individual members. All senators had days for their say before the adoption of cloture by two-thirds of the members. Even afterward, the Rule permitted a hundred hours of additional debate, an hour for each senator to get in that final word.

Senators had previously seen the filibuster as a high wall erected for almost the single purpose of holding back civil rights legislation. Now, seventy-three members had participated in storming the wall on another issue. And, in an ironic twist, the liberals, sworn enemies of the tyranny of talk, had been in this instance the ones silenced by cloture.

Morse and his cohorts were so intent on licking their wounds that they did not notice the glow on the horizon. They did not see that what had been done to them might be done again. They did not immediately make the mental link between their defeat on the COMSAT cloture and the route to victory in the coming struggle on civil rights. Not so with the leader of the southern block. If there was a furrowed brow anywhere in the Senate after the successful vote on cloture, it belonged to Dick Russell of Georgia. For the first time, he had been on the losing side in a cloture vote. To be sure, he was with the winning side in the subsequent vote on COMSAT. To Russell, however, it was a pyrrhic victory. It had been purchased at the price of the adoption of cloture, with both Republicans and western Democrats support-ing the cutoff of debate. Among them were senators whom Russell had counted on in the past not to vote for cloture and in that way help him to bury civil rights bills without having to vote on them. Now the dike had been breached. Senators who had previously turned away from cloture had seen that a vote for cloture was not the end of the world, much less the end of the Senate. Such a perception could well mark the beginning of a major change in the prevailing thought processes of the Senate.

In voting as they had, to sustain Morse's right to unlimited debate the southerners had become separated from their natural allies: conservative Republicans and westerners. Indeed, they had heard nonsoutherners whom they counted on deride and denounce the filibuster, at least as practiced by the liberals on COMSAT. Would these erstwhile allies henceforth react to southerners in the same way? Would there come a time when they might also be prepared to say "enough is enough" to them? In short, was voting for cloture now to become respectable in the "greatest deliberative body in the world," notably on legislation involving race questions and among Abraham Lincoln's political descendants?

Mansfield's unrelenting efforts to build a bridge to the Republicans and particularly to the Republican leader by equal and even deferential treat-ment had paid off in producing the necessary two-thirds vote required for cloture on COMSAT as it had in the earlier vote for ratification of the Nuclear Test Ban Treaty. The accomplishment, however, went largely un-noticed. Mansfield's restrained style remained the subject of a good deal of skepticism, both inside and outside Senate circles. His leadership was vari-ously described as weak, reticent, meek, or even nonexistent.

The skepticism was reinforced by the poor performance of the Senate on other legislation as Kennedy moved deeper into his third year in the White House. Doubts about Mansfield were spreading especially among the lib-eral Democrats who were having increasing difficulty in recognizing the majority leader as one of them. After all, Mansfield had voted against them on cloture and COMSAT. Smarting over those defeats, the liberals began to find fault with the Senate's handling of the Kennedy program to which they avowed faithful adherence. While they refrained from openly blaming the majority leader, their uneasiness was evident. Some of them attributed the difficulty to the Senate's rules and practices. Having indulged themselves so recently with a filibuster that exploited both, however, this line of criti-cism found little support outside their own circle. In any event, there was no groundswell for revision of the Rules.

The rate of absenteeism of senators was, increasingly, a sore point for Mansfield. More and more members seemed to find pressing affairs outside the confines of the Capitol that took precedence over attendance at Senate committee meetings. Committee chairmen complained they could not conduct business because of members' absences. Some chairmen, like the elder Harry F. Byrd of Virginia, of the Finance Committee, refused to give even preliminary consideration to measures that had not yet cleared the House of Representatives. Byrd based his reticence on the Constitution. It is true that the Constitution does provide for the House to act first on revenue bills, but, as other chairmen of the Finance Committee have discovered, it does not forbid the Senate from doing preparatory work while waiting for the House to complete action. The differences in time spans for action in the two approaches can sometimes be calculated in weeks. Nevertheless, Byrd was as adamant as he was gracious, so much so that one might expect that he hoped for no action at all on much of the legislation that came before his committee. Although fond of Mansfield, the Virginia patriarch felt no great urge to accommodate the young president.

Byrd had entered the Senate in 1933 as a reformer and avid supporter of Franklin D. Roosevelt. Soon after, however, he had parted company with the New Deal president and thereafter had fallen farther and farther away from the mainstream of the Democratic Party. In his later years, he became obsessed with the persistent federal budgetary deficits. As chairman of the Finance Committee, he sought to curb the growth in federal expenditures by sponsoring a law that put a ceiling on the federal debt. Over the years the debt ceiling had all the impact of a Band-Aid on a severed artery. It resulted primarily in a time-consuming charade in which the ritual of bewailing the deficit and exchanging political finger-pointing invariably served as a preliminary for raising the debt ceiling higher. When on occasion Congress failed to act in a timely fashion in the latter respect, the government would begin the demeaning process of shutting itself down for lack of funds essential to its routine operation. Byrd's strenuous efforts did not succeed in slowing, much less halting, the juggernaut of mounting federal expenditures, but it did serve to embarrass his party. That was not surprising, inasmuch as, more often than not, his individual position on major issues paralleled that of the Republicans. Still, as a Virginian, he clung to his Democratic identity until his retirement from the Senate in 1965, a year before his death.

As the Senate dawdled through the opening months of 1963, Senate committee chairmen began to feel pressure directly from the administration and the media for action. In the past, the responsibility of the committees for unconscionable delays had been diluted if not obscured by Johnson's eagerness as majority leader to hug the limelight, where the blame as well as the praise fell on him. The press had grown accustomed to seeking answers on the legislative program from the majority leader rather than the committee chairmen. Similarly, the Eisenhower administration talked with Johnson and Rayburn, rarely with committee chairmen when dealing with Congress. Under Mansfield, the situation changed drastically. When, for example, the president summoned congressional leaders to discuss legislative delays, Mansfield insisted on including the relevant committee chairman, often to their discomfort. At regular Tuesday morning presidential breakfast meetings with Kennedy, and later with Johnson, Mansfield was accompanied by both the assistant majority leader and the secretary of the Democratic Conference. When the president's representatives or the press inquired as to the status of a particular piece of legislation, they received assurances from Mansfield as to when the bill would be taken up only if the bill had cleared committee and was on the calendar awaiting action by the Senate as a whole. Otherwise, the inquirer was referred to the appropriate committee chairman. Mansfield rejected suggestions that he intervene in internal committee procedures, stressing the absence of power in the leadership to do so and pointing out that only the Senate as a whole could act if it was dissatisfied with a committee's performance.

In a formal sense, of course, he was correct. Under the Rules of the Senate, the majority leader had no special powers. Indeed, the existence of a majority leader or a minority leader was never even acknowledged in the Senate Rules. Under the precedents of the Senate, they were accorded little more than any member, other than the courtesy of preferential recognition if they were seeking to speak on the floor. That meant little beyond the likelihood that if the leader and a member arose simultaneously to ask for the floor, the chair would recognize the leader. Even then, presumably, it would not be because of his title, but because his desk was front and center and hence in the most direct line of vision of the presiding officer. In Mansfield's view, this distinction was useful but scarcely to be taken as a basis for bold initiatives in conducting the business of the Senate. He continued, therefore, to resist pressures to presume powers in the leadership where they did not exist. Instead, he settled into a prolonged holding pattern, clearing whatever came to the Senate calendar from the committees without delay, meeting from time to time with the chairmen at luncheons and for little more than informal discussions of the legislative program. He was determined that since the Senate as a whole possessed the power, the Senate as a whole would have to exercise it unless he was authorized to exercise it on behalf of the institution.

The Republicans were nonplussed by the massive inaction in the Senate. They enjoyed both the deferential treatment they were receiving from the majority leader and the absence of responsibility that their minority status accorded them. As the Senate ground almost to a halt, Dirksen looked forward gleefully to the weekly editions of the "Ev and Charlie" show for the edification of the press. While he refrained from direct criticism of Mansfield, he flailed away at the do-nothing Democrats in Congress. In due course, he used his skilled buffoonery to pinprick President Kennedy, whose popularity, while still high, was beginning to slip. In sparing Mansfield, Dirksen was not alone. Republicans as well as Democrats continued to extol Mansfield's fairness and integrity. He was providing the kind of leadership for which many of them had pined during the Johnson era. He blamed them for nothing. He had praise for all. His was a leadership well designed to inflate the self-esteem of each member. In return, his colleagues were lavish in expressions of affection for the leader and in acknowledging his good intentions and dedication.

In the corridors, however, the query "Is that enough?" was heard, and it grew more persistent, particularly among members of Mansfield's own party. Some spoke of the majority leader's weakness and indecision. Others thought they had discovered in Mansfield a confirmed liberal concealed in conservative clothing. Still others concluded that he was a conservative in liberal garb. Although they had groaned and railed against Lyndon Johnson's leadership in the past, some senators even began to pine for the "good old days." With few intimates when he was designated leader, Mansfield became more of an enigma to his colleagues with each passing day.

As the situation worsened in the Senate, the majority leader drew ever more deeply into his own counsel. If he was concerned, it was not apparent. As one columnist described it, his demeanor was that of a "cigar store Indian." Growing doubts about Mansfield's leadership were brought sharply into the open by columnist William White and others. White had been an avid admirer of Lyndon Johnson and of the kind of Senate that had functioned in the Texan's corral. He had extolled both in a popular book called *The Citadel,* in which White divided senators into the handful who occupied the Inner Club and all the rest. It was an apt delineation, but a Senate that had all but disappeared under Mansfield's leadership. When Mansfield was seen as Johnson's faithful assistant leader, the columnist had only words of praise for him, particularly for his wisdom in foreign affairs. With the Senate showing no sign of breaking out of its slump, White questioned the viability of Mansfield's approach. More in sorrow than anger, but with no less devastating effect, he expressed doubt about the Montanan's competence as Senate majority leader, drawing a most unflattering comparison of his ability with that of his predecessor.

White's lamentation on the state of the Senate leadership was little different from the whispers that could be heard in hideaways in the Capitol. It was said that the leadership was a role for which Mansfield was patently unsuited and one that he had never wanted. It was rumored, too, that he was looking for a graceful way out. Once again the name of Hubert Humphrey, the Democratic whip, floated aloft as a logical successor, as a man who could snap the whip and really move the president's program in the Senate. Humphrey himself carried on in his usual bubbling fashion, as though he had heard nothing. But his ever-eager staff found allies among their colleagues in the offices of other Democratic senators. As for the southerners, they tended to their committee business as though there was nothing unusual afoot. Whatever his shortcomings, Mansfield suited them in the role of majority leader. From their point of view, the fact that the Senate was doing very little was preferable to a Senate being driven to do too much.

Confronted with an increasingly unstable racial situation, President Kennedy was particularly distressed by the fading hope of civil rights legislation emerging from Congress. After considerable hesitancy, Kennedy was beginning to sense that the situation in the southern states would not hold still for much longer. There was clearly a need to dampen the rising fires of racial unrest. After a massive turnout of all races who gathered on the Mall in August 1963 to listen to Martin Luther King Jr.'s "I have a dream" speech, Kennedy wanted a prompt display of further progress in moving the country toward racial equity. The key was legislative action. Once again he dispatched his brother, the attorney general, and the latter's aides to Capitol Hill to raise with the congressional leadership the question of a comprehensive law that would strengthen his hand in dealing with the crisis. Hard pressed to move even routine appropriations bills, Mansfield could not give Bobby Kennedy any encouragement on civil rights. The only assurance he was prepared to provide was that the civil rights bill would be taken up by the Senate. Even then, he offered no guarantees that it could be passed.

By this point, the first session was running out of time. Members had already begun to raise the question of adjournment. With the exception of a few liberals, such as Clark of Pennsylvania and Jacob Javits of New York, the last thing senators wished to be confronted with was a civil rights bill going nowhere. Some suggested that the best course would be to clear the appropriations bills and noncontroversial measures, close out the first session, and come back in January of the following year to tackle the president's innovative programs. If there were a repetition of the inaction in the second session, it could be attributed to the impending election for the presidency.

At the time, talk of adjournment in early fall was almost a routine of Congress. The two houses usually aimed for a first-session maximum of nine months, with the second convening for an even shorter period. The adjournment target for the first session was not always met, and there were occasions when special sessions of the second had to be convened after an election. The imprecision of the process contributed to an atmosphere of anxiety and anticipation in the Senate that had more in common with a boy's prep school than with what one might expect from a national deliberative body.

Mansfield found it particularly inappropriate for the Senate to be panting after adjournment in the first session of the 88th Congress, one that had done little in the face of a lengthening national agenda. Instead of encouraging such expectations, Mansfield raised the prospect of continuing the session until the end of the year. He did so in the context of what he saw as a need for a permanent change in congressional adjournment practices. He was persuaded that the Senate's responsibilities were becoming year-round; accordingly, he sought to adjust the concept of adjournment to fit that situation. He had already taken a first step in that direction by introducing at the outset of the previous Congress a timetable of regular recesses for the year. It had been welcomed as a replacement for the periodic breaks that previously had been declared more or less at the caprice of the leadership. The change was in accord with Mansfield's innate sense of order. It also responded to members' complaints that the erratic work habits pursued by Johnson unnecessarily complicated their lives.

A schedule of recesses enabled members to arrange their calendars so as to be able to project in advance their returns to their states in order to listen to the people they represented and to carry on other necessary business outside the capital. Mansfield was also concerned with providing some fixed period so that younger members with growing children could count on spending time with their families. Finally, with the Senate moving toward year-round sessions, set periods away from the capital, he thought, might provide legislators with a better perspective of the nation's needs and expectations than that gained in Washington. In return for predictable shutdowns of the Senate, he expected that members could be on hand the rest of the time to do the public's business, an expectation that unfortunately was not always realized.

Elements in the press, as might have been expected, had a field day with tie innovations, often deriding them as an overgenerous arrangement for vacations and junketing even before the Senate had begun working. Notwithstanding the criticism, Mansfield never wavered in his support of the reform. Refined in subsequent Congresses, the recess schedule and all-year sessions have become a regular part of the Senate's practices. And, predictably, some elements in the press continue to deride them.

The Bobby Baker Scandal and Its Aftermath

In the midst of the inactivity in the Senate during the first session of the 88th Congress, a scandal erupted that promised to shake the august body loose from its foundations. Republican Senator John Williams of Delaware took the floor one quiet afternoon and, without prior indication, castigated the majority secretary, Bobby Baker, for certain dubious activities in conflict with his responsibilities to the Senate. Actually, Williams was repeating charges that had appeared in the newspaper column "Washington Merry-Go-Round," the preserve of Drew Pearson, premier muckraker of the era. The initial charges concerned a Baker sideline occupation, something called the Quorum Club, which served as a private gathering place for senators, congressmen, lobbyists, government officials, and assorted hangers-on, including attractive women. The club was located in the Carroll Arms Hotel, a stone's throw from what is now the Russell Senate office building. The hotel was subsequently torn down to make room for a Capital police headquarters.

Senator Williams was a wealthy chicken farmer from Frankfort, Delaware, whose most distinctive feature was a quizzical leer that seemed chiseled into his tightly skinned skull. The leer plus a shrill voice gave him the demeanor of a dreaded inquisitor. He was a petty man who had made it his personal crusade to ferret out shenanigans of a smaller scale in the government. Once within range of a questionable practice, however, he was as relentless in pursuit of its perpetrators as a blue tick hound after a raccoon. In Baker's case, Williams had picked up a strong scent, and he would not be deflected. Once it was known that Williams was coming, the Quorum Club quickly emptied of its members.

The Baker story was soon embellished by reports of wild parties, call girls, payoffs, influence peddling, and a major Baker enterprise, a resort hotel known as the Carousel, in Ocean City, Maryland, one of Washington's favorite summer retreats. Before long, the expanding story even contained a hint of espionage. The practitioner was said to be a friend of some congressional members. She was described in the press as a woman about town said to be not only the mistress of an attaché at the Soviet Embassy but also someone who was of interest to none other than President Kennedy. In any event, the woman was promptly deported to her native Germany by direct order of Bobby Kennedy after the story appeared in the press, and Bobby Baker soon gained the dubious distinction of an appearance as "man of the week" on the cover of *Time* magazine.

In the charges that began swirling about his head, Senate Majority Secretary Baker was quick to see the hand of the other significant Bobby, the president's brother and the attorney general. Baker was convinced that Robert Kennedy not only wanted him separated from the Senate but was out to get him. His surmise may not have been inaccurate. It is likely that Baker was seen by the White House not only as a source of corruption and hence a potential embarrassment to the Democrats but in his role as secretary for the majority also a chief obstructionist of the Kennedy program, particularly on civil rights. Furthermore, Robert Kennedy was certainly ready to repay old debts for Baker's role on behalf of Lyndon Johnson at the Democratic presidential convention. Finally, to devastate Baker was a way of weakening Johnson, with whom Baker had been closely associated in the Senate, if the intention of the White House was to dump Johnson from the Democratic ticket in the approaching 1964 election.

Mansfield remained passive as the scandal swirled about the Senate. He did not make light of the matter, but at the same time he refused to accept Baker's proffered resignation, insisting that the matter had to be clarified. Mansfield arranged a meeting of Senators Williams and Dirksen and other Senate leaders in his office, but Baker, although invited, could not bring himself to confront his accuser, John Williams, and insisted instead that Mansfield accept his resignation. By that point, the FBI had brought into the open indications that Baker was consorting with known U.S. gamblers in a dubious Caribbean gambling enterprise. With the concurrence of Williams, Mansfield decided to turn the entire matter over to the Rules Committee for a full-scale investigation. At the time, the Rules Committee was largely concerned with housekeeping functions of the Senate and was ill equipped to handle the matter. The amiable chairman, B. Everett Jordan of North Carolina, resisted the assignment but against his better judgment was persuaded to take on the Baker scandal. Jordan's reluctance proved well founded. When the report of his Rules Committee reached the Senate floor, it was accompanied by shrill cries of "whitewash" from Senator Williams. As the media took up the cry, even Mansfield could not escape the flack. Senator Case, a progressive Republican from New Jersey, often referred to as the "Mr. Clean" of the period, took the lead in denouncing the report. Although Case frequently saw eye to eye with Mansfield on issues, he denounced the majority leader for attempting to bury the Baker matter.

What Mansfield had done was clearly an attempt at damage control, a course urged on him by Vice-President Johnson and Hubert Humphrey, then the assistant majority leader. It was a futile attempt. The Justice Department pursued Baker relentlessly. Eventually, for his malfeasance as secretary for the Senate majority, Baker served a sentence in a federal penitentiary. His conviction hinged largely on his relationship with Senator Bob Kerr, who was described by Baker as being "on the take," specifically for favors done for the savings and loan industry, a charge vigorously rejected by the dead senator's family.

Mansfield's burdens as majority leader, already weighted down with the sagging legislative program, were aggravated by the Baker scandal. Attracted by the pungent scent of sensationalism, a reinforced media corps descended on the Senate. There they found little more on the Baker affair. But they found a general malaise fueled by heavy absenteeism among the members and drift in the legislative program. The media sought out the majority leader, probing deeply into Senate affairs for the first time during the Kennedy administration. Mansfield did not evade the newspeople but urged patience in passing judgment on the 88th Congress. It had, he noted repeatedly, not yet run a full year. Clearly on the defensive himself, he tried to put the Senate in the best possible light while refusing to pass the blame on to committee chairmen or individual members for the existing state of affairs.

The media were satisfied with Mansfield's intentions and integrity but were not persuaded as to the relevance of either to the Senate's performance. Joe Alsop, a gadfly of the press corps of the period, had been prompted by the fall of Bobby Baker to dash in for a rare appearance at the Senate press gallery. After a brief interview with Baker's designated successor, he dashed out again to pronounce the Senate inoperable without a Lyndon Johnson and a Bobby Baker. Alsop was not alone. Others of the press were still held in thrall by the image of the powerful ringmaster and the nimble fox darting in and out amid the lions, compelling them to do the ringmaster's bidding.

Press comparisons of Johnson and Mansfield remained uniformly unfavorable to the latter. Indeed, some commentaries even attributed the Baker scandal to Mansfield's weakness. Certainly Baker was inclined to blame not himself but Mansfield for his downfall, on the grounds that the majority leader gave him too free a rein to indulge in the temptations of wine, women, and easy money that abounded on Capitol Hill. As for Johnson, the vice president moved as far away as possible from his former intimacy with Baker, avoiding personal contact with him until a few months before Johnson's death.

Criticism of Mansfield's leadership by his own colleagues finally broke into the open during what was for the Mansfield Senate an unusual night session. It was initiated by Senator Tom Dodd of Connecticut. Dodd had come to Washington with a reputation as a brilliant prosecutor, earned at the Nuremberg trials of Nazi leaders at the end of World War II. Serving first as a member of the House of Representatives, he was generally counted among the liberals. After several terms in the House, Dodd was elected to the Senate. Lyndon Johnson lost no time in enticing him into his camp of dependables by giving him choice committee assignments and other perquisites, as well as by effusive flattery, to which Dodd was highly susceptible.

Dodd obtained the floor and then launched into a tirade against the Senate's performance, noting its aimlessness, absenteeism, short hours and wasted time. He then proceeded to lay the blame for this state of affairs at the feet of the majority leader. For the first time, a member of the Senate openly charged Mansfield with failure to lead the Senate. With tears forming in his eyes, Dodd expressed a watery nostalgia for the days under the leadership of Lyndon Johnson. He was joined in his harangue by Senator Russell Long of Louisiana. Long's claims to fame in Senate circles was his uncontrollable outbursts of oratory and his deference to independent petroleum interests in matters of taxation that came before him as chairman of the Finance Committee.

Although only Long and Dodd spoke on this occasion, they were not alone in their opinion. Others were known to saunter onto the Senate floor from time to time, often inspired by little more than an excess of Jack Daniels or Dewars, to give vent to their discontent. But the media pounced on Dodd's theme of Senate dawdling and Mansfield's weak leadership. Editorialists expressed amazement at how little the Senate had done to date. Where were the appropriations bills? What about civil rights legislation? The rest of the Kennedy program? Since they so rarely appeared on the floor, where were the senators, and what were they doing? Finally, what about the leadership? Where was it headed, and why didn't it do something to get there?

Mansfield found himself in the gunsights of the press. It was a position that he had assiduously avoided as majority leader. His stress on the equality of members, one senator one vote, and his readiness to shift the plaudits of the press to others had been deliberately designed to place not himself but the Senate as a whole in the spotlight. Now he felt the attention coming directly at him, and he could do nothing to deflect it. Like a heat-seeking missile, the press homed in on the majority leader.

The enlarged media coverage meant reporters rarely seen in the Senate press gallery with little familiarity with the peculiarities of the institution. They had no interest in searching among its arcane practices for the source of the difficulties. It did little good to point out that what had come from the House in the way of appropriations legislation had passed the Senate but was still resting in limbo, waiting for a conference with the House Committee, with the two chairmen unable to agree on where to meet. How to explain that legislation stuck in Senate committees could not be pried loose because of a reluctant chairman; civil rights measures in particular were still hidden behind the hunched over frame of Jim Eastland, chairman of the Judiciary Committee.

Schooled in the Senate of the Johnson era, the media were seeking a personification of the problem. They thought that they had found one in Bobby Baker. But despite a lot of pumping up by press-carried rumors, the Baker story was fading rapidly as its focus shifted to the Justice Department prosecution. Plainly, Baker was not enough; the press needed another person to blame for the breakdown of the Senate. Nice guy or not, it was plain that Mansfield's system was not working. The Senate was in trouble. Interestingly, a brief flurry of Senate activity followed the first outburst of public criticism aimed at Mansfield. It was as though the Senate were suddenly fearful of losing its fall guy. His colleagues, Republicans and Democrats, closed ranks around the majority leader, and speeches of praise echoed in his ears. Senators showed up at committee meetings and on the floor in greater numbers. A few modest bills were cleared by committees to the floor, where they were acted on with alacrity.

Unfortunately, the new mood was short-lived. Once again a deadly calm settled over the Senate. The lights went on. The lights went out. The summoning bells rang throughout the Senate's domain, two rings for daily convening at noon and to announce quorum calls in between. They rang four times for daily adjournment. But the single ring that would announce a roll-call vote was rarely heard. Exploiting Mansfield's style of leadership, senators freewheeled with less and less hesitation. They came and went as they saw fit. Some even expressed irritation at receiving telegrams from the leader, urging their presence for a possible vote, especially when it necessitated a hurried return from a European meeting or a Caribbean break.

The Senate looked bad to the public. Indeed, it was functioning badly, and Mansfield could do little about it. The character of his leadership was formed out of a tightly reined personality and his anachronistic vision of a classic Senate, a vision that had much in common with its earliest years, when breakaways by horse and carriage were far more difficult than those made possible by automobiles and jet planes.

Mansfield's attempt to re-create that kind of Senate in the second half of the twentieth century could work only if senators were prepared to accept a full share of personal responsibility for what went on and for the image that the Senate projected to the nation. Above all, it required that the Senate's easily abused rules and indulgent practices be used with a maximum of self-imposed individual restraint and mutual consideration. Otherwise, rules intended to facilitate wise decisions became deadly impediments to rational legislative action and covers for inaction and inequity.

Although his approach showed obvious signs of failing, Mansfield would not even consider a reversion to Johnson's tactics, as some of his well-meaning colleagues hinted would be useful. Mansfield was viscerally revolted by the idea of applying such methods and temperamentally incapable of doing so. If his approach did not work, Mansfield would consider no other. And while his restrained and gentle methods had seemed to serve adequately at first, it was clear that they were not working in the third year of the Kennedy administration.

Mansfield Throws Down the Gauntlet

For the first time, Mansfield seriously considered resigning the leadership. He saw no reason, as he put it, "for shortening my life" in an exercise in futility. As far as he was concerned, the Senate could take back the job it had given him. He would be content to be identified as the "senator from Montana" without further embellishments.

As a last resort, he decided to try what he had not tried before, a shock treatment to serve notice that if the Senate did not shape up, he would ship out. As precedent for tendering his resignation as majority leader, Mansfield was familiar with only one example and not a precisely comparable one. Alben Barkley of Kentucky had sought to resign as majority leader when caught between a reluctant Senate and President Roosevelt's incessant and impatient demands for legislation. In that instance, however, Barkley chose to put the blame for his dilemma on the president. Whereupon the Senate rose as one to reject his resignation, to be joined in due course by an apologetic Roosevelt.

In this instance, however, it was not the president but the Senate as a whole that was to blame for Mansfield's predicament. Fully prepared to step down, the possibility of a Senate acceptance of his resignation did not disturb him. He was determined to state his case for the record, however, summing up what he had attempted to do as leader, the methods he had employed, and the results of almost three years of his leadership.

In a speech that he was preparing for delivery, Mansfield acknowledged the criticism to which he was being subjected. True to form, he thanked such critics as Dodd for bringing their complaints into the open. In response to press criticism of the Senate's performance, he asked:

> How do you measure the performance of this Congress—any Congress? How do you measure the performance of a Senate of 100 independent man and women, of any Senate?
> [S]everal Senators, at least, judged it and found it seriously wanting. And with the hue and cry thus raised they found echoes outside the Senate. I do not criticize Senators for making the judgment, for raising the alarm. Even less do I criticize the press for spreading it. Senators were within their rights.

And the press was not only within its rights but was performing a segment of its public duty which is to report what transpires here.

I, too, am within my rights and I believe I am performing a duty of the leadership when I ask again. How do you judge the performance of this Congress—any Congress? Of this Senate—any Senate? Do you mix a concoction and drink it? And if you feel a sense of well-being thereafter decide it is not so bad a Congress after all? But if you feel somewhat ill or depressed, then that is proof unequivocal that the Congress is a bad Congress and the Senate a bad Senate?

Noting the critical references to "time wasting," to "laziness," to "standing still," he asked, "Who are the time wasters? Who is lazy? Who is an absentee? Each Member can make his own judgment of his individual performance. I make no apologies for mine. Nor will I sit in judgment on any other member."

Mansfield rejected the short length of the daily convenings or of the entire session or even attendance on the floor as a measure of performance, saying that it would be

to no avail to install a time-clock at the entrance to the Chamber for Senators to punch when they enter or leave the floor. . . . We will have the Senate sit here day in and day out, from dawn until dawn, whether or not the calendar calls for it to impress . . . the American people with our industriousness. We may not shuffle papers as bureaucrats are presumed to do . . . what we are likely to shuffle are words—words to the president on how to execute the foreign policy or administer the domestic affairs of the nation. And when these words pall, we undoubtedly will turn to the court to give that institution the benefit of our advice on its responsibilities. And if we run out of judicial wisdom, we can always turn to advising the governors of the states or the mayors of the cities or the heads of other nations on how to manage their concerns.

. . . Senators have every right to comment on whatever they wish and to do so on the floor of the Senate. Highly significant initiatives on all manner of public affairs have had their genesis in the remarks of individual Senators on the floor. But there is one clear cut day-in-and-day-out responsibility of the Senate as a whole. Beyond all others, it is the Constitutional responsibility to be here and to consider and act in concert with the House on the legislative needs of the Nation.

Mansfield went on to compare the Senate's legislative performance during his first two years as leader with that of its predecessors at two-year intervals going back to the end of World War II. On the basis of substantive legislative output, the specific record of the Mansfield Senate was the equal, if not the superior, of any, including those under Johnson's leadership.

Mansfield, however, knew that he was being judged not on the legislative record but on a superficial perception of the Senate, as well as by a contrasting of his reticent personality with that of his flamboyant predecessor. He noted that

> descriptions of the Majority Leader, the Senator from Montana, have ranged from a benign Mr. Chips, to glamourless, to tragic mistake. I have not yet seen wet-nurse to the Senate but that, too, may not be long in coming.
>
> It is true, that I have taught school, although I cannot claim either the tenderness or the understanding of Mr. Chips for his charges. I confess freely to a lack of glamour. As for being a tragic mistake, if that means that I am neither a circus ringmaster, the master of ceremonies of a Senate night club, a tamer of Senate lions or a wheeler and dealer then I must accept, too, that title. Indeed, I must accept it if I am expected as Majority Leader to be anything other than myself—a Senator from Montana who has had the good fortune to be trusted by his people for over two decades and done the best he knows how to represent them and to do what he believes right for the nation.
>
> Insofar as I am personally concerned, these and any other labels can be borne. I achieved the height of my political ambition when I was elected Senator from Montana. When the Senate saw fit to designate me as Majority Leader, it was the Senate's choice not mine and what the Senate has bestowed, it is always at liberty to revoke.
>
> But as long as I have this responsibility, it will be discharged to the best of my ability by me as I am. I would not, even if I could, presume to a toughmindedness which, with all due respect to those who use the cliché, I have always had difficulty in distinguishing from soft headedness or simple mindedness. I shall not don any Mandarin's robes or any skin other than that to which I am accustomed in order that I may look like a majority leader or sound like a majority leader—however a majority leader is supposed to look or sound. I am what I am and no title, political facelifter or imagemaker can alter it.
>
> I believe that I am, as are most Senators, an ordinary American with a normal complement of vices and, I hope, virtues, of weaknesses and, I hope, strengths. As such, I do my best to be courteous, decent and understanding of others and sometimes fail at it. But it is for the Senate to decide whether these characteristics are incompatible with the leadership.
>
> I have tried to treat others as I would like to be treated and almost invariably have been. And it is for the Senate to decide, too, whether that characteristic is incompatible with the Senate leadership.
>
> I have done my best to serve the people whom I represent and, at the same time, to exercise such independent judgment as I may have as to what is best for the nation as a whole, on national and international issues. If that is incompatible with the Senate leadership that, too, is for the Senate to decide.
>
> I have always felt that the president of the United States—whoever he may be—is entitled to the dignity of his office and is worthy of the respect of the Senate. I have always felt that he bears a greater burden of responsibility than any individual Senator for the welfare and security of the Nation, for he, alone, can speak for the Nation abroad; and he alone, at home, stands with the Congress as a whole, as constituted representatives of the entire Ameri-

can people. In the exercise of his grave responsibilities, I believe we have a profound responsibility to give him whatever understanding and support we can in good conscience and in conformity with our independent duties. I believe we owe it to the nation of which all our states are a part—particularly in matters of foreign relations—to give him not only responsible opposition but responsible cooperation. If these concepts, too, are incompatible with the majority leadership, then that, too, is for the Senate to decide.

And, finally, within this body I believe that every Member ought to be equal in fact, no less than in theory, that they have a primary responsibility to the people whom they represent to face the legislative issues of the Nation and to the extent that the Senate may be inadequate in this connection, the remedy lies not in the seeking of shortcuts, not in the cracking of nonexistent whips, not in wheeling and dealing, but in an honest facing of the situation and a resolution of it by the Senate itself, by accommodation, by respect for one another, by mutual restraint and, as necessary, adjustments in the procedures of this body.

I have been charged with lecturing the Senate. And perhaps these remarks will also be interpreted in this fashion. But all I have tried to do is state the facts of this institution as I see them. The Constitutional authority does not lie with the leadership. It lies with all of us individually, collectively, and equally. . . . In the last analysis, deviations from that principle must act . . . to the detriment of the institution. And, in the end, that principle cannot be made to prevail by rules. It can prevail only if there is a high degree of accommodation, mutual restraint and a measure of courage—in spite of our weaknesses—in all of us. It can prevail only if we recognize that, in the end, it is not the Senators as individuals who are of fundamental importance. In the end, it is the institution of the Senate. It is the Senate itself as one of the foundations of the Constitution. It is the Senate as one of the rocks of the Republic.

Thus, almost three years after assuming the leadership, Mansfield threw down the gauntlet to the Senate and especially to the Democrats who were responsible for his selection as leader and whose grumbling could no longer be ignored. In laying out "the facts," Mansfield made clear that faced with a choice of adhering to his approach or trying to run the Senate in the style of his predecessor, he would choose to withdraw from the leadership. The choice would actually be the Senate's, inasmuch as Mansfield's approach was heavily dependent on the willingness of the members to act with restraint, a minimum of partisanship, and acceptance of individual and collective responsibility for the performance of the institution. He would not change his ways; it was for the senators to change their ways.

To be sure, Mansfield had succeeded in bringing about a few modifications in Senate practices and procedures that tended in the direction he wished to go. But, he knew that this small achievement owed as much to the pent-up resentment against Johnson and a honeymoon period of accommodation for a new Leader as to any deep acceptance of his vision of the

Senate. To be sure, there were fewer shenanigans on the Senate floor, less flimflam, and a greater degree of mutual trust, at least between the party leaders. Among the Democrats, the Steering Committee had achieved a more equitable distribution of legislative committee assignments. Moreover, the Policy Committee and the Democratic caucus were being used not merely as props for the majority leader but to permit senators to express an opinion or air complaints. With encouragement from Mansfield, younger members were speaking out more freely.

While Mansfield's repeated assertions of his doctrine of equality among members was still largely a pleasant-sounding abstraction, the substructure of power in the Senate was changing. Mansfield's deemphasis of the role of the majority leader was contributing to the rise of other centers of power and enhancing the role of the individual members. The sudden death of Bob Kerr of Oklahoma at the end of 1962 had closed off a significant concentration of financial influence over the Senate. Kerr's access to wealth, his own and others, and his ruthlessness in using money to achieve his ends had been a major ingredient of the Johnson Senate. Even before Kerr's death, Mansfield had shut off another such concentration in the Senate Democratic Campaign Committee. In a period when campaign costs had not yet risen to astronomical levels, the Senate Democratic Campaign Committee was a significant source of financing for candidates. An astute allocation of a few thousand dollars by the committee could give a real lift to a sagging campaign and would leave the recipient indebted to the source. How these funds were distributed to candidates was controlled by Lyndon Johnson, who relayed his wishes to the Committee through Bobby Baker, whom Johnson had designated as secretary-treasurer of the committee. Conversely, Baker was in a position to advise Johnson as to where contributions would do the most good.

In contrast to Johnson's arbitrary use of the Democratic Campaign Committee, Mansfield acted to equalize the distribution of campaign funds. In doing so, he was again responding to the complaints of Democrats who resented Johnson's arbitrary decisions and the personal indenture that went with the funds allotted to them. Mansfield reshuffled the membership of the Campaign Committee, unloaded the staff, and instituted new rules for its operation. He withdrew from the allocation process, at the same time insisting that all Democratic senators seeking reelection—from large states or small, from the North or South, conservative or liberal—receive equal allocations. Those with easy campaigns or other sources of funds could decline the allocation, but that would be their decision. If funds were available beyond the basic allocations, they could be distributed on the basis of need in close races or to help Democrats running for the Senate for the first time.

Such decisions, however, were to be those of the entire Committee and not the majority leaders. In short, any IOUs for the financial help provided to a senator would not be held by the majority leader but by the party in the Senate as a whole.

As a result of the initial changeover of leadership, Bobby Baker, who had served Johnson in many roles, found himself limited under Mansfield to that of secretary for the majority. Left largely to his own devices in that role, Baker proceeded to carve out a domain of personal enrichment based on his putative influence in the Senate. Until his downfall, he exerted a continuing influence on Senate affairs disproportionate to his remaining title. He did so by intensifying his collaboration with Senator Kerr of Oklahoma. After Kerr's death, however, with Bobby Baker facing criminal prosecution growing out of that collaboration and his own independent refinements on wheeling and dealing, the backdoor manipulation of the institution, so essential to the Johnson Senate, was closed.

With key links to the past severed, the Senate was face to face with the question of whether or not it could function with a leadership insisting that every senator share equally in the responsibilities placed on them by the institution. If the Senate did not have a leader who claimed credit for its achievements, neither did it have a leader who could be blamed for its failings. It was a Senate of a hundred members, and the hundred members would decide what kind of Senate it would be. That is what Mansfield intended to tell his colleagues as he worked over the draft of his speech with great care. He discussed his intentions with no other member of the Senate. He distributed no advance copies of the speech to the press.

Satisfied that the time had come, Mansfield took what was for him an unusual procedural step. On Friday, 22 November 1963, he opened the Senate as usual and then left the floor, only to return to the chamber a short time later. He found an angry political discussion in progress. It had been initiated by Minority Leader Dirksen interrupting Joe Clark of Pennsylvania. The latter was seeking to protect President Kennedy from criticism for the bogging down of his legislative program. Clark was trying to shift the blame from the White House to Congress and, specifically, to the Senate's archaic rules, his favorite theme.

Dirksen was determined to keep the heat on the administration and the Democrats. He was in rare form. His partisan blood flowing strongly, he strode before the dais, raising a finger frequently to point at Clark and other targets, including empty desks. In a mixture heavy with humor and sarcasm, he proceeded to turn Clark's complaints around, shifting the blame from the Senate rules and Congress to the Democrats and, especially, Democratic liberals. His denunciation of the latter brought chuckles of approval from

Republicans and some support from southern Democrats, particularly his defense of the Rules. Ripples of laughter ran through the galleries, and even the presiding officer smiled as he gaveled for order. Dirksen's thespian impulses, no less than his partisanship, were stimulated. He grew bolder and more theatrical, finally going further than he intended when he attacked the president without mentioning his name. It was not in his criticism of the president's performance that Dirksen overstepped the bounds; such criticism was commonplace. Instead, it was his mimicry of Kennedy's manner of speaking with its broad Bostonian "A" that was Dirksen's target. It was a form of derision then much in vogue among the president's most vicious critics, with whom Dirksen did not wish to be associated. Clark caught him immediately and Dirksen desisted. In fact, the offending words did not appear in the *Congressional Record* issued the following morning, the minority leader having deleted them.

Mansfield interrupted the Clark-Dirksen exchange to advise the members that he, too, would have something to say on the state of the Senate's affairs and the president's program. He expressed the hope that all members from both sides of the aisle might be there to hear his remarks. Whereupon he took an unusual procedural step for one not inclined to press his words on his colleagues. He announced a specific time for his speech on the coming Monday and asked that a so-called live, or three-bell, quorum be sounded before he began talking. This meant that all members would be notified that he intended to speak and that a minimum of fifty-one members would have to be present to answer the call of the roll before the Senate could proceed. In short, he wanted to be certain that the Senate would get his message.

Despite the elaborate preparation, Mansfield did not make the speech on the following Monday. Instead, he inserted the full text in the *Congressional Record,* with these introductory words:

> The remarks which I had already prepared . . . [were] a statement of what has been achieved, not by any genius of the leadership or by some Senate establishment but by the 100 Members of this body. . . . We all share in the responsibility for its achievement and shortcomings. . . .
> After a while what the Senate appears to have been in any given period will be noted, if at all, only by the scholars. What the Senate does in a legislative sense in any given period will be felt for a long, long time by all the people of the nation. We are not here as actors or actresses to be applauded. We are here as Senators to do the business of the government. It is not we but that alone, in the end, which counts to the Nation.

He paused for a moment and then concluded:

In the light of what has happened I!have no heart to read this report to the Senate. . . . It has now become . . . a final report on the Senate and its leadership during the Presidency of John Fitzgerald Kennedy.

Minutes before Mansfield announced his intention on Friday, November 22, 1963 to address the Senate the following Monday, rifle shots had sounded above the cheering of onlookers watching a presidential motorcade passing through the streets of Dallas. A bullet had pierced the skull of the thirty-fifth President of the United States. Kennedy was dead.

Interlude

A Bleak Day in Dallas

Riding in an open limousine, the president and his wife, and the Texas governor and his wife, led the motorcade through the sunlit streets of Dallas. Following the lead car came Vice President and Lady Bird Johnson and the Secret Service men of the Department of the Treasury. Several hours into the visit, it was already judged to be a highly successful one. The route of the motorcade was lined with receptive Texans. The principals smiled and waved at the spectators, who waved and smiled in return.

Suddenly, an assassin's rifle crackled, and it was no more.

An afternoon of horror stretched into a long night of disbelief and into the following day. Kennedy's body lay in a massive box in the Rotunda of the Capitol. A hundred paces removed Mansfield and then Dirksen addressed their colleagues. Both spoke of life, death, and deliverance. Then both led the others out of the chamber. Only Margaret Chase Smith of Maine remained in a stilled room of empty desks. She took the dark rose from its diurnal place on her breast and placed it on the desk where once sat the senator from Massachusetts; then she moved out of the empty chamber. The Senate assembled around the bier in the Rotunda. So, too, did the House of Representatives, the Supreme Court, the cabinet, the ambassadors and heads of states. As they had done—how many years before or was it only yesterday—to witness the arrival of a new president.

They gathered to confirm his departure after a final flow of words of praise and recollection. Chief Justice Earl Warren spoke of the forces of hatred and malevolence "eating their way into the bloodstream of American life." Speaker John McCormack sang praises to a great leadership. The majority leader of the Senate groped for the human dimension of a national tragedy in these words:

> There was a sound of laughter; in a moment, it was no more. And so she took a ring from her finger and placed it in his hands.
>
> There was a wit in a man neither young nor old, but a wit full of an old man's wisdom and of a child's wisdom, and then in a moment, it was no more. And so she took a ring from her finger and placed it in his hands.
>
> There was a man marked with the scars of his love of country, a body active with the surge of a life far, far from spent and, in a moment it was no more. And so she took a ring from her finger and placed it in his hands.
>
> There was a father with a little boy, a little girl and a joy of each in the other. In a moment it was no more, and so she took a ring from her finger and placed it in his hands.
>
> There was a husband who asked much and gave much and out of the giving and asking wove with a woman what could not be broken in life, and in a moment it was no more. And so she took a ring from her finger and placed it in his hands, and kissed him and closed the lid of a coffin.
>
> A piece of each of us died at that moment. . . .

Once he had spoken, Mansfield passed the paper on which the words were written to Jackie Kennedy even as she reached for it. Later, she called the Senate majority leader to thank him for saying what had not been said and needed to be said. Later, a leading weekly newsmagazine found the Mansfield eulogy out of place, rather in bad taste. But Mansfield received thousands of letters from over the nation and from countries abroad in gratitude for the solace of his words, some containing translations of the eulogy or newly crafted variations on its theme. Later the words would be put into popular songs and into a symphonic tone poem, played on anniversaries of Kennedy's death.

3

A New Senate Approach
to Civil Rights Legislation

Riding in the second car of the motorcade on that fateful day in Dallas, Lyndon Johnson had been a few feet from death when President Kennedy was assassinated. Although shocked by that tragedy, Johnson moved at once to take charge. With Jackie Kennedy and Lady Bird Johnson at his side, he was sworn in as the thirty-sixth president of the United States. When he returned to Washington a few hours later, he found himself the leader of a nation profoundly bewildered by what had happened, a country whose way of life appeared to be on hold. His first responsibility was to reassure the people of the government's stability and continuity. With the confusion over the Dallas tragedy increasing by the hour, he had to find acceptable answers to questions rising on all sides about the why and who of the assassination. The situation was such as to tax the abilities of any national leader.

In the dulling confines of the vice presidency, Johnson's political acumen had seemed to be losing its edge. Before the assassination, he was seen less and less at old haunts on Capitol Hill. Most of his time was passed in the vice president's executive office at the other end of Pennsylvania Avenue. There he tended to withdraw into his own counsel, seemingly fearful that the Bobby Baker scandal might rub off on him. When he emerged, as he did from time to time, it was to carry out some ceremonial mission, a foreign policy assignment, or a political task such as the one that had drawn him and President Kennedy to Dallas.

Once president, Johnson was like a dog released from a leash. His political blood again began to course furiously through his veins, and his ingrained skills came readily back into play. With a sure hand, he shaped the response that would steer him through the aftermath of the assassination. He knew at once what had to be done, not only to put the nation back on track, but also to consolidate his position as president with an eye to election in his own right the following year.

Johnson was fully aware that he would be under the intense scrutiny of the media. Having grown somewhat neglectful of him during his tenure as vice president, the press corps would now descend in full force, anxious to size him up in his new role as president and to compare him in every way with his predecessor. Johnson knew that in these comparisons Kennedy's shortcomings would be all but forgotten, while his own would be ferreted out. A president dead, especially in such tragic circumstances, would be viewed as larger than life.

That image of Kennedy would be reinforced by a resplendent funeral, with Jackie Kennedy directly supervising every detail. The great assemblage of national and international dignitaries, all come to Washington to pay homage to the fallen leader, would be long remembered. Carried by television, the proceedings would engage the attention of the entire world as mourners at the bier of the deceased. In such a vast and tragic tableau, the dead president's successor would be little more than a supernumerary and, in the eyes of some, an uninvited guest. In short, Kennedy would be a tough act to follow.

Until his predecessor's body was in the ground, there was little that President Johnson could do except wait. Nevertheless, while going through the ceremonial ordeal, he began to function as president of the United States. He was presented with legislation that had to be signed. He acted to quell the flood of speculation over the events in Dallas by appointing the blue-ribbon Warren Commission to investigate the assassination. He met with heads of state attending the funeral who were eager to find out what would happen to U.S. foreign policy in the aftermath of Kennedy's death. To their surprise, Johnson's restrained manner and measured responses were at odds with the foreign media's portrait of a raw and impulsive Texas cowboy. The foreign dignitaries went home and spread reassurance about the United States and the new leader of the Free World.

One of Johnson's first acts as president was to ask Robert Kennedy to remain as attorney general. The offer was not an act of noblesse oblige or an arrogant gloating toward an adversary who had had the rug pulled suddenly from under his feet. Nor was the offer a suggestion that they kiss and make up. The reality was that Johnson needed Robert Kennedy to ensure a smooth assumption of presidential power. Looking ahead to 1964, moreover, having Bobby Kennedy close at hand would forestall any slips in the nomination and election to the presidency that he would seek in his own right. The late president's favorite brother remaining in the cabinet would serve not only to keep him in line but also to discourage defections of the more passionate of the Kennedy faithful who, embittered by the president's death, might turn deeply resentful of Johnson's backdoor entry into the White House. If they were kept busy in Washington, they would not be out in the country stirring up political difficulties for him. As Johnson himself would put it in one of his favorite aphorisms, he preferred to have them "inside the tent pissing out than outside pissing in." As for Attorney General Kennedy, he could not refuse Johnson's request if he expected to keep alive his still far-from-satiated political ambitions. While the presidency was obviously beyond his grasp in 1964, the vice presidency might not be. Turning down the president's invitation to remain in the cabinet would simply invite a massive split in the Democratic Party.

Another reason impelled Bobby Kennedy to accept Johnson's offer. His understanding of the civil rights issue had deepened since the responsibility for the administration's handling of civil rights had first been thrust on him by his brother. At the outset Bobby may have been, as James Baldwin, the black novelist, put it, "incredibly naive" on civil rights. That was no longer true. Bobby Kennedy had witnessed the spreading violent and nonviolent protests in the streets and the angry confrontations at the school doors. They were reflections of what was now an unshakable determination by black Americans no longer to accept second-class citizenship anywhere in the land of their birth. Kennedy had learned that the problem was not going to go away quietly. Palliatives such as Lincoln Day speeches or an occasional appointment of a black to high office would no longer suffice. The issue had to be met head-on.

After an uncertain start, Bobby Kennedy had thrown his weight fully to the side of those seeking to end segregation and had persuaded his brother to take that course. As attorney general, Kennedy had acted vigorously to enforce the *Brown* decision on school desegregation. At the University of Mississippi and then at the University of Alabama, he met the diehard segregationists in the Democratic Party and forced them to back down. Incidents such as these highlighted Bobby Kennedy's key role and served to win for him the increasing trust of black leaders. By accepting Johnson's request that he remain as attorney general, Kennedy would be in a position to consolidate that trust and to make a major contribution in the legislative battle over civil rights that lay just ahead.

Bobby Kennedy's decision to stay in the cabinet under Johnson rubbed off on some of the late president's closest lieutenants. With typical persuasiveness, President Johnson had pleaded with Kennedy to stay with him on the grounds that "if he needed you, think how much more I need you." Even those who were less than eager to answer Johnson's call for help were not prepared to break ranks with the late president's younger brother. Whether from a sense of duty, a passion for their function, a desire to stay close to the seat of power, or a genuine change of heart about Johnson, almost all of the "top brains" of the Kennedy administration opted to continue with the new administration. In doing so, they assisted greatly in preserving a sense of continuity with the late president and his policies and helped safeguard the unity of the Democratic Party. With a nation in dire need of reassurance, not to mention a presidential election fast approaching, that was precisely what Johnson wanted.

While holding on to the Kennedy team, however, the new president had no intention of remaining for long at its mercy. Scarcely a year after the close of Johnson's surrogate administration, only Defense Secretary Robert McNamara, Secretary of State Dean Rusk, White House foreign policy expert Walt Rostow, and a few others would remain of the original Kennedy team. In short order, Johnson was surrounded by a cordon of his own reliables, such as George Reedy, Horace Busby, Bill Moyers, and Harry McPherson. Jack Valenti, an old associate of Johnson's, was summoned hastily from Texas to polish the image of the new administration as it separated from the old. Valenti had scarcely settled in when he opted to leave the White House to become head of the Motion Picture Association. Before doing so, however, Valenti was to achieve lasting fame for having set the nation to smiling again by declaring with utter sincerity that he slept better at night knowing that Lyndon Johnson was in the White House.

Johnson acted swiftly to refurbish his links with leading figures in Congress, receiving assurances from them that they would give him all the support that they could "in good conscience." The reservation, a long-established cliché in the lexicon of politics, was synonymous with "I'll do whatever you ask but don't ask me to do anything that is going to cost me." At that moment, however, this assurance of support was more than an empty gesture. In the first place, his old colleagues on the Hill had been deeply impressed by Johnson's humble demeanor and restraint in confronting the tragic circumstances of his elevation to the presidency. It produced a genuine sympathy that induced them to set aside old skepticisms, irritants, and angers. Members of Congress also shared with Johnson an awareness of how deeply the assassination had disturbed the people of the nation. This mutual understanding presaged a period of cooperation, rather than confrontation, between them.

Johnson lost no time in requesting the Speaker of the House and the majority leader of the Senate to hold a joint session as soon as possible so that he might address the Congress. An old admirer of Johnson, Speaker McCormack was delighted to accommodate him. Senate Majority Leader Mansfield reacted in the same fashion. He recognized the need for a message of reassurance from the new president, not only to the nation but to the world. Moreover, he sensed that the shock of the assassination might change the tenor on Capital Hill. It was possible that the Senate might respond to the assassination and the ascension of Johnson to the presidency by getting down to the legislative business that members had been avoiding for so many months. The moment might be at hand to break through the legislative impasse that had led Mansfield to the verge of resigning the leadership.

Johnson came before a joint session for the first time as president on 27 November 1963. He delivered an inspiring address. He spoke with persuasive eloquence of his sorrow at the tragic events that had elevated him to the presidency. With humility, he promised to do his best to carry forward what Kennedy had begun in building a better nation. To the world, he gave assurances of the continuity of Washington's commitments. He talked of peace and barely mentioned Vietnam. Civil rights constituted the high point of the speech. Johnson aligned himself firmly with the advocates of equal rights, not neglecting to mention contributions that he himself had already made as Senate majority leader. He stopped just short of endorsing Martin Luther King Jr. by name in extolling the moderate advocates of civil rights while condemning the violence that the issue was spreading throughout the nation. Johnson also urged Congress to act on a long list of bills having to do with education, youth opportunities, care for the elderly, appropriations, and tax reduction.

The members were satisfied that a new captain had indeed taken over and that, under his hand, the nation would sail smoothly and safely from one administration into another. In that sense, Congress had heard what it wanted to hear. Johnson had struck the right note, and tears of mourning gave way to cheers of reborn hope. Reactions were similar throughout the nation. The *New York Times* was struck, in particular, "by the dramatic force of his delivery, the seemingly sure grasp of the mood and the moment." The *Times* went on to state that the speech was "remarkably similar to the rhetoric of Mr. Kennedy but delivered in a voice as different from his quick Bostonian accent as could be." The juxtaposition of Kennedy content and Texas twang was scarcely surprising. Kennedy advisors and writers in the White House had put the speech together. As for the accents not being Bostonian, it might be noted that, for political purposes, Johnson had at times contended that he was a westerner rather than a southerner. But not in his wildest quest for votes would he have ever tried to overlay his Texas twang with the cadences of Boston in order to woo the voters of New England.

That is not to say that thoughts of politics were absent from his mind on the occasion of his first address to Congress as president. Seated in the family gallery of the House chamber, at the side of Lady Bird Johnson, were the president's distinguished guests, Mayors Robert Wagner of New York City and Richard Daley of Chicago and David Lawrence, the former governor of Pennsylvania. The three men had one thing in common. They were Democratic Party leaders of a special kind, capable of delivering the votes for a favored candidate in quest of a nomination at a national convention and then following through with large Democratic turnouts in general elections. All had come through for Kennedy in 1960. Would they do the same for Johnson in 1964?

Mansfield, who had led the Senate to the House side of the Capitol to listen to Johnson's address, was pleased by the very positive reaction. The new president's initial speech appeared to have a sobering but uplifting effect on the mood of the Senate. The criticism and political acrimony that had been building just prior to the assassination was silenced, at least momentarily. The speech seemed to induce a higher level of sobriety and a greater readiness to cooperate in furthering the business of the Senate. Absenteeism declined. Committees did get down to business. Appropriations bills again began moving through the process. Even Senator Harry F. Byrd, the elder, who could find any number of procedural reasons for delaying a proposed tax cut or expenditure increase, promised to act in committee on the tax bill so that it would be ready for the second session. The majority leader promptly announced that it would be the first order of business after the session opened.

Background of the Civil Rights Bill and Its Passage in the House

Although Mansfield had laid aside thoughts of resigning, the press retained its doubts about his suitability as majority leader. Having seized on the idea of his resignation before the assassination, a few columnists resumed calls for him to step aside. They subsided only when, in a great show of unity, virtually the entire Democratic contingent in the Senate feted the majority leader in a surprise testimonial dinner. Hubert Humphrey, frequently mentioned as a successor to Mansfield, served as the toastmaster, and the president came to Capitol Hill to make a glowing speech in praise of the Senate's majority leader. Thereafter, Johnson remained in close contact with Mansfield for the remainder of the Congress, seeking his views on matters ranging from Vietnam to the state of the legislative program to the selection of a keynoter for the 1964 National Democratic Convention. Their relationship during this period was far closer than it had ever been in the past, even when Mansfield had served as assistant leader to Senate Majority Leader Johnson.

The first session of the Congress ran nonstop almost into the second. Thanks to an end-of-session tieup in the House, Congress continued to meet in 1963 until just two days short of the New Year. Inasmuch as the Senate could not recess until the House was prepared to do so, Mansfield devised a unique procedural tactic of pro forma sessions of the Senate. The procedure enabled all but a handful of senators to depart for the holidays, while a skeleton Senate remained on hand waiting, as required by the Constitution to close out the session officially. This procedural arrangement worked as long as there was no demand for a disruptive quorum count, and there was none during Mansfield's leadership. The pro forma Senate session was, again, an act of thoughtfulness for his colleagues's needs, unencumbered by a demand for a quid pro quo. Out of such acts, Mansfield was slowly building a mood to counter the deep divisiveness of the anticipated debate on civil rights that was closing in on the Senate.

After scarcely a week's recess, Congress reassembled for the second session. As he had previously announced, Mansfield moved promptly to bring the tax bill before the Senate as the first order of business. The bill had languished in committee for the better part of a year, and there was no question that it would pass. Nevertheless, with the reluctant acquiescence of the chairman of the Finance Committee, Harry F. Byrd, the Senate began a perfunctory debate on the virtue of cutting taxes in the face of an economic slowdown and notwithstanding a budgetary deficit.

All the while, the issue that was on the minds of the returning congressmen was civil rights. Members had taken the pulse of their constituencies during the short intermission and what they found was a growing demand for an end to the injustice of segregation of black Americans. To be sure, the federal courts and the executive branch were already tackling some aspects of the problem. The military and the civil service, for example, had been desegregated by President Truman's executive order. Pursuant to the Supreme Court's *Brown* decision, the ending of segregation in public education was advancing "with all deliberate speed." Federal intervention by the Justice Department had had a decided impact on lynching and other revolting practices long used to terrorize blacks. Recently enacted laws had begun to strike at voting practices in southern states that effectively disenfranchised most black citizens. A dent had been made in ensuring equitable access to employment opportunities by requiring it in federal contracts. Notwithstanding these achievements, progress was painfully slow. In 1964, blacks were still far down the line when it came to jobs. As for public accommodations, the situation, particularly in the South, was little changed from the distant past. Blacks were still forced by law to accept separate and unequal services whether in buses, hotels, or at a hotdog stand or public restroom.

What brought the issue to a head in Congress was the emergence among African Americans of a fierce determination to end the injustice by effective organization for social action. The main theater of action was the South, and southern blacks were the shock troops, but their largely nonviolent struggle had the support of black Americans everywhere and a growing element of white America.

Under the inspired leadership of Dr. Martin Luther King Jr., the outrageous practices of segregation were confronted in peaceful marches of protest, boycotts, and sit-ins. Not infrequently, the demonstrations broke down in violence, with local police and militant segregationists using such instruments for "maintaining order" as high-pressure fire hoses, electric cattle prods, police dogs, ax handles, billy clubs, and, in several situations, murder. Through the medium of television, the entire nation saw and was repulsed by the brutality and at the same time was somewhat shamefaced for having permitted it to go on for so long.

Congress could no longer push the issue aside in favor of more pressing or titillating matters. White voters outside the South grew more receptive to the idea of federal action to end what had come to be seen as a downright indecent situation. The civil rights issue emerged, as Senate Republican Minority Leader Everett Dirksen would later describe it, as "an idea whose time has come." More accurately, perhaps, civil rights was an idea that Congress, and especially the Senate, could no longer evade. The majority leader of the Senate knew it. The minority leader knew it. So, too, did Senator Richard Russell, who, despite failing health and personal reluctances, would nevertheless lead the southern senators in a last-ditch parliamentary effort to forestall the inevitable. The impending struggle would engage these three leaders and the rest of the Senate in the most extended debate in the history of the Senate.

While streets in southern cities were seething with demonstrations, the buildup to the legislative confrontation accelerated in Washington. During the closing months of his life, President Kennedy thrust aside the political caution that had led him to accept readily the advice of the congressional leadership and stall for two years on meeting the civil rights issue squarely. During that period, he had confined himself to statements in support of human equality and made clear in various ways where he stood personally on the issue.

By 1963, demonstrations in dozens of cities strongly suggested that the pace of change was too slow to maintain social order in large sectors of the nation. President Kennedy decided to take on the problem of segregation where it had to be met, where it had been stalled since Reconstruction, in the Congress of the United States. It was a moral decision delayed but, in the context of the times, a courageous political decision. Kennedy knew that he was risking an outright break in the fragile North-South Democratic coalition and perhaps destroying his chances for reelection. Moreover, from his own experience, as well as what Majority Leader Mansfield, Vice President Johnson, and other old Senate hands had pointed out to him, he knew that he faced an almost impossible task. Nevertheless, the president sent a sweeping civil rights bill to Congress. The proposed measure was the fruit of many years of drafting and revision in the Justice Department. It called for an end to the principal overt forms of segregation and for strengthening the legal role of the Justice Department in bringing about equal treatment for all Americans.

In the House of Representatives, the president's bill received the number H.R. 7152 and was referred to the Judiciary Committee. A companion measure with identical text was introduced in the Senate jointly by Mansfield and Dirksen, as a courtesy to the president but without commitment on their part, and then referred to that body's Judiciary Committee. The latter move was strictly in accordance with the Senate Rules and established practice. Both the administration and the congressional leadership recognized that the best hope of passage of any civil rights measure depended on completing action, first, on the House measure and then using it as the vehicle for the all-out effort that would be required in the Senate. It would have been irrelevant to have attempted to begin the action in the Senate in the face of the opposition of Chairman James Eastland.

The Kennedy administration's initial efforts, therefore, were concentrated in the House of Representatives. In the first place, a substantial majority of House members was known to support an end to segregation. Moreover, the Judiciary Committee that would handle H.R. 7152 was headed on the Democratic side by a strong advocate of civil rights. The committee's long-time chairman was Emanuel Celler of New York, whose constituency embraced the Bedford-Stuyvesant section of Brooklyn with its overwhelmingly black population. His Republican counterpart on the committee was William McCulloch, a small-town lawyer from Ohio with very few blacks in his district but whose sense of justice and fair play was very strong. The chances were good that the committee might produce a civil rights bill satisfactory to the administration and that a majority of the House could be counted on to vote for such a measure.

Notwithstanding this auspicious beginning, H.R. 7152 had still to travel a long and arduous route in the House. The text of the bill remained in dispute in the Judiciary Committee for months. Even after clearing that body, the bill's route led through the House Rules Committee, with its autocratic chairman, Howard W. Smith, a former Virginia circuit court judge and an unreconstructed segregationist. Smith had a well-deserved reputation for waylaying progressive measures in general. He had no hesitancy in manipulating the committee's practices to prevent bills distasteful to him from ever reaching the floor of the House for a vote.

Passage in the House would be only the halfway mark for H.R. 7152. The text would be carried by messenger down the main corridor of the Capitol to be deposited on the doorstep of the Senate. No preparations were yet visible there to welcome it. As a practical matter, not a finger had yet been lifted to pave the way for dealing with the issue. The president's bill that had been introduced in the Senate by the majority and minority leaders had disappeared without a sound into the files of the Senate Judiciary Committee, as completely as a collapsed star into a black hole. A similar fate could very well await a House-passed H.R. 7152 if and when it reached the Senate and was referred routinely to Eastland's Judiciary Committee. How to avoid that prospect was a question that constantly occupied Senate Majority Leader Mansfield even as he sought to avoid any public discussion of the problem. To repeated inquiries from the press, his set response was that a civil rights bill would be taken up by the Senate before the end of the Congress.

After an initial burst of activity on H.R. 7152, there appeared to be a fall-off of interest in civil rights as it involved Congress. President Kennedy's exhortations on the urgency of the problem brought little response in either house. National enthusiasm for action on civil rights seemed to have reached a zenith with the massive turnout on the Washington Mall to hear the stirring words of Martin Luther King. Thereafter, it had fallen off in a wave of second thoughts. The administration was seen by an increasing number of Americans as pushing too fast for change. Some in Congress were quick to sense an altered public attitude on civil rights. A few weeks after its launching, H.R. 7152 appeared dead in the murky waters of Capitol Hill.

The assassination of President Kennedy gave the bill a new impetus. Many tended to link the violence and viciousness in the resistance to desegregation with the murder of the president. It was as though Kennedy had paid the supreme price for reminding the nation of its better instincts by deciding to move on civil rights without further delay. Suddenly, legislative shenanigans and tricky procedural maneuverings in Congress to avoid the question could no longer be dismissed as clever or amusing, especially when seen against the backdrop of a president lying in state, one of whose final acts had been designed to resolve this critical issue. In short, Kennedy's death took on the appearance of a blood sacrifice in the cause of justice. Members even began to speak of civil rights legislation as an appropriate memorial to the late president.

As his successor, Lyndon Johnson reinforced that concept. He concentrated on rekindling the public's insistence on action on civil rights, speaking generally to the nation and specifically to influential segments of the public on the urgency of the issue. He subjected foot-dragging businessmen and reticent labor leaders such as George Meany to the "Johnson treatment." The treatment was a nose-to-nose hortatory on civil rights that usually ended in an abrupt ushering of the recipient to the door for a speechless departure. Liberals were delighted by Johnson's initiative, and it served to dispel any doubts among them as to where he stood on the issue. Moreover, they found him more approachable than Kennedy. Not only did Johnson meet repeatedly with civil rights leaders, both black and white, he gave them guidance on how to organize a public effort to move Congress to action. In January 1964, at the outset of the second session of Congress, the president used the State of the Union Address to prod a lethargic Congress into action on H.R. 7152. Soon thereafter, the House began a final drive to complete work on the bill.

In a desperate attempt to make the bill unpassable either in the House or Senate, Judge Smith introduced an amendment designed to extend to women the same concept of nondiscriminatory treatment as the legislation promised to blacks. Smith intended his "sex" amendment, as it was dubbed, to embarrass and split the bill's supporters and prevent its passage, if not in the House, then in the Senate. His assumption was not farfetched. Although the handful of women in the House at the time were against segregation and knew that Smith had offered the women rights amendment as a way to jeopardize the bill's passage, they could not resist the temptation held out by the amendment. Much to the consternation of the bill's managers, they banded together and took the lead in support of Smith's amendment. The judge sat back contentedly as male members went along with the women's leadership, either because they shared Smith's dubious motives that the addition would act to defeat the bill or because they genuinely shared the view that the future, along with racial equality, should contain the idea of equal treatment of women. Smith's intended finesse of the H.R. 7152 rebounded when the "sex" amendment was adopted not only by the House but later in the Senate. Thus, in his eleventh-hour maneuver, Smith was hoist with his own petard. His amendment to H.R. 7152 became a legal building block for equal treatment of women as well as black Americans.

On 10 February 1964, the House of Representatives passed what was described in the press as the "most comprehensive civil rights bill in history." The vote was an overwhelming 290 to 130. Much to the satisfaction of its enthusiastic supporters, H.R. 7152 emerged as a far stronger endorsement of federal action than Kennedy had proposed to Congress a few months before his death. Success in the House, however, caused some to lose sight of the fact that H.R. 7152 was still only a bill. The hardest part of its journey lay ahead. The fact that it had been made stronger in the House acted to confound the next step: securing its passage in the Senate.

Mansfield was not pleased by what had been done to Kennedy's civil rights bill. Never sanguine about the prospects of the original bill in the Senate, he saw the final House version of H.R. 7152 as adding to his difficulties. In his discussions with Johnson, as with Kennedy, he was noncommittal about how he would proceed, indicating only that the bill would be brought up in the Senate. Mansfield rejected at the outset suggestions that the Senate be kept on a twenty-four-hour schedule to combat an expected filibuster. He did so on the ostensible grounds that the Senate had older members whose health would be endangered by sessions running through the night.

Mansfield's Strategy in the Senate

Although he had already made up his mind on how to proceed, the majority leader resisted revealing his plans in the Senate. He also refused to discuss them with those from outside who were working for civil rights. Fresh from victory in the House and with the president's encouragement, supporters of the legislation were converging on the Senate in a massive lobbying effort. Black leaders, clergymen, educators, and civic activists sought to meet with Mansfield and when he declined to discuss his intentions, anxieties arose among them. Rumors quickly spread that Mansfield's heart was not in the civil rights legislation. The majority leader ignored the rumors while continuing to plan for the arrival of H.R. 7152 from the House. His approach was based on three premises: (1) the issue of civil rights had reached a point where it could no longer be evaded, and a major legislative response had become crucial for the well-being of the nation; (2) the dug-in position of the southern senators, reinforced by the Senate's antiquated rules and procedures, had to be confronted and overcome or the credibility of the Senate and his leadership would crumble; and (3) not just the leadership but the Senate as a whole, Democrats and Republicans alike, would have to share the credit or blame for the outcome of the impending confrontation.

What this added up to in terms of legislative tactics was that there could be no major compromises with the southern Democrats on the substance of the bill; it was by offering such compromises that Lyndon Johnson as majority leader had been able to persuade the leader of the southerners, Senator Richard B. Russell, to end the filibuster of 1957. With a compromise in hand, Russell had then called off the filibuster, thereby permitting the Senate to pass a watered-down voting rights bill. There was no likelihood that Russell would be prepared to stop the talk in this instance without a similar massive weakening of H.R. 7152 by the Senate. In view of the tenor of the nation on the issue, a compromise of that kind would immediately be labeled a sellout. It would probably raise, rather than lower, the manifestations of discontent in the black community and reduce the Senate to a laughingstock.

Mansfield was convinced that the issue could not be resolved by going the route that Johnson had followed in order to pass the Voting Rights Act of 1957. Mansfield had witnessed firsthand the consequences of that attempt. When Johnson, as majority leader, had used such tactics as "continuous sessions" and manipulation of the Rules, there had been "pajama sessions," with proponents of the bill, dutifully rising from cots in their offices and appearing bedraggled and unshaven to answer quorum calls in the middle of the night. These quorum calls were initiated, as was permitted under the Senate Rules, by two or three southerners who remained on duty while the rest of the filibusterers were peacefully sleeping at home. The Senate stood speechless for hours while the sergeant-at-arms rushed hither and yon attempting to round up the fifty-one members necessary for a quorum so that business might proceed, at least until the next quorum call. Such meaningless interludes delighted the press corps and amused the nation. But the round-the-clock tactics had had no effect whatsoever other than to enhance the ability of the filibusterers to hold the Senate hostage to their determination not to permit passage of a bill of substance.

What the round-the-clock sessions did do was to weaken and confound proponents of civil rights legislation. It fell to them to produce on the Senate floor the fifty-one senators necessary to establish a quorum at any hour on demand of a single opponent. Otherwise, the Senate remained a silent place, stopped from doing any business, even speechmaking, until the necessary number of senators had responded to the call of the roll. Physically worn down after nights of interrupted sleep, proponents of the legislation were forced either to abandon the attempt to obtain a vote on the substance of the bill or to accept a compromise. In the Voting Rights measure, such a compromise was worked out by Johnson. On the one hand, Johnson was hailed for getting any sort of bill passed; on the other, he was berated for selling out the civil rights supporters with a weak compromise. Notwithstanding this experience, it was astounding that many urged Mansfield to follow the same procedural path. On the verge of taking up H.R. 7152 in the Senate, for example, President Johnson called on Mansfield to "get out the cots." Such was the lack of understanding of the Senate's peculiar procedural ways that long-time advocates of civil rights joined in the chorus calling for all-night sessions. Some of the strongest advocacy came from inside the Senate, including a few members who had slept fitfully and awakened grumpily but faithfully for the all-night sessions in 1957!

Mansfield was adamant in rejecting such pressure, even when it came from Johnson. In public, he linked his rejection of the round-the-clock strategy to the jeopardy it posed to the health of elderly senators. Privately he discussed his concern with the demeaning light in which the Senate was cast by "pajama" tactics. Most important, he was firmly convinced that round-the-clock sessions would not work. Certainly there was no indication that that parliamentary maneuver would break the southerners. Such sessions might wear down the proponents of civil rights to the point where they would be prepared to accept a weak compromise. But it was unlikely that the House of Representatives would accept it. In any event, Mansfield could not envision a compromise that would be agreeable to the southerners and at the same time meet the needs of the nation.

To be sure, Mansfield was not certain that any other parliamentary strategy would work better. As he saw it, there was no alternative than to attempt to invoke cloture under Rule 22. Adopted in 1917 to cut off a filibuster against a measure that permitted President Wilson to arm merchant vessels as a preliminary to America's entry into World War I, Rule 22 allowed a preponderance of the Senate to apply a gentle gag to a minority who found it impossible to stop talking. It is appropriately described as "gentle" because even after cloture is adopted by a two-thirds majority, Rule 22 still permits each senator an hour of talk. Only thereafter would the Senate be permitted to decide the fate of a bill on the basis of a simple majority, as provided for in the Constitution.

Despite the mildness of Rule 22, the idea of "unlimited debate" had become so ingrained that the Senate seemed prepared to postpone a vote on a measure forever if the only alternative was to invoke the Rule. This stand was taken not only by southerners, who had long promoted the idea that it was not senatorial to "gag" a colleague, but by members from other regions. The venerable President Pro Tempore of the Senate, Carl Hayden, vowed that he would "never" vote for cloture and, in truth, in a career spanning forty-two years as a senator, he never did. His reason? A filibuster had been instrumental in winning Arizona's admission to the Union in 1912, an event he himself had witnessed as the territorial delegate. Other senators from low-population states, notably from the West and border states, saw in the filibuster a weapon against heavily populated states. Such a view, of course, conveniently overlooked the fact that they had already been provided such protection by the constitutional provision of two senators from each state, regardless of population.

In approaching the confrontation on civil rights, the Senate mindset against proceeding by Rule 22 had already been loosened by the adoption of cloture the previous year. Senator Wayne Morse and his supporters had been silenced, and the Senate enabled to vote on the Communications Satellite (COMSAT) bill. At that time, a number of senators who had not previously shown a willingness to support cloture were persuaded to join the two leaders in producing the requisite two-thirds majority. Mansfield had no way of knowing how much of the change in attitude on Rule 22 that this represented would carry over from the previous year. What was clear to him from the successful experience with COMSAT, however, was that there was no way to put together a two-thirds vote for cloture on a civil rights measure without the minority leader's cooperation.

Everett McKinley Dirksen was the key. Only with his active participation could there be any hope of obtaining the support of additional Republicans beyond the handful, such as Jacob Javits of New York and Hugh Scott of Pennsylvania, who were consistent backers of civil rights measures. It would take a dozen or so additional Republicans if proceeding under Rule 22 was going to work. In conversations with Mansfield and the press, Dirksen had said that he was for a civil rights bill. But what kind of bill? He had not endorsed the Kennedy measure, much less the more comprehensive H.R. 7152 that had emerged from it in the House. Nor did he indicate the point in the Senate debate when the requisite number of senators would conclude that the debate had gone on long enough. The fact that Dirksen had been very cooperative on procedural matters during the previous year and actively participated in the COMSAT cloture were hopeful signs. But the civil rights issue, with its high emotional content, was a different matter.

It is entirely possible that, like Hamlet gazing at the skull, the irrepressible Dirksen may have toyed with the pros and cons inherent in the impending debate on civil rights. How would the position that he took affect the unspoken affinity between southern Democrats and Republicans in the Senate? The attitudes of his white supporters in Illinois and the blacks who had actively opposed his candidacy for the Senate? He might have considered taking refuge in Abe Lincoln and the Republican Party's role in ending slavery in order to conceal his built-in antipathy toward the expansion of the federal role in most matters, including civil rights. He could feign cooperation with the majority leader, shaking his head more in pity than in scorn at the complexities of the procedural situation while faulting the Democrats, whose responsibility as the majority party it was, for failing to operate the Senate properly. All the while, of course, he would know full well that the divided majority, like a confused spider, would become ever more entangled in a procedural web as the filibuster continued. And would the procedural flailings of a Democratic-"controlled" Senate over civil rights legislation result in a public revulsion with the Democrats? And did that, in turn, add up to a substantial Republican gain in the approaching general elections? Perhaps even a Republican president?

When he finished musing over such questions, the minority leader would remember that he had to maintain his ties to the liberal Republicans in the Senate who supported his leadership and civil rights legislation, such senators as the Republican whip, Tom Kuchel of California, Jacob Javits of New York, and Scott of Pennsylvania, who were feeling increased pressure to act on civil rights. Other Republicans, such as George Aiken of Vermont and John Sherman Cooper of Kentucky, possessed a deep sense of national responsibility and strong moral convictions. They sensed that the time was at hand to end the charade and come to grips with the civil rights issue.

Dirksen, as minority leader, was aware of the rising tide among liberal Senate Republicans but he had to contend with his conservative faction, with such Republican senators as Barry Goldwater of Arizona, Carl Curtis of Nebraska, Norris Cotton of New Hampshire, and Bourke Hickenlooper of Iowa. Although each was conservative in his own way, they did agree on one thing: they were rock-ribbed Republicans and, as such, it was not incumbent on them to make life easier for the Democratic majority in the Senate. There was in fact already considerable grumbling over Dirksen's failure to consult with them on his plans for dealing with the civil rights issue.

The minority leader knew that this group, no matter what, could not be stampeded. They would have to be coaxed to the water, and even then he was not sure that they could be made to drink. Without large black populations in their states, civil rights was hardly a life-or-death issue. Nor was it a political elixir. Dirksen knew that apart from their ever-present urge to stick it to the Democrats, they also had concerns with parts of H.R. 7152, concern that centered on a substantial growth in the power of the federal government against the states and the implications for business in dealing with equal employment opportunities. As a senator from Illinois, Dirksen shared some of their views and had others of his own that led him to differ with the text of the bill as it would arrive from the House.

Dirksen would not be pressured, least of all by the president, Lyndon Johnson, his old Senate adversary. Johnson might try his bag of tricks, but Dirksen was impervious to them. Nor would the civil rights activists have any greater success with pressure tactics, as they discovered when they sought to carry the campaign for H.R. 7152 to his home state. He owed no political debt to them. The black voters of Chicago and other black concentrations in the industrial centers of Illinois were not among Dirksen's avid supporters. White religious leaders, who endorsed federal action on civil rights, did carry weight with Dirksen because of the moral implications of the question and because the congregations to whom they preached contained many of his political supporters.

Most persuasive with Dirksen was his awareness that something larger than politics was involved in civil rights as the issue loomed before the Senate in the early 1960s. Dirksen sensed, as did Mansfield, that the outcome of the confrontation on H.R. 7152 in the Senate would say something definitive regarding the soundness of American political institutions and the resiliency of the system that had evolved from them. It might do the same regarding the depth and durability of the unity of the American people. It might try the Senate, as it had not been tried in a century, as a central institution capable of meeting the changing needs of the nation.

Mansfield's Different Kind of Senate Is Key

One other consideration inclined Dirksen toward active cooperation with the Democrats on H.R. 7152. By 1963, the Senate was a changed place. The frenetic keep-them-guessing, egocentric, wheeling-dealing, wheedling, whiplashing style of Johnson's leadership had been replaced by the plodding, self-effacing, laid-back predictability of Mansfield. The almost paranoic suspicion, not only between the two political parties but among Democratic senators who had been exploited by Johnson's tactics, was giving way to Mansfield's insistence on equal treatment for all. Where once the Senate chamber had seethed with anger, frustration, fury, and farce, there was now a degree of mutual tolerance, accommodation, and sobriety. It was as though Johnson's one-man band had swelled into a hundred-voice chorale. If senators did not always sing on key, at least they did manage a loose harmony under the barely visible baton of the majority leader. While all might not yet be equal, in spite of Mansfield's continued avowal of equality, the senators were clearly less unequal than they had been in the past. By 1964, with Bob Kerr dead, Bobby Baker on his way to jail, and the doors of the Inner Club thrown open to all, there was little left of the Johnsonian Senate. What lingered was a dated public perception of the institution, a media caricature that no longer had much in common with the reality on Capitol Hill.

Mansfield attributed the change, as he did almost everything else that happened in the Senate, to all the members. Without the majority leader's persistent efforts and his infinite patience, however, it is not likely that the transformation would have come about. In crediting the entire membership, Mansfield was being entirely sincere. He was the chief agent of the Senate, carrying out, not his own purposes, but the wishes of his colleagues. Certainly Democrats had sought a thoroughgoing change when they elected him as majority leader. In working to provide it, he was the servant of the whole. But in filling that role, he went much further than anyone anticipated. The egalitarianism he sponsored in the Senate was more an expression of his personal vision of the institution. His concept of the Senate was the antithesis of Johnson's. In Mansfield's view, the Senate was a self-governing collegium of equals and not an insider-outsider club run by an awesome director assisted by a cabal of favored insiders.

Mansfield did not draw a distinction between Democrats and Republicans in the Senate, although he never forgot that his authority as leader was dependent on the Democratic majority. He aimed at all senators working together with mutual restraint, reciprocal courtesy, and personal trust. The institution would do the nation's legislative business in an orderly, enlightened, and unsensational fashion, with the Golden Rule transcending even the Senate's quasi-sacred rules. The new egalitarianism would produce an institution in which not just one or a handful of its members but the Senate itself would glow in the nation's political firmament.

However much Mansfield preached equality among senators, he was not naive about the varying capabilities of individual senators. He realized fully that he was not dealing with a hundred Websters, Clays, and Calhouns or a hundred "profiles in courage." He knew his own limitations as well as those of his colleagues. What he saw, then, was a body of ordinary men and women containing the whole repertoire of human strengths and weaknesses—and just possibly something more. The members of the Senate had been elected to serve the people of the states and the nation by passing through the stringent, often vicious filtering process of politics. He felt it incumbent on the leadership to maintain an institutional setting that would permit an equitable opportunity for all members to give meaning to their selection. If some had more to give, they would be encouraged. If some had less that, too, would become apparent. In either event, the responsibility would rest not on the leadership but on the members, individually and collectively, for what the Senate achieved or failed to achieve.

Everett Dirksen had struggled through the complexities of the majority leader's personality and had come to regard him with a genuine affection. There were good reasons for Dirksen to entertain such sentiments. During the three years of Mansfield's leadership, Dirksen had been treated with respect, deference, and consideration. Whenever possible, Mansfield transferred credit for Senate achievements from himself to the minority leader. He did so, moreover, without condescension and without later submitting a tab. Dirksen was as delighted to take the spotlight as Mansfield was reluctant. While the minority leader would have been glad to confound the Democratic liberals over any issue, including civil rights, he had no desire to hurt Mike Mansfield in the process. For him to aid and abet a procedural catastrophe on H.R. 7152 would have meant to precipitate a disaster for Mike Mansfield's leadership. Dirksen was not seeking that sort of advantage at the expense of the majority leader.

Mansfield began to consolidate a bipartisan approach on civil rights in the Senate by requesting that Dirksen join him in a joint introduction of President Kennedy's proposed civil rights bill in the Senate, a bill identical with the original H.R. 7152 that was simultaneously introduced in the House of Representatives. In going along, Dirksen stressed that he was doing so only as a courtesy to the president. He made clear that the introduction in no way bound him to support the president's bill. At the outset, he would go no further than to say that he favored a civil rights measure's being considered in the Senate, a caveat that Mansfield readily accepted. The civil rights measure, jointly introduced by the two leaders, identical in text with H.R. 7152, was referred to Jim Eastland's Judiciary Committee and, as anticipated, nothing was heard from the committee thereafter. Nevertheless, the leadership referral foreshadowed a continuing dialogue between the two leaders and held the promise of eventual bipartisan action.

Thereafter, Mansfield kept Dirksen fully advised on every aspect of the evolving legislation. Underlying the strategy was Mansfield's belief that there was little likelihood that an acceptable compromise could be negotiated with the southern bloc to circumvent a filibuster, as had been done by Johnson in the previous civil rights bill in 1957. Mansfield knew that such a compromise, at best, would be only a cosmetic solution, which would not have served in the situation that existed in 1964. Although the 1957 compromise had been billed as opening the polls to disenfranchised southern blacks, in practice it had proved of little value. Moreover, the 1957 law left untouched the infuriating humiliation suffered on a daily basis in the form of segregated access to restaurants, buses, railroad stations, hotels, beaches, washrooms, and other public facilities. It also had done nothing to foster greater equity for blacks in employment opportunities.

The earlier compromise had irritated not only southern Democrats opposed to desegregation but also civil right activists and Senate liberals, even those who had voted for it. For Mansfield to try to negotiate a similar compromise in the context of the militancy that existed in the black community by 1964 would have been worse than meaningless. A repeat performance that failed to deal in depth with the grievances induced by segregation while once again claiming to have done so would simply have added fury to the spreading discontent. Moreover, another such gesture in the Senate would have angered the House of Representatives. The other body had spent months in strengthening H.R. 7152 even beyond the formidable Kennedy proposed text, and a substantial majority of House members would not have looked kindly on a Senate version that seriously weakened the measure.

There was, in short, no mistaking the fact that time had run out on segregation; there was no margin for another legislative charade. As passed by the House, H.R. 7152 contained the needed substance to resolve the issue. To be sure, there could be changes made to win over a sufficient number of reluctant Senators. Changes in bills as they move through the system are a routine part of the legislative process. In this instance, however, how much change would be too much? At what point would H.R. 7152 as altered by the Senate cease to be palatable to the House? Whatever the case, Mansfield was convinced that a negotiated settlement with Dick Russell, the leader of the southern senators, was no longer a viable alternative.

The second premise of Mansfield's strategy was that once Russell understood that a window-dressing compromise was not possible, he would be relentless in his exploitation of the Senate Rules in order to prevent H.R. 7152 from passing in a form unacceptable to the southern senators. Russell could and would hold up the Senate indefinitely by forcing it to spin procedural wheels. Such tactics had invariably given him dominance of the floor situation on race issues in the past. He could persist for weeks on end, months if necessary, hoping that a sufficient number of his opponents would tire of the struggle and eventually opt to end it on terms that he would be in a position to establish. In short, there was going to be a relentless filibuster. The southerners would pull out all the stops in order to forestall H.R. 7152 from coming to a vote in a form unacceptable to them.

Even if Russell wished otherwise, he and his associates were trapped by the constituencies that over the years had nurtured them. The great preponderance of people who voted in the South were white, and most of them were registered Democrats. They expected from their representatives in the

House and Senate what they had grown accustomed to receiving since the days of the New Deal. They expected economic benefits from the federal government designed to overcome widespread southern impoverishment, the economic inequity bequeathed the region by the Civil War. And they expected successful efforts by their senators to defeat or curb measures designed to undo the legal segregation that was left after the abolition of slavery and was an integral part of southern culture. For a southern Senator to cease delivering on these expectations would be to ensure a quick political demise. If it happened frequently, it would also end the long dominance of southern politics by the Democratic Party.

Mansfield understood the political predicament and had nothing but sympathy for his southern colleagues. But he also knew that it made a prolonged confrontation on H.R. 7152 unavoidable in the Senate. He was aware of the formidable power the southerners could wield through manipulation of the Senate Rules. He knew that all-night sessions could not break a filibuster, even as it had not silenced the southerners in the previous Senate clash on voting rights. He also knew that attempts to finesse the southern resistance by procedural legerdemain or trickery of his own would come to naught; not only was Russell a masterful legislative tactician, even more to the point the Rules were stacked hugely in favor of a determined minority.

Early in the Kennedy administration, Mansfield had reluctantly allowed himself to be persuaded to bring up a civil rights bill almost as a routine matter. He had done so to satisfy Senate supporters of the measure and a still naive Kennedy administration seeking to be viewed by the press as having tried to do something about civil rights. It had been a halfhearted effort on Mansfield's part, and he had promptly abandoned it in the face of an incipient southern filibuster. Mansfield had little patience with such exercises in futility and thereafter turned a deaf ear to pleas that he repeat the attempt from those who thought that round-the-clock sessions or procedural manipulation might achieve their ends. Mansfield had long since concluded that there was only one way a meaningful civil rights bill could be enacted in the Senate. That was to have the patience to endure the filibuster while waiting for public and other pressures to produce the two-thirds majority vote required to break it. This time, the situation was different. To be sure, a two-thirds vote for cloture was not yet in sight, but Mansfield sensed that at least there was a chance to gather the necessary sixty-seven votes. Indicative of the possibility was the way in which H.R. 7152 had swept through to passage in the House of Representatives. There, the coalition headed by Democrat Manny Celler of New York and Republican Bill McCulloch of Ohio had managed to hold together a bipartisanship that strengthened and then passed the bill by an overwhelming margin. The magnitude of the outpouring of support had not been anticipated, and it was correctly interpreted as reflecting a decisive change in the mood of the country.

A change had indeed taken place. Television screens in countless living rooms had provided the nation with an opportunity to witness firsthand the brutal ugliness induced by segregation. Those who were militant in their insistence on racial separatism found themselves shrinking in number and increasingly isolated from the mainstream of American life. From a more or less pro forma belief in the constitutional ideal of human equality throughout the nation, many Americans had been shocked by the reality into a heightened awareness of the moral issue raised by segregation. They were determined to see an end to what they had seen on television, at least an end to its legal practice.

This basic change in outlook meant that mass support for equal treatment was coming not only from blacks but increasingly from the nation's white population, particularly from religious, educational, and other cultural sources. The issue had grown from one of essentially minority concern to one of full national involvement, producing a great increase in the number and influence of those prepared to go all-out to persuade Congress to pass H.R. 7152. The great rally led by Martin Luther King Jr. in Washington was a watershed, presenting striking evidence that the movement had spread far beyond the South and African Americans. Leading activists of a nonviolent kind had even obtained the clear-cut support of the White House. In spite of his personal aversion to segregation, President Kennedy had previously held back, giving only a hesitant endorsement to King and other black leaders. Kennedy was reluctant to move faster or go further because, among other things, he was aware that he would be the one to suffer political repercussions, particularly in the South. His successor had no such inhibitions. Lyndon Johnson also disdained segregation on a personal basis, but in contrast with Kennedy, he had much to gain politically from supporting passage of the pending civil rights measure. His southern-western identity shielded him to a considerable extent from the potential political losses that Kennedy would suffer in that region; Johnson's political concerns lay elsewhere. He feared what might happen, especially in such states as New York, Pennsylvania, Illinois, and California, with large minority populations, if he were to be identified with a failure to pass the civil rights bill. Johnson had no political hesitancy, therefore, in pulling out all the stops in his support of H.R. 7152. He threw open the doors of the White House to the civil rights leaders and even provided them with free advice on how they might accomplish their aims in Congress. He was like a football coach at half-time, lending enthusiastic encouragement to Martin Luther King and other civil rights advocates.

Mansfield's Plan for Passing H.R. 7152

As the time drew near for consideration of H.R. 7152, the Senate felt the increased public pressure for action on civil rights. Senators from states with small black populations outside the South could not ignore the change in national attitude on the segregation question. Formerly, they had enjoyed a certain immunity because civil rights was not high on the list of their constituency's interests. However important it might seem in the abstract, segregation was a problem occurring in someone else's back yard. Indeed, Republicans senators could afford to consider pertinent legislation in the Senate primarily as a way to embarrass the Democrats, divided as they were by the issue. By 1963, however, concern over segregation had become nationwide, and senators were forced to recognize their political stake in the issue. Demonstrations supporting an end to segregation were occurring in dozens of cities throughout the nation, preachers were denouncing segregation from thousands of pulpits, and editorials of condemnation could be found in newspapers everywhere.

Nor could segregation be evaded as an institutional problem within the Senate. Senators who had previously taken refuge in the Senate's Rules and traditions to explain their failure to act on civil rights found the explanations no longer persuasive. By engineering a successful cloture vote on the telecommunications bill the previous year, Mansfield had closed this escape hatch for straddlers. Prior to that, they might explain their refusal to vote for cloture on the grounds of Senate practice, while proclaiming their readiness to support equal rights for blacks if given an opportunity to vote on the question. Breaking the filibuster on satellite communications helped considerably to make a vote for cloture acceptable, regardless of the Senate's aversion to cutting off a colleague from having his say. If cloture had been admissible on COMSAT without bringing down the citadel, what justification was there for finding it beyond the pale on civil rights?

Although developments in the nation and the Senate enhanced prospects for passing H.R. 7152 in the Senate, Mansfield remained very cautious. There was still the practical question of how heightened public enthusiasm was to be converted into a two-thirds vote for cloture. The task was a formidable one whose success would depend heavily on effective organization of the civil rights advocates. Without such organization, it would be virtually impossible to stay with the issue long enough to overcome the advantage that the Rules conferred on the opponents. While listening to stirring oratory calling for immediate action, Mansfield was only too aware of the difference between a speech and a nailed-down vote. He was all too familiar with the legislative phenomenon of great initial enthusiasm followed by second thoughts or limited attention spans.

In designing a strategy for handling the bill, the majority leader proceeded on the assumption that all 100 senators would be present for the critical vote on cloture. Since cloture required a two-thirds vote of those present and voting, the decisive number was sixty-seven. Without that number, there was no way of preventing an indefinite stall by the opponents and the eventual exhaustion of the advocates of the legislation. Only when sixty-seven senators were ready to vote for cloture would Mansfield be able to silence the opponents of H.R. 7152. The number that mattered to him above all others, then, was the sixty-seven.

Initially, he found it necessary to restrain some of the more enthusiastic proponents of H.R. 7152, who clung to the belief that there was an easier or quicker way to pass a civil rights bill. They continued to talk of round-the-clock sessions or clever manipulation of the floor procedures to compel the opponents to yield. Indeed, the astute Russell encouraged such beliefs by presenting himself and the southern block as fighting with their backs to the wall, harassed, driven, and on the verge of collapse even before the debate began. In the circumstances, some supporters of civil rights found in Mansfield's refusal to entertain such an approach reason to believe that he lacked competency as floor leader or was lukewarm in his support of the bill.

Mansfield's initial tally of support for cloture on H.R. 7152 showed nowhere near the required sixty-seven votes. At best, he could add to a bare constitutional majority of fifty-one, mostly Democrats plus a handful of Republicans who, over the years, had been unequivocal in their support of civil rights legislation. An additional fifteen or twenty votes for cloture would have to be found among the less-than-passionate supporters. It was reasonable to expect that some of the shortfall would be made up by Democratic senators from western and border states. Representing as they did states less directly affected by the issue than those in the Deep South, they might be persuaded to swallow their objections to cloture and go along with the leadership in voting to shut off the filibusterers. But this source would still not yield sixty-seven votes.

On the other side of the aisle, Mansfield had already counted in the strong Republican advocates of civil rights. To uncover the balance meant digging into the Republican center that grouped around the minority leader. Dirksen had still to make known what procedural tactics would be acceptable to him, let alone the changes he was prepared to accept in the text of H.R. 7152. Moreover, even if the Republican center, containing such New Englanders as George Aiken and Winston L. Prouty of Vermont and Margaret Chase Smith of Maine, were won over, the votes for cloture might not add up. The search for support would have to penetrate further into the Republican Party, into its more conservative recesses, among senators such as Bourke Hickenlooper of Iowa, Carl Curtis of Nebraska, and other mid-westerners. For them, the political stake in equal rights for blacks was minimal. Hence, bent on political mischief, they had merely to join with the southerners in opposing cloture. At the same time, at Lincoln Day dinners, they could express their dedication to the principle of equality for all Americans under the Constitution. Although the question of civil rights was beginning to intrude into their political worlds, it was not yet a compelling issue in their states. Some of this group, as Mansfield saw it, had to be persuaded to vote to shut off debate.

In seeking votes for cloture, Mansfield was unwilling to use the tactic described in legislative circles as trading "apples for oranges." What is involved in such trades is a commitment to act in a particular way on some unrelated matter in the future in return for a desired vote on the matter at hand. For three years as Senate leader, Mansfield had steered clear of the practice, and he could not bring himself to pursue it in the situation con-fronting him on H.R. 7152. He regarded such "logrolling" as a distortion of the legislative process, as well as demeaning personally. What he was pre-pared to do, particularly on procedural matters, was to appeal to better natures or to statesmanship, and he made such appeals to members from time to time when the Senate found itself wallowing in a procedural jam. Such exhortations, unfortunately, rarely served to translate into specific votes on critical issues.

He was left with the orthodox legislative practice of seeking the neces-sary votes by making changes in H.R. 7152 that would satisfy the specific objections of senators. In return, their votes might be forthcoming, not necessarily for the legislation but, more importantly, for a vote on cloture. Bargaining of this kind is, of course, an integral part of the legislative process in that it serves to reconcile and harmonize many viewpoints as a bill moves toward majority acceptance. In this instance the point of consen-sus, however, would be the sixty-seven votes for cloture rather than the simple majority of fifty-one provided for in the Constitution. That would mean making changes agreeable to a far larger number of holdouts than!would customarily be true. Great caution was necessary lest the bill be so changed as to make the final Senate version unacceptable. There was a point at which watering down would produce a text unacceptable to the House of Representatives, which would have to repass the measure, or to the president, who would have to sign it. If that were to happen, the House leadership could not be blamed; it had already shepherded a bill to passage that had found wide public acceptance. Nor could President Johnson be held responsible; he had campaigned vigorously for the bill and already congratulated the House on the passing of H.R. 7152. If a version of H.R. 7152, as amended by the Senate were unacceptable, it was going to be the reputation of the Senate and its leadership that would bear the consequences. In the process of bartering textual changes for votes on cloture, therefore, great care had to be taken to touch all bases, to keep the House, the president, and civil rights leaders in tune with developments in the Senate.

Mansfield was equipped neither by temperament nor inclination to undertake that kind of effort. He was an atypical legislator with little taste for haggling over differences and engaging in what often is little more than semantic swordplay. He was more than happy to leave to others the precision tuning of the bill's sections, paragraphs, words, commas, and periods, the clarifying or obfuscating of passages, and the adding or subtracting of substance.

In ordinary circumstances, this basic phase of the legislative process would have been assigned routinely to the Senate Judiciary Committee. But usual practice could not be followed in this instance. The committee route had been tried before with civil rights legislation. Such attempts had meandered off into a dead-end under the quiet but wily direction of Chairman Eastland of Mississippi, with an assist from the more partisan Republican Committee members and in spite of the loud but futile cries of protest from liberals.

To have followed routine procedure in this instance would have afforded Eastland an opportunity to sabotage the bill in committee. If he could not bury the measure, he might at least have been able to see to its weakening to the point of unacceptabilty. Given the traditional power of committee chairmen and the conservative composition of the Judiciary Committee at the time, there clearly existed the possibility of his doing one or the other. Whatever the uproar elsewhere, such an effort would have won Eastland cheers from his white constituency in Mississippi. In fairness, it should be noted that although he complained, he was not adamant in demanding that the normal procedure of referral to committee be followed on H.R. 7152. In any event, Mansfield was taking no chances. He was determined to find an orderly means for bypassing the Judiciary Committee.

If the bill did not go to the committee, acceptable textual changes and other adjustments involved in garnering the necessary votes for cloture would have had to be pursued elsewhere. Moreover, since Mansfield could not undertake this task himself, another Democrat, and preferably one readily identifiable as a strong supporter of equal rights, had to be named. It would have to be someone highly schooled in the issues of civil rights and racial segregation who enjoyed fencing with words, matching wits, friendly persuasion, and backroom banter; in short, the kind of horse trading that is a commonplace of the legislative process. Inasmuch as the need to obtain Republican votes was critical, the minority leader, too, would have to be persuaded to designate someone from his party for the same purpose. In fact, it occurred to Mansfield that Dirksen might designate himself to carry out this task. As ranking Republican member of the Judiciary Committee, he possessed the credentials. Moreover, he was by temperament well suited to the task and, unlike Mansfield, found pleasure in the legislative negotiating process.

As the majority leader saw the strategy unfolding, two designees, one a Democrat and one a Republican, would act as substitutes for the chairman and ranking minority member of the Judiciary Committee. The two designees would screen proposals for changes coming from senators. They would select from among them those they could agree on and adjust the bill accordingly. In the end, Mansfield hoped that a version of H.R. 7152 so modified would induce sixty-seven members of the Senate to vote to shut off debate. And it had to be a version that would still be acceptable to the House of Representatives and the president. Not verbalized but still to be hoped for, the version would assuage civil rights leaders, please the editorialists of the media, and keep southern senators from bolting the Democratic Party. Such were the parameters of the challenge confronting the majority leader.

The minority leader was the base on which Mansfield's approach would rest. To be sure, Dirksen's collaboration was not all that was needed to engineer the passing of an acceptable version of H.R. 7152. But without Dirksen's active participation, the majority leader knew that there would not even be a bill—or at any rate an acceptable bill. No matter from what angle Mansfield examined the problem, Dirksen emerged as the essential, the master key.

The majority leader had to have Dirksen's genuine cooperation, and he was prepared to go to great lengths to obtain it. Although the courting of the minority leader had begun at the outset of Mansfield's leadership, there was no farsighted master plan of manipulation in anticipation of what would be required to pass H.R. 7152 three years later. Mansfield's deferential approach to the Senate minority was neither calculated nor specifically related to the issue of civil rights. Instead, it was a consequence of the style of leadership Mansfield was determined to give to the Senate. Mansfield was far more comfortable avoiding confrontation than inviting it. He rarely sought the public spotlight. Throughout his entire career in the Senate, public attention ferreted him out, not the other way round. As a senator and as Senate majority leader, it never occurred to him to engage a public relations expert. Nevertheless, he enjoyed national and international recognition.

Coalition for Cloture: Dirksen

By 1963, the Republican senators and their leader had accepted Mansfield's leadership as not necessarily always effective but at least free of ulterior motive. Almost without exception, Republicans were unstinting in their praise of his integrity and evenhandedness. In the difficult procedural situation involved in H.R. 7152, not a few Republicans were favorably disposed to work with him without consideration of political advantage. Dirksen, in particular, had reason to reciprocate Mansfield's solicitous treatment of the minority. For one thing, it gave Dirksen plenty of access to the public spotlight, and, unlike Mansfield, he relished the attention. With little news being generated by the majority leader, the media found in Dirksen an excellent source of copy.

In return for Mansfield's benign treatment, Dirksen put aside his militant Republicanism. He no longer took delight, as he had with Johnson, in confounding his Democratic counterpart in floor debate. That is not to say that his partisanship had atrophied. Although he spared Mansfield personally, he retained sharp barbs for use against the Democrats. But after three years of Mansfield leadership, so pacific had the Senate floor become that when Dirksen did revert to his old tactics, they seemed almost a welcome relief from the routine. Dirksen eschewed public criticism of the majority leader. He fully endorsed fully Mansfield's efforts to enhance the stature of the Senate in the eyes of the public and fortify the institution's role within the federal government.

After three years of dealing with Dirksen, Mansfield was satisfied that he could count on the minority leader's personal amicability and even his cooperation in the conduct of the Senate's routine business. But with H.R. 7152 he was looking for something more than what had been forthcoming from the minority leader. Dirksen had not had any difficulty supporting the cloture vote on COMSAT. He was a strong supporter of the legislation, as were most Senate Republicans. He also had a personal reason for doing whatever he could to pass the legislation inasmuch as opposition to the bill was coming from a handful of Democratic liberals. To that group, he was ever prepared to give a lecture or teach a lesson. Moreover, this time the liberals were being led by Wayne Morse, a Republican turned Democrat and hence deserving of great disdain in Dirksen's eyes.

The minority leader had entered actively into the COMSAT mélee only when it became apparent that a liberal filibuster was under way. Then, with hackles raised, he had agreed almost without hesitation to Mansfield's insistence that the Senate would have to follow the route of invoking cloture in order to get to the measure. Once having accepted the majority leader's approach, Dirksen had gone all-out in persuading Republican colleagues to support cloture. On the Senate floor, he chose the role of picador, delighting in pricking the hides of the filibusterers, deriding their use of the same delaying tactic they had denounced time and again when employed by southerners against civil rights measures. Dirksen enjoyed his role, finding an audience ever ready to nod in agreement with his blistering thrusts and to laugh at his jabs. But in his determination to stick it to the liberals, he seemed not to have considered closely the implications of joining in *any* successful vote on cloture. What he may have overlooked was the impact that the first such successful vote in decades would have on Senate mores.

Intending to go the same route of cloture on H.R. 7152, Mansfield needed something more than Dirksen had given on COMSAT. He wanted Dirksen's full participation, virtually to the point of co-leadership, in seeking the votes for cloture and final passage of the bill. This posed serious problems for the minority leader, who found the circumstances quite different this time around. To begin with, Dirksen was not prepared to buy H.R. 7152, at least not in the form in which it had passed the House. In addition, co-leadership would mean his active involvement in rounding up cloture votes and, this time, without the gratification of opposing the liberals. He would not be the opponent of Paul Douglas of Illinois, Joe Clark of Pennsylvania, Hubert H. Humphrey of Minnesota, and Wayne Morse of Oregon. He would be their ally.

As co-leader, Dirksen would be obliged to persuade conservative Republicans to vote for cloture, and he would find them reluctant. Some were not nearly as enamored of the cause of equal rights as their Lincoln Day speeches might lead one to believe. At best, many who might vote for a civil rights bill had reservations about various provisions of H.R. 7152 and would be in no hurry to bring the debate to a halt unless changes to their satisfaction were made in the text. Finally, Dirksen was aware that to accept co-leadership might mean a break with the conservative southern Democrats. In the past, that unspoken link had given the Republicans a position of power out of proportion to their minority status in the Senate. A break, moreover, could adversely affect the National Republican Party in its emerging strategy of attempting to spread a two-party system throughout the Democratic South. Members of his party, such as the aspiring presidential candidate Barry Goldwater, who would see in this course something of a sellout.

If Dirksen participated as co-leader, he would be committing himself to joining with Democrats in producing a modified version of H.R. 7152 that would bring a two-thirds majority vote for cloture. He would have to keep his Republican minority on the course laid down by the majority leader.

Only in that way would he avoid the procedural minefield that would be planted by Russell and keep the attention of the Senate fixed on civil rights until the issue could be resolved in a vote. A procedural alignment with the majority leader seemed feasible in the light of the goodwill that Mansfield enjoyed among Republicans. But it was by no means certain how long such an alignment could be maintained. As the debate droned on, the response of Dirksen's conservative cohorts would become less and less predictable. Some were already grumbling at the extent of the minority leader's cooperation with the Democrats and his failure to consult with them. Moreover, even if an acceptable version of H.R. 7152 passed in the Senate, it would require a rerun vote in the House, where it might be subject to delays or outright rejection. Finally, the version would require the president's signature, and that was not likely to be forthcoming if the version did not satisfy the civil rights leaders. In short, the road to converting H.R. 7152 into law would be difficult and protracted, with much of the responsibility for what finally emerged resting on his shoulders. It was a responsibility that, as Minority Leader, Dirksen did not have to take.

Dirksen was indeed in a dilemma. For the writers and cartoonists who knew his penchant for theater, it was easy enough to portray his inner conflict. Would he be remembered as the Republican leader who at the eleventh hour threw a monkey wrench into the legislative machinery to prevent the civil rights bill from passing? Would he retreat to the seclusion of the minority leader's office to wait out the storm, unmoved by the cries for help coming from the Democratic leadership? Would he be content to put the onus on the Democrats even as he tallied his political winnings? Would he stand idly by while the Senate floundered like a helpless giant, unable even to reach the point of a vote on the question of segregation despite the rising public clamor for ending it? Would he turn away from the idea of human equality, this principle that had given birth to his beloved Republican Party? Would he let this moment pass in inaction and find himself thereafter forever haunted by the ghost of a betrayed Lincoln? Or would he thrust aside the sirens of political profit that were contesting within him with those other inner voices, the voices of decency, fair play and, above all, an overriding concern for the nation? Would he heed the call to put on his armor and sally forth to do battle for the right? Would he save not only the Senate from the folly of its antiquated practices but also the nation from the threat of permanent and deepening racial division?

Dirksen's oratory on the Senate floor encouraged such portrayals. Not without reason was he dubbed the "Hamlet of the Senate" or, in a less flattering variation, "the Prince of Ooze." His style bordered on the theatrical, and as he grew older, he seemed to accentuate its thespian aspects. He indulged ever more lavishly in references, accurate and inaccurate, to the classics. He took to striding back and forth before the presiding officer's desk and using all the gradations of his formidable voice. He not only amused the galleries and his colleagues with his antics but seemed also to derive a great deal of personal pleasure from his displays of histrionics.

To see Dirksen in theatrical terms, however, was to miss the character for the caricature. Beneath the twisted quotations, the mellifluous rhetoric, and the clowning, Dirksen was a down-to-earth politician with an ear tuned to the mood of his constituents in Illinois and to the currents of concern in the nation. He also possessed an excellent sense of what was viable in the Senate, especially among his Republican colleagues, who, like the Democrats, came in many ideological hues and with a wide variety of personal idiosyncrasies. He extolled in the most extravagant terms the virtues of small-town America whence he had come, although he had spent most of his life in cities. Urban or rural, he had faith in his countrymen. He believed strongly in the nation's concept, as expressed in the Declaration of Independence and in the constitutional system. He had confidence in the institutions of the federal government and in the relevance of the party system. He was, in short, a bone-deep patriot, a very sophisticated senator, and a proud Republican. In the fullness of his years, his priorities among these characteristics had sorted themselves out in about that order.

Dirksen hesitated before deciding to throw in his lot with the majority leader on civil rights, but not for long. He knew that the inequity suffered by black Americans, especially in the South, was a travesty on fundamental American values. But he also knew that there were many other travesties in the nation. Elected by a predominantly white constituency with many concerns, the ending of that particular travesty had not been a burning political imperative for him. In the past, he had treated it as an issue best left for others to provide the initiatives. Now, his sense of political timing told him that the hour was late. The Senate could no longer seek refuge in the sacrosanctity of its rules if those rules caused it to fail once again to face up to the question of equal racial treatment. To dodge this question, as had been done on other occasions, threatened to do permanent damage to the Senate, to the Republican Party, and in the end to the nation. It was, as Dirksen would express it, "an issue whose time has come." For such issues, Dirksen did not require theatrical trappings. He was ready to grasp the historic moment.

He could deal later with his doubts about parts of H.R. 7152. He could find a way to quiet the rumblings of discontent from within his own party about too much cooperation with Democratic liberals. He could risk the loss of power in the Senate that might be entailed in breaking the conservative

Republican link with the southern Democrats. He could even overlook his personal irritations with black civil rights leaders and the hard time they had given him in Illinois politics. He was still a member of the party of Lincoln. He was still a senator of the United States and one of the nation's political leaders. He had an inescapable obligation to show the way on this critical issue.

Dirksen agreed with Mansfield that going for cloture was the only course offering any prospect for success. This was the cornerstone of Mansfield's strategy for handling H.R. 7152, and it won Dirksen's general concurrence. Dirksen agreed to work in tandem. He continued to leave open an exit for himself by warning that while he accepted H.R. 7152 as an appropriate vehicle, changes in the text would be necessary to satisfy him and other Republicans. Mansfield did not demur in the slightest, urging only that Dirksen work out the changes in the bill with the Democrat who would be designated for that purpose.

Mansfield was prepared to go further in his determination to assure the minority leader's full participation. When Dirksen decided that, rather than designate another Republican, he would personally undertake to negotiate changes in the bill in return for votes, Mansfield welcomed the idea. As if to underscore his confidence in the minority leader, Mansfield proposed setting up the principal venue for handling H.R. 7152 in Dirksen's office in the Capitol. Somewhat overwhelmed by the suggestion, Dirksen hesitated at first, arguing that Mansfield's office was more appropriate. But, pressed by the majority leader, he put aside his reluctance.

Reporters were taken aback by what seemed to be a symbolic act of abdication of leadership, but Mansfield downplayed the matter with a characteristic response of a half-smile. He vaguely attributed the arrangement to convenience of location—Dirksen's office was but a few paces from the Senate floor—plus the fact that Dirksen would be working mostly with his Republican colleagues. He noted that the locus was unimportant in any event because the effort to pass a civil rights bill had now become completely bipartisan.

There was more involved than a deferential gesture or even convenience of location. In the Republican leader's office, negotiations with reluctant Republicans would be conducted in an optimum setting. The ambiance of Dirksen's quarters might very well predispose them to greater flexibility in what they would demand in the way of changes in H.R. 7152 as the price of their votes. Surrounded by Republican memorabilia, under the benign gaze of a Lincoln portrait, with the reassuring drone of their leader's voice in their ears, Republicans could feel themselves safe from being sandbagged. And if there were interruptions in the negotiations while the minority leader was called away on some other matter, they would be kept at ease by

Dirksen's highly competent and long-time aides, Oliver Dompierre and Glee Gomien, who were as reassuringly Republican as the leader himself. Dirksen's office also had a large inner conference room with a bar at one end where serious discussions could take place in seclusion and where toasts to progress could be drunk discreetly; the gregarious Dirksen did not share Mansfield's reticence about the mix of alcohol and politics in the Capitol. As a workplace for H.R. 7152, then, Dirksen's office was an excellent substitute for that part of the legislative process, the give and take, that in ordinary circumstances would have been located in the Senate Judiciary Committee.

Mansfield insisted that the team of Justice Department attorneys under Nicholas Katzenbach, who had been assigned to assist him, make themselves fully available to Dirksen. They had previously moved from the House Judiciary Committee into Mansfield's conference room where they found little to do since the majority leader asked nothing of them and shared nothing with them. Whenever Attorney General Bobby Kennedy became directly involved in the situation, as he did from time to time, he rarely met with Mansfield without being advised to see Dirksen as well. After a while, Kennedy found it simpler to go directly to Dirksen's office. Press people talked with Mansfield on occasion, but they gathered nightly around Dirksen if they wanted to learn the latest developments. Not only Republican senators but also Democrats were drawn to Dirksen's office. Civil rights leaders swallowed hard and, smiling, showed up in his reception room, seeking to heal the political wounds of the past. Sooner or later, all interested parties beat a path to Dirksen's door, deluging him with their queries, complaints, compliments, concerns, and counsel. The genial Republican leader welcomed everyone with open arms.

The arrangement also served to keep the public heat generated by H.R. 7152 centered on the Senate Republicans, the group from whence the bulk of the critical votes had to come. Moreover, by clearly identifying the minority leader as at the center of what was going to be a long process, Dirksen was thrust into a position in which he stood to accumulate a large share of the credit if the outcome was successful or, for that matter, of the blame if it was not. His identification with supporters of civil rights legislation at a critical moment would be significant in determining his niche in history. It was also of relevance to the future of his party, serving as it did to indicate to an expanding black electorate that voting Democratic was not necessarily the only or even the best way of advancing their interests, that there was still a place for them in the party of Lincoln. This reminder was timely because, as black voters were growing in numbers and influence in the political process, the group was gravitating heavily toward the Democratic Party. Dirksen's stand on civil rights would also flag for liberal white independents that there was more to the Republican Party than its noisy right wing. The right wing had been held in check by the presence of President Eisenhower but had found a new and attractive champion in Senator Barry Goldwater, who would be the party's presidential candidate in 1964.

Mansfield had no reason to envy the benefits that would flow to the minority leader because of the bipartisan arrangement he was putting together. He was not seeking applause in connection with H.R. 7152. He had no political need of credit for achievements on behalf of black equality. His credentials on civil rights had long since been established, although he had not been out in front on such issues. Nor had he ever felt compelled to hire a black employee for his state office, a practice beginning to come into vogue in the Senate at the time. But his votes over the years had served to identify him as generally supportive of liberal positions, including those on racial questions. For political purposes in Montana, with its sparse black population, it was enough that he already enjoyed an excellent reputation with another minority group, Native Americans.

The majority leader knew the hour was late. He was aware that action to end segregation was of the highest national importance and that it was now obvious to all that the Senate was the bottleneck. What Mansfield needed desperately was for the Senate to come to grips with H.R. 7152. It was essential to his personal reputation as a senator and the survival of his leadership. It was also essential to the Senate as an institution. Mansfield's seemingly studied indifference sometimes suggested otherwise, but he cared very deeply about his place in history and about that of the Senate in his time. Additionally, he very much wanted the civil rights issue to be dealt with in a manner that would avoid precipitating a devastating breach between the southern wing and other Democrats in the Senate. Ever present in his mind was the possibility of a massive bolt of southern Democrats in the pattern set by Strom Thurmond of South Carolina a few years earlier. While highly unlikely, such a development had been a recurrent nightmare for Democratic leaders for years.

Preventing a break was essential not only to the continuance of the party's majority in Congress, it was also critical to its national status. A split in the Senate Democrats would jeopardize the party's chance of retaining control of the White House. By engaging Republicans in a united front on civil rights, Mansfield was taking out insurance against this possibility. With Dirksen out in front in support of desegregation, where would the southerners go if they bolted? Mansfield also had to keep in mind the possibility that the southern Democrats would agree to halt the filibuster in return for changes in H.R. 7152 that would be face-saving for them but still acceptable to proponents of the bill. To be sure, the chances were remote, but Mansfield was not one to close the door against a compromise. By standing outside the day-to-day maneuvering over the bill, he placed himself in a better position to engineer one if the opportunity presented itself. Dirksen's profit in the arrangement, then, was also Mansfield's gain. Moving Dirksen to the forefront served the interests of both leaders, the two parties, the Senate, and, in the end, the interest of the nation. It was a prime example of the effective operation of the American political system acting to prevent a drastic shift toward extremism and a dangerously divisive situation. It was possible because, in the last analysis, two responsible political leaders understood the stakes involved and acted on that understanding with a high sense of patriotism.

Choosing a Floor Manager: Humphrey

With Dirksen's full participation assured, one other major place remained to be filled in the pattern that Mansfield was drawing for handling H.R. 7152. A Democratic senator had to be named to work closely with Dirksen on a day-to-day basis in the negotiations with unpersuaded members for changes in the text that, he hoped, would produce enough votes for cloture without destroying the bill's acceptance to its supporters. What was needed, in effect, was a highly competent alternative to the chairman of the Judiciary Committee, Jim Eastland, who was a mainstay of the southern opposition. Mansfield's designee would have to be deeply knowledgeable about the general background of the struggle for equal rights and well versed in the specific issues of segregation lodged in H.R. 7152. On the Democratic senator that he chose for this assignment would rest the responsibility for defending the measure that emerged from the negotiations against attempts on the Senate floor to subvert it by sophistry and ridicule. What sort of senator would serve for this assignment? Most Members possess certain personal characteristics that make for effective legislators. They include a sharpness of perception sufficient to discern the common denominator of agreement among opinionated men and women, good-fellow amiability and flexibility, plus a readiness to keep commitments. The characteristics are commonplace in legislative bodies and are to be found not only in the Senate and Congress but in statehouses throughout the nation, and indeed in legislatures in other countries. They are built-in traits of the trade.

Mansfield wanted a Democrat who possessed these traits in full measure and more. Once H.R. 7152 was before the Senate as a whole, it would take someone with physical endurance to stay with the legislation over weeks of attempted procedural manipulation and delay. He would have to have a sense of humor and the patience to explain the myriad details of the legislation over and over again to senators having only a passing acquaintance with the bill. He would also have to have the mental acuity to be able to discern when to accept minor adjustments in the text in order to accommodate a member or soothe specific anxieties of another member without damaging the substance of the bill. Among such members would be the "nitpickers" of the Senate, who delighted in engaging in lengthy discussions of seeming profundity in order to wrench a minute and often meaningless change from a weary manager. Having succeeded, they might still vote to reject the measure.

Above all, Mansfield wanted an outstanding senator who would be instantly recognized as one whose heart as well as head was engaged in the cause of equal rights. Less than that would fail to reassure the vigorous advocates of H.R. 7152 that their views were represented and their interests safeguarded. Mansfield could count on the support of such advocates of the bill, but he also wanted their enthusiasm and anxieties restrained during the process so that compromises might be possible. That was something that could be done only by someone they trusted fully. Otherwise, he feared that in the exuberant expectations stimulated by a House victory on H.R. 7152, they might throw a monkey wrench into the negotiations in building the necessary vote total in the Senate. Moreover, Mansfield had no desire to be charged with a "sellout" if the inevitable compromises that were going to have to be made fell short of the expectations of militant civil rights leaders. A well-chosen floor manager for H.R. 7152 would stand between him and that outcome. His predecessor had not acted with such prudence and suffered the consequences. When Lyndon Johnson, as Senate majority leader, insisted on personally undertaking to pass the "first civil rights" measure since Reconstruction, he had emerged with a weak compromise dictated by Senator Russell that embittered civil rights advocates. That may have been all that was possible at the time, but Johnson's hyperbolic claims for the compromise served only to embitter the militant liberals, who dumped their anger at what they saw as a failure on Johnson's head.

From the outset, there was one obvious choice for floor manager and Mansfield had no hesitancy in making it. Indeed, it had been a choice foreordained three years earlier when the majority leader gave the nod to Hubert Humphrey over George Smathers for the position of Majority whip. Humphrey's position as assistant leader as much as his reputation as a civil rights activist made his choice both logical and politically effective. Even southern opponents of the measure could not fault the selection. They might denounce riding roughshod over Committee Chairman Eastland as unseemly. They might shed tears over the unorthodox procedure, but the choice of the assistant leader to act on behalf of the majority leader on the Senate floor was proper. Humphrey found himself, personally, in an unassailable position insofar as the southern Democrats were concerned.

As for the advocates of civil rights, there was no question of Humphrey's acceptability. Indeed, his designation was reassuring to those who were suspicious of the extent of Mansfield's commitment to equal rights. No other senator enjoyed a greater trust among black leaders than Humphrey. His credentials stretched back to his years as mayor of Minneapolis. They were underscored by his key role in adding a strong plank on racial equality to the platform of the National Democratic Party in 1948. His efforts won him national recognition and an impassioned following in liberal circles and mobilized black voters behind President Truman even as the platform plank they produced heralded the North-South split in the Democratic Party.

Humphrey moved from the local politics of Minneapolis to the Senate in the elections of 1948. On his arrival in Washington, he was given a much coveted assignment on the Foreign Relations Committee. By treating Humphrey and other newly arrived liberals in a generous fashion, Lyndon Johnson as Senate majority leader sought successfully to reassure them of the thrust of his leadership and to consolidate his support among the Democrats. Nonetheless, Johnson kept the fiery Minnesotan and other liberals at arms' length when it came to the inner workings of the Senate.

As for the conservative Democrats already ensconced in the party's leadership, they greeted Humphrey by his first name and with the other ritualized courtesies that senators extend to new arrivals. At the same time, they regarded him from the outset with considerable suspicion. Some saw him as a potential Henry Wallace, who had served as Roosevelt's vice president and had bolted the party in the 1948 elections and then sought the presidency as a third-party candidate.*

Humphrey never fully overcame the initial impression among Senate conservatives that he was a leftist radical or, equally to be deplored, a young man in too great a hurry. They regarded him in the way that college students sometime look on the superachievers in their midst, with a mixture of disdain and envy. The Minnesotan was not unaware of these reactions, but he made few changes to accommodate them. As a senator, he was

---

*Such was the hostility to Wallace that the bronze bust by which the Senate honors all vice presidents who are also presidents of the Senate was removed from its pedestal in a public corridor of the Capitol and placed in a remote location in the building. Only later, at Johnson's insistence, was Wallace's likeness restored to its earlier location.

satisfied that he had a solid home base built on the support of labor unions, stubborn dairy farmers, and independent businessmen. At the same time, his appeal was strong to national labor leaders, intellectuals, blacks, and ethnics in the liberal wing of the Democratic Party.

Humphrey loved politics to the point of obsession. He breathed politics like a dragon breathes fire. Whether in Minneapolis or Washington, in New York, Los Angeles, or Charlestown, West Virginia, he talked politics non-stop. He played politics with a fierce enthusiasm and relentless persistence; for him, the name of the game was always the next rung on the political ladder, leading ultimately to the presidency.

By 1963, Humphrey had gained a degree of tolerance even among those conservative colleagues who had regarded his initial arrival in the Senate as little short of a disaster. After serving with him for a decade, none could deny the depths of his political passion. On that score, he was clearly one of them. Nor could they ignore his brilliant grasp of public issues. He had a consummate ability to move audiences with persuasive speeches that often began at the drop of a hat and then went on for an hour or more without reference to notes. The brashness that had first aroused their apprehension came to be seen as tempered by a lively sense of humor, including Humphrey's readiness to laugh at himself. His simultaneous pursuit of a multitude of issues continued to rub the wrong way, as a somewhat un-seemly ebullience for a senator. In due course, however, even this was recognized not so much as an unpardonable grab for power inside the Senate but as a reaching for something outside and thus more acceptable to senatorial sensitivities.

Humphrey possessed towering qualifications for leading the floor fight on H.R. 7152. He was completely conversant with the issues of equal rights for blacks. He had dealt with them, both as a teacher and in the mayor's office in Minneapolis. His contacts were firm with all the leading person-ages, black and white, in the civil rights movement. Humphrey's door was always open to them, and he lent them not only a sympathetic ear but political leadership in their pursuit of equal treatment. They had recipro-cated with strong support for him. Humphrey was not a lawyer, and H.R. 7152 was a bill drawn up by lawyers. The absence of a legal background, however, did not phase him in the slightest. After a short period of intense study, he was completely at home in the complex text of the measure as it had arrived in the Senate. As the debate unfolded, it became evident that his command of the bill's details easily rivaled that of lawyers. Moreover, he brought to the dispassionate text the intensity of a religious evangelist. Citations to sections, paragraphs, and lines rolled off his tongue with the fluidity of an impassioned preacher citing chapter and verse. Humphrey dominated discussions on the Senate floor, drawing assistance from the staff of the Democratic Policy Committee, which functioned with great effectiveness not only in providing legal assistance to Humphrey but also in liaison with Dirksen's staff coopted from the Senate Judiciary Committee.

If there was any cause for anxiety over Humphrey's designation as floor manager, it lay in his tendency to dash peripatetically over the whole legislative field. He was ever ready to respond to the pleas or proposals of anyone who had managed to impress him or whatever cause had caught his eye. No issue was too small to escape the attention of the senator from Minnesota, or none too large. His interests ranged from the care of the Capitol grounds to nuclear disarmament, from a tax on margarine (in order to help the butter producers of Minnesota) to the establishment of the Peace Corps. He was prone to deal not with one issue at a time but with a dozen. Like a juggler adding more and more balls to his performance, Humphrey was forever pushing his political hand-eye coordination to its outer limits. As a speaker, his quick mind and seemingly inexhaustible energy permitted virtuoso performances that astounded audiences. But his rapid shifts of interest, from one subject to another, was also cause for consternation, since it suggested a certain superficiality.

Mansfield knew that the impression was erroneous. Humphrey may have been overeager, but he was never superficial. Even as a disinterested sideliner, if a debate on the Senate floor happened to catch his attention, he would plunge into it without hesitancy. These sudden intrusions often revealed that he knew more about the issues than its active proponents and opponents.

It was not shallowness, then, that spread Humphrey so thin but a deep interest in all aspects of government, a sincere concern for the left-outs and overlooked of an affluent nation. Humphrey was open to any noble cause. If a call went out for a white knight to champion the cause, he was ever ready to mount and ride forth. In these sallies, he sometimes arrived on the scene too soon and sometimes too late. His tendency to overextension and his bad timing were more often cause for amusement than concern. In the case of the civil rights legislation of 1963, however, Humphrey's ability to put aside the extraneous and stay in step with the essential would be critical to the fate of H.R. 7152. It was vital that he concentrate on the passage of the bill to the virtual exclusion of all else.

In the end, such concerns proved unwarranted. Humphrey knew that the outcome of the Senate debate on H.R. 7152 would govern the direction of civil rights in the United States for many years to come. What happened to the bill, moreover, was also critical to his own political future, especially to his chance at the presidency. Not only the eyes of Washington and Minnesota would be fixed on him; he would be under the scrutiny of the entire nation. In the circumstances, converting H.R. 7152 into law superseded all other claims on his time. He would subordinate other activity and give his full attention to achieving that goal. He would put in mothballs the myriad causes that preoccupied him and foseswear, at least for a time, taking on any new ones. The Capitol lawns could turn brown and shrivel from neglect; margarine might replace butter in the American diet; but Humphrey would not be sidetracked from passing H.R. 7152. All his energy and ability would be concentrated on that issue. This was, indeed, the moment for which Humphrey was born.

Mansfield's Final Strategy: Russell

Having designated Humphrey to act as floor manager and persuaded Dirksen to serve as a virtual co-leader on H.R. 7152, Mansfield was ready. One other preliminary remained before raising the curtain. At the eleventh hour, Mansfield invited Senator Russell to come to his Capitol office. Russell responded promptly. The two met privately in what was neither a scowling confrontation nor a cozy tête-à-tête. Instead, like most Mansfield meetings, it was brief and to the point. The majority leader outlined in some detail the ground rules he had set for himself in seeking passage of H.R. 7152. Russell could rest assured that there would be no duplicity, no parliamentary tricks, no end runs. Orderly procedure would be followed, as it had been for as long as Mansfield had been majority leader. The rights of the minority equally with those of the majority would be fully protected.

Nevertheless, Mansfield wanted Russell to know that after H.R. 7152 reached the floor, it would remain the business of the Senate to the exclusion of all else, pending its disposal. Until the members had an opportunity to make up their collective mind on H.R. 7152, the Senate would come to a full stop on every other question. As majority leader, Mansfield would not lay the measure aside even temporarily to consider some other question. To compel the Senate to stick to the business at hand might be an unusual practice, but it would be entirely in accord with the Rules. In fact, there would be no attempts to circumvent the Rules in any way, shape, or form. As for all-night sessions or other attempts at parliamentary legerdemain in order to coerce the minority, that was entirely out of the question. There would be no tactics employed that might endanger the health of older members or demean the Senate.

Russell listened to the majority leader without making any comment. What was there to be said to a general who, on the eve of battle, invites his opponent to sit in on a final intelligence briefing? It was as though George

Washington had sent word to the British commander at Trenton that not only did he intend to cross the Delaware on Christmas Eve but that he would also detail the how and where of the crossing. Russell heard from Mansfield that the procedure he would follow for H.R. 7152 not only did not challenge the southerners but appeared to dovetail perfectly with Russell's own style. How on earth did the majority leader expect to stay within the Rules, eschew surprise tactics, proceed in proper order, and still pass a civil rights bill? Where was the stealth, the "no holds barred" maneuvering, the parliamentary tricks, the determination to exhaust the southerners by endless sessions—all tactics that Russell had confronted time and again and, it might be added, had confounded time and again. None of these tactics was even hinted at in the approach outlined by the majority leader. To be sure, they had not succeeded in the past. But they had provided a perfect target for Russell's tongue-in-cheek denunciations. He had thundered against their use as outrageous, overbearing, and completely at odds with the Senate's traditions. His opponents, most of whom had been caught up in the myth of the Gentlemen's Club, or appeared to be, were stung by these criticisms. They found themselves denying sheepishly any such intention, even as they began to draw back.

What Russell never mentioned in his repeated beratings of his opponents was the reason why he never had any difficulty in preventing the Senate from coming to a vote on issues of racial equality. Behind his small but singleminded band stood all-powerful allies—the Senate's Rules, customs, practices, and pretenses. So little understood in their complexity by outsiders, and even by many members of the Senate, the Rules were heavily stacked in favor of inaction, an arrangement presumably designed to compel senators to perform the deliberative function more fully. Whatever constructive impact the concept may have had in other situations, in the area of racial equality its main purpose for decades had been to prevent passage of any bill that would threaten the racial status quo in the South. By giving widely disproportionate power to a determined minority to talk or dawdle indefinitely, even a handful of members, with powerful lungs and physical stamina and large bladders, could force the Senate into a prolonged stalemate.

If the proponents of civil rights measures sought to defeat the filibuster by the tactics of exhaustion, the daily sessions would have to be extended through the night, compelling them to listen to hours-long speeches by filibusterers organized like soldiers to hold the floor in regular shifts, going on and off duty at regular intervals, with ample time for rest between changings of the guard. Still more hours would be squandered in frustrating silence while awaiting the assemblage of a quorum that could be called by a single filibusterer. The call might come at any time, even in the middle of the night; proponents of civil rights would be compelled to rise bleary-eyed from army cots set up in their offices or off the Senate floor and straggle into the Senate chamber, some in pajamas, to answer "present" at the call of their name by the reading clerk. It was not uncommon for an occasional "off-duty" southerner, returning from a dinner party to appear in evening clothes, refreshed from a relaxing evening, to announce himself present. His presence would make little difference in assembling the quorum because the rest of his colleagues could remain at home or elsewhere. They would be under no compulsion to answer the roll call unless the Senate, under its Rules, ordered that they be arrested and brought forcibly to the Senate for that purpose. But such an order flew in the face of the Senate's gentlemanly traditions and was rarely resorted to. After trying for days and nights and from every conceivable angle to break through such obstacles, the bewildered, beleaguered, confounded, weary, and harassed proponents of civil rights legislation would be reduced to utter confusion, and finally they, not the filibusterers, would be exhausted. They would then be ready to do whatever might be needed in the way of compromise or acceptance of defeat in order to escape from the procedural nightmare.

What Russell had learned from his meeting with Mansfield was that this time around, something different would be forthcoming. Whatever might lie ahead, it would not be the same battle as in the past. Indeed, it had sounded as though there would be no battle at all. Mansfield was not another presumptuous, overbearing opponent intent on passing a civil rights measure at all costs; that kind could be quickly cut down to small size. Instead, it was clear that Mansfield would play by the same Rules—the Senate Rules—as the southerners; he had even gone so far as to promise to protect the rights of the southerners, along with all other senators, under those Rules.

Although he had known Mansfield for many years, Russell was taken aback by his candor. He trusted Mansfield's integrity enough to know that the leader was not being deliberately deceptive. But was it possible that Mansfield had not laid out the full scope of his strategy during their brief meeting? Was he holding back something? Was Mansfield more friend than foe to the South, as in fact some militant civil righters suspected? Might this conversation be preparing the way for a later bid from the majority leader for a compromise that would be acceptable to the southerners? Perhaps Mansfield had neglected to mention the finale of the scenario, the point down the road of a protracted debate and repeated modifications of H.R. 7152, the point at which the majority leader might proclaim victory while, in reality, suffering a defeat at Russell's hands? After much sound and fury, such indeed, had been the way out when Johnson was majority leader. Russell had agreed to the accommodation then, and he might be prepared to do a repeat if that was what Mansfield was seeking. Still, that could hardly be the case, since Mansfield had said in public as well as directly to Russell that charades would not be a substitute for a formidable bill on racial equality. The majority leader must have known that Russell was not prepared to concede more than a face-saving agreement to anyone. Did Mansfield really believe that H.R. 7152 could be passed over southern resistance? Had the majority leader fine-combed the Rules and made some serendipitous discovery? Had he stumbled on a road through the procedural quicksand? After years of blocking civil rights legislation, Russell was highly unlikely to have overlooked any such possibility. Even if he had, it was more unlikely that Mansfield would have found it. Mansfield was the first to admit that he was not an authority on the Rules. On the contrary, he seemed to have little interest in them or in floor procedures except to get through the Senate's business each day as quickly as possible.

From Russell's viewpoint, the Senate's Rules provided the last refuge for the dying mores of the southern states. Russell had masterminded the defense of those mores for years, yielding minimal ground to the encroachments forced on the southern establishment by the courts. A decisive test was now at hand, what with the courts, the president, the House of Representatives, and national opinion all heavily weighted against the South. Russell was determined that the southern citadel would not fall—at any rate, not on his watch. Whatever tactics the majority leader might have in mind, Russell was adamant in his belief that they would not prevail.

Russell was convinced that only one procedural approach was a real danger to the southerners. That was the "gag" rule, as he chose to call Rule 22. Whatever disdain he may have felt for it, Russell had to recognize that the Rule of cloture offered the only way to follow the orderly approach to which Mansfield had committed himself.

The fact that the ending of the debate under Rule 22 required a two-thirds majority mitigated this danger; it was not easy to produce sixty-seven votes, tantamount to overriding a presidential veto, on any controversial measure in the Senate. Moreover, while the southern forces by themselves did not have the votes to defeat a cloture attempt, in the past Russell had always been able to count on sufficient support from outside the Deep South to make up the shortfall.

There was an intangible factor that would work to Russell's advantage if Mansfield chose to follow the cloture route. Over the decades, it had become part of Senate lore to regard cloture as an unbecoming procedure, somehow at odds with the senators' self-image. To cut off a debate abruptly by cloture had come to seem like an unsightly ruffle on the otherwise smooth hide of the institution. Russell and others concerned with frustrating a majority, of course, never passed up an opportunity to strengthen this shibboleth, and it weighed heavily on the Senate's behavior in 1963. True, cloture had been achieved the previous year on the Communications Satellite bill. But that vote could be seen as something of an aberration because it represented the first such successful application of Rule 22 in decades. In that case, Mansfield had filed the cloture petition with the presiding officer, but the main movers in obtaining the required sixteen signatures required to cut off the debate had been Republican Leader Everett Dirksen and Oklahoma Democrat Bob Kerr.

Much of the support for that cloture vote had come from conservatives on both sides of the aisle. Additional votes had been provided by senators who had tired of Morse's scolding lectures, as on senators' drinking habits in the Capitol and other senatorial shortcomings.

While Russell shared the sentiments of Dirksen and Kerr on the desirability of passing COMSAT, he had not been among those who voted for cloture in order to bring it to a vote. Nor had he cheered the adoption of cloture against Morse. Russell's position remained consistent with his repeated denunciations of the "gag" rule. With his eyes ever fixed on the main task of holding back the tide of desegregation, he refused to be a party to lending respectability to any vote for cloture, regardless of its objective. When cloture was adopted notwithstanding, it was cause for deep concern to Russell. It reduced the awe with which cloture had previously been regarded and suggested that the vaunted tradition of unlimited debate might no longer be enough to hold back civil rights legislation. Russell could still seek comfort in the different cores of strength enjoyed by civil rights legislation on the one hand and the COMSAT on the other. Morse had been able to count scarcely a dozen colleagues prepared to join him in holding back the latter. Russell had twice that number as core supporters in opposition to H.R. 7152. Even though that was still short of the votes he needed to block a cloture attempt, Russell had room to maneuver in order to make up the shortfall.

Other than the outside chance of an adoption of cloture, Russell had little to fear in the impending consideration of H.R. 7152. Nevertheless, he was not given to overconfidence, and this time it was readily apparent that something different was afoot. While he thanked the majority leader for his frankness, the furrowed brow that Russell bore as his discussion with the majority leader ended suggested that the conversation had left him perplexed.

His perplexity may have derived from Mansfield's disarming openness, the very essence of his leadership. As majority leader, Mansfield did not believe in overwhelming opponents by surprise or nimble maneuvering. His approach in this instance was based not only on his personal distaste for such tactics but also on a realistic appraisal of the formidable restraints imposed by the Senate's rules and practices. Advising Russell in advance of his strategy was an expression of his determination to operate the Senate in the only way he knew how, that is, as an open Senate, without guile or procedural pyrotechnics, and by moving all measures, particularly those sought by the president, through the legislative process to a decision with all deliberate speed. What he would not do was to take shortcuts or end runs, unless so ordered by the Senate.

As leader, moreover, Mansfield had no intention of differentiating between colleagues who were with him or those who were against him on H.R. 7152. His view was that all senators were entitled to the same treatment from the leadership. If the Rules of the Senate gave an advantage to some, as they clearly did to those bent upon unconscionable delays, it was not for him to circumvent the Rules. It was for the membership as a whole to face up to the inequities and rectify them. His conscience was clear. Unfurling the Golden Rule as his heraldry, he treated all senators in the same way as he would hope to be treated. If his colleagues did not respond in kind, they would have to answer not to him but to themselves and the institution as a whole. Slowly, almost imperceptibly, this Mansfield dictum was making its weight felt in the Senate. To be sure, some members were so immersed in their own egotism as to be impervious to Mansfield's repeated pleas for mutuality. Vestiges of the Johnsonian era still lurked in Capitol corridors and hideaways. But, by 1964, the clouds of suspicion were lifting, and the worst of the throat-cutting had subsided. The general tone of the Senate was closer to Mansfield's liking—and to that of most of his colleagues. In appearance at least, it was a far different Senate from its predecessor. It remained to be seen whether the note that Mansfield had sounded would survive the supreme test of H.R. 7152.

4

Passing the Civil Rights Act, 1964

At noon, on 17 February 1963, the Senate was called to order, and a chaplain lifted a prayer to God over the bowed heads of the senators. Mansfield shuffled papers impatiently while standing at his desk through the chaplain's recitation. Then, at the prearranged moment, the official version of H.R. 7152, as adopted by the House of Representatives, entered the Senate chamber, hand delivered by a messenger from the other end of the Capitol. After the bill had been transferred to the presiding officer, the majority leader moved to shut down the routine operation of the legislative mill. Instead of going automatically to the Judiciary Committee, as would have otherwise been the case, H.R. 7152 was held, at Mansfield's insistence, at the presiding officer's desk. There It would remain until the entire Senate was prepared to decide by vote the future course of its journey.*

---

*The opening steps in the legislative process in the Senate normally involve automatic referral of a House-passed measure to committee by authority of the Chair. As a practical matter, most bills are routed in this fashion, with the professional parliamentarians actually handling the mechanics of referral on behalf of the presiding officer. Once a bill has been handled in this manner, it remains within the jurisdiction of the committee of referral and no further action can be taken on the measure by the Senate until the committee reports the bill or is discharged from responsibility for the measure by a vote of the Senate.

"Stopping the bill at the door," the procedure Mansfield followed, although rarely used, was entirely in order under the Rules. He chose to pursue it because he saw only unacceptable delay in following the usual practice of automatic referral to committee, in this case the Judiciary Committee, chaired by Senator Eastland of Mississippi. While H.R. 7152 remained buried in the obscure recesses of the committee, Mansfield feared the loss of the substance of the issue in a confusing blur of parliamentary pontificating, endless wrangling, points of order, and countless procedural votes leading nowhere. This travesty on the legislative process would take place at the very moment that the nation's eyes were fixed on the Senate. He knew that as majority leader he would be held responsible for the spectacle, even as the Senate was reducing itself to a laughingstock. The risks involved in referral of the measure to Eastland's Judiciary Committee, both to Mansfield and to the institution's integrity, were more than he was prepared to take. It was essential to bypass the committee process and in that way keep responsibility for H.R. 7152, from beginning to end, where it belonged, with the entire membership.

Mansfield expected that there would be a challenge to his strategy. What he did not anticipate was the source of the challenge. When Mansfield stopped the customary procedure of automatic referral, he was not surprised that Russell was on the Senate floor waiting to assail the move. But opposition also came unexpectedly from Wayne Morse of Oregon. From his filibuster the previous year, Morse had gained new insights into the immense power that the Senate Rules bestows on unremitting dissenters. Although unsuccessful, the talkathon had helped convert him into a passionate defender of procedural orthodoxy. To Mansfield's chagrin, Morse chose this critical moment to express his newfound faith. Although a firm supporter of the substance of H.R. 7152, Morse subscribed to Russell's complaints about irregularities and proposed that the bill be referred to the Judiciary Committee. As though that were not enough, the majority leader received an aftershock when Dirksen made a similar proposal.

To be sure, in endorsing referral both Morse and Dirksen reaffirmed their support for civil rights. Nevertheless, they insisted that committee consideration was necessary, lest there be second thoughts. Since civil rights was of national importance, they agreed that H.R. 7152 deserved nothing less than the full procedural treatment. Some members interpreted the Morse-Dirksen intervention in less monumental terms. Morse was seen as expressing gratitude to Russell for his support against cloture the previous year. As for Dirksen, since he was a member of the Judiciary committee, some thought that he was seeking a better venue than the Senate floor to work out changes in the text of the bill. Others, less generous, saw

Dirksen's plea for referral as a gesture to conservative Republicans, who were growing increasingly restless with what they perceived to be Dirksen's excessive cooperation with the Senate's Democratic majority. Others, even less generous, regarded his move as coming from an inability to resist a last-ditch political attempt to throw the Senate into confusion as a prelude to bringing the spotlight fully on himself. They expected Dirksen to emerge then as the man of the hour to rescue the Senate from public wrath.

Morse and Dirksen received effusive praise from Russell for their unexpected assist. The Georgian appeared to find, particularly in Dirksen's stand, a glimmer of hope that the minority leader might still be separated from his newfound civil rights collaborators. Indeed, Russell hinted strongly that he was ready to sit down at any time to listen to whatever might be on Dirksen's mind in the way of a reasonable solution. What Russell did not mention was that delay for any reason and from whatever source is invariably welcomed by filibusterers. It is axiomatic in the Senate that the longer and more snarled the procedural process, the greater the distance a bill will have departed from its original intent when it finally passes, if indeed it passes at all.

Mansfield remained nonplussed in the face of Morse's objection, having long since concluded that Morse was predictable only in his unpredictability. But he was deeply dismayed by the position taken by Dirksen. Mansfield had hoped Dirksen would be fully aligned with him on procedural matters. The latter's unexpected proposal of an alternative caught him off-guard. If it meant that Dirksen was having second thoughts on bipartisan collaboration, the prospects were harrowing. From the outset, the minority leader had been the cornerstone of Mansfield's strategy. If that was lost, the prospects of passing H.R. 7152 in a meaningful form were likely to collapse in a heap. Whatever Dirksen had in mind, it was too late for the majority leader to shift gears. Mansfield could not see referral to committee as anything but a charade that, at best, would be a waste of time and, at worst, would open the way for further mischief. It was conceivable that Dirksen had had a change of heart and was now seeking to gut the bill by amendments added in committee. Even so, it would be better to have the sabotage take place in full view of the Senate and the nation and not behind the obscuring curtains of Eastland's Judiciary Committee. Mansfield could not yield on the question of committee referral, not even in the name of Senate orthodoxy, not even to palliate Dirksen.

Dirksen appealed to the Senate to send H.R. 7152 to the Judiciary Committee. Mansfield urged that it be kept under the direct control of the entire Senate. On the procedural question, the Senate upheld the majority leadership by a vote of 54 to 37. Although the first test had been won, the margin was far short of the two-thirds that would be needed later to invoke cloture. Nevertheless, the vote was reassuring, mainly because twenty Republicans had crossed over to supply the winning margin. George Aiken of Vermont was one of the twenty who chose to follow Mansfield rather than his own leader. Aiken attributed the outpouring of Republican support for the majority leader not to the issue but to the high regard in which the opposition held Mansfield. It was, in effect, a vote of confidence in Mansfield's integrity, a kind of unsolicited payback when desperately needed for the fair and impartial manner in which he had conducted the affairs of the Senate for three years.

The vote also suggested a basic change in the mood of the Senate on civil rights. It was as though the members had come to recognize that the nation was face to face with a grave issue and that it was incumbent on them to rise to the occasion. It implied, too, considerably less tolerance in the Senate for tactics of delay, contrived confusion, and playful politics. The change was not lost on either Dirksen or Russell. Thereafter, while still maintaining his independent position on H.R. 7152, Dirksen's cooperation with the Democratic leadership grew closer. As for Russell, the vote confirmed what he had already learned from his prior meeting with the majority leader. This would not be a rerun of previous Senate confrontations on civil rights. He faced a different situation, one in which appeals to Senate traditionalism packed considerably less punch than in the past. Moreover, the situation was one in which the majority leader could count on more support from the Republican rank and file than had been true in previous confrontations on civil rights. Mansfield had prevailed and, significantly, had done so in spite of a determined dissent from Dirksen. It was clear that, in contrast with his predecessor, Republicans harbored no built-in itch to embarrass Mansfield and that some were even inclined to help him. Russell had no illusions. He knew that he had lost the first skirmish. His only solace was to find Dirksen aligned with him in this instance.

After the initial test of strength, Mansfield took a time-out to let the victory sink in while he turned the Senate's attention to a tax-reduction bill being pressed by the president and then to a farm bill urged by Senator Humphrey. With these measures out of the way, Mansfield moved to take H.R. 7152 from the presiding officer's desk and place it directly before the Senate as the pending business. The southerners immediately gave a demonstration of the ease with which the Senate could be brought up short. To frustrate Mansfield's motion, they engaged in a continuing display of such tactics as refusing to approve the accuracy of the previous day's Senate journal (a routine action usually requiring less than a minute) until it was read in full by the clerk (a procedure requiring an hour or more). They also called for live quorums, which involved wasted hours spent in rounding up

Senator Mansfield meeting with Chief Minister Penn Nouth in Pnom Penh, Cambodia, September, 1954. Photo by Frank Valeo.

French General Cogny (right) receives Senator Mansfield in Hanoi shortly before the disastrous defeat at Dien Bien Phu in 1954 that ended France's attempt to restore colonial administration in Indo-China. Photo by Frank Valeo.

Joint House and Senate leadership lingering with Vice President Lyndon Johnson after meeting with President Kennedy, who inscribed this photo, "For Mike, who knows when to stay and when to go" (July, 1962). Left to right: Representatives Carl Albert, Hale Boggs, and John McCormack, Vice President Lyndon Johnson, Senators George Smathers, Hubert Humphrey, and Mike Mansfield. Photo no. 88–76, K. Ross Toole Archives, The University of Montana-Missoula.

President Kennedy throwing out the first ball at opening day at D.C. Stadium, April 9, 1962. Behind him are Lawrence O'Brien, special assistant to the President (l.), and Mansfield. Photo no. 1998–1298, K. Ross Toole Archives, The University of Montana-Missoula.

Majority Leader Mansfield shares a joke with Republican Senator George Aiken and a group of their constitutients. U.S. Senate Historical Office.

Mansfield and Minority Leader Everett Dirksen joined forces in a bipartisan effort to pass the civil rights bill of 1964. U.S. Senate Historical Office.

Mansfield and President Pro Tem Senator Carl Hayden attend a Majority Policy Committee luncheon in the office of Secretary of the Senate Frank Valeo (center), January, 1966. Photo no. 98–2225, K. Ross Toole Archives, The University of Montana-Missoula.

A gathering of Democratic committee chairmen after the passage of the Civil Rights Act of 1964. Visible around table from left: Kenneth Teasdale (Majority Policy Committee staff), Frank Valeo (Secretary of the Senate), J. William Fulbright, Stuart Symington, John Sparkman, unknown aide, Richard Russell, Mansfield, Carl Hayden, unknown aide, John McClellan, Joseph Hill, Allen Ellender, James O. Eastland; June, 1964. Photo no. 98–1848, K. Ross Toole Archives, The University of Montana-Missoula.

President Nixon being received at the Senate, 1969. Left to right: President Pro Tem Richard Russell, Minority Leader Everett Dirksen, Nixon, and Mansfield. U.S. Senate Historical Office.

President Johnson is escorted on a visit to the Capitol by the two women in the Senate during the 1960s, Margaret Chase Smith of Maine (l.) and Maurine Neuberger of Oregon. U.S. Senate Historical Office.

Minority Leader Hugh Scott and Mansfield jointly notifying President Johnson of their readiness to end the first session of the 90th Congress, December, 1967. U.S. Senate Historical Office.

First Lady of the Philippines Imelda Marcos is received at the Senate by Majority Leader Mansfield and Secretary of the Senate Frank Valeo. U.S. Senate Historical Office.

Congressional leaders greet a former colleague, President Gerald Ford. From left: Minority Leader Hugh Scott, President Pro Tem James O. Eastland, Ford, Mansfield, House Speaker Carl Albert, and Majority Whip Robert C. Byrd (Mansfield's successor as Senate Majority Leader). U.S. Senate Historical Office.

Receiving an early delegation from the People's Republic of China, 1973. Frank Valeo (l.), members of the delegation, Mike and Maureen Mansfield (r.). U.S. Senate Historical Office.

absent members. Then they launched protracted tirades against H.R. 7152. These delaying tactics were not greeted by Mansfield with a tearing of hair and gnashing of teeth. He reacted with his usual sober restraint and a refusal to be drawn into what he knew would have been a futile clash.

Mansfield made no immediate effort to force the issue of taking up the civil rights bill as the pending business, choosing instead to wait for the Senate to grow restless with the delay. The days rolled by with little more than a drone of speeches interspersed with the reading clerk intoning the roster of senators being assembled for repeated live quorums. Signs of impatience appeared, as Mansfield expected, and they grew more urgent as the time for the Easter recess drew closer. The delaying tactics became a source of increasing irritation to the rest of the Senate. There were flashes of anger at the waste of time, even among those who had been highly tolerant of filibusters in the past. Mansfield appeared not to notice these warning flashes, but Russell weighed them carefully.

Never one to flaunt power aimlessly, Russell took council with his forces. The southern bloc reached the conclusion that it would be counter-productive to persist in holding up the Senate any longer over a procedural question, especially one that a clear majority had already spoken on when it rejected referral of the bill to the Judiciary Committee. There were other places down the road where it would be better to make a stand. They decided to permit a vote on the question of taking up H.R. 7152. Interestingly, Mansfield had already received private assurances from Russell that he did not plan to persist indefinitely in debating the procedural question. Mansfield was delighted by these assurances, seeing in them a hopeful sign that consideration of H.R. 7152 would unfold, as he devoutly hoped, not as a duel unto death between enemies but about differences that, however deep, would be faced, reconciled or otherwise dealt with as colleagues.

Maneuver and Debate

The southern delaying tactic ceased and then, more than a month after it had arrived from the House, the Senate voted 67 to 17 to take up the civil rights measure. Only the southerners and a handful of other senators were registered in opposition. Once again, Dirksen intervened at the eleventh hour as he made a final attempt to have the bill referred to the Judiciary Committee. This time, he attached a fixed date for reporting the measure back to the Senate as a kind of insurance against burial in committee. But Mansfield was not persuaded. Having concluded that the time for such gestures had long since expired, he insisted that the bill be considered directly on the floor. Once again, the Senate backed the majority leader.

The attention of the Senate was at last fixed on H.R. 7152, and Mansfield was determined that it remain there. To ensure that members would not stray, deviate, or be sidetracked, he relied on two principal safeguards. First, he objected to all committees meeting while the Senate was in daily session on the civil rights bill. As did his earlier move against referral to the Judiciary, this action touched a highly sensitive nerve in the Senate power structure, that of committee prerogatives. Ordinarily, the committees themselves, without consulting the Senate leadership, decide when to meet, and it is common for their meetings to coincide with daily sessions of the Senate as a whole. Simultaneous meetings result in most members attending committee sessions and therefore not being present on the Senate floor unless a vote or some other important matter is under consideration.

Mansfield's objection meant that committees would be forced to schedule meetings only in the early mornings, late evenings, and on weekends, when the Senate was not in session. He insisted that H.R. 7152 had been stamped with the highest priority by the Senate by its vote to forestall a committee referral. The work on a bill normally done in committee would have to be done by the entire Senate acting, in effect, as a Committee of the Whole. Therefore, all members had an overriding obligation to participate on the Senate floor in perfecting H.R. 7152.

Russell was taken aback by the majority leader's move. Indeed, preventing committees from meeting while the Senate was in session was another perplexing Mansfield usurpation of Russell's style. The southern leader had raised the same objection time and again during civil rights debates in the past, effectively bringing all committee proceedings to an abrupt halt. But, he had used the tactic briefly and selectively to punish advocates of civil rights measures, to induce support from nonsouthern sources, and generally to persuade the Senate of the futility of pushing a civil rights measure. By preempting the tactic and applying it uniformly and for the duration of the consideration of H.R. 7152, Mansfield denied an important option to Russell. Henceforth, if one committee suffered from the ban on meeting, all would suffer, and suffer as long as the filibuster went on.

The Mansfield move also raised the hackles of other senators. In the past, when forced to sit idly by at southern insistence, members with little interest in civil rights tended to hold proponents responsible for wasting their time by persisting in pressing a bill that could not be passed. By contrast, the predominant reaction to Mansfield's use of the tactic was the opposite. A majority having followed him on the initial procedural votes, the Senate could hardly object to his imposing a prohibition on committee meetings while the bill was being discussed and debated on the floor. Moreover, in view of the growing concern in the nation over the consequences of segregation, who would dispute the top priority Mansfield had assigned to H.R. 7152? Members refrained, then, from blaming the majority leader for cutting off their committee meetings. On the contrary, the longer the prohibition remained in effect, the more the filibusterers came to be seen as the source of their idleness. In turn, this led to a growing predisposition to support cloture as the only way around the impasse, even among those traditionally opposed to the procedure.

The second tactic Mansfield used to lock the Senate's attention on H.R. 7152 was to call on proponents of the bill to organize themselves in order to produce a live quorum promptly. The organized southerners had no difficulty in covering the floor with regular shifts of only two or three members, that number being sufficient to prevent any action of consequence. In contrast, proponents needed a half-hundred members on tap at all times in order to produce a quorum so that the Senate might operate at all. Initially, barely that number of ardent advocates of civil rights could be counted on to answer a quorum call at any time, night or day. After Mansfield gained the cooperation of Dirksen, however, additional members, still undecided but inclined toward H.R. 7152, agreed to lend their support.

The task of organizing the Democratic proponents was assigned to Humphrey and the staff of the Democratic Policy Committee. Dirksen designated the assistant minority leader, Tom Kuchel of California, to handle the Republican share of the responsibility. Thanks to their joint efforts, Humphrey and Kuchel were able to maintain a high level of cohesion between the parties. Throughout the long debate, it was usually possible to produce an "instant" quorum, with at least fifty-one members assembling within a half hour to answer to their names on the roll call. To obtain that number in that time made it necessary for almost all determined supporters of H.R. 7152 to remain promptly available while the Senate was in session. The organized quorum was not only necessary to keep the Senate in session but had the virtue of building an esprit de corps among Senate advocates of H.R. 7152 across party lines. It served to bring fully into play the oratorical, legal, and other talents of the proponents of civil rights.

Day after day, the Senate met on the bill in an atmosphere of sustained sobriety that discouraged the buffoonery that had been present in previous civil rights filibusters. Few personal clashes took place. On the contrary, a surprising measure of goodwill persisted throughout. Senators immersed themselves in H.R. 7152 and debated both its legal meaning and its significance to the nation. They delivered erudite speeches, setting forth views that often were laced with passionate conviction. Almost all sensed the historic significance of the moment and groped for words to cement their place in its recording. There were those who expressed their deep repugnance to racial segregation and those who wanted to affirm their segregationist credentials. Some speeches were brief; others went on at great length. Before the debate came to an end, 4 million words were logged in the *Congressional Record.*

The southern bloc did try to throw the civil rights advocates off balance by calling for live quorums and by employing ensnaring procedural tactics. In the face of these provocations, Mansfield clung stoically to his determination not to let the debate degenerate into a physical endurance contest. He turned a deaf ear to periodic rumbles from the White House urging that he initiate all-night sessions. As leader of the southern bloc, Russell ran through a repertoire of parliamentary wizardry that had served the southern cause so well in earlier contests. But this time he seemed to lack eagerness for the fray. When it became apparent that his astute needling would not provoke foolish impatience or anger, his provocative tactics became half-hearted. Such efforts would have been meaningless in any event, since it was obvious that Mansfield had no hidden agenda. He meant simply to mark time awaiting the vote estimates that would tell him that the propitious moment to attempt cloture on H.R. 7152 had arrived. Against that approach, Russell's previous style of parliamentary maneuver lost much of its meaning. In due course, Mansfield would either have the sixty-seven votes or he would not and, in the interim, there was little that could be done to throw his slow train off the track.

Humphrey as Floor Manager

Throughout the long debate, Hubert Humphrey dominated the situation on the Senate floor. Humphrey's profound knowledge of the issues underlying H.R. 7152 gave great authority to his verbal dexterity. His skills in debate and his quick wit seemed especially honed for this occasion by his deep personal convictions. On the Senate floor, he was like a dedicated college professor as he explained the intricacies of the bill. Over and over, he repeated the arguments for passage. At the same time, he wielded a sharp mental whip with great precision, to flick the flaws from opposing arguments for the benefit of the unpersuaded. It is doubtful, however, that even his superb talents would have been sufficient had he not managed to keep his enormous energy centered on bringing H.R. 7152 to a vote. Whatever concerns there may have been at the outset that he would stray into other realms of interest were soon laid to rest. His perseverance in pursuing the debate was unwavering, and it carried him to what surely was the apex of his political career.

Humphrey worked closely with Senators Warren Magnuson of Washington, Phil Hart of Michigan, and John Pastore of Rhode Island. They were stalwarts in producing the senators who, like firemen answering the bell, appeared for the "instant" quorums. When he was not engaged on the Senate floor, Humphrey was busy outside the chamber promoting passage of H.R. 7152. Humphrey briefed the press for the Democratic side on the nuances of day-to-day developments. He remained in continuous contact with the White House staff, the attorney general, and Justice Department attorneys. He kept up a steady exchange of views with President Johnson, who was often restless with the progress in the Senate and was constantly seeking to become involved without appearing to do so. Humphrey served as his line of contact, introducing as much of the president's thinking into the process as he felt would be acceptable to the majority leader and providing him with feedback. Johnson was careful to remind the press that Mansfield and Humphrey were running the show in the Senate.

Humphrey was also the Senate's contact point for the principal private interest groups, such as the National Association for the Advancement of Colored People, that were supporting the bill. His door was always open to the NAACP and similar organizations. He listened attentively to civil rights leaders and their Washington lobbyists. He briefed them on developments. He gave them guidance on which of the senators to pressure and which to leave alone. He smothered their doubts and anxieties with his optimism. He lifted their spirits with his enthusiasm and humor even as he commiserated with them over setbacks. The central role that Humphrey was playing in seeking Senate passage of H.R. 7152 served to reassure the black leaders. They swallowed hard at times when he made concessions in the text of the bill that caused them concern. But they knew that with him their cause was in the best possible hands.

Dealing with civil rights activists came easily to Humphrey. He had had a long association with such leaders as Clarence Mitchell of the NAACP, Joe Rauh of the Americans for Democratic Action, Walter Fauntroy of the Southern Christian Leadership Conference representing Martin Luther King Jr., and Whitney Young of the National Urban League. These well-established contacts were a major asset in seeking passage of H.R. 7152 because the private organizations served to undergird the entire effort by their activity. They put time, money, and heart into keeping the pressure of public attention on the Senate, and it was imperative that they not become discouraged or turn bitter during the protracted filibuster.

Recognizing the importance of Humphrey's tie with the activists, Mansfield urged him to maintain a close liaison with the civil rights leaders. But Mansfield chose to remain at a cautious distance. He resisted meetings with pressure groups, and when circumstances compelled such encounters, the exchanges were courteous but stiff, brief, and noncommittal. It is not surprising that some civil rights leaders came away regarding Mansfield as cold and distant, if not downright unsympathetic. His seeming aloofness was in part a reflection of a certain diffidence in his nature or, in any event, an understated political style. More to the point, whenever he sensed that he was being importuned to do what he did not wish to do, his visceral reflex was to freeze, with political antennae alert. At the same time, his vocabulary constricted to yes, no, and maybe, interspersed with long, silent pulls on his pipe. And what he did not wish at that moment was to identify himself intimately with the activists. As he saw it, his past votes were enough to certify him as a consistent supporter of equal treatment.

Moreover, Mansfield saw no useful purpose in engaging himself with the civil rights leaders in the small talk of wishful thinking. He sought nothing from them in the way of personal praise or favor. Such help as they could give to the job at hand was already being extended through their liaison with Humphrey. In truth, whatever the depth of his feelings on the subject of civil rights, at that point Mansfield's most pressing preoccupation was the struggle to prevent the Senate and himself as majority leader from falling into disrepute over H.R. 7152. The only way he could hope to avoid that was by bringing the situation to the point where sixty-seven senators would vote for cloture. The core advocates of civil rights alone could not produce anywhere near that number, and to the degree that he was identified closely with them, his ability to maneuver among the undecided would be diminished. Moreover, although it appeared hopeless, he could still not rule out the remote possibility of an acceptable compromise with the southern Democrats somewhere down the line. If there were to be any chance for Mansfield to bring it off, he could not give the appearance of being bound tightly to militant supporters of H.R. 7152, lest he lose viability as a go-between. The southern segregationists still saw Mansfield as a moderate on civil rights who was merely carrying out his duties as majority leader, and he did not wish to disabuse them of that perception.

Humphrey was under no such inhibitions. His close identity with the civil rights cause had long established him as a crusader against segregation, and no one expected him to change his colors. Humphrey could not move from where he was to a less militant posture without subjecting himself to derision. In any event, no useful purpose would have been served thereby; not a vote would be gained. Instead, by maintaining the full trust of the civil rights leaders, Humphrey could put this intimacy to good use on behalf of H.R. 7152. It would permit him to engage freely in hard negotiations with senators still waffling on the question of cloture. He could offer the undecideds tangible inducements in the form of changes in the bill in order to bring them around to voting for cloture. And he could do so without arousing the unsettling specter of a sellout among the core supporters of civil rights. This freedom to maneuver enabled Humphrey to work easily with Minority Leader Dirksen, whose purposes remained suspect in the eyes of civil rights leaders.

In negotiating with Humphrey, Dirksen had the help of Senator Roman Hruska of Nebraska. Hruska was a solid midwesterner, trusted not only by the minority leader but also by Republicans more conservative than Dirksen. A punctilious attorney from Omaha, Hruska had studied carefully both H.R. 7152 and the exceptions taken to it by various Republicans. As a result, he was able to make a significant contribution to the passage of the bill by negotiating acceptable changes in the text. The task confronting Dirksen and Hruska on that score was formidable; at one point the minority leader was compelled to announce somewhat ruefully that he had a collection of forty amendments being proposed to H.R. 7152 by various Republican senators. To be sure, some of these were minor changes and others clearly untenable, so the number was quickly reduced to less than a dozen in the course of the filibuster. Nevertheless, some amendments having to do with equal employment opportunities, federal intervention in state functions, and legal procedures including the right to jury trials represented deep-seated philosophical differences and were not readily bridgeable. Disposal of them called for extended negotiations by Dirksen with Humphrey, and for protracted discussions with Bobby Kennedy and the Justice Department lawyers, and, finally, clearance with Republican Representative Bill McCulloch. As ranking minority member of the House Judiciary Committee, McCulloch had taken a lot of political criticism for his cooperation with the Democrats in redesigning the administration's bill and in its passage in the House. He was in no mood to accept major adjustments by the Senate. His resistance involved a far more serious consideration than pride of authorship or personal stubbornness. He knew that if the Senate made only limited alterations, House acceptance of the revised version could probably be obtained without great difficulty. But if the changes were substantial, resistance in the House might very well rise to the point of rejection of the Senate version. That, in turn, could require a virtual rerun of the entire process in both houses, an appalling prospect.

Debate and Compromise

While negotiations on amendments were going on principally in Dirksen's convenient Capitol office, formal consideration of H.R. 7152 continued on the floor of the Senate. Day in and day out, week after week, the debate went on, to the exclusion of all other business. A couple of weeks after they had begun, the floor proceedings had become perfunctory, repetitious, and largely irrelevant. It was obvious that the Senate would not—could not—proceed without further clarification of the procedural question. The Senate was waiting for Mansfield to lay down a cloture petition, and the majority leader would not do that until the carefully kept vote tallies reached the number needed to shut off a filibuster.

Marking time on the Senate floor was not entirely time wasted. For one thing, the nation's interest in H.R. 7152 remained high, thanks in part to the extensive coverage of the proceedings by the media. Not only were the American people exposed to the issues surrounding civil rights but also to some of the unusual ways of the Senate. The interest in H.R. 7152 was reflected in a sharp increase in public attendance at the Senate's Visitors Gallery. At the same time, the usually near-empty Senate Press Gallery overflowed with unfamiliar faces. The new arrivals were mostly journalists who did not make a habit of covering the Senate. Indeed, when the expected procedural free-for-all that had marked past encounters on civil rights did not materialize, most of them disappeared. With their departure, the Press Gallery reverted largely to Associated Press representative Tony Vaccaro and Warren Duffy of United Press International, plus other regulars. The Diplomatic Gallery, empty in normal times except for an occasional lower-ranking diplomat, saw a sharp rise both in attendance and rank. The Family Gallery played host to a greater than usual number of wives, relatives, and friends of members. In the Visitor's Gallery, interest groups supporting H.R. 7152 were in constant attendance. They were augmented by a large increase in regular tourists and high school youth, many visiting Washington for the first time on class trips. These visitors were shepherded in and out of the galleries in organized shifts by the Senate guides. During the entire debate, only one untoward incident of any consequence occurred in the galleries. At one point in the proceedings, a spectator from the heights of the gallery joined uninvited in the debate on the floor below by providing comments from above. The guards quickly ejected the offender. Otherwise, the crowds were orderly and peaceful, notwithstanding the absence of metal detectors and the rest of the complex technology that had not yet been installed for protecting the security of the Capitol and its occupants.

A major stimulator of public interest during the filibuster was Roger Mudd, a popular news commentator at the time. Mudd set up his television paraphernalia in the driveway outside the entrance to the Senate wing of the Capitol for the duration. From that vantage point, he received the latest word on developments from Humphrey and Dirksen. He also conducted interviews with senators coming and going from the Senate chamber. His reports were broadcast throughout the country night after night on the CBS network, helping the public to understand what was happening. Also working to maintain popular interest in spite of the long hiatus were civil rights advocates, who came to Washington in a continuing stream from all over the nation. Thousands of all races were drawn to the Capitol to register their endorsement of H.R. 7152.Many were mobilized by religious groups. Young seminarians, for example, organized a twenty-four-hour vigil at the Lincoln Memorial and vowed to remain until the Senate voted on the bill. Their determination was reinforced by a unified religious movement that, on one occasion, brought together 5,000 Roman Catholic, Jewish, and Protestant clergymen for a prayer rally at Georgetown University. Labor Unions, the B'nai B'rith women, and other organizations mounted demonstrations in support of the legislation. Individual supporters of civil rights took time out from their vacations in Washington to visit the Senate office buildings and make known their views to their senators. To be sure, opponents of H.R. 7152 also exercised the right of petition in Washington that spring, but their efforts were not nearly of the same magnitude.

The public demonstrations of support for H.R. 7152 in Washington were sustained throughout the filibuster. They indicated the direction of the flow of public sentiment and helped maintain the Senate's determination to come to grips with the legislation, notwithstanding the filibuster. In past legislative clashes on civil rights, there was a quick dissipation of public enthusiasm and hence Senate interest, as debate was sidetracked into the labyrinth of Senate procedures. This did not happen in the spring of 1964. On the contrary, the manifestations of public support for H.R. 7152 in Washington were a constant reminder to the Senate of both the nationwide scope of the civil rights movement and its multiracial and nonsectarian character.

Public support was welcomed by senators favoring the bill as positive evidence of popular support for their position. The demonstrations also had a telling impact on senators who, while avowing their support for civil rights, still managed to drag their feet on voting for cloture. In the past, these members had enjoyed political immunity on the civil rights issue because their states contained few voters interested in what was regarded as a black cause. But, by 1964, the character of the issue had changed, and these senators were now faced with answering to voters of all colors and creeds who supported action to end racial discrimination. There was no escaping the fact that awareness of the issue had taken on a moral dimension that extended far beyond the black community. In that larger context, political immunity on the issue became largely a thing of the past. Even southern senators found the new breadth of support for civil rights legislation disconcerting, to say the least, especially since it now included many white religious and other leaders from the South. That is not to say that the civil rights movement had already grown far enough to persuade the southern senators to bring the filibuster to an end; their voting constituencies remained largely white and predominantly segregationist.

Notwithstanding the enormous waste of time, the weeks of the filibuster in the Senate did provide opportunity for work on the bill that would normally have taken place in committee. Since members were estopped from doing anything else, they had no choice but to participate in the consideration of H.R. 7152 or sulk in their offices. Those who chose to do so could educate themselves on the legislation at hand. Few matters ever to come before the Senate were so thoroughly understood and worked on by so many before being adopted. The long stall on the Senate floor permitted the real issues in H.R. 7152 to come into focus. After weeks of debate, the generalities had all been exhausted. All that could be said about the evils of racial discrimination had been said, not once, but over and over again. Whatever defense could be made for segregation in the South had been made and made again. Nor could anyone, not even Russell, contend that the Senate majority had run roughshod over the rights of the minority, that insufficient time had been provided to argue the southern position. Instead, thanks to the long lapse of time, the debate narrowed down to very specific questions, to the bread-and-butter issues that still divided the Senate. Was "Mrs. Murphy's Boarding House" in Brattleboro, Vermont, for example, equal with the Hyatt Hotel in Atlanta as a "public facility" within the meaning of the legislation? Would Mrs. Murphy, with three rooms to let in her own house, have to take in black guests, as would be the case with the Waldorf-Astoria Hotel in New York city? Under the Fair Employment Practices provision of the bill, would the black errand boy at Mom and Pop's corner grocery store in Richmond, Virginia, be entitled to the same protection from discrimination as a black assembly-line worker in a General Motors plant in Detroit; or would there be some cutoff in numbers of employees, below which the law would not apply? What of jury trials for those charged with violations of the voting provisions of the legislation; would they be guaranteed? Should the "sex equality clause," inserted in the bill almost as an afterthought on the floor of the House of Representatives, be retained by the Senate? And did the equal treatment clause mean that women could be compelled to use the same toilet facilities and public showers as men? Or was the sex clause aimed only at such problems as equal access to employment opportunities, equal wages for men and women for the same work, nondiscriminatory treatment of women in public accommodations, and equal opportunity for promotions in the workplace?

It will be recalled that the initiative for including the so-called sex equality clause had come, not from proponents but from confirmed opponents of desegregation. The intent had been the mischievous one of making the legislation more unpalatable to some fence sitters in the hope of defeating H.R. 7152 in the House or gumming up consideration of the bill in the Senate. But the ruse backfired when female House members embraced the proposal and launched a determined campaign among their male colleagues for its acceptance. Much to the consternation of the segregationists who had perpetrated the sex clause, it had not only passed the House but was on the way to passage in the Senate. An eleventh-hour effort to excise it ran into the unyielding opposition of Republican Senator Margaret Chase Smith of Maine. Thanks largely to her determination, the provision remained in the legislation and became law. Thereafter, it evolved in the courts into a solid legal bulwark for equal rights for women.

Even after such issues had been refined in extended discussions on and off the Senate floor, opponents still forced a continuance of the debate. In time it became obvious to even the most doubting that the Rules were being used, not to protect any reasonable rights of individual members or the integrity of the Senate as "the greatest deliberative body in the world," but solely to prevent a decision on a matter long since ripe for decision. By any count, an obvious constitutional majority was being held at procedural gunpoint. The choice had narrowed down to a constitutional majority yielding to the minority or, alternatively, acknowledging a humiliating inability of the Senate to function as a proper legislative body because of its rules. There was one way out: two-thirds of the members could vote for cloture. In the circumstances, a vote for cloture had become virtually synonymous with a vote for extending full and equal rights to all Americans. Members could scarcely profess to be for the one without also being for the other.

As that reality took hold, not only in the minds of the senators but also among the media and the public, it began to be manifested in an increasing level of irritability, particularly among moderates in the Senate. Mansfield found the whole drawn-out procedure "disgusting" and described the filibuster as a display of "adult delinquency." He laid the blame not so much on the southern opponents but on those who professed to support civil rights and still held back on cloture. He lengthened the daily sessions by several hours as a gesture to an impatient President Johnson, who continued to press through Humphrey for twenty-four-hour sessions. As Mansfield knew would be the case, the extension of the debate went nowhere, and he soon discontinued it. Such was the nature of the bind in which the Senate was being held that a defiant Russell was able to laugh off the majority leader's gesture.

Nevertheless, there were indications that the southern fortress was being

152 / Chapter 4

undermined. To be sure, their ranks remained steadfast around Russell's leadership. But allies who had previously bulwarked their position by refusing to vote for cloture began to announce their readiness to do so. Careful vote counts led Humphrey to conclude in early May that fifty-five members were definitely prepared to vote to shut off the debate and several others leaned in that direction. Dirksen sensed the change when he wrote in his personal notes that certain factors were predisposing the Senate to vote for cloture. Among them, he listed the growing logjam of legislation, the weariness with the aimless debate, and outside pressure for action. He also observed that 1964 was a presidential election year, and the Republican convention was scheduled to open 13 July, only weeks away. Russell, too, sensed changes in the wind and started to prepare his constituency for what had begun to look like the inevitable. Speaking before a meeting of the Georgia Junior Chamber of Commerce, he acknowledged that he did not have the votes necessary to prevent passage of the bill.

After the arrival of H.R. 7152 from the House, days had stretched into weeks, weeks into months. By 12 May the measure had preoccupied the Senate for almost three months, long enough to tie a record filibuster set in 1846. Still, Mansfield refrained from attempting cloture against the filibusterers. His hesitancy was well founded. Without first nailing down a dozen more senators, a successful outcome of a vote for cloture was highly uncertain. To lose on an initial test could strengthen the position of the opponents and bring increasing demands for a face-saving but inadequate compromise. As he had from the beginning, Mansfield regarded Dirksen as the key to obtaining the two-thirds majority for cloture. He said so on every possible occasion, thus turning public attention increasingly to the minority leader and the still-reluctant Republicans. Dirksen responded by assuring the press that more votes for cloture would soon be forthcoming from his side, even though he had yet to announce his own readiness to vote for cloture. The heat was on the minority leader. After working with his party and with Humphrey, Dirksen was able to announce on 13 May that he was in full agreement with the administration, the Justice Department, and the Democratic leadership on a comprehensive revision of H.R. 7152. McCulloch and Cellar in the House and congressional civil rights advocates such as Javits of New York hastened to make known their approval of the revision. Mansfield announced his full concurrence.

The revised text introduced in the Senate on 26 May was immediately dubbed the "Dirksen Substitute" by the media. The title was apt because the Republican leader had worked indefatigably to bring about most of the changes from the original text of H.R. 7152. At the same time, he had not pushed the changes to such a length as to alienate supporters of the House text. He swallowed some of his own objections and persuaded other Republicans to do the same. In short, it had taken a long time, but Dirksen had done much to achieve an acceptable compromise text. In so doing, the national interest had been served at a critical moment, and the Republicans were identified with the achievement.

Russell perceived at once the decisive nature of the "Dirksen Substitute." Indeed, he had tried desperately to forestall it, offering to talk over whatever it was that the minority leader had in mind and indicating his willingness to accommodate him in every way. When Russell's overtures were ignored and Dirksen remained aligned with Mansfield, the Georgian could scarcely suppress his fury. In one of his less sure-footed political conclusions, he remarked of Dirksen's move: "Unless I am badly fooled, he has killed off a rapidly growing Republican Party in the South, at least so far as his party's prospects in the presidential campaign are concerned."*

As subsequent developments proved, Russell was, indeed, "badly fooled." Not only did the Republican Party continue its rapid growth in the South, but thanks to the Senate Minority Leader, the party also managed to keep faith with Abraham Lincoln.

The emergence of the "Dirksen Substitute" marked the beginning of the final assault on resistance to H.R. 7152. Not one to pass up a spotlight, Dirksen redoubled his efforts to close out the struggle successfully. He was in constant motion, seeking in direct meetings with individual senators and in party caucuses to persuade his Republican colleagues to accept the revision and with it the necessity for supporting cloture. The names of Carlson and Pearson of Kansas, Miller of Iowa, and Cotton of New Hampshire were soon listed among those ready to vote to cut off debate; other Republicans moved closer to that point.

In spite of Dirksen's best efforts, however, the most difficult Republican holdout remained unconvinced and uncommitted. With Bourke Hickenlooper of Iowa, senior to Dirksen in the all-important Senate hierarchy of seniority, the minority leader carried little weight. At one time called "the gloomy pragmatist" by a *New York Times* writer, Hickenlooper indeed gave the impression that he was trying to live up to the name. By nature, he was taciturn almost to the point of surliness. Without ever having put a hand to the plow, he had the midwestern farmer's suspicion of the unknown and a defensive shrewdness in dealing with people like Dirksen. In the political arena, he found himself repeatedly classified with the far-right wing of the Republican Party, although he eschewed labels. He held his personal views

---

*Charles Whelan, *The Longest Debate*, p. 189.

like guarded cards in a poker game and brought them into play only with the greatest caution. He rarely spoke on the Senate floor, but rarely missed a vote. Preferring to wait in the cloakroom, he would appear just long enough to cast his vote and then disappear.

Despite his reticence in displaying them, Bourke Hickenlooper possessed many of the stylized attributes of the successful politician of the period. When in an outgoing mood, he was a warm handshaker and an excellent raconteur. He could be humorous, amiable, accommodating, and charming. He was an effective shirtsleeve campaigner, highly regarded in Iowa, where he was repeatedly elected to public office.

He was a conscientious senator ever cognizant of his responsibilities to his Iowan constituency. With accumulating years of Senate service, Hickenlooper's viewpoint broadened beyond Iowa's borders. He served as chairman of the Joint Atomic Energy Committee, a committee representing the first congressional attempt to assert an influence over the development of what then was widely regarded as an inexhaustible source of power for peaceful uses even though it came wrapped in images of mushroom clouds set off by the nuclear detonations over Hiroshima and Nagasaki in World War II. Hickenlooper had experienced a major personal setback for leading an unsuccessful attack on David Lilienthal, an outstanding bureaucrat of the New Deal era and the first chairman of the Atomic Energy Commission. He suffered a second loss in a contest with then Senate Democratic Leader Lyndon Johnson over Eisenhower's appointment of Admiral Louis Strauss as chairman of the Atomic Energy Commission. In spite of Hickenlooper's strong support for Strauss, Johnson succeeded in blocking confirmation of his appointment. The defeat added another layer to Hickenlooper's sense of frustration.

After these setbacks with atomic energy matters, Hickenlooper shifted his principal interest to the Senate Foreign Relations Committee, where he served for many years as the ranking Republican member. Extensive travel abroad for the committee fed his growing curiosity about the rest of world and helped him reconcile its realities with his heritage of midwestern isolationism. He aligned himself, reluctantly but irrevocably, with the main thrust of U.S. foreign policy after World War II. He was instrumental in ensuring the survival of the U.S. Information Agency and the Voice of America when both were on the verge of disappearing in the face of the onslaughts of Senator Joe McCarthy. Hickenlooper developed an excellent working relationship with Chairman William Fulbright. Despite ideological differences, the two men were generally in agreement on the role of the United States in world affairs. In any event, they were equally emphatic in their insistence on an activist contribution from the Senate in shaping that role.

In contrast to the cordial relationship he enjoyed with Democratic Chairman Fulbright, Hickenlooper kept a distance between himself and Everett Dirksen. Highly sensitive to personal slights, Hickenlooper resented Dirksen's failure to take cognizance of his seniority through consultation, deference, and other traditional indications of appropriate respect. Reticent by nature, Hickenlooper also found Dirksen's flamboyant style distasteful. This clash of attitude was papered over by the Senate's code of acceptable modes of surface interaction, especially the comradely use of first names. Such conversation as there was between the two men was always interspersed with seemingly affectionate "Evs" and "Bourkes." Nevertheless, the reality was that differing temperaments and attitudes acted to keep them at arms' length, a distance accentuated by Dirksen's handling of H.R. 7152.

Hickenlooper was no crusader for equal rights and initially was reluctant even to acknowledge an urgent need for comprehensive federal legislation to deal with segregation. Over the years, he had shared the Republican delight in the North-South split of the Democrats on the issue. He probably would not have been averse to using H.R. 7152 as a way to exacerbate the split. To be sure, he would not have led such an effort, but he might well have supported it, something he could have done with relative political impunity. The black population of Iowa was small, and the state was quite free of racial intolerance. Public facilities were not separated. High-quality integrated public education, from kindergarten through university, was available to all races. Blacks not only voted freely in elections but were also active in politics. Indeed, Hickenlooper and other Republicans received considerable support from organized Republicans in the black community.

Dirksen's course of cooperation with the Democratic leadership on H.R. 7152 evoked only a grumbling acquiescence from Hickenlooper. For his part, Dirksen was at a loss as to how to deal with the sullen Iowan. As a result, he avoided him and concentrated on reconciling less reticent Republicans to his position. That served only to deepen Hickenlooper's disdain for what in his eyes had become the dubious path down which the Republicans were being led. Even after protracted negotiations had produced the acclaimed "Dirksen Substitute" for H.R. 7152, Hickenlooper remained a snarling holdout. It was not easy for him to maintain that position. The growing irritation of his Senate colleagues with the filibuster, the negative public reactions to the Senate's inability to put an end to the unconscionable delay, the moral pressure from religious groups and criticism from the media were making it increasingly uncomfortable for him. Still, he gave no signs of budging, showing only disdain when his junior colleague from Iowa, Jack Miller, openly threw in his lot with Dirksen and announced his readiness to vote for cloture. Hickenlooper's refusal to climb aboard the

"Dirksen Substitute" bandwagon was a source of inspiration to a handful of other conservative Republican holdouts, who had yet to announce their positions on cloture. The four or five votes in this group represented a margin of safety without which Mansfield was reluctant to launch a final assault on the filibuster. So the Senate proceeded to mark time, even as Hickenlooper continued to sulk in the Republican cloakroom.

At that point, an inadvertent intrusion by President Johnson set off a chain of events that was to lead to the decisive breakthrough. With the "Dirksen Substitute" stalled, Johnson made known his impatience with the situation not only to Humphrey and other leaders but also to staff acquaintances on the Hill. Reluctant to discuss the matter directly with Mansfield, he asked for ideas from the secretary for the majority as to what further he might do to break the logjam. Word was sent back to him through his White House liaison officer, Mike Manatos, that the time might be right for him to try to contact Bourke Hickenlooper. Earlier, Johnson had received the same advice from other sources but had not acted on it. On hearing the suggestion again, Johnson had thrown up his hands in a gesture of despair and exclaimed, "Persuade Hickenlooper to vote for cloture? Jesus Christ, that's like asking me to get Strom Thurmond to vote for cloture!"

At the time, Thurmond of South Carolina was the personification of diehard southern resistance to desegregation. Indeed, his opposition had caused him to leave the Democratic Party in the 1948 elections. Thurmond's political acumen in placing himself in the vanguard of the emerging Republican Party in the South was confirmed subsequently by his repeated reelections and by his consequent elevation through seniority to President Pro Tempore of the Senate. In the course of his long career, moreover, he was able to accommodate to the addition of black voters to the rolls in South Carolina and draw his share of support from that source. This was not surprising because Thurmond's reputation among black people was far from malevolent. Many recognized the vehemence of his segregationist stand as a form of inescapable expediency in an otherwise decent southern politician. Neither that nor the defense of states' rights deterred him from seizing every opportunity to bring the benefits of federal programs and projects to both races in South Carolina. This formula of enunciating a militant segregationist and states' rights position while harvesting federal benefits for blacks as well as whites was also pursued by most of the political survivors among the southern Democrats, even by those who were loudest in their denunciation of H.R. 7152. Thurmond had no difficulty ignoring his affiliation with the party of Lincoln when confronted with H.R. 7152. He was the lone Republican who joined the southern Democrats in actively pursuing the filibuster to the end.

The linking of Thurmond and Hickenlooper by the president provided Mansfield with an unexpected opportunity on H.R. 7152. Johnson's comment was immediately relayed to Hickenlooper by the majority secretary who, despite differences in party affiliation, enjoyed a friendly relationship with the Iowan. Reclining in a leather chair in the Republican cloakroom, Hickenlooper was in an amiable mood when the president's reaction was recounted to him in jest by the secretary. The senator did not find the story at all amusing. He stiffened and sat upright. His face, which flushed easily in any event, turned red as he growled: "Johnson doesn't know what the hell he's talking about. I'm not against cloture. The problem is in the bill. They won't listen around here [an obvious reference to Dirksen] but if they would make some changes, get rid of some of the things in it—it's the bill not cloture that I'm opposed to."

The incident in the Republican cloakroom was relayed to Mansfield, who immediately grasped the significance of the Republican's reaction. In an instant, Mansfield was on the phone, inviting Hickenlooper to come in and discuss whatever it was that was troubling him in connection with Dirksen's substitute, no commitments, no arm twisting, just a discussion. In the few minutes before the Iowan's arrival, Mansfield directed the Justice Department attorneys, led by Nick Katzenbach, who were holding forth in the majority leader's conference room that they were, in no circumstances, to argue with Hickenlooper but were merely to listen, take note of his proposed changes, or concur in their desirability if that were possible. Mansfield received Hickenlooper with all the warmth that he could muster and escorted him into the conference room. Before leaving him with the attorneys, he urged him to speak frankly about his reservations concerning the bill. Hickenlooper was somewhat taken aback by finding himself the center of attention in the Democratic leader's office and, unexpectedly, in the midst of the Justice Department's legal talent. He growled through the lengthy bill, noting here and there a point that he found distasteful. With few exceptions, the indicated differences were minor. The Justice Department attorneys, wedded to the text that they had labored so long to devise, barely managed to avoid a confrontation. Instead of doing legalistic battle, however, they contented themselves with an occasional nod of agreement, here and there a winced comment, and some barely perceptible negative head shaking.

Hickenlooper emerged from the meeting clearly pleased with what had transpired. "With those changes," he commented, "it would be a lot better bill." Before taking his leave, he admonished Mansfield not to interpret the discussion that had taken place as an indication of his readiness to vote for cloture. He received in return Mansfield's assurances that not only would his position on cloture be construed as still open but that if he cared to offer any amendments, the leadership would personally see to it that they received full consideration on the Senate floor. Hickenlooper glowed as he expressed his appreciation for the consideration shown him and then departed. True to his promise, Mansfield never counted Hickenlooper as a nailed-down vote and instead cleared the way for him and his conservative Republican associates to take up their amendments to Dirksen's substitute on the floor. In due course, the amendments of these holdouts did come to a vote, and all were defeated.

Even without a commitment, Mansfield knew that the door had been opened, and there was now a good chance that not only Hickenlooper but other Republican mainstays for the southern Democrats would end their resistance to cloture. Russell, too, recognized what was afoot. The southern leader had even more cause than Mansfield to nail down Hickenlooper's vote. Having already lost Dirksen, his only hope of avoiding defeat lay in Republican allies from among the most conservative of the minority. Russell made clear that he was prepared to bid high. He assured Hickenlooper that he was not only prepared to clear the way for his amendments to be taken up but was also ready to consider any and all other matters of interest to the Iowan. When this invitation was brushed aside, it was evident to Russell that the Hickenlooper cluster of Republicans could no longer be counted on to support the filibuster. Russell sensed that the game was over. With shoulders slumped, he left the Senate floor via the rear doors and slowly walked the fifty paces to the senators' private elevator, which was located immediately adjacent to the majority leader's office. He encountered there the majority secretary but scarcely seemed to notice him, even as he smiled a rueful smile. "What a hell of a way to make a living," he said, shaking his head as he disappeared into the elevator.

The Vote for Cloture and Its Aftermath

What had transpired with Hickenlooper was sufficient to convince Mansfield that the time had come to strike directly at the filibuster. Several more days were to elapse, however, before the decisive vote would take place. In the interim, Humphrey brought back word from the White House that the president had persuaded certain western Democrats, such as Bob Bartlett of Alaska and Howard Cannon of Nevada, to vote for cloture by providing federal public works projects or other plums for their states. In his exchange with the media, Dirksen grew ever more expansive in expressing confidence in the outcome.

Outside pressure on the Senate to end the filibuster reached a climax when former President Dwight D. Eisenhower broke his cautious silence to come down firmly on the side of H.R. 7152. His new position contrasted with what he had maintained during his presidency. At that time, he affirmed his determination to enforce the Supreme Court's *Brown* decision on school desegregation as the law of the land but avoided judgment in public on the merits of the Court's action. This time, there was no ambiguity. In a statement to the *New York Herald Tribune,* then a citadel of Republican respectability, Eisenhower embraced desegregation as vital to the nation's interests.

On 8 June 1964, Dirksen joined Mansfield in filing a cloture petition on H.R. 7152. It contained the signatures of twenty-seven Democrats and eleven Republicans. The number was more than sufficient to satisfy the requirements of Rule 22, but Mansfield had kept the list open to accommodate all those wishing to sign. Many sought to record their position for posterity on what they perceived to be an historic document, a kind of Magna Carta in the evolution of civil rights in the United States. Under the Rule, two days had to elapse before the petition could come to a vote. The forty-eight hours were filled by the introduction of numerous additional amendments that would have to be disposed of after cloture was adopted and by speeches, on the whole conciliatory, as befitting a group that had been drenched in words for months and understood that they would still have to live with one another regardless of the outcome.

Then, before a packed gallery in an utterly silent chamber, the alphabetical call of the roll was intoned. On reaching the letter *E,* supporters of the measure looked up from their tally slips toward a desk that had not been used for weeks. They were reassured when the clerk paused to record the vote of Senator Clare Engel of California. Engel was known to be a strong supporter of civil rights but a question remained as to whether his health would permit him to be present. With great effort, he had risen from a hospital bed and, attended by physicians, reached the Capitol in an ambulance. A small man, Engel was barely visible in the cluster of aides and attendants who held him upright as he took the few steps from the lounge into the Senate chamber. Too weak to speak, Engel managed a feeble smile as he pointed to his eye in a gesture of "aye" for cloture in response to the call of his name. Engel repeated this performance in the vote on the civil rights bill. It was a final gesture of triumphant dedication. Within a few weeks, Engel was dead of cancer.

When John Williams of Delaware called an "aye" in a voice less strident than usual, his was the decisive sixty-seventh vote. The tension broke, and a scattering of applause ran through the chamber. Visitors were gaveled back into silence by Senator Lee Metcalf, the acting President Pro Tempore. The call of the roll continued until all 100 members had been recorded. While the count was in progress, President Pro Tem Carl Hayden of Arizona waited anxiously in the Democratic cloakroom prepared, if necessary, to cast his first vote ever for cloture. After much cajoling, Hayden had promised Lyndon Johnson that he would do so but only if his vote were absolutely essential. With the issue decided, Mansfield called out to him in a voice that could be heard in the galleries, "It's all right, Carl. You can come out now." A greatly relieved Hayden emerged from the cloakroom to vote "nay," thus preserving a half century of consistency in opposing cloture. The junior senator from Arizona, Republican Barry Goldwater, joined him in voting against cloture. Their motives were not necessarily the same. For Hayden, opposing cloture was an ingrained habit. Goldwater later contended that he had something similar in mind. However that might be, there is no doubt that his "nay" also served what was then his consuming personal ambition. His eyes were zeroed in on the Republican nomination for the presidency. The Goldwater "nay" resounded throughout the South, assuring him of the decisive support of delegates from that region as against Nelson Rockefeller of New York in the impending Republican National Convention in San Francisco.

The filibuster had endured for more than 500 hours, making it the longest debate in Senate history. It was only the sixth time ever that the Senate had agreed to silence itself by invoking Rule 22. In twelve previous tries on civil rights legislation, the Senate had failed to muster the required two-thirds majority. The final tally showed seventy-one for and twenty-nine against, four more than needed.

Although the most critical milestone, the cloture vote was still merely concerned with a procedural question. It was not a vote on the substance of H.R. 7152. Only after yet another delay provided for in Rule 22 would the Senate vote on the actual bill. After the adoption of cloture, each senator could still claim one hour of nontransferable time, thus adding the specter of another 100 hours of debate before the final vote. Some members elected to use their allotted hour for one last declamation on the civil rights issue. Others decided not to waste any more time and, with the leadership's blessings and gratitude, chose to remain silent and yield back their time. Still others, mostly in the southern block, were prepared to call up amendments they had taken pains to file before the adoption of cloture so that subsequently they would be in order. As a harbinger of what was to come during the postcloture period, one member had introduced dozens of such amendments during the final two days preceding consideration of the substance of H.R. 7152. Mansfield and Dirksen, working in the closest harmony, lengthened the daily sessions and called on their colleagues to beat down all amendments without debate. Russell and other southerners challenged the approach by calling up some perfecting amendments; all were abruptly defeated. Some of the southerners complained of being persecuted into silence by this treatment. Such complaints might have been taken seriously a few months earlier. Now they were laughed off by a Senate liberated at last from the tyranny of endless talk. Moreover, since the time it took to make the complaint was now to be charged against the complainant's single allotted hour, the protests soon ceased.

It was clear that the Senate wanted no more of delays. It soon became clear, too, that Russell would no longer seek to evade the wall of silence closing in on his losing cause. Stunned by the defeat, the first he had suffered in years of holding back the tide of desegregation, he was not of a mind to pull any more parliamentary surprises. His southern colleagues were generally in agreement. Together they had done everything possible to represent the predominant position of their voting constituencies, and it had not been enough. They were resigned to a vote on the civil rights bill and to the certain defeat it would bring.

There was one significant exception. Sam Ervin of North Carolina was not ready, despite the adoption of cloture, to throw in the towel. Ervin was a sophisticated Harvard Law School graduate camouflaged as a county court-house lawyer. Years of service in the Senate had acted to perfect his style, which was at once shrewd, humorous, garrulous, gracious, and unyielding. Beyond opposition to H.R 7152, the same style was evident on other issues that enlisted his interest. Recognized as an authority on the Bill of Rights, for example, Ervin was a relentless thorn in the side of those seeking to chip away at the barricade imposed by the Constitution between church and state. He was also a powerful advocate of the individual's right to privacy and had done pioneer legislative work against bureaucratic snooping in that area. He achieved his greatest fame, however, in the sunset of his career as the immensely effective chairman of the Special Senate Committee that investigated the Watergate scandal for the Senate. His light but firm touch in conducting the televised hearings was a devastating factor in bringing about the disgrace and resignation of President Richard Nixon.

Regarded as an enlightened southerner by many, Ervin's opposition to H.R. 7152 still came as no surprise as he joined his southern colleagues in the protracted filibuster. In the context of the times, the fact was that southern senators who desired to continue as senators had no choice but to stand against any legislation intended to change the existing pattern of race relations in the South. The alternative was to accept the principle of integration and with it the virtual certainty of defeat in the next election. Indeed, for most southern senators, it was not enough merely to oppose change in the existing pattern of racial relations. They felt compelled to offer dug-in, all-out determined resistance to any suggestion of change. Such a stance was the first requirement for political survival in the region. Regardless of his other meritorious characteristics or achievements, for a sitting senator to have pursued any other approach on racial questions would have been tantamount to announcing his retirement.

Whatever their personal convictions on racial questions, there was really no other road open. To be sure, it was the road of expediency and pursuing it could be faulted on moral grounds. But to do so was to close one's eyes to the contributions of such outstanding and politically durable senators of the era as William J. Fulbright and John McClellan of Arkansas, and John Sparkman and Lister Hill of Alabama. These men left enduring marks in such diverse fields as foreign relations, education, crime control, housing, and health.

Indeed, Ervin made many constructive contributions and at the same time upheld the prevailing racial patterns of southern society. When it came to asserting his segregationist credentials, Ervin was at least the equal of any of his peers. His words and actions in the Senate defined him as a pillar of the status quo on this issue.

In confronting H.R. 7152 he was not only aligned with the last-ditch resistance to desegregation, he was also among the most militant in defending the existing situation. His formidable legal talents were used to argue the constitutional case for segregation even as his ever-ready tongue and inexhaustible energy were substantial factors in sustaining the long filibuster. However misguided one may consider these exertions, they were at least understandable in the context of southern political survival. That was hardly the case, however, with the extent to which Ervin persisted in them after cloture had been achieved on H.R. 7152.

It may be that his anxieties with regard to reactions in North Carolina were such that he felt compelled to go far beyond his colleagues to affirm his personal views on segregation and his dedication to its preservation. Or perhaps it was merely an inability to accept defeat gracefully on an issue that had been central to his career for decades. In any event, after most of his southern colleagues had concluded that enough was enough, Ervin could not bring himself to do the same. Using the hour of time provided by Rule 22 after cloture, he proceeded to bring up amendment after amendment from the dozens he had filed just before the cloture vote. The great bulk of them were of little consequence. Yet he demanded on each amendment that senators first appear to answer a quorum call and then be present for a second run-through of the roll in order to record their votes on each amendment. Such a demand was rarely heard except for purposes of delay. Senators appeared repeatedly on Ervin's insistence, hour after hour, first to answer the roll call, then to listen to the reading of the amendment, and then most to vote no on its adoption. To make matters worse, his example inspired other southerners to follow the same procedure.

Ervin's intent was purely dilatory. Although seventy-one senators had already said that it was time to end the matter, he had no difficulty in compelling his colleagues to dance to this time-wasting tune. Such is the nature of the Senate's indulgence of each member that it was feasible to go on in this ludicrous fashion indefinitely, even after the adoption of cloture on a procedural matter that already had consumed 500 hours!

When Russell became aware of what was transpiring without interference from the chair, his reaction was simply, "If that's what cloture means then I'm not afraid of it anymore." Mansfield was irritated by what was happening but confined his response to lengthening the sessions still further. In time, Ervin did call off his postcloture filibuster. He subsided not because he had run out of energy or amendments, and certainly not because the Senate had lifted a finger to stop him. He did so only after the media had had plenty of time to became aware of his antics and to spread the image of his Custer's Last Stand against desegregation across North Carolina. However effective the impression created in his home state, it was achieved at great cost to the Senate. Additional days of wasted time were piled on top of the weeks that had already been expended to obtain cloture. Even more destructive, his tactics threw into doubt the value of the Rule of cloture itself, the last resort that the Senate had assumed it possessed against the filibuster. By his successful manipulation, Ervin had opened the door to a repetition of the trick by others in subsequent years. What had begun as one senator's personal indulgence, supported by an off-the-cuff commentary of a Senate parliamentarian on the verge of retirement, was duly incorporated thereafter into the precedents of the Senate, to be elevated in a short time to the status of procedural gospel.

After the exhausting filibuster on civil rights, the tactic of tieup by talk, or threat thereof, began to be used almost routinely on a host of contentious issues in addition to civil rights. It became obvious that the tactic, accentuated by the postcloture filibuster, was a threat to the viability of the Senate as a legislative body. There was a backlash from those who did not wish to see the Senate reduced to an absurdity by the concept of "unlimited debate."

With the experience of H.R. 7152 still fresh in mind, majority leader Mansfield pressed his long-standing advocacy of a reduction in the requirement from two-thirds to a three-fifths majority in order to invoke cloture. The change was swiftly adopted and served adequately during the remainder of the period of Mansfield's leadership to discourage any major holdups in the Senate's business. Subsequently, under majority leader Robert C. Byrd, additional measures against dilatory tactics had to be adopted to counter the post cloture filibuster. At the same time, it became virtually routine to threaten or launch a filibuster on virtually all seriously controversial measures, thus effectively resetting the point of Senate legislative decision at three-fifths rather than a simple majority as provided for by the Constitution.

Final Passage of H.R. 7152

After Ervin ended his last stand, the Senate passed H.R. 7152 by an overwhelming vote of 73 to 27. Hickenlooper and Curtis, both of whom voted for cloture, voted against the bill itself. Bennett of Utah, Young of North Dakota, Bible of Nevada, and Hayden, all of whom had opposed cloture, voted for the bill on final passage. H.R. 7152 was returned to the House. There the principal proponents were successful in steering it by the shortest possible route to acceptance with the changes made in the Senate. There remained only the need for the president to sign it. He did so on 2 July, one year and thirteen days after President Kennedy had requested the legislation from Congress. Johnson invited those who had been most instrumental in passage of the measure to witness the signing. With dozens of witnesses grouped around him, Johnson put his signature to the legislation. He used seventy-two pens, passing them out afterward as souvenirs. H.R. 7152 was now the law of the land.

Enactment of the Civil Rights Act of 1964 was a landmark in the nation's continuing effort to realize the constitutional ideal of equal treatment and opportunity for all. The measure activated legal weapons powerful enough to end government sanction of segregation wherever it persisted. While designed primarily with the inequities in mind that burdened blacks, the legislation has been applied to other minorities and to women. The impact of the Civil Rights Act of 1964 can be seen in the vast changes that have taken place in the nation's political life, educational structure, workplaces, public facilities, and social mores. To be sure, the act has been supplemented by other laws and its effect spread by judicial interpretations. Nevertheless, the Civil Rights Act of 1964 stands as a beacon in the long struggle to ensure that the American promise of equal regard for all would not be lost in the continued fragmentation of its people on the basis of race or sex.

5

Mansfield and Vietnam: The Johnson Years, 1964–1968

With Congress about to recess for the 1964 Democratic National Convention, President and Lady Bird Johnson gave a lawn party at the White House to honor the Democratic members of Congress. The gala was a way of saying thanks to the legislators for past performance, as well as a sendoff for those who were about to enter the election arena. At the other end of Pennsylvania Avenue, the Senate found itself in a procedural wrangle, with most senators, including Majority Leader Mansfield, remaining at the Capitol awaiting the unraveling of the knots. Their absence was scarcely noted at the presidential reception because of the Texas-size turnout of House members with spouses and others of the party faithful. Hundreds of guests strolled in the glare of floodlights that made the night air more sultry than usual. But the heat, the mosquitoes, and the fireflies were ignored as guests stopped here and there at a table for a cool drink or a tidbit. All the while, loudspeakers regaled the gathering with a program of political songs from past presidential election campaigns. Narrating the program were three prominent television news commentators of the period—Walter Cronkite, Nancy Dickerson, and Howard K. Smith—all favorites of the Johnsons. As a memento of the occasion, each guest received a phonograph record of old political campaign songs.

President Johnson delayed addressing the assemblage, hoping for the appearance of the absent senators, especially Majority Leader Mansfield. As the hour grew late, he could wait no longer. His remarks were generous in praise of the 94th Congress and its leadership. Johnson had reason to be pleased. What was being dismissed shortly before Kennedy's death as one of the worst Congresses in history was now being hailed as among the greatest. No small part of this revised evaluation by the media was credited to Johnson. In the few short months that he had occupied the presidency, the erstwhile hard-nosed ringmaster of the Senate had acquired an updated image that enlarged his reputed legislative skills and gave him a new dimension. He was now seen as a firm but rather benign, even-tempered father-figure for the nation. This new version of Johnson was shared by leading allies abroad. Having studied him close-up at the Kennedy funeral, various allied heads of state went home breathing easier. Unlike his reputation as a cowboy who shot from the hip, Johnson had given them the impression of a sober, rather stolid and serious man, a dependable leader of the Free World. His restraint in foreign affairs in the months immediately following Kennedy's death seemed to confirm that first impression.

A key factor in the transformation of Johnson's image had been the successful outcome of the civil rights struggle. During the weeks of the filibuster in the Senate, the attitude toward the president among black leaders and in liberal circles had shifted from suspicion to unabashed admiration. Johnson had taken to using Martin Luther King's theme of "we shall overcome" in his speeches. He was perceived among civil rights advocates as having acted with passionate dedication to the cause while exercising great skill in extracting the Civil Rights Act of 1964 from Congress and, particularly, from the Senate, with the assistance of Hubert Humphrey.

Enactment of the law had served to quell the rising anger of black Americans and to rekindle their faith in the American Dream. At the same time, the new law was something of a catharsis for white Americans, relieving their moral discomfort over the anachronism of legal segregation. Especially satisfying to Democrats, moreover, was the fact that the achievements had been recorded in a manner that would keep most of the southern states in the Democratic fold in the coming election. Johnson's handling of the still small but irksome Vietnam question was seen as an astute mixture of firmness and restraint. In this respect, he seemed to be a president who knew how to keep the communists at bay without getting the nation's feet sullied in the gore of a bloody war, as had happened in Korea. In his readiness to face up to nagging social and economic inequities, Johnson was readily identified as in a direct lineage from Franklin D. Roosevelt, a lineage that also included the already quasi-legendary John F. Kennedy.

On the eve of the 1964 election campaign, then, Lyndon Johnson stood tall. His shoulders appeared broad enough simultaneously to bear the burden of concern over racial violence, communist threats, nuclear extinction, and the nation's inner social and economic imperfections.

All the while, the economy continued to bubble along, distilling for most Americans a lifestyle of personal freedom and considerable material wellbeing and the hope for an even better tomorrow. The public mood, in short, was decidedly upbeat, one of unusual contentment with Washington. The contentment, moreover, was freely ascribed to Johnson's performance after the death of Kennedy. In the summer of 1964, even the most casual observer of the American scene could see that Johnson's political star was very high and still rising.

The more earthbound Democrats in Congress were following in Johnson's wake, already tasting victory in the approaching elections. It was indeed a moment for the faithful of the party to savor to the full, as they were doing at the White House lawn party. The president shook as many hands as he could reach. For more intimate exchanges, he gently grasped a few coats by the lapels and firmly drew the wearers close in order to entrust confidences to them.The Democrats were one big happy family that night. Never had they felt more in tune with one another, never more confident of their party and its political mission. They enjoyed the food. They applauded the entertainment. They were effusive in their praise of Johnson's political leadership and Lady Bird's deft hospitality. When the music ended, the congressmen and their wives went home and the Johnsons retired for the night, all transported by warm feelings of affection for their country and each other. Hosts and guests were content and primed for the election campaign of 1964.

The 1964 Campaign and Election

The enthusiasm of the White House reception remained with the participants as they made their way to Atlantic City for the Democratic Party's National Convention, which opened three days later. Legalized gambling had not yet arrived in the New Jersey beach resort, and so delegates were content to stroll the boardwalk, where they encountered other Democrats, who were arriving from all parts of the nation. As the thousands of delegates and onlookers poured into Convention Hall, the air became supercharged with their exuberance. Like fuel in a rocket on a launch pad, they waited to be fired by a powerful partisan speech.

To provide the ignition, Senator John O. Pastore of Rhode Island had been handpicked by Senate Majority Leader Mansfield to give the keynote

address. In selecting the fiery Pastore, Mike Mansfield displayed his un-
canny astuteness for matching politician with purpose. The senator from
Rhode Island was indeed the right man in the right place at the right time.
Sensing that a well-based optimism would prevail among the Democrats at
the convention, Pastore had spent days fine-tuning his remarks to that
tempo. The delegates, having surmounted the grief of John F. Kennedy's
death, were ready to get on with the nation's political life under a new
leader. Pastore's theme was an appropriate *"Le roi est mort, vive le roi,"*
with somewhat more emphasis on the living over the deceased. Standing on
tip-toe as though to lift his height to the level of his eloquence, Pastore used
his powerful voice to drive that message into the eager ears of the convention delegates. They roared a thunderous concurrence.

Johnson's nomination at Atlantic City was a foregone conclusion. There
was not the shadow of an opposition lurking anywhere in Convention Hall.
Indeed, all the elements of a Johnson nomination were in place even before
the arrival of the delegates. George Meany, president of the American Fed-
eration of Labor, and a powerful force in the Democratic Party at the time,
was satisfied with Johnson. Black activists were now enthusiastic about
Johnson. Liberal leaders were excited by Johnson's reassuring performance
on civil rights and his accent on peace. The dwindling ranks of Democratic
big-city bosses knew a winner when they saw one, and what they saw was
enough for them to give their full support to Johnson. Notwithstanding what
he was saying on civil rights, the southern delegates recognized that
Johnson's political roots in Texas gave them about the most sympathetic ear
they could expect to have in the White House. As for the most conservative
Democrats, anyone would be better than a Kennedy, but they could hardly
say so openly.

Johnson was nominated by acclamation, and tens of thousands of voices
burst forth in a thunderous rendition of "Hello Lyndon" sung to the tune of
"Hello Dolly." Johnson's acceptance speech reflected his mastery of the
moment. He paid brief but generous homage to the late president, linking
his caretaker administration to his predecessor's ideals. As he went on,
however, it became clear that Johnson was moving out from under the
shadow of John F. Kennedy. Whenever and wherever it would help in the
coming election, he would bring into play the political magic of what was
fast becoming the Kennedy legend. But the victory that lay ahead would be
Lyndon Johnson's victory. The administration taking office in January 1965
would bear Johnson's stamp.

When it came Bobby Kennedy's turn to speak, he tipped the emphasis
rather in the other direction, toward the memory of the dead over the aspirations of the living. He referred to what brother John had done for the nation

and what was left undone by his tragic death. Bobby's very presence on the speaker's platform was a poignant reminder of how recent was the Democratic Party's tie to the Kennedys. Bobby spoke not for himself alone but for the Kennedy clan and the myriad Kennedy admirers who were not yet ready to let go of their grief. What he had to say, however, was in no sense a hail and farewell for himself; he was not about to fold his tent and quietly slip away into an early retirement. On the contrary, there was enough reference to President Johnson to confirm his Democratic credentials and the continued involvement of the Kennedys with the party's future. That much was clear. They would join in the party's efforts to retain the presidency.

Despite their differences, neither Lyndon Johnson nor Bobby Kennedy was inclined to carry them to the point of a rupture in the party. Both were practical politicians who recognized the need for enough comity to win the impending election and to lay the basis for another Democratic victory four years later.

The certainty of Johnson's nomination did not carry over to the selection of a vice-presidential running mate. With Bobby Kennedy out of the running, the convention waited anxiously to see who the president would draw out of the hat. Numerous trial balloons floated upward, only to be lost in the rafters. Although most delegates seemed to favor Hubert Humphrey from the outset, Johnson's hold on the convention was such as to ensure an ecstatic acceptance of his choice, whoever it might be. Johnson played the guessing game to the hilt, withholding his preference from the drooling delegates until the last possible moment. The drawing out of the selection served to provide some drama to an otherwise cut-and-dried convention. For a few days, it was the old Johnson, stage managing a political show in much the same way that he had done as majority leader in the Senate.

The president hinted at any number of potential vice presidential candidates, dangling them as so many puppets on strings. The names that surfaced most frequently, in addition to Hubert Humphrey, included Gene McCarthy of Minnesota, Mike Mansfield, and Tom Dodd, an old Johnson favorite. Humphrey professed to enjoy the guessing game and played along with it eagerly. He teamed up with Gene McCarthy to open a joint headquarters for Minnesota vice presidential aspirants, vowing to bring the nomination to the state through one or the other's selection. If Johnson saw the main requirement in a running mate as someone who could turn up the enthusiasm of labor, blacks, and liberals, what better choice than Humphrey? Alternatively, would not Gene McCarthy serve nicely to rekindle the interest of Catholic voters in the Democratic Party, an interest that had been dealt a bad blow by the assassination?

Notwithstanding the joint headquarters and the humor, it was obvious that of the two, Humphrey was the probable candidate. The moment was decisive in his lifetime quest for the presidency. It was now or never for him to position himself within striking distance of the prize, and the vice presidency would be an ideal steppingstone for that purpose. By 1964, Humphrey had a firm and expanding base of support not only in Minnesota but with farmers and organized labor throughout the nation. Moreover, the political mood of the entire country had shifted sharply in the direction of his pioneer stand on civil rights, a shift that served to enhance his appeal to black and liberal voters. At the same time, his performance in the Senate over the years had dispelled some of the anxiety among conservative southerners that he was some sort of wild man. True, Humphrey would not have been their initial choice, but they could appreciate the realities of the situation; he was needed and was therefore tolerable to them on a ticket headed by Lyndon Johnson.

Perhaps more to the liking of southerners as the vice presidential candidate would have been Senate Majority Leader Mike Mansfield. Although his voting record was not that much different from Humphrey's, when filtered through his restrained personality and accommodating manner, his votes seemed to grate less on conservative nerves. He stood in sharp contrast to the flamboyant and hectic Humphrey; Mansfield was more sober, more stolid, more like a Lee than a Grant. To be sure, Mansfield was a Roman Catholic but that taboo had been removed from the deep political freeze and thawed by the late president's victory. If Catholicism was what Johnson needed in a vice presidential candidate in 1964, Mansfield would have been an ideal choice to the southerners.

Before the convention opened, the press had flagged the Senate majority leader as a serious possibility for the vice presidency. Passage of the civil rights bill had been followed immediately by a rapid output of pent-up legislation in the Senate such as to vindicate Mansfield's approach to the leadership. A change had begun to take place in the press perception of the majority leader. Mansfield was now seen as quietly astute and highly effective, something of a political alchemist who could stir together liberals, conservatives, Republicans, and Democrats and produce an almost effortless flow of legislation.

What made references to Mansfield as a vice presidential candidate of more than passing interest was that some came from William S. White, then the political columnist of the *Washington Star,* who a few months earlier had been calling for the resignation of the Senate majority leader. White was a great admirer of Johnson. He had written a book on the Senate that extolled Johnson's dominance over his Senate colleagues. When Johnson moved to the vice presidency and then into the presidency, White continued to enjoy an inner-circle rapport with him. After a meeting with the president, White had reported that the idea of Mansfield on the Democratic ticket was no mere self-serving Washington floater of the majority leader but had actually originated with Johnson. It was a plausible assertion, inasmuch as a Catholic Mansfield on the ticket would have provided insurance against criticism of Johnson's passing over Bobby Kennedy. White did not attribute the president's interest in Mansfield as a candidate to a reevaluation of the latter's capabilities after the successful passage of the civil rights legislation in the Senate. But that, too, was a possible motivation. Just as possible might have been a presidential desire to get Mansfield out of the leadership of the Senate and into the obscurity of the vice presidency from which he himself had just emerged. Several years after the election, Mansfield confirmed that the president had offered him the vice presidential nomination, and he had rejected it.

Such a rejection would not have been decisive if the president had been adamant in having Mansfield on the ticket. Johnson was well aware that Mansfield possessed a visceral inhibition against doing anything that might seem designed to enhance his personal political status. Years before, for example, the Montanan had, at first, resisted a Johnson proposal to make him majority whip but after some urging he had accepted the offer. The same resistance surfaced again when Johnson joined President Kennedy in pressing Mansfield to permit himself to be elected Senate majority leader. Confronted with an opportunity for political aggrandizement, such as most politicians would welcome, Mansfield's normal reaction was to fall back and wait, as though unsure that he had heard correctly. Over the years, this personal restraint that bordered on self-abnegation had been absorbed into his political stock in trade. So complete was the integration that it was impossible to separate the one from the other. The built-in reticence served to protect him from precipitate actions and set him apart from the eager scramblers for power so common in U.S. politics. Whatever else might have motivated his refusal, Mansfield had no intention of permitting himself to become one more puppet dancing at the end of a string in a Johnson puppet show.

In any event, the phone did not ring a second time for Mansfield on the vice presidential nomination. Instead, after maintaining silence about his preference until the eleventh hour, Johnson gave the convention's delegates a lift in spirit by selecting the man who was clearly their overwhelming favorite. He named Hubert H. Humphrey as his running mate and asked Mansfield to second the nomination. Whether disappointed or relieved, Mansfield complied without ever changing expression and then joined wholeheartedly in acclaiming Humphrey the ideal candidate.

Unlike Johnson, who enjoyed united Democratic support, his opponent in the 1964 election, Barry Goldwater of Arizona, was a controversial figure among Republicans. Goldwater's enthusiastic acceptance by the expanding but still feeble southern wing of the party hardly compensated for the alienation that he induced elsewhere in the Republican ranks. Goldwater's vote against cloture on the civil rights bill grated on such liberal Republicans as Jake Javits of New York and Tom Kuchel of California. Something of a loner, Goldwater waged a swaggering campaign against Johnson. Building on his fighter pilot service in World War II, Goldwater's speeches sounded as though he were itching to take on not only the Soviet Union but also Red China and any other communists that might be lurking in the shadows of the world. His fortissimo anticommunist approach to international affairs found a rapt audience among the frustrated armchair warriors of the right. It also met with acceptance from many World War II veterans and their contemporaries, who were beginning to populate the sun-filled retirement communities of Arizona, southern California, and Florida.

Lyndon Johnson took the road of caution in a campaign that contrasted sharply with Goldwater's tendency to shoot from the hip. Senate Democratic candidates followed Johnson's lead, staying close to the main themes of the convention in Atlantic City. They harkened back to the still vivid memory of John F. Kennedy while pumping up the promise of continuing peace and progress under the firm hand of President Lyndon B. Johnson. It was a sure-fire approach. Kennedy's political shrouds in death were a more powerful attraction to the American voter than his coattails had been in life. Even his erstwhile Republican detractors found it in their interest to praise the fallen hero or, at any rate, to speak no evil of the dead.

Major Campaign Issue: Vietnam

During the campaign, the sharpest divergence between Goldwater and Johnson came over Vietnam. At the time, the U.S. role in Vietnam was minimal, especially as compared with the military undertaking in Korea a decade earlier. Johnson passed off Vietnam as a relatively minor matter, well under control in his hands. By contrast, Goldwater, while supporting what was being done to stop communism in Southeast Asia, complained that the Democratic administration was pussyfooting and indecisive in handling the situation. To be sure, he did not go so far as to demand that President Johnson dispatch major U. S. military forces to Vietnam. Nor did he offer any other specific remedy, unless it was to stick out the nation's military chest further with the expectation that that would be enough to frighten the communists into collapsing. In short, he sought to create the impression that the Democrats were once again in the process of caving in to communism. As Goldwater framed the issue, it seemed more contrived than actual, and most of the voters in the 1964 election could not be persuaded to fix on it. Nevertheless, Goldwater persisted to the end in hammering at Vietnam. He sometimes sounded like a child who goes on raising the decibel level if an initial banging on pots and pans fails to evoke a sufficient response.

The Republican attempt to rewrite the "who lost China?" theme of two decades earlier into a new melodrama, "Who is about to lose Vietnam?" involved putting together a new cast of villains, this time headed by Ho Chi Minh, instead of Mao Zedong, and shifting the main setting from Beijing to Hanoi. The effort met with little success in the 1964 campaign, in part because the popular remembrance of the Chinese revolution was fading and the involvement in Vietnam was very limited. Moreover, scarcely a decade after the inconclusive war in Korea, Americans were still leery of any politician who seemed eager to take the nation on another military crusade in Asia. The popular inclination was to engage communism from afar with words while enjoying the affluent state of affairs within the nation.

With the public thus focused, the Democrats had little to fear from Vietnam as an issue in the 1964 election. Actually, they were able to go on the offensive against Goldwater, raising questions about his jet-jockey brashness, all the while extolling Johnson's mature restraint. Instead of Vietnam becoming central to the campaign, Goldwater himself was put on the spot.

To keep him there, Democrats devised a television commercial that was to become a classic in political campaigning. The opening frame of this paid-for advertisement showed a lovely child seated in a field of wind-rustled flowers on a sunny day. Smiling dreamily at the daisy she held in her hand, the little girl provided viewers with a winsome personification of the security and contentment of American life. In the next frame, however, this bucolic scene was obliterated by the mushroom cloud of a detonated nuclear bomb. The sequence of horror devastating innocent bliss was linked by implication to a trigger-happy Barry Goldwater. The commercial made what was perceived to be the sharp contrast between the two candidates come alive for the nation. Johnson emerged as the defender of America's peace and contentment. Three decades later, the commercial stands as a milestone in the progressive corrosion of politics by television commercialization.

The Democratic victory in the 1964 election was a signal for a sweeping change of personnel in the Johnson administration. Ted Sorenson, who had drafted Kennedy speeches for many years and stayed on to help Johnson in the transition, moved out of the White House. In his place came such

Johnson phrase makers as Horace Busby, Harry McPherson, George Reedy, and Bill Moyers. At the same time, other new faces were emerging at an accelerated pace throughout the administration, bringing with them changes in policy. Soon the key Kennedy carryovers dwindled to McGeorge Bundy and Walt Rostow in the White House, with Robert McNamara remaining as secretary of defense and Dean Rusk as secretary of state.

By contrast, few changes took place in the Senate in the aftermath of the election. The principal impact there was one of consolidation. Most of the Senate leaders in both parties were returned to office with their prestige greatly enhanced. Particularly noteworthy, Republican Leader Everett Dirksen won reelection in Illinois despite a Johnson landslide in the state. Among the Democrats, the party leadership, including the committee chairmenships, was little affected. Mansfield himself was chosen by acclamation for a third term as majority leader in a Senate already attuned to his style of leadership. The outpouring of Democratic support for Mansfield was not surprising inasmuch as few politicians are inclined to quarrel with success, and the Senate Democrats had been successful beyond their expectations in the 1964 elections.

The election did leave a vacancy in the Senate Democratic leadership hierarchy under Mansfield. With Hubert Humphrey moving to the vice-presidency, a new Democratic whip had to be named by the Democratic caucus. As majority leader, Lyndon Johnson would have filled such a vacancy by designating a replacement with routine confirmation by the caucus; Mansfield himself had been chosen Democratic whip by Johnson and, in turn, had been succeeded by Humphrey by the same procedure. It seemed, then, a foregone conclusion that John O. Pastore of Rhode Island would be the new assistant leader. Pastore had been one of Mansfield's strongest supporters, giving him cooperation and full support at the low point of his leadership. Mansfield had handpicked Pastore to deliver the keynote address at the Democratic National Convention in 1964, an opportunity that had turned the former Rhode Island governor into a national political figure overnight. No name other than Pastore had surfaced in the media as successor to Humphrey.

When Pastore returned from Atlantic City, it was with the tumultuous applause of the delegates still ringing in his ears. Outgoing by nature and buoyed even more by his success at the convention, Pastore made no secret of his interest in the Humphrey vacancy. Indeed, the press had all but named him to the post and Senate colleagues were already patting him on the back in congratulation. Pressed by the media to confirm its expectation, Mansfield's reply was unexpected. He reminded the media that the caucus had the power to elect all party officers, and while it was his intention to endorse any incumbents already in the leadership for a two-year term, he would remain neutral in the case of a contested vacancy because it was not his intention to seek to usurp the electoral function of the caucus. He underscored the point by making clear that the election of the assistant leader would be by secret ballot.

Russell Long of Louisiana was quick to take Mansfield at his word and began actively to solicit support of his candidacy for assistant leader. Pastore was caught by surprise by Mansfield's decision not to intervene and could only concur in its technical correctness. Russell Long, chairman of the Finance Committee, won the contest easily. While he never complained openly, Pastore was humiliated by the defeat, and his irritation with the majority leader remained evident until his retirement from the Senate.

The reasons for Mansfield's refusal to name a preference as a replacement for Humphrey perplexed many observers. Some regarded his silence as a way of dealing with the continuing intraparty struggle between southerners and northerners; had Pastore been selected by Mansfield, southerners would have been excluded from the top leadership of the party. Others regarded the majority leader's reticence as a dodge to keep himself out of the line of fire in an intraparty struggle. More likely, Mansfield's refusal to dictate a choice for whip was another reflection of his avowed determination to continue the divestiture of personal power as the majority leader, an integral part of his approach to leadership. Mansfield persisted in the approach, remaining aloof from intraparty contests for the remainder of his tenure. The practice went further perhaps than he had anticipated. Contested elections became commonplace not only when vacancies occurred but whenever there appeared to be a possibility of toppling an incumbent. Four years after his victory over Pastore, for example, Russell Long was challenged and unseated by Ted Kennedy. In turn, Kennedy was defeated by Robert C. Byrd of West Virginia, who served as assistant leader until Mansfield's retirement in 1976.

With many new faces coming into the Senate in the 1966 midterm elections, the democratization of party procedures was extended by Mansfield to include a final say by the caucus on the Democratic designees to the standing committees of the Senate. Such assignments continued to be made in the first instance by the Democratic Steering Committee, largely on the basis of seniority. Mansfield insisted, however, that the committee's lists be subject to actual confirmation by secret ballot in the caucus. This procedural adjustment served as a pointed reminder that all assignments to committees, including the designation of chairmen, were not preordained on the basis of seniority. Nor did the power to make the final selections rest with either the majority leader or the Steering Committee. The power of assignment rested in the end with the party caucus. In this instance, Mansfield provided a unique opportunity to curb the rigidity of the seniority system. It opened the door to the establishment of other criteria for making committee assignments. Despite perennial complaints about the seniority system, however, particularly from younger members, none was prepared to bell the cat. Thereafter, no slate prepared by the Democratic Steering Committee and presented by Mansfield for confirmation was ever challenged by the caucus. That is not to say that the exercise was meaningless. If it had no other value, it did quell carping criticism regarding committee assignments. It also made clear that if the Democratic senators chose to accept the Steering Committee's proposed committee assignments, that was their choice, not the majority leader's. At the same time, it provided a sobering reminder to committee chairmen and other senior members that they did not hold their assignments by Divine Right of Seniority but were accountable to the party caucus.

With organizational preliminaries completed, Congress assembled in Joint Session on 3 January 1965 to hear the State of the Union message. Johnson delivered a speech to the new Congress that differed markedly from his previous statements as fill-in president after the assassination. There was no mistaking it; Johnson was out from under the Kennedy shadow. Whereas previously he had stressed continuity with his predecessor, now his references to Kennedy, while respectful, were brief. His resounding victory over Goldwater had cleared the way for him to put his own brand on the incoming administration. In doing so, however, the president did not revert to the style he used when Senate majority leader; there was none of the endearing cornpone of the shirtsleeve Texas politician or the glibness of the wily legislative activist. Instead, it was as though a new Johnson meant to aspire to the heights of presidential statesmanship. It was a Johnson with vision, a populist vision to be sure, but a vision of a "Great Society" into which he would seek to transform the nation. The foundations of this Great Society might rest on Roosevelt's New Deal. The details to a large extent might be found in draft legislation already prepared by Kennedy's intellectuals for the New Frontier. But the whole would be cast in a kind of Olympian vision. Johnson's approach would be charismatic, bold, and steeped in what was an almost religious fervor.

To the extent that he dwelt on international questions, he also struck a new note. His call for aid to foreign nations was presented as a sort of worldwide outreach of the Great Society and no bones were made about its applying only to those who accepted American leadership. Moreover, for those nations who might oppose us, there was a kind of snarled warning, like the North Carolina revolutionary flag that unfurls a rattlesnake poised to strike and containing the caption "Don't tread on me."

The situation in Vietnam that had figured so prominently in the election campaign was scarcely mentioned in the Inaugural Address. But Lyndon Johnson had already reset the course in Vietnam in a direction, unfortunately for him, that would lead to the destruction of his presidency. Unfortunately for the nation, it would inflict extensive damage on the U.S. economy, compound the difficulties of racial integration, and polarize the American people between "hawks and doves." These and other damaging repercussions would be reflected in U.S. politics for many years. As his White House incumbency drew to a close, Johnson would rue the fact that he was not going to be remembered so much for civil rights or the Great Society. These accomplishments were overshadowed by popular disillusionment with the war into which he was about to lead the nation, and in the end he would find himself with the albatross of "Vietnam President" hung round his neck.

The Beginning of the American Involvement in Vietnam

What precipitated his fatal decision on Vietnam was a naval incident off the Indochinese peninsula. Just as the presidential election campaign began to gather momentum, the Pentagon alerted the White House to what was described as an attack on two U.S. naval vessels in the Gulf of Tonkin. Neither damage nor casualties were reported as resulting from the attack. Indeed, a formal Senate inquiry into the incident months later cast doubt on whether it was even an attack that had taken place, although the investigators stopped short of saying that the incident had been manufactured. In any event, there was no doubt that the U.S. warships were cruising close to North Vietnamese coastal fortifications in the vicinity of the city of Haiphong, which contained a major military base of the Vietminh and served as the seaport for Hanoi. Although the U.S. military was not directly involved in the fighting in Vietnam at the time, substantial military assistance was being supplied to the south by the United States. In the circumstances, the U.S. naval sail-by could hardly have been categorized as a courtesy visit. Its purpose, apparently, had something to do with showing the U.S. flag to the North Vietnamese to discourage them from interfering with freedom of the high seas. Johnson decided that a firm expression of displeasure was called for. He ordered an aerial bombing of north Vietnamese coastal fortifications. The attack marked the first time that U.S. military forces had acted directly against North Vietnam, a course that President Eisenhower had firmly rejected a decade earlier and one that Kennedy had avoided.

Immediately after ordering the bombing, Johnson called on congressional leaders to reinforce his message to Hanoi. He asked both houses for a formal resolution drafted by the administration stating that Congress approved of the action and asserting that peace in Southeast Asia was vital to our national interests. At the time, there was wide congressional acceptance of the president's verbal assurances that the resolution would not involve an expansion of the U.S. involvement in Vietnam but, on the contrary, would help to forestall it.

In the House of Representatives, Speaker McCormack applauded Johnson for his firmness, and the resolution passed immediately by a unanimous vote. Although somewhat less enthusiastic, the Senate was not disposed to take too much time for deliberation. The proposed resolution was rushed through the Foreign Relations Committee with minimal discussion and, with the concurrence of the majority leader, was taken at once by Chairman Fulbright to the Senate floor.

In the outpouring of congressional support for the president, a discordant note came from Wayne Morse of Oregon. For months, Morse had been criticizing the U.S. aid-involvement in Vietnam, limited though it was. Like a voice crying in the wilderness, Morse had been prophesying that the nation was headed into an undeclared war. Ernest Gruening of Alaska concurred with Morse in opposing the Tonkin Gulf Resolution, and Wisconsin's Gaylord Nelson expressed his concern about the deepening of the involvement implicit in the resolution. These three senators were alone in raising a warning flag. As for the majority leader, Mansfield had sought on previous occasions to focus attention on the realities of Indochina and the dangers of a military involvement. But in spite of personal doubts, when the Tonkin Gulf Resolution came before the Senate, he joined Chairman Fulbright in supporting the president, both accepting Johnson's assurances that the proposed resolution was to be regarded simply as an expression of national unity at a moment of foreign challenge. Other senators also harbored reservations, but they guarded their silence either out of a sense of loyalty to President Johnson or because they felt something ought to be done to stop communism in Asia. Still others applauded the resolution as an "it's about time" assertion of our military might against upstart nations that would "kick us around."

The Senate was comfortable with the idea of standing behind the president as commander in chief in the face of what was presumed to be a military challenge. In truth, like most Americans at the time, senators knew very little about Vietnam and Indochina. Before the Tonkin Gulf incident, few had voiced much interest in the region. They were disinclined to second-guess the executive branch, especially when it was acting against "communist aggression." They had no reason to doubt Johnson's assurances that the resolution would not widen existing U.S. involvement in

Vietnam. In truth, they did not appear to attach great importance to what they were being asked to vote on, nor were they encouraged to do so by the administration. For the most part, they regarded the resolution as a show of unity that called attention to America's military might in the hope of causing the communists to have second thoughts. With a national election fast approaching, they were inclined simply to give the president what he wanted and get to the political hustings as quickly as possible. After a brief floor debate, therefore, the Senate joined the House in passing the Tonkin Gulf Resolution, with only Morse and Gruening voting "nay."

Whatever Congress may have thought it was doing, the administration knew what was being sought in the resolution. More was being asked than a "rally round the flag" at a time of a presumed crisis. Later, the president and his advisors would read into the resolution not only an endorsement of Johnson's handling of the Tonkin incident but also legislative support for whatever military follow-through might be necessary to underscore it. Subsequently, the administration would use the resolution as something of a postdated declaration of war, tantamount to advance approval for whatever further military commitments might be necessary.

Many members of Congress professed shock at the administration's interpretation. Had they remembered the Korean experience a decade earlier, they would not have been shocked. After World War II, it had become fashionable in foreign policy circles to regard a formal congressional declaration of war as an anachronism. In the face of the anxieties generated by nuclear weapons, the president's constitutional powers to make war had come to be seen as virtually unlimited. That view was tested in dealing with the North Korean invasion of South Korea. On that occasion, without any prior notification to Congress, President Truman had ordered U.S. armed forces to support the Seoul government in resisting the attack. His order was at first limited to the use of U.S. naval and air forces. When that quickly proved insufficient, Truman expanded the military commitment to include U.S. ground forces under General Douglas MacArthur's command. Korea quickly became an American war in every sense except that it lacked a formal declaration by Congress.

Notwithstanding Johnson's assurances to Congress on its limited purposes, the bombarding of the Haiphong fortifications served notice on Hanoi that the United States was deepening its commitment and that henceforth the communists might expect to confront not only Saigon's forces but also the military might of the United States if they persisted in their "aggression" against the south. Previously, Washington had refrained from defining its role in Indochina as that of a military participant. Part fiction, perhaps, the maintenance of this official position in both Democratic and

Republican administrations had helped to confine the Vietnamese conflict to an on-again, off-again guerrilla war in the south involving only Vietnamese.

Johnson's decision to deepen the U.S. role in response to the Tonkin Gulf incident was in line with a widely held view in the United States at the time. The view was that unless the United States intervened militarily, what had happened in China would be repeated again and again in Asia, that is, other governments would collapse in succession into communism. Under this so-called domino theory, if South Vietnam were to fall to "communist aggression," the other states of Indochina would follow. In turn, additional southeastern nations such as Thailand, Malaysia, Singapore, and Indonesia would then fall "like dominos," until all of east Asia was absorbed into the communist monolith. Just precisely what made the communists so irresistible or exactly how far the United States should go in trying to keep "the cork in the bottle" was rarely specified. Only the most passionate of anti-communists went so far as to say outright that the United States should even use nuclear weapons, if necessary, to stop the advance of communism in Asia. More commonly, the American role, as projected in this concept, seemed to have something to do with providing vast amounts of encouragement and other aid, especially military aid, to any self-proclaimed noncommunist political elements that could be found in the region. Most of all, it was necessary for the United States to stop trying to negotiate settlements and instead "stand up to the communists." Presumably, if this country assumed the proper stance, it would strike enough terror in the communists to make them fall down or, at least, back off.

So pervasive was this view in U.S. politics at the time that it obscured the inner determinants of political developments in Southeast Asian societies. These included Asian revulsion with the remnants of pre–World War II colonialism and the attempts by European colonialists to regain their political and economic footholds in the region in the wake of the withdrawal of the defeated Japanese. Also overlooked were outdated indigenous institutions that had been tolerated or even reinforced under colonialism and had managed to survive the Japanese occupation. Ignored, too, were gaping economic and social inequities within the Asian societies that had grown even wider during World War II. Most significant was the failure of U.S. policy to come to terms effectively with an emergent nationalism. This sentiment, particularly passionate among Asian youth, contained a powerful undercurrent of antiforeignism. After World War II, it was so strong that even well-intentioned activities of Western nations in the region became highly suspect.

Oblivious to these elements in Asian attitudes, Johnson may well have seen his decision on the Tonkin Gulf incident as nothing more than one

more increment in a long-standing commitment to communist contain-
ment in Indochina. Whether he realized it or not, however, the U.S. air
attack on the Haiphong installations represented a quantum jump in involvement. To be sure, under his predecessors, Truman, Eisenhower, and
Kennedy, there had been increments added from time to time in the form
of increased aid to those resisting communism. But after the Korean
War, both Democratic and Republican administrations had assiduously
avoided direct military participation in the various struggles on the
Asian mainland. Indeed, except in immediate self-defense, the use of any
sort of weapons by U.S. personnel in Vietnam had been ruled out. Eisenhower had said no when the Pentagon proposed U.S. carrier-based air
strikes against the Asian mainland. And even Kennedy's dashing "Green
Berets" were not supposed to be direct death dealers, their official role
being confined to that of trainers and advisors to the South Vietnamese
armed forces.

Whether he realized it or not, then, Johnson's handling of the Tonkin
Gulf affair marked a fundamental shift in policy. The bombardment of the
Haiphong fortifications was the first clear-cut military initiative undertaken
by U.S. forces in the Vietnamese conflict and the first extension of the war
into North Vietnam after the departure of the French. For Vietnamese, both
north and south, the decision was tantamount to an announcement that the
United States would intervene militarily to make its will prevail in Indochina. Certainly, Ho Chi Minh and the Vietminh in Hanoi understood that
to be the case. Nor is there any reason to doubt that Johnson intended the
incident to be understood in any other way.

Johnson had long been persuaded that a bristling confrontation with the
communists in Indochina was the right approach. This conviction came from
an oversimplified version of the situation that, in turn, was derived from his
limited experience with foreign affairs. Throughout his legislative career,
Johnson had shown only passing interest in the subject. While in the House,
the closest Johnson had ever come to Asia was a visit to the South Pacific
theater of operations during World War II. As a senator, he usually went
along with the prevailing generalities in matters of foreign relations; with
Truman and then Eisenhower in the White House, he accepted the practice of
"bipartisanship" then in vogue. As majority leader, Johnson spoke of the
chairman of the Foreign Relations Committee, William Fulbright, as "my
secretary of state" and expressed his admiration for Assistant Majority
Leader Mansfield's knowledge of foreign affairs. On defense-laden international questions, he followed the lead of Senator Russell, chairman of the
Armed Services Committee. Johnson took care of Texan economic interests
in defense appropriations and worked with Senator Kerr of Oklahoma on

setting up a space program and in securing federal funds for the lucrative race to make it better than that of the Russians. As if to round out his image, he sponsored the establishment of the East-West Center, a largely federally supported intellectual center at the University of Hawaii designed to promote understanding and friendship among the Pacific Rim nations.

As vice-president, Johnson appeared convinced that the United States had to resist what he saw as the march of communism into Southeast Asia. Otherwise, as he propounded to friendly Asian leaders, "If we don't stop them in Indochina, we will have to stop them in California." His bypassing of Hawaii in this manner appeared to be an unintentional oversight rather than a desire to read out of the union a state that had only recently gained statehood, thanks in part to his effort as Senate majority leader. During another flight of rhetoric, in a conversation with the prime minister of Thailand on how communism was to be dealt with, Johnson likened communism to a bonfire and asked rhetorically: "And how do you handle a bonfire?" When the prime minister's response was a blank stare, Johnson answered his own question: "You do it by taking out your hose and putting out the fire. That's how you do it." Whereupon he yanked with both hands at an imaginary hose of substantial size in the vicinity of his crotch and aimed an imaginary stream of water at high pressure in a looping arch over the heads of the numerous aides seated in a horseshoe around the principles, causing some to duck reflexively. The face of the Thai prime minister lit up with comprehension, and he greeted the explanation with grunts of approval even before the Thai interpreter could find words to convey its meaning.

These incidents occurred during Johnson's first direct exposure to Asia, when in May 1961 President Kennedy asked him to undertake a mission to Southeast Asia. While Johnson was in Southeast Asia, stories appeared in the press at home suggesting that Johnson's uncouth antics were regarded as damaging the U.S. image in Asia. Uncouth or not, Johnson's swing through the region added the authentic color of political populism in the United States to his mission, and the response to him personally was clearly a favorable one. The problem with the future president's mission, was not so much with Johnson's exuberant political style. The serious flaw was that his campaigning against communism did nothing to open his eyes to the complexities of the transition then in progress in Southeast Asia. The Southeast Asian leaders were not inclined to disabuse Johnson of the oversimplifications. As for U.S. diplomatic and military personnel in the region assigned to brief Johnson, they tended to reinforce his snapshot view of Southeast Asia. Among the professionals, Johnson's style created the strong impression that what he really sought was not so much advice but confirmation of conclusions he had already reached. To what extent Johnson's subsequent course in Vietnam grew out of "facts" found in this fashion can only be conjectured. What is certain is that Johnson, as vice-president, already shared the prevailing view of many Americans that the advance of communism in Asia could be turned back by little more than a combination of greater emphasis on military aid to anticommunist governments, a greater show of U.S. determination to stand by anticommunist elements, and a brandishing of U.S. military power in the region. Johnson received little advice to the contrary from American officials in Southeast Asia.

Kennedy sent other missions to Vietnam, and their findings did not differ greatly from Johnson's except in how much additional support would be necessary. One such group, headed by General Maxwell Taylor, a trusted military advisor, assured the president that a prompt expansion of U.S. aid, coupled with political and economic reforms undertaken by the Vietnamese government, could lead to a victory in South Vietnam without the necessity of a U.S. takeover of the war. As a form of insurance, Taylor recommended sending an additional 8,000 U.S. troops to Vietnam to help train the Vietnamese forces and to serve as a demonstration of U.S. power and commitment. By the time Johnson succeeded to the presidency, his predecessor had already raised the total of U.S. military personnel in South Vietnam to 15,000, a fifteen-fold increase over the maximum of 1,000 that Eisenhower had permitted. This precipitous growth, however, had failed to make a dent in the communist position in South Vietnam. The fundamentals in the situation remained the same. The standoff strongly suggested that the road ahead would grow more, not less, difficult for the United States, a reality that appears not to have registered on Johnson prior to his assuming the presidency.

The clamor for more U.S. involvement in Indochina rose under President Kennedy, its echoes reaching the Senate. There it encountered the reticence of the majority leader. Mike Mansfield was eminently equipped to provide leadership to the Senate in confronting the problems that were gathering in Southeast Asia. His authority as majority leader had been confirmed in 1962 by his reelection by the Democratic caucus after the mid-point general elections during Kennedy's presidency. Moreover, he enjoyed the respect and trust not only of his Democratic colleagues but also of the Republican minority whose leader, Everett Dirksen, had just been reelected. Mansfield had learned much of both the potential and limits of the Senate's powers in the federal system and of his own role as majority leader, particularly in dealing with international issues.

As a former teacher of Far Eastern history, moreover, Mansfield maintained a continuing interest in developments in Asia. He had a personal exposure to Asia, having served in the U.S. military in the region before

World War II. Moreover, he had served on the Foreign Affairs Committee in the House of Representatives and had been entrusted with a special one-man mission to China during the Truman administration. Like other politicians after World War II, he had personally felt the impact of the victorious Chinese Communist Revolution on politics in the United States and had become extremely circumspect in dealing with any matter touching on China.

With regard to the Vietnamese problem, Mansfield had a special claim on the attention of his colleagues. Soon after his election to the Senate in 1952, Mansfield set about familiarizing himself firsthand with the situation. He traveled widely in Indochina in 1953, and again in 1954 and 1955, visiting Vietnam, Cambodia, and Laos, and reporting his findings through the Foreign Relations Committee to his Senate colleagues. Mansfield's emergence in later years as a leading questioner of U.S. policy on Vietnam was rooted in these and subsequent missions to Indochina undertaken at the request of Presidents Kennedy, Johnson, and Nixon.

What Mansfield learned, first and foremost, from these travels was that the American awareness of what was transpiring in Asia lagged perilously behind the reality. He found, for example, that three tides of nationalism—Vietnamese, Cambodian, and Laotian—were rising in the region in the aftermath of the withdrawal of the defeated Japanese. To the extent that these movements were united, it was in a common determination to prevent the return of the pre–World War II colonial system. He saw, too, that the French military was engaged primarily in attempting to hold back these tides in order to reassert France's political dominance over the entirety of Indochina. Mansfield was skeptical of this attempt and what amounted to U.S. back-door cooperation with it via a military aid program routed through the French, ostensibly to help develop noncommunist forces. This aid program had been initiated by President Truman and his secretary of state, Dean Acheson, and was enlarged by the successor Eisenhower administration. It consisted mainly of the transfer of surplus World War II military equipment and supplies to the French military and, subsequently, to the Vietnamese.

When the attempt to regain control of Indochina was defeated at the disastrous Battle of Dien Bien Phu in 1954, the French agreed at the first Geneva Conference to withdraw from Indochina. Faced with the need to redesign U.S. policy, the one alternative that the Eisenhower administration found inadmissible was to come to terms with the communist-led Vietminh revolutionaries. As a practical matter then, Secretary of State John Foster Dulles was left with only two choices. On the one hand, the United States might have to cut loose entirely from the situation by ending the aid program and closing down what was then a small U.S. mission in Saigon where what was left of the resistance to the communist-led Vietminh was gathering. Alternatively, an attempt might be made by the United States to put together a noncommunist government in Saigon to take over from the departing French. This alternative offered a slim chance of establishing a noncommunist political structure for South Vietnam that would be able to keep the "cork in the bottle" against the further spread of communism. Dulles won Eisenhower's support for the second alternative. It was a course that required a continuance of a U.S. aid program, redirected from the French to Vietnamese nationalists but one that did not contemplate direct U.S. military intervention.

In Congress, the Eisenhower administration's approach drew the support of the Republicans. As for the Democrats, they were no more ready than the Republicans to urge a complete U.S. withdrawal. Hence, they had little choice but to go along with Eisenhower and Dulles. To buttress the administration's position with Congress, Dulles sought a channel of communication to the Democrats. The then Senate majority leader, Lyndon Johnson, had little interest in Asian affairs and, in any case, was preoccupied in trading rebuffs with President Eisenhower over which party was responsible for the failure to balance the national budget. In Dulles's eyes, Chairman J. William Fulbright of the Foreign Relations Committee was not a suitable channel of contact to the Democrats; Fulbright had shown little interest in cooperating with Republicans on Indochina and did little to conceal the low esteem in which he held John Foster Dulles.

As for the other members of the committee, only Mansfield had shown serious concern with Indochina. The secretary was persuaded that Mansfield's overall approach to foreign policy was free from extreme partisanship; indeed, the senator had even expressed on the Senate floor a sympathetic appreciation for the travails of Secretary of State Dulles.

In 1954 Dulles invited Mansfield, then the lowest-ranking Democrat on the Senate Foreign Relations Committee, to join him in Manila in signing a Southeast Asian defense treaty. The relationship between the two was cooperative. Mansfield's advice was sought and given, notably in the selection of a Vietnamese nationalist, Ngo Dinh Diem, to receive U.S. support in heading up a noncommunist government in Saigon. Mansfield had advised and then fully supported U.S. diplomatic recognition of nationalist governments in Cambodia and Laos, as well as South Vietnam as legitimate successors to the collapsed French colonial structure in Indochina.

From the point of view of the Eisenhower administration, that was a sufficient adjustment of U.S. policy for the region. It was far better certainly than a direct U.S. military involvement to hold back the communist

Vietminh operating out of Hanoi or the alternative of doing nothing in the face of communist success against the French, thus permitting the whole of Indochina to be absorbed into the communist maw. Thereafter, in Washington, references to "toppling dominos" and popping the "cork in the bottle in Southeast Asia" receded, and in Hanoi, the talk was of the U.S. replacement for the French colonialists.

With some trepidation, Congress went along with the new Eisenhower-Dulles policy, voting increased but still modest aid to help the three emergent nation-states in Indochina to establish themselves. New U.S. aid missions were joined to the new U.S. embassies in Laos and Cambodia. In Saigon, the United States extended aid to a new Vietnamese nationalist government, while a small U.S. military aid group began to supply the nationalist armed forces of South Vietnam.

During the remainder of the Eisenhower administration, that was about as far as the U.S. involvement went in the standoff between the rival Vietnamese governments in Hanoi and Saigon. There were no challenges to Hanoi from Washington, and any use of firearms by the American military was strictly limited to self-defense. U.S. personnel found themselves free to move about with minimal precautions in Saigon and other southern cities. Vietcong guerrilla raids on the small U.S. installations in the south were rare and were not regarded as justification for a deeper U.S. involvement. The Eisenhower administration, in short, showed itself ready to stop communism in Vietnam by the proxy of aid programs but not by direct U.S. military intervention.

With the situation reasonably stable, Congress seemed to lose the interest in Indochina that had been aroused briefly by the French collapse. After Ngo Dinh Diem's installation as president of South Vietnam, Mansfield stayed in touch with the situation, his ear frequently sought by those concerned with Indochina. He listened to the various viewpoints but generally upheld the approach of the Eisenhower administration.

Shortly after Kennedy's inauguration, the new administration was greeted with a coup d'état in Laos. It was perpetrated by a Lao general with ties to the U.S. mission in the capital of Vientianne. The civilian prime minister, Prince Souvanna Phouma, was compelled to leave the country hurriedly, and the king remained closeted in the Royal Palace in Luang Prabhang. The coup provoked a threat of invasion of Laos from North Vietnam, and Kennedy sent a small U.S. military detachment to northern Thailand as a precaution. At the same time, he agreed to refer the problems brought on by the coup to a second Geneva Conference, this time with the United States as an active participant. The conference produced a solution based on neutralization of Laos, the return of

Souvanna Phouma as prime minister, and the stationing of an international peacekeeping team in Laos.

No sooner had the Laotian crisis been quieted in this fashion when reports began to reach President Kennedy of increased guerrilla activity against the Diem government in South Vietnam. There were also other indications that the Hanoi government, having concluded that Diem would not participate in an all-Vietnamese election as provided for in the first Geneva Accords, had decided to use military force to take over the south. These ominous developments revived concerns in the United States about the communist threat in Indochina. They were concerns, moreover, that were underscored by Vice-President Johnson's mission to Southeast Asia in 1961 and his outspoken support for increased military aid to South Vietnam. Like Eisenhower before him, Kennedy was not disposed to take a chance on another "Who lost China?" syndrome. He reacted by affirming strong U.S. support for an independent South Vietnam and dispatching special missions to evaluate the situation.

A consensus of serious doubt concerning the capabilities of the Diem government took hold of the Kennedy administration. The administration concluded that the situation in Vietnam called for something more than a further loosening of the purse strings of the aid program. To be sure, more U.S. aid was offered, but it was now coupled with an insistence that Diem accept additional U.S. personnel in Vietnam and give the U.S. military establishment a greater training role in regard to Saigon's armed services. Washington also insisted that internal reforms be undertaken in the Saigon government, reforms that hinted strongly at the need to restrain the influence of Ngo Dinh Diem's relatives. One relative, the Roman Catholic bishop of Hue, visiting the United States at the time, sought out the Senate majority leader. In addition to conveying personal greetings from Ngo Dinh Diem, he informed Mansfield that Diem's inclination had been to reject the proffered increase in U.S. aid rather than accept the proposed expansion of the U.S. role in Saigon's affairs. He ascribed Diem's reluctance to go along with Washington's conditions to a growing fear of compromising his nationalist credentials among his own people and being dismissed by them as a puppet of the United States. Nevertheless, the bishop assured Mansfield that after an all-night discussion, he had convinced Diem to accept the conditions.

The bishop's account suggests that the growth of the U.S. role in Vietnam that took place during the Kennedy years was hardly a response to desperate pleas from Diem for more U.S. help. Instead, it suggests that the expansion of the U.S. involvement was largely generated in Washington based on assessments of the Vietnamese situation within the Kennedy administration, including those of the U.S. Embassy in Saigon as well as the Johnson and other missions dispatched by the president. Taken together, they portrayed a South Vietnam in imminent danger of collapsing into communist hands unless the United States did something substantially more than it was doing to change the odds in favor of Saigon.

In any event, as Eisenhower had before him, President Kennedy was confronted by his advisors with the unthinkable—Vietnam falling to the communists and then the rest of Southeast Asia following suit. Finding himself face to face with this political specter, Kennedy responded by increasing the aid program and enlarging both the U.S. military presence and the scope of its functions in Vietnam. With the dispatch of several thousand Green Berets, the commitment of Americans to military involvement was brought very close to a point of no return; that is, of direct U.S. participation in the fighting and, hence, deep responsibility for the outcome of the conflict. In following this course, President Kennedy received praise from both Democrats and Republicans in Congress and virtually no opposition from the press. For President Diem, the rapid expansion of the American role had serious consequences. As he had feared, it tarnished his aura of uncompromising nationalism among his own people, lending credence to Hanoi's charge that he was a tool of the United States for reintroducing colonialism. Moreover, it suggested to the South Vietnamese military that Diem as president was no longer an indispensable funnel for the flow of U.S. assistance. The more U.S. personnel became directly involved with South Vietnamese military leaders, the more the latter were convinced that the United States would sustain South Vietnam with or without Diem as president. As a result, they felt freer to indulge in their contempt for Diem, his ubiquitous family, and his close civilian advisors. Largely French educated, the Saigon generals adjusted readily to a growing intimacy with the U.S. military advisors and trainers who were appearing in ever-increasing numbers. Indeed, they found a sympathetic ear when venting their frustrations with the presidential palace.

While not necessarily encouraging a shift of loyalty away from Diem, U.S. officials in South Vietnam did not discourage it. The U.S. mission in Saigon at the time was particularly concerned with the role of Diem's younger brother, Ngo Dinh Nhu. Viewed as the president's alter ego, Nhu and his wife exercised great power in palace circles. They were in disfavor at the U.S. mission, particularly, for interposing themselves between the president and key Vietnamese on the one hand and U.S. officials in Saigon on the other. Moreover, Ngo Dinh Nhu was suspected of opening contacts with Hanoi leaders, seeking an arrangement between the north and south as an alternative to U.S. aid. Many American officials in Saigon were convinced not only of Nhu's incompetence but also of the reliability of his anticommunism. As time went on, the U.S. mission found it increasingly difficult to work with him or around him. His wife, Mme. Nhu, was widely regarded as an evil influence who dominated the bachelor president and affairs within the presidential palace. Mme. Nhu lent credence to her critics when she chose to mock the immolation of several Buddhist priests who set fire to themselves on the streets of Saigon. The sacrificial suicides were pictured widely in the Western press as a protest against the Diem government. In reaction, Mme. Nhu insisted on applauding the fiery deaths of the priests and expressed her disdainful delight with "barbecued monk." The American public was shocked by the juxtaposition of these ill-chosen words and gruesome photos of Buddhist priests seated with crossed legs, engulfed in flames. It was a dramatic factor in raising doubts about the Diem government and acted to facilitate the public acceptance of its overthrow.

Mansfield's Trip to Indochina and Its Consequences

The deteriorating situation in Vietnam prompted Mansfield to return to Indochina in late 1962. Informed of his intention, Kennedy requested that the majority leader proceed as a presidential emissary, accompanied by a small Senate group. Mansfield agreed and chose as participants in the mission Claiborne Pell of Rhode Island, later chairman of the Foreign Relations Committee; Ben Smith of Massachusetts, a close friend of the President who was serving out his unexpired Senate term; Ed Muskie of Maine, later secretary of state; and Cal Boggs of Delaware, a highly respected Republican. None had previously been to Indochina, and Mansfield arranged for extensive briefings of the group by the State Department, the U.S. embassies, and local leaders in the three Indochinese states. Seeking independent evaluations, Mansfield met confidentially with American journalists in Saigon and others outside official circles for informal exchanges of views.

Comparing his observations with his previous experiences in Indochina, Mansfield found that only in Cambodia were there encouraging prospects for realizing the original Eisenhower policy of building stable and independent governments in the three Indochinese states by aiding indigenous noncommunist political leaders. Under Prince Norodom Sihanouk's highly personalized leadership, Cambodia had emerged from a backwater of colonialism into a modernizing state with a strong sense of cultural unity, relatively free from the ideological bitterness that plagued its neighbors in Indochina. Sihanouk also had been successful in steering a course of neutrality among the conflicting pressures bearing down from Vietnam, both north and south, and from Thailand to the west. With the agility of a ballet dancer, he had fended off the embrace of both the Soviet Union and the United States designed to pull Cambodia in one-sided directions. In time, however, he found developments, particularly insistence on greater involvement in the anticommunist crusade from Washington, moving beyond his control. At that point, Sihanouk rejected further U.S. aid and chose to break diplomatic ties with the United States rather than change his policy of trying to keep Cambodia neutral.

Mansfield respected the prince's refusal to be shaken out of that course, not only because it appeared to be working for his country but also because Cambodia's neutralism might have conceivably served as a model for other nations in the region, as an alternative to the costly and bloody confrontations with communism. There were indications that President Kennedy also had begun to consider neutrality among Southeast Asian states as an acceptable alternative to rigid anticommunism as a course better attuned to U.S. interests in the region. When the threat of expanding war developed in Laos, for example, he dispatched Averell Harriman to a second Geneva conference. Harriman, a former governor of New York and a prominent figure in American diplomacy during several Democratic administrations, met with representatives of the Soviet Union and China and worked out an agreement to neutralize the remote kingdom. Kennedy chose to accept the agreement rather than pursue the alternative course, that of direct U.S. military intervention to "save" Laos from the communists. Although the agreement was later largely ignored, it did forestall a U.S. military involvement for the balance of Kennedy's presidency.

On his presidential mission to Indochina, Mansfield was most disturbed by the situation in Vietnam. On the one hand, his meetings in Saigon with President Diem gave him no cause to alter his earlier impression of the president as a dedicated Vietnamese nationalist. On the other hand, he perceived what he took to be a change in Diem's alertness. It was as though the Vietnam president had atrophied in his past political achievements and was losing touch with what was taking place in the power structure in Saigon. While Diem's condition was troubling, Mansfield came back from Vietnam still regarding Diem as the linchpin of U.S. policy. The implications of his findings were clear: if a viable noncommunist government could not be built during the Diem presidency, U.S. interests might better be served by beginning to look for the least painful way out of Vietnam. What Mansfield saw happening in Vietnam was the reverse.

Within the U.S. mission in Saigon, many were growing impatient with Diem, but few were suggesting that the alternative for the United States was finding a way out of Vietnam. Instead, U.S. officials were becoming more deeply immersed in Saigon's affairs. The U.S. military contingent was growing and assuming new functions. Special forces were moving from the rear of the fighting between Vietnamese toward the front. In short, Americans were being drawn ever closer to direct participation in the war.

While the Mansfield mission delivered a unanimous report with somewhat pessimistic conclusions to the Senate Foreign Relations Committee, Mansfield in a private meeting with President Kennedy provided an even more blunt picture of the danger to American interests in the deepening U.S. involvement. According to Kenny O'Donnell, President Kennedy's appointments secretary, who was present at the meeting, the Senate majority leader's findings were very disconcerting to Kennedy. O'Donnell describes the president as being, at first, irritated by Mansfield's report and then angered because he found himself agreeing with it, while feeling himself unable to change direction. He thought that with respect to Vietnam, his hands were tied, at least during his first term as president.

After reporting to Kennedy, Mansfield sought to focus public attention on the disturbing developments in Vietnam. From time to time, he gave voice to his concerns in press interviews, statements, and speeches, and in private memorandums to the president. He was restrained in his public utterances. In private, however, his was a countervoice to the pressure being exerted on Kennedy from within the executive branch to expand the U.S. role in Vietnam. For his part, Mansfield sought to hold back what he saw as a thoughtless slide into a wrong war in a wrong place. His recurring nightmare, shared by some U.S. military leaders, was of the United States locked into a military crusade moving ever deeper into the Asian mainland in pursuit of an elusive victory over an ideological abstraction.

Mansfield's efforts to flag the growing danger to the United States in Vietnam engendered a modest degree of attention in the Senate and the media, and in Saigon, where the mission's report was sharply criticized by Mme. Ngo Dinh Nhu. Mansfield's caution, however, seemed to have little affect on the administration. U.S. military aid personnel continued to expand in numbers and in the scope of their activities in South Vietnam. As the United States moved ever more deeply into the situation, relations between U.S. officials and the Diem government deteriorated. American advisors working with the Vietnamese military command would urge certain tactics regarding the Vietcong guerrillas, only to have their advice countermanded or redirected by the presidential palace. As the American presence loomed larger, the frustrations of the U.S. mission also increased, triggering temper outbursts against the Diem family, particularly Ngo Dinh Nhu and Mme Nhu. Underlying the friction was the basic question of who was going to run the show. It was asked on both sides and with increasing frequency.

As the mutual irritations between Washington and the Saigon government continued to rise, Kennedy designated a prominent Massachusetts Republican and former senator, Henry Cabot Lodge, as ambassador to Vietnam. Enlisting someone from the opposing party in this fashion may have reflected an appreciation of the appointee's unique skills for dealing with a confounding situation. It might also have been, as it frequently is in American politics, a form of political damage insurance.

In any event, not long after his arrival in Saigon, Ambassador Lodge received instructions from Washington to advise Diem that the United States could no longer tolerate the interference of his brother Ngo Dien Nhu in the work of the U.S. military aid mission. Lodge's representations seem to have had little impact. Relations with the presidential palace continued to deteriorate, until they were abruptly terminated during a military coup d'état. President Diem and his brother Nhu were murdered while in the custody of the Vietnamese High Command.

There were references in the press at the time to CIA complicity in the assassination. The reports were at first categorically denied by the Kennedy administration. Perhaps the most plausible explanation of the U.S. role was the subsequent revelation that, before launching the coup, the Vietnamese military leaders had assured themselves in conversations with U.S. officials in Saigon that the end of the Diem government would not mean the end of U.S. support of South Vietnam in the fight against the communists.

Majority Leader Mansfield denounced the assassination of Diem and called for an examination of U.S. policy in its aftermath. He had long regarded Diem as the only civilian leader in the south with any prospect at all of maintaining an independent noncommunist state. He judged that the coup that had taken Diem's life would be followed by an attempt to synthesize a new political leadership out of the Vietnamese military, assisted by selected carryover bureaucrats from the Diem government. It was, moreover, only the first in a series of reshufflings. In subsequent minicoups within the military, new faces appeared in the leadership of the Saigon government. Each reshuffling was duly endorsed by the United States as the legitimate government of South Vietnam, and U.S. aid continued to flow as though nothing had changed. The longer this process went on, the more the "government of South Vietnam" seemed to lose what little contact it had had with the Vietnamese people.

Whether Kennedy would have stayed with this arrangement beyond a transitional period and then shifted to a new policy of U.S., disinvolvement is a matter of conjecture. As previously noted, Kennedy had openly expressed second thoughts about trying to do in Vietnam what the Vietnamese could only do for themselves, and in a press conference shortly before his death he had mentioned Burmese and Cambodian neutralism as possibly a model for Vietnam, other than alignment. In any event, the decisions that would set the U.S. course in Vietnam passed into other hands when less than a month after the violent death of President Diem, Kennedy was assassinated.

On assuming the presidency, Lyndon Johnson at first stood firm against abrupt changes in his predecessor's course on Vietnam. In this as in other matters, he portrayed himself accurately as a surrogate, attempting to carry on with Kennedy's policies. Johnson as president approached the problems of foreign policy, particularly Vietnam, with a kind of pedestrian caution, playing down even the Tonkin Gulf Resolution as merely a sort of insurance against a spread of the war to embrace the United States. Unfortunately, the Hanoi leaders seemed to have concluded that the incident was confirmation of their suspicions that the United States was bent on replacing the French with its own version of colonialism in Indochina.

Instead of backing away from confrontation with the United States, the Ho Chi Minh government stepped up support for the Vietcong in the south. Then, a few days before the U.S. elections of 1964, the Vietcong launched a fierce guerrilla raid on American installations at the Bien Hua Air Base in South Vietnam. Five Americans were killed, seventy-six wounded, and six B-57 bombers were destroyed in the attack. Despite the extensive damage suffered at Bien Hua, Johnson turned down proposals for immediate retaliation. With the election behind him, however, Johnson was ready to listen to suggestions from his advisors on how to respond to the Bien Hua attack and bring the war in Vietnam to an end. There is little to indicate that the advice he received was anything less than a very enthusiastic call for action. At that point, his principal advisors on Vietnam were holdovers from the Kennedy administration who had been parties to the expansion of the U.S. role in Vietnam that had already taken place. Moreover, with the abrupt ending of the Diem government, they had already persuaded themselves that a greater role for the United States would be necessary to provide breathing space during which to stabilize the military regime in Saigon and, in time, democratize it.

The strategy Johnson settled on was that of "measured escalation." Under this concept, the U.S. role would be enlarged to include, first, direct U.S. military involvement designed to stabilize the situation in South Vietnam. Second, U.S. airpower would be used to interdict supply routes from the north to the communist combatants in the south. Third, U.S. air strikes would be launched in an escalating pattern on targets in North Vietnam. What the plan added up to was a progressive tightening of the screws on the Hanoi-led Vietnamese primarily through the introduction of U.S. military power into the conflict; the intensification to be divided into stages marked by brief olive-branch pauses. The process would continue until Hanoi reached the "breaking point" or until Ho Chi Minh came to his senses, if not his knees, and agreed to a settlement.

Before he adopted the plan, Lyndon Johnson met with several members of Congress, including Majority Leader Mansfield and Richard Russell of Georgia, both of whom sought to maintain their distance from the plan. The president also directed General Maxwell Taylor to advise the Foreign Relations Committee on what was being considered. The immediate reaction of Chairman Fulbright was a negative one. Several members of the committee also joined with him in criticizing the proposed plan, especially the idea of using U.S. combat forces to pacify South Vietnam. Beyond making known to General Taylor their individual reactions, however, the committee took no formal action at the time to discourage the President from putting the plan into effect.

Independent of the committee, Majority Leader Mansfield communicated his concerns about the proposed military escalation directly to President Johnson. In a memo dated 6 December 1964, Mansfield noted that escalation would take the nation "further out on a sagging limb," and sooner and or later it was going to have to be faced that "the preponderant responsibility for what transpires in South Viet Nam rests with us . . ."

> If a significant extension of the conflict beyond South Viet Nam should occur then the prospects are appalling. Even short of a nuclear war, an extension of the war may well saddle us with enormous burdens and costs in Cambodia, Laos, and elsewhere in Asia. . . .

Mansfield's memo called for an effort to put together a government in Saigon that "can speak with some native validity and authority" for the south in terms of *peaceful* unification of all Vietnam, rather than in terms of either liberation of the north or establishing an isolated independence in South Vietnam. "The first is illusory, without total United States involvement. The second, an independent and isolated South Vietnam is also illusory . . . since it would require such a vast United States involvement as to negate the meaning of independence."

Mansfield concluded that if it were not possible to assemble a Vietnamese government in Saigon able to negotiate a peaceful settlement with Hanoi, "we had better begin now to face up to the likelihood of years and years of involvement and a vast increase in the commitment and this should be spelled out in no uncertain terms to the people of the nation."

In reply, the president wrote Mansfield: "I think we have the same basic view of this problem . . . differing on only one point: Given the size of the stake, it seems to me that we are doing only what we have to do."

The president's reply had dismissed lightly the basic difference on Vietnam between Johnson and Mansfield. In a sentence, Johnson believed that "further in" was the way out; Mansfield was convinced the way out was "no further in." Unlike Johnson, Mansfield did not think the stake in Vietnam was anywhere near large enough to warrant the lives and resources he sensed would be expended in asserting it. Thenceforth, this fundamental difference would be ever-present in the exchanges on Vietnam between the president and the Senate majority leader and in the end would prove irreconcilable.

Mansfield's blunt memo was an attempt to turn the president away from deepening the U.S. involvement. It sought to persuade him, instead, to try for a settlement with Hanoi that would provide an acceptable U.S. exit from Vietnam before the only way out would be by U.S. military victory or defeat. Failing that, Mansfield wanted the president to pause long enough to spell out to the American people the potential cost of military escalation in the hope that a negative reaction might cause Johnson to have second thoughts. Or, if the public were as sanguine about military action as the administration seemed to be, at least the American people would know in advance what might be coming and steel themselves for a bloody conflict of indefinite depth and duration.

In pressing ahead on military escalation in Vietnam, the administration ignored such views as those advanced by Mansfield. There is nothing to indicate that Mansfield's approach was even seriously considered in the administration's planning prior to the military escalation. The president seems to have heard nothing from within the executive branch about the negative side of military escalation. What he received was confirmation of his own preconception, namely, that the United States could prevail quickly by a demonstrative deployment of its vast military might and sufficient evidence of a readiness to use it.

Mansfield's concern that this would not work in Vietnam may have caused the president some hesitancy; if so, it was fleeting. Johnson was predisposed by his restless temperament to retaliate forcefully for the Bien Hua attack, and the course of military escalation appeared to offer a controlled way to do so. His view was reinforced by what appears to have been a virtual unanimity of opinion among his immediate advisors.

Johnson did not actually give a go-ahead to military escalation until after his inauguration in January 1965. In the interim, the Defense Department was busy preparing for a major deployment that eventually would put American combatants in all three countries of Indochina. In February, with Johnson's approval, U.S. bombers were unleashed against Hanoi's supply lines in the southern part of North Vietnam. Within a month, such bombing runs had become routine. At the same time, American ground forces were making their initial landings along the coast of South Vietnam. With rifles at the ready, marines spewed out of landing craft and fanned out into combat positions along the beach. Although they encountered no opposition, the landings created ample photo opportunities that brought back to the American public exhilarating recollections of World War II. The landings also marked the end of the prohibition on the use of weapons except in self-defense by American personnel in Vietnam, a stricture that had remained in force throughout the Eisenhower and Kennedy administrations.

Having unsheathed the sword, Johnson was ready to extend the olive branch. In a highly publicized speech at Johns Hopkins University on 7 April 1965, the president stood proudly by what he had begun and vowed that military action would continue in Vietnam until communist aggression was halted once and for all. As an antiphony to this militancy, he set forth a proposal for a multipurpose engineering project of Tennessee Valley Authority proportions for the Mekong River. Intended to benefit all Southeast Asia, the offer specifically included North Vietnam. The proposal stirred considerable interest in Southeast Asia, mostly among countries that had already been receiving U.S. aid for years. As for Hanoi's response, the Vietminh government dismissed both the proposal and the South Vietnam regime as fraudulent.

Hanoi's rejection of the olive branch was hardly surprising. With the possible exception of Johnson, few in the administration expected the first turn of the military screw to produce a scream for talks from the Hanoi communists. Nor did the rejection shock Congress or American public opinion. If it raised any doubts about the efficacy of escalation, they were smothered by a patriotic desire to stand behind America's fighting men and their commander in chief. The only discernible flicker of dissent was produced by an obscure group known as Students for a Democratic Society (SDS). The organization held a public demonstration in Washington attended by less than a hundred people. Barely large enough to draw the attention of the media, it created scarcely a ripple in official circles, where the SDS was dismissed as "some kind of communist front."

Total U.S. Involvement

Once having taken the first step in military escalation, the defense of South Vietnam, for all practical purposes, became the primary responsibility of the United States. U.S. combat forces in Vietnam grew by the tens and then hundreds of thousands. Johnson dispatched General William Westmoreland, a combat specialist, to serve as supreme commander of the military forces. Westmoreland was an able and conscientious field commander. Unfortunately, his orthodox military background was not necessarily the best preparation for dealing with the complex political situation in Saigon or an enemy in the field that could not only "swim among the people" in the rice fields but mingle undetected with U.S. personnel in the cities. In this generally hostile setting, U.S. combat forces took the lead in campaigns to wipe out the Vietcong guerrillas in South Vietnam. The ground war grew in intensity. U.S. combat teams undertook countless "search and destroy" missions along the Mekong River and its numerous tributaries, seeking the Vietcong guerrillas in hamlets and hidden tunnels. Other U.S. ground patrols probed the scattered villages of the highlands looking for infiltrators from the north and rarely finding them. There were few formal battles, only skirmishes and pursuits, ambushes, snipers, and booby traps. Advanced military technology was deployed by the U.S. forces, including the use of chemical defoliants and heavy air bombardments, in an attempt to intercept supplies and reinforcements coming down from the north. U.S. air and naval units not only supported ground forces in the south but also initiated attacks on targets in North Vietnam, attacks that grew routine and soon were expanded to include daily runs of B-54 bombers from bases on Guam more than a thousand miles away. In time, the strategy of measured escalation gave way to wholesale immersion of the U.S. armed services in the Vietnam War.

Each major escalation, such as the introduction of B-52 bombers, was invariably accompanied by a burst of optimistic reports from the Pentagon and the White House on its efficacy, leading the public to expect that the war would soon end. Time and again, expectations of imminent success were built up only to be followed by letdowns. Johnson's approval ratings began to see-saw. As the promised "light at the end of the tunnel" faded, the zeniths on the fever chart of Johnson's popularity grew fewer and shorter and the nadirs deeper and longer.

Primed by misapprehensions inherited from the Eisenhower and Kennedy administrations already embedded in policy, the Johnson administration added a few of its own. It underestimated the difficulties of coping with Vietcong guerrilla warfare, while overestimating the speed with which Saigon's organized military forces would be able to take back from the U.S. forces the main burden of the war in the south. Moreover, the United States relied heavily on aerial warfare and exotic technologies in its military operations; both proved of limited relevance, notably in disrupting the primitive transportation system—bicycles, foot portage, tricycles, fishing junks, and the like—that moved supplies and combatants down from the north. Little advance thought was given to the significance of increased military aid from China and the Soviet Union that materialized to bulwark Hanoi's resistance and increased the effectiveness of its well-led regular forces. The routes by which this aid was funneled into North Vietnam were relatively impervious to interdiction from the air without a direct U.S. military confrontation with China.

As the U.S. involvement deepened, such miscalculations were buried under inflated reports of success in the antiguerilla war in the south, the interdiction of the supply routes from the north, the efficacy of such high-tech innovations as night vision, and pinpoint bombing of North Vietnam's war-making capacity. Again, these glowing reports added to the unwarranted expectations of a quick victory that the administration had kindled in the American people. Presiding over this formulation for a disaster, Lyndon Johnson not only had a weak grasp of the political and military realities in Vietnam but also, apparently, of the durability of the nation's enthusiasm for an anticommunist military crusade in Asia. Initially, this did not present a serious question, since the anticipation was that Hanoi would fold quickly. When that proved not to be the case, Johnson was forced to deal with a situation of increasing complexity that slipped further and further beyond his comprehension. In time, the abstract objective of "stopping communism" was no longer enough to sustain popular enthusiasm for the war. Administration spokesmen were reduced to blaming the war's continuance on Hanoi for being unwilling to come to the conference table and to chastising those in the growing opposition at home for not being "tough" enough or unwilling "to stay the course."

Nor could the Johnson administration delineate specific vital national interests that warranted the mounting human sacrifices involved. The best that could be offered in the way of a rationale for prolonging the war was "in order to end it." As a last straw, the administration trivialized the entire undertaking by invoking a winning-at-all-costs idiom of the sporting world to justify the continuance of what had become an aimless pursuit. All the while, the graphic media was making clear to Americans the gruesomeness of the conflict. As the human and material costs continued to pile up in the inconclusive struggle, public enthusiasm gave way to bewilderment, then revulsion, and, finally, to bitter anger with the White House and its chief occupant.

Mansfield saw the administration's fundamental failure as the failure to recognize that there were rational limits to the use of U.S. military power in Indochina. He saw that the U.S. commitment was deepening until the ratio of possible benefit to cost was totally askew. By then, however, it was too late to heed Senator Aiken's advice just "to declare victory and get out."

Unlike his predecessors, who had resisted being pushed into a situation where the United States would bear prime responsibility for the war, Johnson had jumped into it with both feet. Eisenhower and Kennedy had authorized aid programs, funneled first through the French colonialists and then the Vietnamese nationalist regime in Saigon, in the hope that they would check the communist advance in Indochina. In their administrations, the prime responsibility for success or failure remained lodged in the Vietnamese, rather than the United States. Once in the presidency, Johnson found insufferable the self-imposed restraints on the direct use of American military power that his predecessors had accepted as part of this arrangement. He wanted the Vietnamese interlude closed out cleanly and quickly; to that end he accepted, and perhaps even sought, the conversion of the conflict from a war between Vietnamese into a war between the United States and the Vietnamese. The initial expectation that a brief U.S. military engagement would bring a prompt resolution of the struggle disappeared quickly. The war spread throughout South Vietnam and into the north. It was extended secretly by the United States to Laos, overwhelming the neutrality of that country that had been negotiated by the Kennedy administration. It exploded into Cambodia under Johnson's successor, Richard Nixon, destroying what had been the only oasis of peace in Indochina. In short, all of Indochina was set aflame and the war degenerated into an aimless killing game. It was pursued not in terms of national objectives but in weekly "body counts" of destroyed enemies, tonnages of ordnance dropped, and other statistical irrelevancies. It became a war, moreover, from which the administration could find no exit, a war that would persist for years after the Johnson administration had become history. Johnson's decision to resort to direct military action derived only in part from a major concern of U.S. foreign policy that had to do with the spillover of the Chinese Revolution into Southeast Asia. It also reflected a response to a national anxiety over the "spread of communism" following World War II. After the collapse of Nationalist China in 1950, this fear was stimulated by politicians and the media until it bordered on hysteria. It predisposed presidents and their advisors and members of Congress to serious errors of judgment and costly overreactions to developments elsewhere in the world. It engendered a quasi-ritualistic requirement among government careerists and elected officials not to pass up any occasion to "stand up" to the communists in confrontational posturing. In the atmosphere of the time, it was a rare politician who would not leap at an opportunity to shake a menacing verbal fist at Moscow or Beijing. If nothing else, such posturing served as insurance against being labeled "soft on communism."

Indeed, as he settled into the White House, President Johnson received reminders of the risks in neglecting this ritualistic performance. The reminders came with particular force from Richard Nixon. Nixon had done much to make the threat of communism the central motif of U.S. politics after World War II, having used it to establish his career in California politics and then pursuing it in Washington in both houses of Congress. After being defeated narrowly in the 1960 presidential election and then losing a subsequent race for governor of California, Nixon did not retire from politics as many expected. Instead, he began preparing for a comeback, building his strategy around the then remote Vietnam situation.

Soon after Johnson became president, he began to be badgered by Nixon to take a "harder" line against the "communist advance" in Indochina. Nixon's political speeches carried the implication that if Vietnam were "lost," it would be because the Democrats were still "soft" on communism, as they had been in China. Although Nixon never called for direct military action, such action was about the only way left to reinforce the American position in Vietnam. Nixon's demand for a hardening posture on Vietnam was echoed by other Republicans, notably Representative Melvin Laird of Wisconsin, a highly partisan leader of the Republicans in the House of Representatives, who would later be named by Nixon as secretary of defense. With an eye to the 1968 election and Nixon as his likely opponent, Johnson had no intention of permitting himself to be labeled as soft on communists—in Vietnam or anywhere else.

As early as 1963, however, there were counterpressures against enlargement of the United States commitment in Vietnam, coming from the Senate. Mansfield had expressed the need for caution in deepening the commitment, lest the United States become directly involved. He had done so publicly and in private communications with the White House. Wayne Morse of Oregon had repeatedly objected to the U.S. course in Southeast Asia. Morse's objections were rooted in an earlier reversal of his position on U.S. foreign aid. After years of support for the program, he had denounced it mainly because of what he saw as its loss of focus after the success of the Marshall Plan for Europe. Most of all, he was concerned with the nation's accumulating entanglements all over the world when the aid program became involved in the "fight against communism." His critics found it easier to ignore Morse as a maverick and neoisolationist than to challenge him on the substance of his opposition. Although Morse was aware of these disdainful reactions, he was unmoved by them. He was fond of saying that his concern was with the historic record, and he showed no inclination to dilute his views for the sake of greater acceptability in the eyes of his colleagues or the administration. Morse underscored this position when he joined with Ernest Gruening of Alaska to cast the only negative votes on the Tonkin Gulf Resolution.

As time went on, Democratic senators who originally supported the president on the Tonkin Gulf Resolution swelled the growing ranks of the dissidents. Several made fact-finding treks to Vietnam to see for themselves and came back to express their doubts. There were also those, such as George McGovern of South Dakota and Eugene McCarthy of Minnesota, who at an early date drew away from the president. Some, like Stuart Symington of Missouri, were moved to shift to the opposition by a growing concern with the human casualties and the financial drain on the U.S. economy. With the war coming more and more into disrepute, liberal Democrats, such as Church of Idaho, Moss of Utah, Inouye of Hawaii, the Kennedys of New York and Massachusetts, and Ribicoff of Connecticut, shifted from support to opposition. On the other hand, John Stennis of Mississippi, Gale McGee of Wyoming, and a scattering of other Democrats continued to uphold presidential leadership. McGee, in particular, was unwavering in his support and worked hard to restrain the rising congressional pressure for withdrawal. He was identified unofficially as the Senate spokesman on the issue for the Johnson administration and the State Department's viewpoint. Among the Republicans, Javits of New York and Cooper of Kentucky joined Aiken of Vermont in opposing the policy on Vietnam. The most outspoken Republican supporters of presidential policy on Vietnam were Bob Dole of Kansas, whose scars from World War II lent weight to his position, and Bob Griffin of Michigan, the minority whip. Both men were rising stars among Senate Republicans and potential successors to Minority Leader Dirksen. They sought to forestall any action in the Senate that might be construed as weakening military escalation, taking turns in opposing legislative expressions designed to encourage the president not to overlook the possibility of negotiations.

Some applauded this Republican support for Johnson's policies as an expression of bipartisan statesmanship. With a political backlash already forming on Vietnam policy, however, the more cynical were inclined to ascribe it to a Republican determination not to let Johnson off the hook. In the midterm congressional elections of 1966, senators of both parties showed signs of wanting to put some distance between themselves and the president's course on Vietnam. The tendency was first evident among members of Johnson's own party. Republicans still seemed to be taking their cue from Richard Nixon and House Minority Leader Mel Laird, both of whom continued to prod Johnson in the direction of more active U.S. intervention in Vietnam.

During the 1968 presidential campaign, however, candidate Nixon, in a shift from his earlier prodding of Johnson, called for peace and announced that he had a "secret plan" to end the war and bring back the U.S. forces. Without knowing precisely what it was that they were supporting, many Republican senators hastened to embrace Nixon's "secret plan." In any event, with Hugh Scott of Pennsylvania replacing Dirksen as minority leader, the dominant position on Vietnam of senators of both parties was to support a U.S. military withdrawal from Vietnam.

By the summer of 1965, however, it had already become clear that Vietnam was an American war and that there would be no easy exit. The Johnson administration clung to its expectation that military escalation would produce a victory. With the Vietnamese conflict turned into a war between Americans and Vietnamese this estimation began quickly to undergo a recalculation. Popular exuberance over Johnson's policies cooled rapidly. Vietnam became a taboo subject at dinner tables in Washington. A few months after the initiation of escalation, a vague fear burgeoned that this remote and little understood military involvement was going to hang over the Great Society for the indefinite future. The Johnson administration redoubled its assurances that the nation could have both "guns and butter." Johnson himself pointed the way, moreover, to curbing the costs of the federal government by ordering a program of conservation of electricity in all federal buildings in the capital, beginning with a "turn off the lights" drive in the White House. The admonition included a blackout of the annual Christmas tree on the White House grounds, much to the chagrin of the tourist industry.

With the war gathering momentum, the media detected a rift between the president and Senate Majority Leader Mansfield. As early as April 1965, Johnson was reported to be referring to Mansfield in exasperation as "that man from Montana." Although both denied the rift, each was calculating the political fallout from Vietnam. The core of their differing approaches was revealed in a passing exchange between them. At one point, Johnson touched a sensitive nerve by reminding the majority leader that the American people did not want "another China." The reference was to the political battering that the Democrats had suffered from being accused of "losing China" to the communists during the Truman administration. Having barely survived that experience during his first campaign for the Senate, Mansfield did not need or appreciate the reference. He answered quickly, "No, Mr. President, and they don't want another Korea either," a reference to an indecisive conflict with very heavy American casualties, uncomfortably similar to Vietnam, that also damaged the Democrats.

Sources close to the president continued to deny that his irritation with Mansfield arose from differences over Vietnam. In leaks to the press, the White House dismissed Mansfield's opposition to Vietnamese policy disparagingly as deriving from pique over the administration's closing of a veterans' hospital in Miles City, Montana, that he resisted. To be sure, Mansfield was angry over the closing, but to link that with his stand on

Vietnam was to trivialize his deeply felt opposition to the war. As if to underscore the absence of a connection between the two situations, Mansfield hastened to reiterate very forcefully his concerns on Vietnam, and he did so immediately after the administration reversed itself on Miles City and decided to leave the hospital open.

In public, Mansfield continued to avoid any direct criticism of Johnson over Vietnam. He upheld the president's role as commander in chief of the armed services, and his authority in making the difficult decisions. He differed openly only with the Johnson administrations's interpretation of the Tonkin Gulf Resolution as the equivalent of a declaration of war and therefore a Congressional endorsement of military escalation. Beyond that, Mansfield refused to be drawn into a discussion of his disagreements with the president. In private encounters, however, Mansfield politely but relentlessly pressed Johnson to halt the escalation and consider negotiations. A principal focus of this effort was Mansfield's strong endorsement of the "enclave theory" advanced by General James Gavin. Gavin's proposal called for limiting the U.S. military presence in South Vietnam to several fixed areas, mostly along the coast. Because of their accessibility to naval and air cover, Gavin argued, such enclaves could be held at minimal cost in lives and provide a basis for a negotiated settlement with Hanoi. Notwithstanding Mansfield's endorsement, the enclave theory appeared to carry little weight with the president and was brusquely dismissed by the administration. Instead, Johnson permitted the U.S. military effort to be pushed deeper and deeper into Indochina.

Second Presidential Mission to Indochina

In a further effort to put to rest the rumors of a break between them, Mansfield proposed that the president ask him, as Senate majority leader, to head a fact-finding mission of senators to Indochina, as Kennedy had done several years earlier. Although he could have pursued such a mission on his own authority, Mansfield wanted the presidential linkage in the hope that it would intensify the impact of its findings on the executive branch. The proposal confronted Johnson with something of a dilemma. To reject it would have been to suggest irreconcilable disagreement with the majority leader while he was still hopeful of winning Mansfield's active support for his approach. It is also possible that Johnson already sensed that something was not working as intended in Indochina and that a Senate mission of several members might provide some help in determining what to do next. Finally, he may have felt that rejecting the majority leader's proposal would complicate his problems with the Senate, where Mansfield now enjoyed

wide personal acceptance. Johnson agreed to a presidential mission of senators headed by the majority leader. Mansfield handpicked the Senate participants; they included Democrats Muskie and Inouye and Republicans Aiken
and Boggs. The four enjoyed reputations in the Senate for personal integrity, a high level of political independence, and minimal partisanship. Except for Boggs, none had ever been to Indochina. Nor had any of them yet
taken a public position on Vietnam that was at serious odds with that of the
administration.

The Senate group went to Indochina in late December 1965. Mansfield
was appalled by the changes since his visit several years earlier. He was
particularly disturbed by the degree of Americanization of the military situation that had taken place. In Laos, for example, efforts at neutralization in
line with the second Geneva agreement, for all practical purposes, had been
abandoned by the American mission. With the king of Laos sulking in the
royal capital of Luang Prabhang, the "neutral" government, headed by
Prime Minister Souvanna Phouma in the administrative capital of
Vientianne, was no longer neutral and had become something of an irrelevancy. Through the aid program, the U.S. mission was in effective control
of the prime minister's government and the Lao military forces. The embassy, moreover, was serving as a command post for a secret U.S. air war
against North Vietnamese targets.

Cambodia remained at peace in the midst of the widening war in Indochina. But Prince Sihanouk, the popular prime minister, was finding it
increasingly difficult to maintain a semblance of the neutrality on which
that peace had rested. In the remote, sparsely inhabited northeastern sector
of the country, North Vietnamese human supply trains frequently crossed
the border into Cambodia. Sihanouk could do nothing to stop them, and the
U.S. air strikes seeking to interdict those lines sometimes hit Cambodian
villages. When that happened, he could no longer ignore them. Also under-
mining Sihanouk's independence was the whispered ridicule to which he
and his neutralist policy had long been subjected by U.S. officials, echoes
of which invariably reached his ears.

The most striking changes since Mansfield's earlier visit had occurred in
Vietnam. In Saigon, the mission found a political structure under the control
of Vietnamese military officers with little experience in government.
Vietnamese officials who had survived the overthrow of the Diem government had been converted into appendages of the Vietnamese military command. After several reshufflings of the military regime, two younger
military officers had emerged as the equivalent of head of state and a
prime minister. Sustained by U.S. aid, they were amenable to direction by
the U.S. military command. As the war became the paramount U.S. con-

cern, the theoretical head of the entire U.S. mission in Saigon, Ambassador Henry Cabot Lodge, was quick to defer to General Westmoreland on all matters affecting the war. In meetings with the Mansfield mission, Westmoreland was optimistic. Ambassador Lodge was optimistic. Lessor U.S. officials, with rare exception, were optimistic. The senators, however, found it hard to reconcile this optimism with the bombing of an American military officers' billet in the heart of Saigon on the very night of their arrival. Nor could they find a basis for optimism in the heavily guarded and barbed-wired isolation of the U.S. Embassy, or in the thump of mortar shells that sounded throughout the night from clashes with Vietminh guerrillas in Saigon's outskirts. In the end, the most significant source of the optimism among U.S. officials seemed to be derived not from the way the war was going but from the anticipation of a continuing enlargement of the American role.

Neither the unanimous report of the senators to the Senate Foreign Relations Committee nor the majority leader's private report to the president on his return endorsed the optimism of American officials in Saigon. On the contrary, the Senate mission reported no likelihood that military escalation would end the war in the foreseeable future. They anticipated a prolonged U.S. military involvement and demands from the U.S. command in Vietnam for a doubling or even larger increase in the U.S. troop deployment. The only discernible restraint on a rapid buildup that they had encountered was the capacity of Westmoreland's command to cope with the logistics of the rapid deployment. In one year, the U.S. military presence had increased from less than 25,000 to 200,000. At the end of 1965, the Saigon waterfront was sagging under the weight of U.S. troops and supply ships and U.S. naval vessels of all kinds.

Mansfield was blunt in his confidential report to the president. He noted that the involvement of U.S. armed forces was already very deep and rapidly going deeper. As he saw it, that was precisely the wrong direction in which to be headed.

The president made no direct response to Mansfield but circulated his report among his chief advisors. They were exasperated by its pessimistic tone, attributing the gloomy findings to "a frozen position" on the part of the majority leader. In their view, his conclusions were based not on an accurate reading of the current situation in Indochina but on his preconceptions. Secretary Dean Rusk was reported to have commented only half in jest that Mansfield could have filed his report even before he left Washington.

The only suggestion of a change to accommodate Mansfield's views or, perhaps, to point up their irrelevancy was a presidential order for a brief pause in the bombing of North Vietnam at Christmas 1965. This gesture was coupled with impatient demands on Hanoi to negotiate with Saigon. Hanoi spurned the demand, scornfully dismissing the Saigon government as a nonentity and renewing its denunciations of U.S. policy. Seemingly impatient to get back to the war, the administration lost no time in resuming bombing operations at the end of the holiday.

The first request from the administration to the second session of Congress in January 1966 was for an additional $12.8 billion for the war, a figure that, at the time, represented an explosive add-on to the budget. The request seemed to validate the pessimistic conclusion of the Mansfield mission that the U.S. course in Vietnam would be long and costly. Released to the public shortly thereafter, the Mansfield mission's public report circulated widely and received careful consideration from the media. It brought home the fact that the policy of escalation had converted what had been a remote conflict in Indochina between Vietnamese political factions, one of peripheral interest to Americans, into a full-scale U.S. war. With American youths pitted against Vietnamese, the public perceived that there would be no quick or easy exit from Vietnam for the United States. This change of focus clearly posed the nagging question of what a war in Indochina had to do with vital U.S. interests. Generalities offered by the administration offered little solace to compensate for the mounting casualties.

Mansfield's Attempts at Persuasion and Remedy

The inability to make a clear connection between substantive U.S. interests and the magnitude of the military effort had an immediate consequence in the Senate. Led by a scattering of Democrats that did not include Majority Leader Mansfield, an attempt was made to repeal the Tonkin Gulf Resolution that a near-unanimous Senate had had no difficulty in supporting a year earlier. The vote to reverse, however, failed by a wide margin. Unfortunately, the administration concluded from this legislative victory that, except for some liberals, the policy of military escalation enjoyed widespread support in the Senate. The reality was quite different. Many members who opposed repeal of the Tonkin Gulf Resolution did so only out of a reluctance to part company with the president at a time of heightened appeals to patriotism in the nation. But a strong undercurrent of national uncertainty over Vietnam was already flowing toward Washington. Although the major portion of the mail being received in congressional offices was still hostile to opposition to the war, it was becoming less so.

The discontent implicit in this trend was muted in the House of Representatives by the ringing support that President Johnson received from Speaker McCormack. The same was not true in the Senate, where the majority leader had already taken note of the changing response of the public to the war. Mansfield's style of operating the Senate encouraged Democrats and Republicans alike to speak their minds freely on Vietnam. Moreover, even though he avoided criticizing the president, Mansfield refrained from faulting those who did. Moreover, his own public comments made clear his growing reservations about the administration's policies. His refusal to be drawn further into a break with the president bewildered the media even as it bewildered administration officials.

Initially, the debate in the Senate over Vietnam revealed a kind of role reversal for the two parties. It was Republican leader Dirksen, rather than Democratic leader Mansfield, who was most articulate in upholding the White House on Vietnam. Similar support on the Democratic side for Johnson was supplied largely by Gale McGee of Wyoming, a western progressive with strong ties to the State Department. He was joined by conservative John Stennis of Mississippi. As acting chairman and long-time member of the Armed Services Committee, Stennis was listened to particularly by his southern colleagues in the absence of Chairman Richard Russell. The latter was terminally ill and on his infrequent appearances in the Senate tended to avoid the subject of Vietnam.

After the release of the Mansfield report in early 1966, members of both parties began to question the direction of U.S. policy openly and with rising vehemence. The Foreign Relations Committee initiated a series of widely telecast "educational" hearings on the Vietnam War. The hearings disseminated the views of respected witnesses carefully drawn from American business, educational, and other circles. Although their credentials were unimpeachably patriotic, their comments to the committee were often laced with doubts about the course of the war. Vice President Humphrey appeared before the committee as a star witness for the administration. In spite of his nimbleness of mind, Humphrey was hard-pressed to explain U.S. policy to the satisfaction of committee members. Nevertheless, his defense of the administration drew him closer to President Johnson, even as it diminished his political stock with many of his supporters in Congress and throughout the country.

Although doubts about Vietnam continued to multiply, they took a long time producing a consensus in the Senate on what to do next. Senators were quick to recognize that something was seriously wrong with Vietnam policy, but they were nowhere near in agreement on remedies. During 1966–67, the period of rapid expansion in the U.S. military commitment, most senators chose simply to deplore the war, commiserate with anxious constituents, blame the problem on the communists, and accept the president's assurances that he was trying to end the war as soon as possible. Some upholders of the prevailing wisdom found troublesome both the Mansfield report and the hearings of the Foreign Relations Committee. Political orthodoxy still required a militant assertiveness in confrontation with communism anywhere. That and the wreaking of more, rather than less, military destruction was viewed as the way to end the Vietnam War. Indeed, some very militant subscribers to this approach complained that military escalation was not proceeding fast enough with large enough increments of fury.

A few senators who began to have doubts about where the administration was headed were examining more closely the position pioneered by Morse of Oregon that the United States had no business in Vietnam, should not have become involved in the first place, and should get out forthwith. Embracing variations on this theme, they were inclined toward negotiations with Hanoi leading to a compromise and U.S. withdrawal from Vietnam sooner rather than later—an approach implicit in the Mansfield report. In the same breath, however, they were at pains to warn Hanoi that the United States would not be "forced" out of Vietnam. It was a view that earlier would have been scorned as "appeasement." As time went on, it became the respectable view in Congress. But in 1966 it did not command even a bare majority of the Senate, not to mention the House, where McCormack still managed to shut it out almost entirely.

As the war intensified, Mansfield walked a political tightrope, not endorsing escalation but not openly divorcing himself from Johnson. Mansfield was more than ever convinced that a meaningful resolution of the Indochinese political conflict could not be dictated by U.S. military action. Nor could he accept the view that the direct use of U.S. military forces in Vietnam was serving some substantial national interest. In short, the policy of escalation, as he saw it, had led the United States into a bottomless pit, with U.S. forces not only pursuing communism all over South Vietnam but having to continue the pursuit to Hanoi. And beyond, perhaps to Beijing and conceivably to Moscow. As he said at every opportunity, Mansfield believed the way out of Vietnam was not to go farther in. Even after the administration had reacted negatively to his report on Vietnam, Mansfield still clung to the hope that Johnson could be persuaded to change direction. Thus, even as he avoided public criticism of the president, in private he pressed Johnson to restrain the military buildup. Mansfield was convinced that this approach would maximize whatever part he could play in minimizing the damage that the war was doing to the United States.

To strengthen his hand with the president, Mansfield turned to the Senate Democratic Policy Committee that he had come to rely on as an instrument of collective leadership. As reconstituted by the majority leader, the committee was well suited to that purpose. It was no longer a preserve of Senate patriarchs but contained both older and younger Democrats, who together encompassed the broad geographic spread of the party—northern and midwestern liberals, southern conservatives, and western progressives. The committee had become an accurate spectrum of Democrats in the Senate and, indeed, in the nation. Despite its diversity, members worked in excellent harmony with one another and responded well to the light touch of the chairman.

The committee had no difficulty in recognizing the strains that the war in Vietnam was placing on the social and economic fabric of the United States. As astute politicians, they recognized that the "Who lost China?" syndrome, while not a dead issue, was receding. They knew, too, that there would be serious political consequences to the Democrats if the party was to be saddled in Vietnam with another unpopular war, as in Korea. Even if not yet prepared for a withdrawal from Vietnam at any price, the committee was ready to listen attentively to alternatives to continuing military escalation. With no easy end in sight, there were no longer any fierce "hawks" eager for more of the same on the Democratic Policy Committee.

The committee had become receptive to a range of attitudes toward Vietnam that mirrored the differences among Democrats in the Senate. The spread extended from the southern conservatism of a Talmadge of Georgia to the Michigan liberalism of Phil Hart; falling in between was a mix of Democrats that included Robert Byrd of West Virginia, Dan Inouye of Hawaii, Ted Moss of Utah, Ed Muskie of Maine, Fritz Hollings of South Carolina, John Pastore of Rhode Island, and Warren Magnuson of Washington. All were conscientious senators with deep concerns about Vietnam; but each was still clinging, to personal views as to the source of the problem and possible remedies. Mansfield searched constantly for a common ground on which the group might stand together. Throughout the remainder of Johnson's presidency and into Nixon's, he sought to express through committee advisory resolutions the ever-rising level of common concern and commonly acceptable remedies among the Senate Democrats.

Although he sympathized with senators who were prepared to try something stronger than advisories to the president in the form of legislation that would compel Johnson to end the war, Mansfield resisted these attempts at first. He knew that the Senate, let alone Congress as a whole, was far from agreeing on any strong course of action. Mansfield was reluctant to assert a position on Vietnam that lacked the votes in the Senate to undergird it. He had little patience with the illusion or pretense of Senate power that underlay the early demands for Senate action to end the war. In a constitutional sense, to force a change of policy that the president was disinclined to make required at least a majority, not only of the Senate but of both houses of

Congress, and more likely a two-thirds vote of both Houses to override a presidential veto. By contrast, a unilateral decision by the president could change policy on Vietnam by the stroke of a pen. With the experience of trying to repeal the Tonkin Gulf Resolution still fresh in his memory, Mansfield was unable to discern anywhere near sufficient numbers in the Senate, let alone in a House dominated by Speaker McCormack. As the U.S. war in Vietnam moved further into its second year, the majority leader judged that the antipathy at home to the war had reached a point where Senate Democrats as a whole just might be prepared to support a nonconfrontational but still formal statement of concern, such as the one Mansfield had already managed to obtain from the Democratic Policy Committee. If that were so, he reasoned, it might cause the president to look more closely at negotiations without further escalation. His reading of the Senate Democrats was accurate. He obtained an overwhelming endorsement in the Democratic caucus upholding the Policy Committee's position and formally expressing concern with the U.S. role in Vietnam. This was followed at intervals by similar expressions obtained in both the Policy Committee and the caucus.

Although without the force of law, the party resolutions reflected a gathering consensus among Democrats. They served as a kind of escalation of pressure on the president to intensify the search for peace. They also acted to give the Democrats, at least the Democrats in the Senate, an identity as peace seekers on Vietnam. In so doing, they accentuated the growing separation of the Senate majority from the administration.

In these resolutions, Johnson was hearing the whole range of Senate Democratic voices telling him that something was going very badly in Vietnam. To be sure, the chorale included liberals such as the Kennedys and Gene McCarthy. But it also contained old Senate hands, wise in the ways of political survival, senators like Russell, Magnuson, and Symington. Russell abhorred "half wars" but knew that Indochina was no place for the United States to be involved in a whole war. Magnuson envisioned for his state of Washington not conflict with the Asian land mass across the ocean but a vast trading network. Symington was convinced that the war would undermine the nation's economic position in the world and because his grandchildren had laid on him their moral objections to Vietnam. Inouye was leery of the racial implications of another U.S. war against Asians. Among Senate Republicans, the disquiet over Vietnam had spread to Javits, Aiken, and Cooper. In the House of Representatives a scattering of congressmen, ignoring Speaker McCormack's withering glare, had begun to express their doubts about Vietnam.

The sounds of popular protest in the nation's cities also reached Washington. A demonstration of 100,000 occurred in New York. A few months later, 50,000 antiwar protesters marched on the Pentagon. A major factor underlying such public demonstrations was the growing number of U.S. casualties. At the end of 1966, the total numbers of Americans killed in action in Vietnam was close to 7,000, more than a sevenfold increase over a year earlier. A year later, with 500,000 GIs in Vietnam, the number killed jumped to almost 16,000. The colleges grew ever more restless, with student strikes and demonstrations spreading throughout the nation, military draft cards being put to the match, and young draft eligibles slipping out of the country to seek asylum in Canada, Sweden, and elsewhere. Students in Europe joined in sympathy with American youths. A flood of mail inundated official Washington. Much of it was directed to the Senate, with Mansfield's office as one of the focal points. At first, the tone of Mansfield's incoming mail on Vietnam had been scathingly critical of his talk of peace. Within a few months, the tone had begun to shift to an expression of angry and anguished doubts about the war. At the end of 1967, public opinion polls showed for the first time that more Americans opposed than supported the U.S. involvement in Vietnam.

To counter complaints that the war was going nowhere, Johnson sought from his leading advisors more tangible evidence to the contrary. The Pentagon promptly supplied him with up-to-the-minute printouts on the number of bombing runs and the tonnages of explosives dropped by U.S. planes on North Vietnam; these were soon seen as rivaling in magnitude similar statistics for the European theater in World War II. The computers also spewed out massive "body counts" of Vietnamese, presumably combatants, slain by U.S. forces in the south. Johnson found in the reports of destruction what he needed to persuade himself that all was well with the policy of escalation. He carried this documentation of success around in his pocket as visible evidence of "light at the end of the tunnel." It failed to convince skeptical reporters and reassure anxious members of Congress.

Domestic Complications and Consequences

The president also kept close tabs on public opinion polls that indicated popular support for his policies. After each escalation of U.S. military action, the polls would show a sharp rise in Johnson's approval ratings. What Johnson was less inclined to see was the prompt decline in the ratings when the escalation failed to be decisive in bringing the war to a close. Moreover, each successive escalation tended to produce a peak of approval that was lower than its predecessor. Despite the elaborate attempts to document the effectiveness of the policy, military escalation provided little discernible impact on Hanoi.

A serious domestic consequence of the war was its impact on race relations at home. The Civil Rights Act of 1964 had opened up a period of mutual discovery and warm interaction between the races. It was a reaching out on both sides, led by the churches, schools, and various other communities of moral awareness. Somewhat naive, perhaps, it was nonetheless a sincere popular attempt to make desegregation work and to bridge the economic and social gaps that had long divided Americans along racial lines. That this would not be easy was brought home by an eruption of rioting by blacks in the impoverished Watts area of Los Angeles soon after the Civil Rights Act of 1964 became law. The depth of the underlying alienation was further reflected on many campuses, where grouping by color persisted and impatient demands of black students and intellectuals for change in educational practices were not met quickly.

These were early warnings that there was no time to lose in dealing with the social and economic problems implicit in the ending of legal segregation. Unfortunately, the Vietnam War intervened at this point to complicate the learning process. Its demands on the attention of the public and on the resources of the federal government superseded all others. Moreover, the new racial relations were further complicated when it became apparent that the gut fighting and, hence, the casualties in Vietnam involved a significant disproportion of blacks. These side-effects of the war intensified the inchoate anger of blacks at the long-suffered inequities of segregation. At the same time, it revived some of the power of those ready to exploit that fury as an "I-told-you-so" way to reverse the progress in racial integration.

By the summer of 1967, the outbursts of racial violence had become so serious that Minority Leader Dirksen and the only black senator since Reconstruction days, Republican Ed Brooke of Massachusetts, joined in urging a Senate investigation. Johnson dispatched Attorney General Ramsey Clark, to ask Mansfield to head off the demand, fearing that a Senate inquiry would complicate the problem. As an alternative, Mansfield urged the administration to set up a commission of inquiry. His suggestion was not acted on, however, until after the assassination of Robert Kennedy a year later.

· Mansfield believed that Vietnam was at the heart of the inner difficulties of the nation because it exacerbated racial tensions and wasted federal resources that could otherwise be used to deal with the societal problems that lay beneath the riots. The longer the war went on, he was convinced, the more pronounced would be its repercussions at home.

In the fall of 1967, Mansfield made another trip abroad to take a sounding of reactions to Vietnam from nations in East Asia closely linked with the United States. He found that Japan, Hong Kong, and the Philippines, as well as Taiwan, were reaping economic benefits from expanded U.S. military activity in the region by providing supplies, maintenance facilities, and various services to the U.S. armed forces. As in Western Europe, a certain sympathy for the United States existed in the Asian countries but, except for Taiwan, there was little inclination to join Johnson's military crusade against communism in Southeast Asia.

After his return to Washington, Mansfield saw the president repeatedly on Vietnam, reiterating long-held views on seeking to negotiate an end to the war and urging Johnson to invite the United Nations to play a role, a course that the administration had avoided from the outset. Although the president continued to receive the majority leader politely, he gave no indication of a readiness to move in a new direction. Instead, he hosted a series of dinners at the White House for members of the Senate, using the occasions to try to win support for the executive branch's thesis that military escalation was working and to reiterate his conviction that there was "light at the end of the tunnel."

Although it placed him ever more obviously in disagreement with the president, Mansfield continued his stubborn resistance to expansion of the war. He received criticism, as well as support, from the public in assuming this position, with support in time far outweighing the criticism. Endorsements came to him from elements in the media, intellectuals, and specialists in foreign affairs, some of whom had previously held the view that, constitutionally speaking, foreign affairs was virtually the exclusive business of the executive branch. As for the role of Congress, the less said about it, the better. Almost in desperation, they turned to Mansfield to lead in bringing the war to an end. But the majority leader had no desire to stand at the head of a populist movement against the war, holding steadfastly to the view that his responsibility lay in the Senate. Young people and other opponents of the Vietnam War also turned to Mansfield for guidance, consolation, or reassurance, particularly with regard to the military draft. In responding to these entreaties, Mansfield took the position that he was sworn to uphold the law of the land, and the military draft was the law. He cautioned those who would ignore or flee from the draft, even as a matter of conscience, to be fully cognizant of what they were about to do and to be prepared to accept the consequences.

The public's initial exuberance for Johnson's leadership on Vietnam began to fade when it became apparent that the war would be prolonged and would carry a heavy price in American lives and resources. The new view of where Johnson had led the nation was formed in great part by the nightly television projections into America's living rooms of returning flag-draped caskets, and the unloading of the sick and maimed from hospital planes. As

1967 drew to a close, fewer and fewer Americans were seeing the light at the end of the tunnel. Many were no longer even bothering to look for it.

For Democrats in the Senate, the shift of public sentiment on Vietnam posed a political problem of the first order. How could Democrats support Johnson for reelection and at the same time divorce themselves from the consequences of his Vietnamese policy? The question became even more acute when Democratic Senator Gene McCarthy of Minnesota indicated that he could not do so and that, because of the war, he was considering opposing Johnson for the presidential nomination. With young Americans rushing to back him, McCarthy was dismissed at first with a note of amusement as a "pied piper" or the leader of a "children's crusade." His threat to Johnson turned serious when he began to be seen as a "stalking horse" for Senator Robert Kennedy of New York. On 3 January 1968, McCarthy formally announced his candidacy and entered the New Hampshire primary.

Several weeks after the New Year of 1968, the war took an unexpected turn that accelerated the political downfall of Lyndon Johnson. During the Tet Holiday marking the New Year on the moon-based ancient Vietnamese calendar, forces infiltrated by Hanoi and the southern Vietcong guerrillas launched coordinated uprisings in three-fourths of the forty-four provincial capitals of South Vietnam, including the former royal capital of Hue. In the heart of Saigon, the U.S. Embassy was attacked.

Hanoi paid a heavy price in casualties, and most of the captured positions were quickly relinquished as surviving guerrillas faded back into the general populace or withdrew to rural bases. But the demonstration of their widespread power in the south came as a severe shock to the people of the United States. Media portrayals of bleeding American personnel staggering around the damaged embassy and the cold-blooded shooting of a captured guerrilla in the streets by a South Vietnamese officer after the attack had been repulsed raised more pointedly than ever the question of the role of Americans in Vietnam. Subsequent attempts by General Westmoreland and the Defense Department to portray the Tet offensive as a severe setback for the communists and, actually, a victory for "our side" evoked more derision than concurrence from a deeply concerned American public. Ironically, shortly after the Tet "victory," Westmoreland was asking President Johnson to increase the American forces in Vietnam by another 200,000 men—above the 500,000 already engaged.

The repercussions from Tet were felt quickly in American politics. Among the first to react was Richard M. Nixon, who announced his candidacy for the Republican nomination for president. A few weeks later, Eugene McCarthy won 42 percent of the vote against Johnson's 48 percent in the

New Hampshire Democratic primary. The vote was interpreted by professional politicians and the media as a clear indication that Johnson could not be reelected. Bobby Kennedy nailed down Johnson's political fate by announcing his candidacy for the Democratic nomination, a move that promised to split major elements in the Democratic party and throw even Johnson's renomination into doubt. Although entered on the New Hampshire ballot, Johnson had not campaigned personally in the primary, insisting that he was too preoccupied with the problems of the nation to pay attention to politics.

One of these problems, of course, was the request from Westmoreland for 200,000 more troops. In a private meeting with the Senate majority leader, Johnson showed Mansfield the request. The president asked Mansfield bluntly what he thought should be done. Equally bluntly, Mansfield replied: "Don't do it, Mr. President." He went on to say one more time that the way out of Vietnam was not to go further in and that the situation could not be brought to a satisfactory conclusion by military means. The president lapsed into a silence that Mansfield took to signify that the discussion was over. As he was going out the door, Johnson called after him: "I would appreciate some support from my majority leader." Mansfield turned and replied: "Mr. President, I'm not your majority leader. I'm the Senate's majority leader."

Johnson laid aside Westmoreland's request for more forces. In March 1968, Johnson announced the deescalation of the war and his irrevocable decision not to run again for the presidency.

6

From China to Watergate:
The Nixon Years, 1968–1974

The war in Vietnam was the dominant issue in the election of 1968. The Republican candidate, Richard Nixon, attacked President Johnson's handling of Vietnam, and Hubert Humphrey, the Democratic candidate, attempted a vigorous defense of Johnson on Vietnam almost to the end of the campaign. Largely unmentioned was the role that Nixon played in deepening the U.S. involvement by prodding Johnson into ordering direct U.S. military participation, a step that would prove to be the undoing of Johnson's presidency. Not that the president needed much prodding. Long before sinking into the Vietnam quagmire, he was acutely aware of the potential for political disaster in Indochina. Notwithstanding, he set out on a course that ensured his downfall.

As with most Democratic politicians of the period, Johnson could readily recall the impact on American politics a decade earlier when China collapsed into communism. In that situation, President Truman, guided by General George C. Marshall and Dean Acheson, successive secretaries of state, had tried to stand clear of the avalanche, only to find that the Democratic Party had to pay a heavy price for "losing China" to "godless communism." The political impact of the China collapse was doubled when, in a reversal of course, U.S. forces were thrust into what was to become the undeclared "Truman's war" in Korea.

Johnson was convinced that a repeat of the China scenario in Vietnam would be devastating to the Democrats and to his reelection in 1968. As with generals portrayed as still fighting the last war when planning for the next, politicians also tend to be guided by the sharp sting of attacks suffered in past elections while trying to arm themselves to contest the next. Johnson was deeply concerned that unless a communist takeover were stopped quickly in Vietnam, the old Republican political slogan of "Who lost China?" would emerge in a new version as "Who lost Vietnam?" And the finger would point directly at Johnson and the Democrats.

Johnson was primed, then, to use U.S. military power in Vietnam if necessary to prevent a communist victory. The political pressure applied by Nixon during his comeback was an added factor, prompting the president to bring U.S. forces actively into the war in Vietnam. All presidents in those years of Cold War confrontation were faced with trying to deal with whatever real threat communism abroad posed to the nation while looking back over their shoulder at political repercussions at home. Nixon's tactics in pursuit of the Republican nomination in the elections of 1968 prompted Johnson to take what was to be a tragic misstep in Vietnam, and when Johnson decided not to run in 1968, Nixon turned the Vietnam issue against his hapless Democratic opponent, Hubert Humphrey, who felt compelled to go "all the way with LBJ."

Other factors, of course, underlay Nixon's victory over Humphrey. After the racial harmony that followed enactment of the Civil Rights Act of 1964, national anxieties over race relations emerged once again to disturb the nation's internal stability. Long-pent-up black resentments against segregation were released in widespread protests. Rioting, looting, and burning broke out in cities throughout the nation, particularly after the assassination of Martin Luther King Jr. in 1968. With the riots, unspoken fears welled up in white Americans, lending a new respectability to random calls for "law and order" directed primarily at blacks. The wedge of racial division was driven deeply again, sending powerful reverberations through the nation's politics. To make matters worse, another political assassination ended the life of Robert F. Kennedy and, in so doing, seemed to dash any prospect of reviving the youthful enthusiasm and hopeful idealism that had been tapped a decade earlier by John F. Kennedy.

Racial division and other national problems worked against incumbent Democrats in the election of 1968 even as Vietnam emerged as the decisive factor. In voting for Nixon, whatever else may have motivated them, American voters were clearly expressing a deep dissatisfaction with Johnson's handling of the war. "Hawks" demanded a clear-cut military win, "doves" urged a dignified "out," and Johnson and his advisors were unable to produce either. To be sure, a sop was thrown to opponents of the war by opening contact in Paris with representatives of Hanoi. This "peace" gesture, however, stalled almost before it started, over who was to sit where at the conference table. Tied up by procedural symbolisms of that kind at the outset, the talks went nowhere and were soon dismissed by U.S. antiwar elements as representing, not a shift in policy to peace, but a charade designed to placate growing numbers of Americans fed up with what began to look more and more like an aimless, half-hearted U.S. military adventure of indefinite duration.

As the presidential campaign of 1968 drew near, many Democrats and independent voters, alienated by Johnson's leadership on Vietnam, attached themselves to Senator Eugene McCarthy's early candidacy for the Democratic nomination. Dismissed by the bemused media as a "Children's Crusade," this largely youthful opposition to the war coalesced as a major element within the Democratic Party. Later, its support shifted en masse from McCarthy to Robert F. Kennedy after the latter decided to seek the Democratic nomination. The enthusiasm of Bobby Kennedy's supporters rose to a crescendo after a victory in the California primary promised to sweep him into the Democratic nomination. The shock of his assassination in June 1968, produced such disarray among Democrats that control of the national convention in Chicago was for all practical purposes left in the hands of Lyndon Johnson.

Even before the convention opened, it was a foregone conclusion that Humphrey would receive Johnson's blessings as the Democratic nominee for president. Not necessarily hostile to Humphrey but hostile to the continuance of the war, antiwar Democrats converged on the Chicago convention determined to make their voices heard for peace in Vietnam. Johnson held out no olive branch to them beyond the stale generalities about peace even as the fighting continued. The noisy demonstrations against the war that broke out in the streets of Chicago were suppressed by the Chicago police with what seemed to be a relished brutality. The police force, it should be noted, was closely controlled by Mayor Richard Daley Sr., and Daley was a political ally of Johnson. Thus, Humphrey, as Johnson's hand-picked successor, suffered the loss of support not only of the militant antiwar Democrats but also of many of the undecided throughout the nation who were revolted by the vicious treatment of the demonstrators or put off by the manifest chaos within the Democratic Party.

After the Chicago convention, the election boiled down to a choice between Humphrey as the defender of an increasingly unpopular policy on

Vietnam and Nixon, the Republican candidate self-portrayed as bent on bringing an end to the war and the return of U.S. forces from Vietnam. Try as he might, Humphrey was unable to shift the focus of the campaign to other issues. Nixon emerged ironically as the "peace candidate," modeling his campaign after that of Eisenhower's in the 1952 election. At that time, with the United States enmeshed in the unpopular "Truman's war" with North Korea and a revolutionary China, the Republican presidential candidate pledged to go to Korea to find a way to bring the war to a close. In a similar vein, Nixon assured the public that he had a "secret plan" to end the war in Vietnam. His political star rose quickly above a Humphrey burdened by his unqualified endorsement of Johnson's Vietnam policy, a burden that he could not bring himself to shed until the closing days of the campaign. By then, confronted with almost certain defeat, he sought in desperation to establish a separate identity for himself on the Vietnam issue. Thereafter, the gap between the candidates began to close, but not fast enough to overcome the early Nixon lead. In the end, Humphrey suffered the defeat that very likely would have been Johnson's had he sought reelection in 1968.

Those who knew Humphrey had difficulty in ascribing his stand on Vietnam to his personal conviction as to the rightness of U.S. policy. As a member of the Senate Foreign Relations Committee, he had shown little interest in the Vietnamese question. But as vice-president, he had defended the Johnson administration vigorously before the same committee. While a vice president is inevitably linked to an incumbent administration, many have managed to maintain an independent identity on specific presidential positions. Humphrey made no such effort. His support for Johnson on Vietnam was unqualified and active. Many observers saw this as the price Humphrey had to pay for the president's backing for the nomination. That may have been a consideration, but it was not clear why Humphrey continued to carry the full weight of Vietnam after he was deep into the race with Nixon. Was it fear of the reach of Johnson's wrath or concern that he might be vulnerable on "stopping communism" even though he had, as a senator, sponsored legislation to ban the Communist Party? Or was it yet another manifestation of the poor sense of timing on major issues that had plagued the Minnesotan at critical moments during his lifelong quest for the presidency?

Humphrey's difficulty is illustrated by an incident involving one of his strong supporters, John Pastore of Rhode Island. Pastore, a raconteur with an earthy sense of humor, joined in an informal postmortem after Nixon's victory. Senator Pastore told several Democratic colleagues of a phone call from Humphrey shortly after the Chicago convention had nominated him for the presidency. Humphrey was seeking not only assurances of Pastore's support in New England but also advice on how best to shape his campaign against Nixon. Pastore reassured Humphrey of his strong personal backing and then went on to offer two pieces of advice. "First, I told him to put some distance between himself and the President on Vietnam." I said, "You don't have to break with Johnson, but neither do you have to sit in his lap" on this issue. The second point I made was that he needed to shorten his speeches: "Great speeches, but you tend sometimes to exhaust your audience." Theo he added: "Do you know what he did? He thanked me and that very night Hubert went out and delivered a very powerful defense of Johnson on Vietnam. And would you believe, he did it in the longest speech I ever heard him make!"

After his election, Nixon reiterated his campaign's main theme in his Inaugural Address. Even though his secret plan to end the war proved to be nothing more than a campaign gimmick, as Nixon himself acknowledged after leaving office, it had created the impression that Nixon was bent on restoring peace in Vietnam in short order. The "hawks" assumed that Nixon's plan would intensify the use of U.S. military power to bring Hanoi to its knees. By contrast, the "doves" supporting Nixon had persuaded themselves that his plan involved serious negotiations leading to an armistice with Hanoi that would permit a withdrawal of U.S. forces. Either way, by more war or less, a prompt finale to the U.S. military involvement seemed to be the public's expectation. Instead, the war continued through the entire four years of Nixon's first administration and well into his second term. A final withdrawal took place only during the surrogate administration of President Ford after Nixon's resignation.

Continuation of the War in Vietnam

On assuming the presidency, Nixon picked up the threads of the same policy pursued by Johnson. Indeed, the roots of this policy stretched back through successive administrations—Democratic and Republican—all the way to Truman, each president rearranging details of American policy in Vietnam, with one eye fixed on the issues and the other on meeting the domestic political imperative of "stopping communism." Until Johnson's presidency, however, the rearrangements of Vietnam policy were accomplished without direct commitment of U.S. military forces and hence with minimal U.S. casualties and limited strains on the national economy. Indeed, the rearrangements were scarcely felt at home, and public support for overall Vietnam policy as an element in "stopping communism" remained at least adequate. But Johnson's rearrangements amounted to a conversion of policy from indirect to direct U.S. military participation. In addition to the adverse impact of escalating U.S. casualties and costs, Johnson's decision changed the nature of the conflict in Vietnam. It became impossible to maintain even the fiction that the war was a struggle among Vietnamese factions, with the United States helping a nationalist faction turn back a takeover by world communism. Instead, after the assassination of President Diem and his brother, the war came to be widely seen as a confrontation between Vietnamese defenders of the Vietnamese people and a foreign military power that, not unlike the French imperialists, was aided by Vietnamese mercenaries. What had previously involved a U.S. policy on Vietnam underwritten largely by U.S. aid programs became a commitment from Washington to do whatever might be necessary to keep Vietnam out of the control of the Communist leader Ho Chi Minh. Pursuit of this enlarged objective called for a huge increase in U.S. expenditures and direct U.S. military participation on the ground in the south. It also resulted in the progressive extension of the conflict into the north by U.S. air and sea power.

Johnson's rearrangement of Vietnam policy was based in part on a desire to bring the war quickly to an end; he found insufferable the indecisive holding action of his predecessors. The Tonkin Gulf response had not been sufficient to convince the communists that the United States was serious about its determination to remain in South Vietnam until a noncommunist situation could prevail there. A more powerful statement of the U.S. position would have to be made. This took the form of the deployment of U.S. forces plus the willingness to engage U.S. military power directly in the conflict. Johnson expected it would prove decisive. At the time of his departure from the presidency, however, this extension had failed to persuade Hanoi even to enter into talks with the Saigon military that had replaced the Diem government. At the same time, in the United States, the strain of direct U.S. military approach was felt in inflationary pressures that forced the successor Nixon administration to resort to price controls even as it weakened the international financial position of the United States. Most significantly, heavy U.S. military casualties brought the cost of the war home to the American people in a way that had not occurred since Korea. The level of public concern regarding the wisdom of Vietnam policy rose steadily, especially since the Johnson administration was unable to spell out tangible national objectives of a kind that might have justified the massive costs. By the time Nixon assumed the presidency, popular support for the war was in rapid decline in the United States, even as open civil defiance spread rapidly across the land. Indeed, soon after his inauguration, Nixon complained to Mansfield that Johnson had had three years to come to grips with the Vietnam problem while he had a margin for maneuver of only a matter of months.

On assuming the presidency, Nixon made no move to abandon his predecessor's policy, as many had expected. Instead, he continued to press military action while talking of peace in generalities. At the same time, he sought ways to curb the growing impatience with the war at home by gestures suggesting a reduction of the U.S. military role. Less than ninety days after the inauguration, Secretary of Defense Melvin Laird announced the "Vietnamization" of the war. This change was generally taken to mean that the great bulk of the fighting would be shifted to Saigon's military establishment, and the direct U.S. military role would revert to what it had been before Johnson's presidency: largely one of supply and training for Saigon's own military establishment. The change was responsive to the major popular concern in the United States about the war because it promised to curb U.S. casualties among the half million military personnel that had been deployed in Vietnam during the Johnson administration. By the end of Nixon's second year in the White House, his new approach had succeeded in lowering that peak to 334,000. A year later, there would be a further drop, to 150,000.

The shrinking deployment of personnel in South Vietnam, however, did not equate with a decline in the U.S. military contribution to the war and its destructiveness. Seeking to counterbalance the draw-down of forces on the ground in South Vietnam, Nixon intensified air and naval warfare against North Vietnam. This involved stepping up the secret air strikes directed from the U.S. Embassy in "neutral" Laos and the relentless long-range bombing runs from Guam over North Vietnam. In time, the port of Haiphong was mined and the B-54 air strikes reached deep into the capital city of Hanoi. The new emphasis on U.S. airpower appears to have stopped just short of the destruction of the Red River dikes, an undertaking advocated in some Washington circles that could have caused the deaths of untold numbers of Vietnamese peasants and the destruction of much of the main food source for the population in North Vietnam.

Mansfield's Reaction to Nixon

At the outset, Mansfield felt that the chances of ending the war promptly would be greater with Nixon as president than they had been with Johnson. For one thing, Nixon was not under the same political pressure at home to emerge with a military victory. He had assumed responsibility for the war only after it was already widely regarded as a lost cause. Almost anything he might do to end it was likely to escape severe public criticism. By that point, there was no great victory to be claimed as a solace for the huge costs of the war, but Nixon could hardly be blamed. He was more likely to reap political credit for ending the loss of American lives and the huge expenditures for the war.

In his initial encounters with Nixon as president, Mansfield had judged him to be personally insecure and, notwithstanding his assurances about a secret plan, uncertain of the road out of Vietnam. In spite of these reservations, Mansfield was persuaded that Nixon was sincere in his desire to bring the war to a prompt end. At first, Mansfield thought that the new president would veer toward the view that "the way out was not to go further in," and Nixon's quick announcement of a reduction in U.S. ground forces seemed to be a step in that direction. As an encouragement for the president to stay on this course, Mansfield started at once to look for ways to alleviate Nixon's insecurity in the White House, reasoning that it would be helpful if Nixon were reassured that insofar as the Senate was concerned, Nixon had room for maneuver on Vietnam. He need not keep looking over his shoulder for fear that Senate Democrats would try to do him in politically for seeking a negotiated peace with the communist Vietminh. To that end, Mansfield began exploring within the Democratic Policy Committee the possibility of passing a resolution that would be expressive of the committee's agreement with Nixon that if he embarked on a peace initiative, it would not later be used against him in a political sense. What he found was that while committee members were not prepared to make a formal endorsement of such a policy, members were not inclined to seek political advantage by challenging it. With Mansfield's encouragement, they were prepared to restrain their criticism. A similar attitude prevailed among Democratic senators as a whole. The Senate, it seemed, was ready for a short period of relative silence on Vietnam.

Against that background, Nixon traveled to Guam to deliver a speech on foreign policy. Although couched in generalities, the speech had major ramifications for Vietnam. Nixon declared that his administration would hold to the following principles as the guiding lights of U.S. policy in the Far East:

1. To honor all U.S. treaty commitments against those who might invade the lands of allies of the United States;
2. To provide a nuclear umbrella against threats of other nuclear powers; and
3. To supply weapons and technical assistance to countries where warranted *but without committing American forces to local conflicts.*

As applied to Vietnam, these principles were part of a continuum of basic premises that had been in effect from the Truman administration until the moment when Johnson decided to plunge U.S. ground combat forces directly into the conflict in Vietnam. Nixon's statement suggested a step back from Johnson's decision. It was also at variance with the politically correct course for all politicians of the period, which seemed to require even local armed conflicts anywhere in the world to be attributable to the international communist conspiracy. Nixon's Guam statement offered an opportunity to see the Vietnam conflict in a different light. Moscow's or Beijing's involvement would not necessarily be at the core of the conflict but an add-on to an essentially local conflict among Vietnamese; indeed, that later proved to be true. In these circumstances, direct U.S. military intervention as sponsored by President Johnson might very well be reexamined, especially by a successor Republican president without the political obfuscation of being branded as "soft on communism."

Mansfield may have read into Nixon's words more than was there. But the Guam speech permitted the Senate leader to give enthusiastic support to the president on his new Vietnam policy. Mansfield pressed his interpretation of the Guam remarks at every opportunity. He extolled the speech as a major departure in U.S. foreign policy. He even sought to give the speech a historic dimension by labeling it the "Nixon Doctrine." Not to be confused with the Monroe Doctrine, this "sound bite" took hold with the media whose repeated use of it aroused considerable interest and some consternation both at home and abroad. In the Far East, the Nixon Doctrine, as espoused by Mansfield, engendered favorable reactions in some nations. In others, the response was more cautious, indicating a concern lest it foreshadow a retreat of the United States into a new isolationism and a curtailment in the flow of U.S. aid. The president apparently was not sure what Mansfield had in mind but found nothing objectionable in the sound of "Nixon Doctrine," as it resonated over the airwaves.

Nixon's relationship with the Senate majority leader continued to grow warmer. Mansfield saw the president frequently, refrained from criticizing him on Vietnam, and constantly sought ways to reassure him of backing from the Senate in his efforts to bring the war to a close. The majority leader worked to supplement his personal support by raising the Vietnam question repeatedly in meetings of the Democratic Policy Committee, invariably citing the Nixon Doctrine in a favorable light. The president, in turn, endorsed a Mansfield visit to East Asia, designed primarily to elicit from leaders of that region their reactions to the new doctrine. Nixon also asked the majority leader to go to Cambodia in view of his personal rapport with Prince Sihanouk, as a way of facilitating the restoring of U.S.–Cambodian diplomatic relations that the Prince had broken at what he regarded as U.S. threats to Cambodia's independence and neutralism.

The president also requested that Mansfield serve as his primary point of contact in the Senate, complaining that there was too much loose talk from the Foreign Relations Committee to use it in that fashion; he did not mention the disdain with which he was regarded by Chairman Fulbright. The request placed Mansfield in a difficult position because a main component of his style of leadership was deference to the committees and their chairmen. This not only pleased the chairmen but also kept Mansfield out of most disputes between the president and Congress. Nevertheless, in this instance, he placed the president's request before the Democratic Policy Committee as one to be considered not by himself alone but by the Senate Democratic Leadership as a whole. Senator Russell was the first to endorse the proposal. Breathing with great difficulty because of the emphysema from which he would soon die, the Georgian informed the committee that he had recently had a private meeting with Nixon and that the president had expressed great confidence in Mansfield's judgments on foreign affairs. Russell added that he felt the same way about Mansfield. As for Vietnam, Russell saw no reason why Mansfield could not represent his views to the president. The committee was not prepared to go quite that far, but it did authorize Mansfield to communicate its sentiments on Vietnam orally to the president and to establish the kind of rapport with Nixon that would minimize partisanship.

Mansfield then discussed the president's request with Chairman Fulbright, explaining that he intended to represent the Senate Democrats as supportive of the president's efforts to close out the war. While Fulbright raised no objection to Mansfield's serving as Nixon's point of contact with the Senate, he warned that he would not hold back criticism if Nixon did not move fast enough to end U.S. military involvement. For the most part, the Senate Democrats endorsed Mansfield's efforts to marshal support for presidential peace efforts. As for the Senate Republicans, they went along with the majority leader. Minority Leader Dirksen had initially endorsed Johnson's deepening of the commitment. But with his death imminent, Dirksen was no longer able to keep abreast of developments in Vietnam and changing public attitudes on the issue. His successor as Senate Republican leader, Hugh Scott of Pennsylvania, had a long and deep personal interest in the Far East, having served there as a young naval officer during World War II. Scott recognized the need to get out of Vietnam and was happy to defer to Mansfield, particularly when he was attempting to support a Republican president. Other Republicans, such as George Aiken of Vermont, John Sherman Cooper of Kentucky, Mark Hatfield of Oregon, and Charles McC. Mathias Jr. of Maryland, were in agreement with Mansfield on the need for a military withdrawal from Vietnam, as were an ever-increasing number of Republican senators who had initially followed Dirksen in un-critical support of Johnson's move toward direct U.S. participation in the war and were now prepared to endorse the Nixon Doctrine as a way out.

Growing Public Outrage

Notwithstanding bipartisan restraint in Congress, the patience with the new Nixon approach quickly wore thin in antiwar circles. Scarcely two months into Nixon's presidency, the Women's Strike for Peace staged a massive demonstration in Washington. It was clearly intended to remind the new administration that Nixon had been elected to end the military venture. By autumn, huge crowds were being drawn into demonstrations throughout the nation to denounce the war. In some cities, counterdemonstrations led to clashes between opponents and proponents of the military involvement. Then came the killing of four students by National Guardsmen who fired into a crowd staging a protest against the war on the campus of Kent State University in Ohio. The media spread news of this act throughout the nation and world in heavy coverage that included a dramatic photo of a young women pleading for help as she knelt beside a dead youth on the campus. The incident raised deeply disturbing questions about what the war was doing to the nation's values and the unity of its people.

So, too, did the revelation of widespread drug use by American service-men in Vietnam and "fraggings" of U.S. military officers, the term being used to describe a practice of setting off a grenade under the cot of a sleeping officer by disgruntled enlisted men under his command.

In the midst of this intensifying disintegration of standards and discipl-ine, the My Lai massacre came to light, an incident in which U.S. soldiers rounded up and gunned down indiscriminately the inhabitants of a small Vietnamese village. The atrocity was attributed to the weariness and frustra-tion of U.S. servicemen, engendered by weeks of futile pursuit of Vietcong guerrillas. To be sure, the Vietcong was an elusive enemy that moved with ease in the same environment that offered sullen hostility to Americans. Nevertheless, the conscience of the nation was shocked by the deliberate killing of old men, women and children.

As the war went on, the opposition at home became more outspoken. There were defiant public burnings of draft cards and an exodus of young Americans seeking asylum in Canada, Sweden, and elsewhere rather than respond to the military draft. The Nixon administration sought to deflect the rising discontent by reducing draft calls and liberalizing military deferments and similar palliatives, all the while assuring the public that the United States was getting out of Vietnam as fast as possible.

Nixon shut himself up in the White House, refusing even to acknowledge the protests. When the administration's attempts to deaden the pain of Vietnam proved insufficient to lift the national discomfort, he did order the resumption of talks with Hanoi in Paris. Initiated by Lyndon Johnson for much the same domestic reasons, these talks had gone nowhere and had remained in suspension for months. In resuming them in February 1970, Nixon bypassed Secretary of State William Rogers, entrusting the responsibility instead to Henry Kissinger, the National Security Council advisor. Kissinger had brought with him into the White House an impressive reputation. He was known as a brilliant teacher of international relations at Harvard University and had written extensively on questions of national security and foreign policy. He had also served as an advisor to New York Governor Nelson Rockefeller when the latter was contemplating another try for the presidency. Kissinger's personal manner was easy-going and charming and illuminated by flashes of a sharp wit. These characteristics made him an effective negotiator with the Vietnamese, but they also concealed a view of the war that was at first as taut and unbending as that of Lyndon Johnson.

Kissinger's good humor and readiness to make light of procedural formalities failed to budge his Vietnamese counterparts in Paris. Hanoi continued to regard the United States as the successor to French colonialism in Indochina, and its spokesmen insisted that all U.S. military activity in Vietnam had to come to an end as the first step in negotiations. For his part, Kissinger sought to uphold the legality of the Saigon government and to make the acceptance of its leaders part of the peace process. He also called for the ending of North Vietnam's aggression against the South. Kissinger's initial position in the negotiations indicated that the Nixon administration was not prepared to abandon the strategy of measured military escalation as the way to handle Hanoi. When the Kissinger talks proved no more fruitful than the earlier round under Johnson, they were once again broken off by the United States, only to be resumed at intervals, usually after periods of intensified U.S. bombing of North Vietnam.

It was the composition of U.S. military activity rather than the aims or direction of U.S. policy that changed at the outset of Nixon's presidency. His administration did move to reduce the heavy U.S. involvement in the ground conflict in the south. At the same time, U.S. air and naval action against the north was increased, a heavily destructive tactic but one that involved fewer American casualties.

Congressional Action to End the War

At one point, the new approach appeared to suffer an unexpected interruption when Nixon abruptly ordered an invasion of Cambodia. The order was accompanied by considerable ballyhoo that was widely interpreted as a major expansion of the war. Nixon quickly backed away from that interpretation, seeking to reassure the nation that the action was not an invasion but merely an incursion, intended to capture the high command of Hanoi's forces in South Vietnam who were said to be holed up in headquarters in the Cambodian jungles close to the South Vietnamese border. But the U.S. armored column that rolled into Cambodia encountered neither resistance nor the Vietnam high command. At one point they did stumble onto a military compound of empty buildings, presumably the hastily evacuated enemy headquarters. After the press had been afforded an opportunity to take pictures of the buildings and a pile of documents said to have been Hanoi's secret orders to its commanders in the South, the U.S. column turned around and made a leisurely return to Vietnam.

Although Republican Senator George Aiken of Vermont labeled the incident "politics" and dismissed it as almost laughable, the seemingly abrupt shift in direction caused an uproar. Other members of the Senate described it as an expansion of the U.S. involvement in Indochina. To Mansfield, the Cambodian incident was a deep disappointment. He was greatly concerned that Nixon might have reversed course and, instead of continuing to shrink the U.S. military presence, was on the verge of plunging the nation more deeply into Indochina. Mansfield asked for and received instructions from the Democratic caucus to seek a meeting with the president for himself and Senator Hugh Scott, the newly designated Republican leader, to ascertain which direction Vietnam policy was headed, in or out. As events developed, the Cambodian incident did appear to be more of an incursion than an invasion and had no effect on the course of the war in Vietnam. On the one hand, the action served to placate those elements in the American electorate that thirsted for tangible demonstrations of the omnipotence of U.S. military power. On the other hand, the action provoked intensified criticism from opponents of Vietnam policy as a further spread of the war. It precipitated another wave of street and campus protests against the Nixon administration.

It also foreshadowed a coup d'état against Prince Sihanouk and an end to his efforts to maintain Cambodian neutrality with regard to the war in Vietnam. A few months later, while the prince was undergoing medical treatment in Paris, his chief military aide, General Lon Nol, seized control of the government in Pnom Penh. With embarrassing haste, the Nixon administration embraced Lon Nol and immediately began infusions of costly military aid and direct air support to keep him in power. Despite the U.S. prop, Lon Nol's regime lasted only until the end of the war in Vietnam. The general was then flown by the United States to the safety of Hawaii. Sihanouk returned to his battered country from exile in China only to be held a virtual prisoner in the Royal Palace by the Khmer Rouge, who had seized control of the country in a hideous bloodbath. In turn, the Khmer Rouge was forced from power and, once again, Prince Sihanouk returned, this time with Washington's concurrence, as a funnel for the U.N.-sponsored effort to build a democracy in an independent and neutral Cambodia.

Although joining other U.S. spokesmen in rejecting the charge that the coup against Prince Sihanouk had been engineered by the United States, Mansfield denounced the overthrow of the prince by Lon Nol. Almost alone in Washington, Mansfield had long argued that a neutral Cambodia served U.S. interests in Southeast Asia far better than another military satrapy maintained largely at U.S. expense. For him, the upsetting of Cambodian neutrality and the administration's quick acceptance of Lon Nol marked a turning point in his relationship with Nixon. Thereafter, Mansfield abandoned whatever expectation he may have had that the Nixon administration could be encouraged to negotiate out of Indochina. That expectation had led him to offer Nixon assurances of his concurrence and support of a good faith effort. After the upsetting of Cambodian neutrality, Mansfield decided that it was time to try by formal congressional action to force an end to U.S. involvement in the war in Indochina, a course already advocated by Senate colleagues in increasing numbers.

Mansfield reached this conclusion with great reluctance. Apart from the parliamentary problems involved, he had a personal aversion to congressional interference in the conduct of foreign policy, particularly in the midst of a war. To be sure, Congress, particularly the Senate, shared a constitutional responsibility with the executive branch in formulating policy. But its execution, in the absence of overriding reasons to the contrary, Mansfield felt, was best left to the president and the executive branch. The Cambodian interlude was to the majority leader a clear indication that the executive branch had lost its way in Indochina, and a strong effort had to be made by Congress to restrain the other branch's continued pursuit of a "wrong war in a wrong place." Although under strong pressure from his colleagues and the public to act swiftly, Mansfield moved with great caution. He was acutely aware that any attempt to legislate an end to the U.S. military involvement could involve a confrontation between the president and Congress and carry a high risk of failure. For the legislative branch to be effective, there had to be, first of all, a dependable majority in both the Senate and the House for ending the U.S. involvement. These majorities would have to be not only of one mind on this objective but also in general agreement on specific legislative steps to be taken to reach it. Although Congress could declare war, it could not declare peace, and there was no indication that Nixon was prepared to accept a congressional initiative for peace that differed from his own. Without such acceptance, the required majorities in the two houses to bring about a legislatively designed peace would rise to two-thirds in order to prevail against the president's constitutional power of the veto.

Notwithstanding these difficulties, decreasing popular support for the war convinced Mansfield that the time had arrived to try to force an end to the U.S. military involvement in Indochina. Developments within Congress at the time reinforced his conviction. For one thing, Hugh Scott's succession to the Senate Republican leadership opened the way for a bipartisan approach on Vietnam similar to what Mansfield had pursued in securing passage of the Civil Rights Act of 1964. On the House side, too, Carl Albert of Oklahoma had replaced John McCormack as Speaker. That change, plus the midterm elections that brought in many new members who were outspoken opponents of the war, had increased greatly the possibilities of cooperation between the House and Senate on Vietnam. Mansfield was quick to exploit this opening by initiating regular meetings of the Democratic leadership of both houses of Congress. Speaker Albert was enthusiastic about this liaison, in contrast with McCormack, who rarely deigned to discuss anything with the Senate leadership except adjournments of Congress.

Having concluded that it was time for Congress to attempt to end the war, Mansfield turned to an approach sponsored jointly by Democratic Senator Frank Church of Idaho and Republican Senator John Sherman Cooper of Kentucky. The two senators were proposing, first, legislation to nail the lid shut on any further expansion of U.S. military activity in Cambodia and then to force the executive branch to shrink the U.S. role in steps by placing increasingly stringent legislative limitations on the use of U.S. forces and appropriated funds for Indochina. When the first Cooper-Church measure was brought before the Senate, with Mansfield's support, it was bitterly contested by the Nixon administration. When its passage was thrown into doubt, Mansfield offered a softening amendment to make the measure more palatable to the administration, and it carried. It also carried Mansfield's message to Nixon: Mansfield had gone as far as he would go to cooperate with the president on Vietnam, and the White House could no longer count on the Senate to underwrite the continuance of the U.S. military involvement in Vietnam. Other legislation, advanced by Mark Hatfield of Oregon, George McGovern of South Dakota, and others of both parties, as well as by Cooper and Church, forced adherence to that message by tightening the screws on the president's freedom of maneuver in Indochina, a form of legislative escalation for peace. In December 1970, over executive branch protests, Congress voted to prohibit the use of U.S. combat forces or advisors in Cambodia and Laos. Next, all U.S. bombing in Cambodia was forbidden. In time, Hatfield and McGovern succeeded in fixing specific dates for the completion of the withdrawal of all American combat forces remaining in Vietnam. By December 1972, U.S. military strength had declined from a peak of about 500,000 during the Johnson administration to 24,200. A year later, Congress restricted the size of the U.S. military contingent in Vietnam to a maximum of fifty. While the downsizing was in progress, Nixon appointed his White House National Security Advisor, Henry Kissinger, to replace William Rogers as secretary of state. Combining both offices in one person helped align the bureaucratic apparatus in the executive branch and to strengthen the president's control over policy. Nixon ordered Kissinger to reopen negotiations with Hanoi's representatives in Paris. At the same time, he called for the escalation of the bombing of North Vietnam to a point just short of the devastation of the city of Hanoi. When this final escalation, too, failed to shake the North Vietnamese, Nixon reluctantly acceded to Hanoi's key demand and halted all U.S. military action in Vietnam. Thereafter, Kissinger was able to negotiate a cease-fire agreement that permitted an orderly withdrawal of the remaining U.S. ground forces. To reassure the skeptical South Vietnamese military leaders of America's continuing concern, he held out to the Saigon authorities the possibility of an increased aid program if the increase could be steered through Congress, at that point a remote possibility at best. With the United States out of the war, the Saigon authorities were left to deal with Hanoi as best they could. By that point, Saigon still had forces that had been built up through conscription and U.S. military aid to more than a million well-equipped men. Such expansion, pursued in earnest during the Johnson administration, had served essentially as a supplement to direct U.S. military action. The buildup fit in well with Nixon's policy of "Vietnamization of the war" and was strengthened and synchronized with the draw-down of U.S. ground forces.

Nevertheless, Saigon remained deeply concerned with the rapid reduction of the U.S. forces. The anxiety about the dwindling U.S. military presence proved well founded. In December 1974, North Vietnam launched massive coordinated attacks in the South. Saigon's armies evaporated almost overnight when the conscripts simply threw down their weapons and returned to their villages or faded into the cities. Within a few months, the entire southern half of the country was in the hands of Hanoi's forces. The president of South Vietnam, General Thieu, fled into exile in France, together with members of his government. His military associate, General Nguyen Cao Ky, fled to the United States and opened a liquor store in California.

When the northern armies reached the outskirts of Saigon, the U.S. Embassy in Saigon closed its doors, and the remaining American officials departed hastily by helicopter, sometimes with panicking Vietnamese employees clinging to the landing gear. The speedy exodus from Vietnam was matched in Laos and Cambodia. In the ensuing months, the American withdrawal from Indochina was followed by the flight of tens of thousands of Vietnamese and tribal people from the highlands, many of whom had been recruited by the CIA or had otherwise collaborated with the Americans during the war. They were joined by thousands of Chinese, mostly from families that had been settled in Indochina for generations. These escapees fled to Hong Kong, the Philippines, France, the United States, and elsewhere, giving rise to a massive international refugee problem that would persist for a decade or more. The aftershocks of the debacle would continue for years and not cease until after Nixon had left the White House. The agony of the Vietnam War was at last brought to a close during the Ford administration.

Nixon in China

Before the curtain was finally drawn, however, President Nixon had launched another major initiative in Asia. In the third year of his first term, and despite the continuing involvement of U.S. airpower in the Vietnamese conflict, Nixon shifted his focus in the Far East from Vietnam to China. In doing so, Nixon acted to reverse a national mindset that for three decades had seemed designed to block awareness of the very existence of a Chinese government in Beijing. During that long period of "waiting for the dust to settle" after the Chinese Revolution, U.S. China policy continued to recognize as the government of all China the nationalist regime headed by Generalissimo Chiang Kai-shek that had retreated from the Asian mainland to Taiwan before the communist onslaught. For decades, the United States not only armed, supported, and protected the Chiang regime as the government of the Republic of China, it also sought to universalize both its quarantine of the Chinese mainland and the denial of the legitimacy of the Beijing government. Although not completely successful, the U.S. effort did discourage many nations from entering into diplomatic relations or other contact with China and was instrumental in denying to the Beijing government the permanent seat reserved for China on the UN Security Council. Until the Nixon administration, that seat remained occupied by the Chiang government on Taiwan.

Nixon had done much to uphold this U.S. policy on China over the years. Nor did he shift the policy until Henry Kissinger, his chief advisor on foreign policy, had completed all the preliminaries in complete secrecy for effecting the change. When it became known, the reversal astounded the American public. Nixon was accompanied to China by a large press corps. Covered by worldwide television, the ceremonial journey dazzled the world and had a powerful impact on the United States that completely shut out potential critics, silenced political carping, nailed down the shift in policy, and even inspired the composing of an opera!

Several considerations could have prompted this master stroke by Nixon. In the first place, the opening to China was a prerequisite to closing out the Vietnam War; Hanoi could scarcely have negotiated without the concurrence of Beijing, since China was a main source of military supply and the route for much of the military aid coming from the Soviet Union. Until the war was finally over, in short, Hanoi was in no position to risk antagonizing China.

A second consideration was that the U.S. attempt to universalize its boycott of China had failed. The Beijing government that had appeared almost to welcome the quarantine at first as a way of building self-reliance had begun to encourage commercial foreign ties and other contacts. The door was opened for Japan and European countries to scout for trade opportunities, and they were doing so with increasing eagerness. As this process went on, the quarantine's principal effect seemed to be to hurt U.S. business without producing commensurate diplomatic results. One consequence of the boycott was that it precluded private U.S. citizens from entering China, much to the chagrin of the American press. In retrospect, the policy can perhaps best be described as one of self-imposed blinders on the nation's perception of what was transpiring within China. Without direct observations by qualified Americans, official judgments rested on antiquated or second-hand information filtered through other nations, Hong Kong, or Taiwan.

The atrophy in policy is illustrated by the American reaction to the monumental ideological split that took place between Joseph Stalin and Mao Zedong. This bitter face-off was accompanied by repercussions in the relationship between the Soviet Union and the People's Republic of China that profoundly disrupted trade and military collaboration and brought an end to Soviet aid. Border disputes in the northeast carried the two nations to the edge of war. Despite these developments, discussion of Chinese-Russian relations in U.S. political circles remained circumscribed by the continued use of such wornout clichés as "Communist Monolith," the "Moscow-Beijing Axis," and "partners in world communism." As President Nixon may well have understood, removing the self-imposed blinders was a necessary precondition for updating U.S. policies with both the Soviet Union and China. Finally, Nixon may have concluded that there was nothing more to be gained even in U.S. politics by clinging to the "Who lost China?" theme, and that it was time to stop beating a dead horse, especially with a Republican administration trying to end the Vietnam War. He may have sensed that the national mood was changing in a way that would permit a president, notably a Republican president, to pursue a long overdue initiative in Asian policy, a new policy based on international realities rather than political sound bites.

Whatever his motives, President Nixon found a ready-made ally for a new U.S. approach to China in Senate Majority Leader Mansfield. Mike Mansfield was highly sensitive to the political risks of the China issue. "Who lost China?" had almost ended his Senate career before it began. His political opponents pulled out all the stops on this theme during his first campaign for the Senate, almost defeating him in Montana where, after a decade of service in the House of Representatives, he was otherwise generally deemed unbeatable.

After Mansfield entered the Senate, he steered clear of the China issue, concentrating instead on Indochina. For several years, he joined the Washington mainstream in waiting "for the dust to settle" in China, the policy pursued by Secretary of State Dean Acheson during the Truman administration and one that was intensified into a rigid "quarantine" of China by Secretary John Foster Dulles during the Eisenhower administration and continued by Kennedy and Johnson. The China policy of the United States through four administrations headed by both Democratic and Republican presidents, in short, was based on the premise that the Beijing government was a temporary phenomenon that would soon fall of its own shortcomings or be toppled by a nationalist military return to the mainland from Taiwan.

During the Eisenhower administration, Mansfield joined most Democrats in the Senate in acquiescing in Secretary Dulles "pactomania," voting to approve numerous defense agreements aimed at building an isolating wall to contain the newly established People's Republic of China, as well as the Soviet Union. Democrats were at least as eager as Republicans to mark billions of dollars of military and other aid for this purpose and to strengthen the "real" Chinese government of the Republic of China on Taiwan.

While overtly supporting the Dulles-Eisenhower policy, Mansfield remained alert for politically feasible opportunities to ease U.S.–Asian policy into harmony with what, as an historian and observer, he believed to be the realities of the situation in the western Pacific and the long-term interests of the United States. Most of all, he wanted to free the U.S. government from a self-imposed exclusion from these realities on the Chinese mainland. From time to time, he spoke out against the straitjacket into which U.S. policy had been fitted. Thus, when an American journalist was threatened by the executive branch with criminal action for ignoring a passport ban that had been imposed on travel to China, Mansfield was quick to take up his cause by denouncing the attempted intimidation in a speech on the Senate floor.

With American politics still dominated by anticommunist themes, however, the relationship between China and the United States remained frozen for years in mutual mistrust, a mistrust exacerbated by the war in Korea and developments in Indochina.

By the time Lyndon Johnson became president, however, memories of the Chinese Revolution were already becoming hazy in the United States. The Korean War had been on hold for many years, thanks to a truce negotiated during the Eisenhower administration. The Chinese "volunteers" in North Korea had returned to China, with the heavily fortified dividing line at the thirty-eighth parallel becoming something of a macabre tourist attraction for visitors to Seoul. In the United States the passing years had eroded the significance of "Who lost China?" in American politics. During the Johnson administration, China was further diluted as a source of American anxiety by the expansion of the Vietnam problem. Unexpectedly, the "Who lost China?" theme did not mutate into "Who lost Vietnam?" as many older politicians, including Johnson, feared would be the case. After the nation was immersed in the war and American casualties began to mount, the principle question asked of politicians became "How and when do we get out of Vietnam?"

Mansfield sensed that answers to the Vietnam question would not be forthcoming without cracks appearing in the granite wall that had stood between Beijing and Washington for a decade and a half. He was convinced that the wall would give way, but only after Americans had a more accurate comprehension of what was going on inside China and particularly of the significance of the second great upheaval taking place there, that of the Cultural Revolution. This involved, he believed, more than collected rumors originating in not necessarily disinterested sources and filtered through Hong Kong or Taiwan listening posts. It was time, he thought, to put aside the bitterness and recrimination and reopen the question of U.S.–China relations to rational and informed discussion.

To precipitate that process, he began by surmounting his own concerns about political repercussions and making a major speech in a nonrecriminatory vein on China. The occasion was the first lecture on public affairs offered by the newly established Mansfield Foundation at the University of Montana. He urged Americans to look anew at the relationship with China and to take the first steps to replace the hostility with acts of conciliation such as cultural and educational exchanges. Having broken with the main line of American policy, Mansfield anticipated that his words would have wide media coverage, especially in Montana. He waited for the caustic political repercussions that such a speech would certainly have engendered a few years earlier. Instead, it drew cautious but almost uniformly favorable reactions from the media, particularly in Montana. Washington barely noticed it.

Reassured by the reaction, Mansfield decided to take the initiative himself by seeking to open a contact with Chou En-lai, the Chinese premier. During World War II, Mansfield had become familiar with Chou's reputation, particularly in Chungking, where Chou received much of the credit for bringing the Chinese nationalists and communists together, and with the United States, to pursue the war against Japan. At the time, Chou was serving as the Chinese communist liaison with Chiang Kai-shek's provisional capital of "Free China." Mansfield remembered him as highly intelligent, modern-minded, and dedicated to the war against Japan. Moreover, he had seemed then to have had a deep interest in promoting good relations with the United States. While Mansfield worked alone in attempting to open a channel to Beijing, he did advise President Johnson and his secretary of state, Dean Rusk, of his intentions. The president, preoccupied with Vietnam, appeared to attach little significance to the Mansfield initiative. As for Secretary Rusk, he saw no real prospect of anything coming of it. While neither Rusk nor Johnson endorsed Mansfield's proposed initiative, at no time did either seek to sidetrack it. The Mansfield overture to Beijing, in short, was that of one senator acting alone but with the knowledge of the president and secretary of state.

Mansfield attempted to contact Chou through the good offices of Prince Sihanouk of Cambodia, asking the prince to make clear to Premier Chou that if he were prepared to receive an American senator, Mansfield was prepared to go to China for that purpose. This initial feeler seemed to have been ignored by Beijing, coming as it did from a solitary voice in the U.S. Senate while U.S. official policy remained one of minimal tolerance for the new China. Mansfield's initiative was further hampered by the situation inside China at the time. The entire mainland was in the throes of the Cultural Revolution, a massive social-political upheaval—some described it as a second revolution—led by the young and most militant of the Chinese communists. Mobs of frenzied people took to the streets in the cities, towns, and villages throughout China, aimed at destroying vestigial reminders of feudal China and exposing and purging "betrayers" of the revolution who had escaped detection in educational and other cultural circles. In what was at times a violent campaign of revolutionary "purification," major figures in the Chinese Revolution, including Communist Party members such as Deng Xiaoping, were booted out of office, paraded through the streets, humiliated, and subjected to "reeducation."

The fury of the Cultural Revolution may have begun to recede at the time Mansfield began to look for an opening, but widespread xenophobia still exercised a fearful hold on the country. Anyone who had informal contact with foreigners, particularly Russians or Americans, was fair game. Chinese officials and intellectuals, in particular, might become suspect of backsliding on Maoist principles at the whim of the youthful street mobs. It was, to say the least, not the easiest time even for a Chou En-lai, Mao's long-time collaborator, to consider overtures from abroad.

So the Mansfield quest rested until after Nixon became president. An opportunity to reopen the matter was provided suddenly by an unexpected initiative from the Chinese side. A crack American table-tennis team happened to be traveling in East Asia, playing a series of matches with leading teams in friendly countries in the region. Without forewarning, the American team received a widely publicized invitation to extend their tour to China where table tennis had long been a popular sport. Without objections from Washington, the American team accepted the invitation, journeyed to China, and engaged in a series of matches with outstanding Chinese players. The event was widely covered by the Chinese and foreign media. The Americans returned home, praising the friendly reception they had received in China.

The U.S. press interpreted the exchange as evidence of a Chinese readiness to emerge from isolation. In a variation on this theme, Mansfield also decided that the time had come to renew his efforts to establish contact with Chou En-lai. He informed President Nixon of his earlier attempts during the Johnson administration and of his intention to resume pursuit of the matter. To Mansfield's surprise, the president raised no objection but urged the majority leader to continue his efforts, offering to help in any way that he could. Mansfield moved promptly, again through Prince Sihanouk of Cambodia. This time, he received a reply from the Chinese premier, although a negative one, telling Mansfield that "the time was not yet ripe." When informed of Chou's response, President Nixon found it not at all discouraging and urged the majority leader to continue his efforts.

During the ensuing months, the administration provided tangible indications that Nixon himself was seriously considering a new approach to China. The president advised Mansfield that, following the latter's recommendation, he was withdrawing the U.S. naval patrol that had continued to show the flag off the Chinese coast in the Taiwan Straits. He also withdrew U.S. objections to replacing Taiwan with Beijing in the Chinese seat at the United Nations, thus ending the diplomatic quarantine that had been the linchpin of U.S.–China policy for two decades. Such modifications of policy tied in with the majority leader's initiative, and Nixon sought and received Mansfield's support for them.

Mansfield's initiative, the table-tennis players, and other unofficial efforts to gain entry to China were the early winds of change. The actual shift in U.S. China policy, of course, had to come from Nixon as president. And with the assistance of his chief advisor, Henry Kissinger, Nixon discharged this responsibility with no little political and diplomatic skill. Because of powerful pockets of resistance to the change, even within the executive branch, the president felt compelled to play his cards very close to the chest. He left preparations for his visit in the hands of Kissinger, concealing them not only from the press but also from the executive branch and Congress, including the Senate majority leader, despite the fact that Mansfield was already in the process of opening the door.

Along with the rest of the nation, Mansfield was surprised when Nixon announced that he was going to Beijing. The news was all the more astounding to the majority leader because only a few weeks earlier he had been informed through Prince Sihanouk and the French ambassador in Washington that Premier Chou was prepared to receive him in Beijing. Even when he discussed this development with the president, Nixon made no reference to his own plans but continued to encourage Mansfield to pursue the opening. While Mansfield was in the process of trying to establish direct contact with Chou, Kissinger traveled secretly to Beijing to make the arrangements for the presidential visit. When Chou and Mansfield met in Beijing a few weeks after Nixon's journey, the premier explained that he was confronted with two proposals for a visit, the first from Mansfield via Sihanouk and the other directly from President Nixon. In the circumstance, he had concluded that the Nixon proposal took precedence. Chou was assured by Mansfield that he had made the correct choice.

Nixon's visit to Beijing in the winter of 1972 was a triumph, serving as it did to dramatize and personify the historic change that was taking place in China policy. Relayed by the television cameras, it made millions of Americans virtual participants in the event. It fascinated an American public that had begun to grow tired of the half-truths, distortions, and anachronisms that had long been the staple fare on China. The Nixon dramatization of the event did much to make the shift in U.S. policy palatable to the people of the nation even as it greatly enhanced Nixon's stature a few months before the next presidential election.

Shortly after his return from China, the president sought out Mansfield and apologized for his preemption of the senator's slowly evolving plans to visit China. He further advised the majority leader that he had made arrangements with Chou En-lai for Mansfield and the Senate Republican leader, Hugh Scott, to follow in his footsteps in order to keep up the momentum and give China an expression of American bipartisan unity to the new approach.

When the two Senate leaders did arrive in Beijing a few weeks later,

Premier Chou inquired of Mansfield in their first encounter: "Where were you, Senator? We were expecting you several weeks ago but instead Mr. Kissinger came to make arrangements for the President." Mansfield replied: "Yes, and I am glad that he did. It was more important that the President himself be the first to open the door."

Subsequent to his joint visit with Senator Scott, Mansfield made two other trips to China, accompanied on each by a bipartisan delegation of senators. Each visit was covered by Mansfield reports to the Senate and the nation that reflected his growing knowledge of what was transpiring within China and the issues that Washington and Beijing would have to deal with before the reopened contact could be consolidated by the restoration of full diplomatic relations. The public reports on these undertakings underscored Mansfield's growing conviction that China was in the midst of a great transition and that it was in the interests of the United States to lay aside old attitudes and seek not only an accurate understanding of the new China but also nonconfrontational contacts of all kinds with the Chinese. Mansfield's position was matched in China by Chou En-lai. On his second mission, Mansfield, accompanied only by his wife, visited Chou, who was terminally ill in a hospital in Beijing. The Chinese leader, who had requested the meeting, ended the conversation by remarking that "the break between the United States and China should never have happened."

Mansfield saw as the most serious political drawback to full rapprochement with China the question of the status of Taiwan. He drew assurances from Deng Xiaoping, who had replaced Chou as premier, that China could wait a long time for reunification of the island with the mainland, provided that there were no serious challenges to Taiwan's generally accepted international status as a part of China. On this question, as well as other issues that had been resolved by the Nixon visit, Mansfield endorsed the Republican administration's new China policy. Together with Minority Leader Scott, he took the lead in clearing away the megislative impediments to constructive contact that had accumulated during the long estrangement. In doing so, he had to deal with the resistance of some senators, notably Barry Goldwater of Arizona and "Scoop" Jackson of Washington. Jackson feared that the change in China policy was but a harbinger of rapprochement with the Soviet Union. Other than Jackson on the Democratic side and Goldwater on the Republican, resistance to Nixon's new China policy was minimal in the Senate. In a political sense, Republicans could hardly seek political gain from the shift, if for no other reason than that it carried the imprimatur of a Republican administration. Nor could Democrats politicize the change without risk of reawakening the "Who lost China?" question to their own disadvantage.

Politics notwithstanding, the handling of the shift in China policy sat very well with the American electorate. The staged spectacle in Beijing, what with the clinking of glasses by Nixon and Chou En-lai in the Great Hall of the People and the president's much-photographed visit to the Great Wall, greatly facilitated acceptance of the new China in the United States.

The door was opened farther by the first waves of American visitors to China, who returned after whirlwind tours, like so many Marco Polos, with stories aglow with what they had seen. Then came expanding cultural exchanges endorsed by both governments and the opening of the doors of American academia to a flood of Chinese students eager to catch up on two decades of isolation. A base for mutual understanding, acceptance, and cooperation quickly began to take form. These early contacts were dwarfed by the rapid growth in U.S. trade and investment after the death of Mao and the ascension of Deng Xiaoping's liberal economic views within the Chinese Communist Party. The establishment of full diplomatic relations between the two countries, however, did not come about until the Carter administration.

The 1972 Campaign and the Watergate Affair

As the presidential election of 1972 drew closer, Nixon was in a powerful position to seek reelection. He could claim credit not only for moving closer to the end of the pain of Vietnam but also for a bold and what proved to be a highly popular initiative with regard to China. These achievements, coming on top of an Anti-Ballistics Missile Treaty he negotiated with the Soviet Union, set the stage for his reelection. True, there were difficulties in the economy, but they could be ascribed to "Johnson's war" in Vietnam, which Nixon was doing his best to bring to a close.

Nixon's reelection was further facilitated by deepening schisms within the Democratic Party, especially as the New Deal generation of whites were replaced by a generation that, more and more, was finding the Republican Party better attuned to its increasing affluence and growing political conservatism. Moreover, just as the influence of the liberal wing was reaching a post–World War II apex within the Democratic Party, "liberalism" was taking on a derogatory connotation in American politics.

The Democratic nominee, Senator George McGovern of South Dakota, was a man of great social sensitivity and compassion, who had given full support to both Kennedy's New Frontier and Johnson's Great Society during his Senate career. A bomber pilot in World War II, McGovern had opposed the U.S. military involvement in Vietnam almost from the outset.

He had also been one of the leaders in the Senate's later effort to end the war by legislation. McGovern became a made-to-order target for the rising political hostility toward liberalism. He was opposed by large elements within the Democratic Party and, increasingly, by industrial blue-collar workers, the northern backbone of the party, many of whom turned to George Wallace of Alabama, a segregationist governor of Alabama. Wallace campaigned vigorously in the North for the Democratic nomination until he was paralyzed by a would-be assassin's bullet. To add to McGovern's burdens in the race, a muckracking Washington journalist discovered that his running mate for the vice presidency, Senator Tom Eagleton of Missouri, had been hospitalized at one time for mental depression, which was seen by many as a disqualification for high office. Panicking campaign advisors urged the replacement of Eagleton on the Democratic ticket and McGovern accepted their advice with great reluctance. Eagleton was replaced by Sergeant Shriver, a brother-in-law of President Kennedy. Interestingly, Mansfield had been offered the candidacy but had turned it down, ostensibly on the grounds of age and health. In private, he recognized that accepting the offer would be tantamount to political "suicide."

In the election of 1972, the Republicans campaigned against "liberalism" as though it were a dirty word, and, aided by the schisms among the Democrats, their arguments gained popular acceptance. By contrast, the denunciation of Nixon as the perpetuator of the war in Vietnam, the Democrats' main issue, had a hollow ring, what with U.S. military participation in South Vietnam visibly winding down and Nixon proudly portraying the new China policy as a diplomatic triumph. The ticket of Nixon and Agnew easily won reelection, but, again, the Democrats retained their congressional majorities. Moreover, the Democrats were successful in holding a majority in the Senate despite a vicious campaign by Spiro Agnew to discredit the institution over which he presided. Agnew built his campaign around such harsh and spurious alliterations as "nattering nabobs of negativism" to belabor Senate Democrats.

The Nixon-Agnew landslide quickly turned into a pyrrhic victory. Within months of the inauguration, Agnew was forced to resign in disgrace from the vice-presidency or face the prospect of going to jail for acts of malfeasance perpetrated while he was governor of Maryland. Nixon designated Gerald Ford of Michigan, then Republican leader of the House of Representatives, to replace Agnew.

The dust had scarcely settled on the Agnew affair when the public's attention was refocused on the possibility that President Nixon himself was linked to certain criminal acts that had taken place during the recent election. These had to do with a break-in at Democratic campaign headquarters in the Watergate Hotel in Washington, D.C. The purported criminal act was masterminded by a former CIA agent, G. Gordon Liddy, who after serving prison time for the Watergate crime, was to be welcomed as host of a radio talk show, where he gained new fame by attacking liberalism and promoting conservative causes.

The Watergate break-in had come to light before election day, when Liddy and several associates were caught red-handed at the Watergate headquarters of the party, attempting to make off with Democratic campaign documents. At first, Watergate seemed to be just one more case of political sleaze in what was a very sleazy campaign. It created only a short-lived stir that had little, if any, effect on the outcome of the election. Later, however, thanks to the doggedness of two newspaper reporters, the ramifications of the break-in were seen to extend to the White House and, perhaps, might even involve the president. There were widespread demands for a thorough inquiry, a responsibility that devolved on the Justice Department. After several key investigators of the Justice Department had either been abruptly dismissed by Nixon or had resigned in protest at the president's interference, a special prosecutor was found to pursue the Watergate affair.

As public interest mounted, incipient investigations sprouted like springtime flowers on Capitol Hill. In the Senate, Mansfield moved quickly to cut off what he feared would become a huge political sideshow. He won House Speaker Carl Albert's agreement that the best prospect of avoiding an unseemly congressional scramble would be to designate a single committee in each of the two houses with exclusive control over all matters pertaining to the Watergate affair. Both congressional leaders, moreover, recognized from press reports that the Watergate affair might contain grounds for criminal action against high officials in the administration, not to speak of the possibility of impeachment of the president. Their joint approach was readily accepted in the House, where the investigation fell to the Judiciary Committee, headed at the time by Peter J. Rodino, a respected lawyer and long-time representative from New Jersey.

In the Senate, Mansfield had sensed correctly that there were a number of aspirants for the presidency among his Democratic colleagues who would welcome the national spotlight promised by a Watergate investigation. Mansfield did not relish a spectacle of their vying with one another for a piece of the action. His concerns were validated when the media quickly focused on Senator Ted Kennedy, the surviving brother of the Kennedy family, as a logical designee to head an investigation. Although his career had suffered severe personal blows after the violent death of a third brother, the name Kennedy still contained a certain mystique. Mansfield was convinced that if Kennedy headed a Watergate investigation, it would be impossible to prevent the inquiry from taking a decidedly political direction. If that occurred, it would risk discrediting the Senate and, in the end, probably do Ted Kennedy more harm than good.

Most serious, Mansfield was concerned lest Ted Kennedy, as the central figure in a highly charged Senate investigation, would be at great risk of suffering the same fate as brothers Jack and Bobby. Sufficient Kennedys, he thought, had already been sacrificed in service to the nation. Mansfield had previously indicated his concern for Ted Kennedy's vulnerability to assassination in connection with the preliminaries of the presidential campaign of 1972. Although undeclared at the time as a presidential candidate, Kennedy seemed to be testing the waters by making numerous public appearances that attracted large crowds. On that basis, Mansfield quietly pressed the Nixon administration to give Kennedy the Secret Service protection extended to presidential candidates. Such protection had been provided for by law immediately after the assassination of Bobby Kennedy. At first, John Connally, who as secretary of the treasury was also head of the Secret Service that provided the protection, demurred because Kennedy had not specifically declared himself a candidate. A declaration of candidacy was one of the criteria the department used in deciding who should receive Secret Service protection. Mansfield suspected that Connally's refusal was dictated more by the administration's desire to smoke out Kennedy's presidential intentions. Mansfield's repeated efforts to obtain protection for Kennedy were ignored until George Wallace, another highly controversial Democratic candidate in the primaries, was severely wounded in an assassination attempt. Whereupon the Secret Service, on Nixon's direct orders, reversed its position and immediately deployed a team of Secret Service agents to provide Kennedy with twenty-four-hour protection!

Nixon's Resignation

To deflect the mounting pressure for Kennedy to head the Watergate investigation, Mansfield urged a reluctant Sam Ervin, of North Carolina, to take the task. Ervin, who was second only to Russell in his influence among southerners in the Senate, had been a judge in the North Carolina courts for many years. He was both a brilliant lawyer and a shirt-sleeve politician who had managed to remain afloat for many years in North Carolina's rough political seas. During his long career in the Senate, Ervin steered a course that carried him, on the one hand, toward a deep conservatism and, on the other, toward the outer boundaries of liberalism. Like Rodino of the House Judiciary Committee, Ervin was approaching the end of his career and entertained no aspirations for higher political office. Mansfield was confident that with the North Carolinian in charge, the handling of the Watergate affair would be thorough and nonpolitical. Having persuaded Ervin to serve as chairman, Mansfield called for the creation of a Select Committee on Presidential Campaign Activities with exclusive jurisdiction over the Watergate affair. The arrangement precluded infighting among Democrats and was accepted at once by the Democratic caucus. Mansfield's approach also won the immediate concurrence of the Senate Republican leader, thus forestalling any attempt to discredit the investigation on the grounds of political manipulation.

Under Ervin's gavel, the Watesgate inquiry unfolded with dignity, appropriately peppered with the chairman's homespun humor. Although conducted with judicial restraint, Ervin was at pains to keep the investigation from becoming a mock trial. Despite the criminal culpability of several witnesses, the proceedings were not designed to prove anyone's guilt or innocence. Instead, it was a model legislative inquiry, sorting out the components of the Watergate affair and the role of the White House. It threw light on problems of deep import to the nation's constitutional system, such as the legal accountability of the president and his highest appointees. In so doing, it laid the basis for legislation providing for designation of special counsels from outside government to deal independently with questionable acts of high officials. Although there have since been questions raised about the specific actions of special prosecutors, who are designated by a panel of three justices, there is little quarrel with the need for some such arrangement if the president and other major political officials are to be held accountable under the law. As chairman, Senator Ervin did not permit the Watergate Committee to become ensnared in trying to put the White House staff or the president himself on trial. That is not to say that the Senate Watergate inquiry was without influence on that question. While Rodino's House Judiciary Committee was already deeply immersed in considering the applicability of impeachment proceedings, the Ervin Committee's inquiry became a clear and authentic statement of what the Watergate scandal was all about, and its disclosures and findings pointed to those who might be criminally culpable. That reinforced the House Judiciary Committee's finding for impeachment and the public's belief that the system could be depended on to deal effectively with abuses of power at the highest levels within the government. The Senate inquiry, moreover, underscored a growing conviction that Nixon was not the victim of ruthless politics but of his own misconduct and that, if impeached in the House of Representatives he should face trial in the Senate, as provided for in the Constitution.

When Nixon first entered the White House, Mansfield had misgivings about the new president's stability, but he had laid them aside as Nixon seemed to grow more comfortable in his responsibilities. Mansfield's concerns returned when it became apparent that Nixon had not only been aware of the Watergate escapade but would eventually be seen as primarily responsible for its perpetration. As the prospects of impeachment loomed ever larger, Mansfield observed of the president that "you have to be very careful with this fellow. If you get him in a corner you don't know what he'll do. You have to treat him very carefully." Although he did not specify what he feared from a cornered Nixon, the possibilities seemed to range from suicide to an attempt to use the powers of the presidency for a preemptive strike at both Congress and the press.

Against the unknowns of a "cornered" Nixon, Mansfield heightened his precautions. He moved to knit closer the rapport of the leadership of both houses. By doing so, he believed Congress would be in the strongest possible position to deal with a confrontation with the president should the Watergate affair lead to a constitutional crisis. To that end, he intensified his efforts to develop close liaison with Speaker Carl Albert and the Democratic majority leader of the House, Thomas "Tip" O'Neill. Both sides saw the virtue of staying together in the face of an unpredictable president. Mansfield sponsored meetings with leaders of both houses, finding common ground among them on the need to give unwavering support to the inquiries going forward under Rodino in the House and Ervin in the Senate. Pending the outcome of these preliminaries, the congressional leaders agreed to maintain continuing and confidential contact with one another. Within the Senate, Mansfield discussed his concerns with the Democratic Policy Committee and the committee chairmen. The problem of succession was raised in the event Nixon followed his vice president, Spiro Agnew, out of government. Under Senator Bayh's recently adopted amendment to the constitution, Speaker Albert would be next in line for the presidency, followed by the President Pro Tempore of the Senate, Jim Eastland of Mississippi. As an alternative, the senator from Maine, Edmund Muskie, who had himself aspired to the presidency and then dropped out of the primaries, raised the possibility of holding a special election. Senator Talmadge warned against precipitous acts on the part of the Congress.

On the basis of such discussions, Mansfield was satisfied that the Democrats would hold together. His primary concern was to maintain a solid front with the Republican leadership in the face of what was becoming the virtual certainty that the House Judiciary Committee would recommend to the House of Representatives that Nixon be impeached. This proved easier than anticipated. At no time did Republicans seek to cast doubt on the integrity of Ervin's Watergate inquiry or its necessity. Moreover, Republicans began to draw away from the president. Barry Goldwater of Arizona, a one-time candidate for the presidency and leader of the right wing of the Republican Party in the Senate, had already raised the question of Nixon's resignation. Other Republicans were emboldened to do the same.

In dealing with Republican Minority Leader Hugh Scott, Mansfield already had received Scott's full support in establishing and upholding the work of the Senate Watergate Committee. Scott also joined the majority leader in quietly laying down a format for the trial of the president by the Senate in the event of a House vote for impeachment. The projected arrangements included opening the Senate to television coverage, a practice that the majority leader had previously opposed. Under discussion, too, was the role of the chief justice of the Supreme Court, who would preside over the Senate during the trial. Mansfield's chief concern was that Warren Burger, chief justice at the time and a Nixon appointee, be restrained from dominating the proceedings or denigrating the Senate's role.

The Senate leaders were spared the necessity for resolving such questions by what transpired after the House Judiciary Committee voted overwhelmingly to recommend that Nixon be impeached by the House of Representatives. Thereafter, Republicans openly called on the president to resign before the House voted on the committee's recommendation. When Nixon continued to hesitate, Senate Republican Leader Scott visited the president at the White House and advised Nixon that there was no way out. The same advice was forthcoming from Senator Goldwater and House Republican Leader John Rhodes. Nixon was told bluntly that if the matter came to a vote, the House of Representatives would decide for impeachment, the Senate would try, and, in all probability, would find him guilty. Nixon was asked to spare the country, his party, and himself further trauma by tendering his resignation.

On 9 August 1974, Nixon resigned. He was replaced immediately by Gerald Ford of Michigan, formerly a Republican leader in the House of Representatives, whom Nixon had appointed to the vice presidency on Agnew's resignation. In due course, Nelson Rockefeller of New York was designated to fill the vacancy in the vice presidency. As president, Ford placed *Air Force One* at Nixon's disposal for a quick departure from Washington. Nixon waved good-bye to the nation via television from the door of the plane and left for his home in California. Later, Ford pardoned his predecessor for any crimes or misdemeanors that he may have committed while in the presidency. The game of musical chairs in the highest reaches of the federal government had come to an end after what Mansfield described as "an incredible year, an incredible month, incredible weeks and days."

7

Legislating the Great Society

When Mansfield described himself as the Senate's majority leader, rather than Johnson's, it was after several years of effort to bring the Senate into something closer to his vision of the institution. By then, most of the irritations carried over from the Johnson era had been dispelled. Mansfield's orderly conduct of business and emphasis on cooperation over confrontation had taken hold. The leaders of the Democratic majority and the Republican minority were attuned to one another in an excellent working relationship as well as a strong sense of institutional cohesion. Mansfield's pride in the Senate and his zeal in safeguarding its integrity and uniqueness inspired emulation among his colleagues. In sum, members of both parties had grown to appreciate what his approach had meant and had responded with confidence and trust.

The long filibuster on civil rights had left the Senate calendar with a huge backlog of legislation awaiting action. Although the accumulation consisted largely of routine bills, most of the calendar had to be cleared before adjournment of the Congress in order to assure the orderly operation of the government. The bills were of a kind that were often deliberately held hostage by a senator or group of senators seeking to serve some special state interest in a kind of end-of-session legislative blackmail.

Such delays did not materialize as Congress headed for adjournment in 1964. Instead, with the Civil Rights Act out of the way, other bills remaining on the calendar moved through the legislative mill at a very rapid pace. So smoothly did the Senate function that Mansfield, fearing a loss of momentum, called only for a brief interruption to permit attendance of senators at the Democratic National Convention. A week later, the Senate returned to pick up where it had left off, bill after bill was disposed of with minimal controversy.

Medicare Legislation

Of those passing through the legislative process, one bill towered in importance above the others, although its significance went largely unappreciated at the time. Without fanfare, Senator Albert Gore of Tennessee, whose son was later to serve in the Senate and as vice president, introduced the measure as an amendment to a routine Social Security bill. At the time, virtually the only major function of the Social Security program was to provide modest annuities for those older Americans who had paid into the national retirement fund during their working years. Senator Gore's amendment proposed to extend the program's coverage to include hospital and medical care for Social Security annuitants. At that time, financing such services, with rare exceptions, was not considered a function of the federal government. As a general practice these costs were met by the individual or private charities, with state and local governments sometimes making up any shortfalls.

Gore's proposed expansion of Social Security to cover health costs served the dual purpose of relieving hospitals and, to some extent, doctors of worry about collecting their bills from the elderly, even as it freed the elderly from anxiety over how they were going to pay their bills. In sum, the Gore amendment was an attempt to provide an orderly way to cover a major part of the health costs that were beginning to rise beyond the capabilities of most Social Security recipients. It was a far cry from universal health coverage, a practice already well established in most economically advanced nations throughout the world. Limited though it was, the Gore amendment was a first step in what was to be a continuing search for a workable system of health coverage for all Americans. When Gore introduced his amendment, such legislation, even though it applied only to the aged, had been held back for years, primarily by the unyielding opposition of the American Medical Association and other powerful health-care interests. But a relentlessly rising accumulation of unpaid medical-hospitals bills began to eat away at this opposition until, by 1964, it was reduced to murmured grumbles about the evils of "socialized medicine."

Gore saw an opportunity to bypass the Senate Finance Committee that had been the major block to action by Congress on the problem. In bringing the issue before the entire Senate in the form of an amendment to a major bill, he had the full support of Majority Leader Mansfield, who in turn sought and received the procedural cooperation of Minority Leader Dirksen. With the Senate facing the issue head-on and under the twin pressures of public support for action and an approaching election, the Gore amendment passed easily. In this almost casual way, without fanfare, a beginning was made on the federally sponsored health insurance program of the United States.

To pass the Gore amendment and other measures of consequence, Mansfield kept the Senate in session until the 1964 election was scarcely a month away. It was as late as he dared, since members confronted with an election at home were threatening to bolt from Washington. When adjournment finally came in early October 1964, just weeks short of the presidential elections, the 88th Congress was being hailed as one of the great Congresses. Scarcely a year earlier, it had been dismissed as one of the worst. The rapid flow of legislation in the closing months of the 88th Congress was a harbinger of what would prevail in the remaining decade of Mansfield's leadership. The majority leader had worked from the outset to ensure an orderly flow of legislation, and this approach held for the remainder of his tenure.

Other Significant Legislation Under Mansfield

The list of measures enacted in this pattern was headed by the Nuclear Test Ban Treaty and the Civil Right Act of 1964. But during the Mansfield years, the Senate also passed an extraordinary list of innovative measures that included legislation underlying:

- A U.S. Arms Control and Disarmament Agency
- A Peace Corps
- The Man on the Moon program and the huge expansion of exploration of Outer Space
- A Trade Adjustment program designed to assist workers and industries adversely affected by changes in national trade policy
- A legal basis for enforcing equal pay for women
- A prohibition on nuclear military activity in outer space and under the seas
- A follow-up civil rights bill to strengthen enforcement of the right to vote
- An economic opportunity program to counter poverty through community education and training programs

- Major new federal funding of improvements in primary and secondary education
- A sweeping program for the development of impoverished Appalachia
- The first federal scholarship program for college students
- A national teacher corps to serve in poverty-stricken areas
- The nation's first nutritional breakfast program for school children
- A demonstration cities development program to rebuild slums and deteriorating urban neighborhoods
- A third civil rights bill prohibiting discrimination in housing and containing a bill of rights for Native Americans
- An air-quality program for research on air pollution and clean-air standards

Even the capture of the White House by the Republicans in the 1968 election did little to curb the legislative outflow. With Nixon in the White House, greater responsibility for rounding out the Great Society shifted from the presidency to Congress. There, the Democrats remained in control of both houses. In the Senate, the effort of the Democrats was supplemented by and, in truth, dependent on the cooperative working relationship that Mansfield had established with the minority. The cooperation became, perhaps, even closer when the minority leadership passed to Hugh Scott of Pennsylvania upon the death of Everett Dirksen in 1969. Scott was a vigorous Republican with a sharp wit and an acerbic tongue when his partisanship was aroused. But his personal views on social issues were more closely attuned to the Democratic majority than those of his predecessor. In addition, he stood squarely with Mansfield, as had Dirksen, on all matters affecting the status of the Senate and its powers and prerogatives within the government.

The Nixon administration could do little to reverse the new social and economic directions delineated by the legislation passed in the prior eight years other than by liberal use of the constitutional veto power. Nixon employed it forty-three times during his tenure, and his successor Gerald Ford rejected sixty-six bills during his brief presidency. These vetoes, many of which were overridden or circumvented, were aimed at such typical Great Society bills as vocational rehabilitation, community health services, educational aid to nurses and nursing schools, and strip-mining control.

Nixon also attempted by executive fiat to exercise what amounted to a line-item veto, that is, impounding specific items in appropriations legislation and refusing to spend the funds provided by Congress. This attempt, of dubious constitutionality, was foiled by legislation designed by Senator Sam Ervin of North Carolina. Thereafter, the idea of a line-item veto as a tool to control federal expenditures lay dormant for many years.

With Nixon as president, the Senate continued to churn out a vast amount of domestic legislation. Adding to what it had achieved during the Johnson administration, the output of the Senate during the Nixon and Ford incumbencies included the following:

- Required environmental impact studies and reports on development projects involving the federal government
- Aimed at enhancing water quality, controlling dumping of pollutants into the oceans, regulating sale of pesticides, and protecting marine animals
- Lowered the voting age from twenty-one to eighteen
- Curbed the draft law and increased its equity
- Promoted occupational safety and health by applying federal safety and health standards
- Established programs against alcoholism and drug abuse
- Set up the first Federal Elections Commission aimed at controlling expenditures in elections and providing partial federal financing of presidential campaigns
- Proposed a constitutional amendment calling for equal rights for women
- Established safeguards against the misuse of information on individuals contained in government databanks
- Estopped the federal bureaucracy, in the Freedom of Information Act, from arbitrarily withholding records from public access
- Insured workers' vested rights in private pension plans against corporate mismanagement
- Set up the Energy Research and Development Administration, precursor to the Department of Energy
- Opened up meetings of federal government heads to the public
- Empowered special prosecutors, under the Watergate Reform Act, to investigate and prosecute top federal officials for criminal acts
- In the War Powers Resolution, sought to prevent the executive branch from engaging in "secret" wars and to assert the congressional role in the exercise of the Constitution's war-making authority
- Terminated all prior legislative grants of special authority to the presidency for dealing with national emergencies, required periodic congressional review of presidential declarations of a national emergency, and provided for congressional termination of such declarations

- Gave enforcement powers to the Commission on Equal Employment Opportunity
- Reasserted congressional control over federal expenditures through the Budget Reform and Impoundment Act

Of the enormous amount of legislation cleared during the period of the Mansfield Senate, the Civil Rights Act of 1964 and approval of ratification of the Nuclear Test Ban Treaty were pivots in a redirection of the nation's orientation at home and abroad and both were peculiarly dependent on action in the Senate. In addition to these key measures, legislation enacted under the banner of the Great Society served to pick up the cadence of social action of the early Roosevelt's years in the White House. The legislation emerging from the Mansfield Senate provided correctives, updatings, and add-ons to programs of social and economic welfare established during the New Deal. In addition, it marked the commitment of the federal government to action on new sources of national concern. Environmental deterioration, for example, was defined clearly as a national problem and brought within the continuing purview of Washington. Groundwork was also laid for dealing with the nation's ever-growing dependence on petroleum. The role of the federal government in education deepened sharply. Something similar occurred with regard to the nation's health, as well as the rights of labor and the welfare of the poor.

In the ensuing years, to be sure, gaps opened up between the expectations engendered by this huge output of legislation and the delivery under federal programs derived from it. That was hardly surprising inasmuch as the democratic process, like any other governmental system, produces its share of flaws and duds. The political engineering of a Great Society, or even one of more modest pretensions, is hardly an exact science. When good intentions expressed in political terms are spelled out in administrative follow-through and legal practice, they invariably reveal the limits of perception and foresight on the part of those who inspire the laws, as well as those who later interpret them. Moreover, the good intentions of one era are often confounded by unpredictable shifts in the public's values and vogues at a later date. In legislating, as in other human activities, yesterday's innovation is sometimes today's obsolescence and tomorrow's albatross. In an ever-changing American society, the need to throw out or supersede from time to time what was done in the past in a legislative sense is continuous.

That does not detract from the profound importance of what was achieved by Congress during the Mansfield Senate. The legislative output of those years enabled the nation to catch up with what was required in a legal sense to maintain a stable, responsive, and responsible political system in the United States. At the close of his leadership, Mansfield alluded to an extraordinary record through two Democratic and two Republican administrations with characteristic understatement. In a summation of the Senate's work during his tenure as majority leader, he said: "The legislation written in the past 16 years has brought changes in every aspect of our lives. I am hopeful that it has done much good."*

President Kennedy did not live to see the explosion of legislation that reverberated through the Senate in the wake of the Civil Rights Act of 1964. Ironically, however, Kennedy's supreme sacrifice appeared to have had a great influence in precipitating this outpouring. Much of the legislative activity took place in his name. Some of the support it received seemed a kind of expiation of guilt over his shocking death. A sense of remorse seemed palpable in the grieving of some who had spoken ill of him while he was alive, and it may well have contributed to the acceptance of his program.

Nor should one underestimate the role of Lyndon Johnson in using the powerful emotional force contained in Kennedy's death in combination with his own skills to prod the legislative process. Johnson built on the grief over the assassination, intensified as it was by the moving funeral arrangements designed by Jackie Kennedy and televised throughout the nation. Johnson deftly tuned into the national mood in order to advance the legislative program of the Great Society. At the outset, he was persuasive in portraying himself as the faithful surrogate of the tragically dead president. He talked humbly of his limitations and pleaded with the Kennedy intellectuals to stay with him on behalf of the nation. He was passionate in asserting the theme of "I need you more than he did." The Kennedy intellectuals responded readily and, with Johnson cheering them on, worked out their own horror, disbelief, and fury at the sudden crumbling of Camelot in federal programs. With Johnson's encouragement, they drove hard to retrieve the New Frontier, the Kennedy Grail, in the form of the Great Society.

In dealing with the public, Johnson intensified his personal humbleness while vowing to carry out Kennedy's wishes. At that point, the public was receptive to almost anything bearing the initials JFK and agreed vigorously with Johnson when he said, "I am going to do what he wanted," without always knowing, specifically, what it was that Kennedy wanted.

In confronting Congress, Johnson was somewhat less self-effacing. While he equated attentive consideration of the administration's legislative

---

*94th Congress, 2d sess., Document No. 94–269, *Summary of Major Achievements,* p. xxxi.

program with respect for the dead president, he also sought support for his program as a former leader of Congress. His approach appealed to liberals in the Senate, who were rallied to action on behalf of the Kennedy-Johnson program. Their efforts were anointed by President Johnson, from whom, initially, they did not know what to expect in view of mutual animosities in the past. In turn, they showed a surprising willingness to temper their more extreme demands to protect their stake in Johnson's success. Johnson's legislative astuteness also carried weight with the traditionalists, especially southern conservatives, who knew Johnson better than they had known Kennedy. They had been nominal at best in support of Kennedy as president, but they wanted very much for Johnson to succeed in the White House. To be sure, they could not subscribe to many of the social measures he was endorsing. All saw him, however, as the best the South could hope for in the way of understanding from the Democratic Party. After the prolonged filibuster of the civil rights bill, then, the southern conservatives were very restrained in using obstructionist tactics against legislation that did not please them but was sought by Johnson's administration.

A mutual stake in Johnson's success as president served to hold together the conservative and liberal wings of the Democratic Party in the Senate. In that adhesion, both factions could hope to retain the prerogatives of the Senate majority and ready access to the White House. Prompted by such incentives, the Democratic liberals exercised restraint in pressing for the more innovative measures of the Great Society. Conversely, the conservative Democrats avoided manipulating the Rules as a way of defeating them. This forbearance was not all that difficult for them in many cases. With much of the Great Society legislation such as health care, which was long past due, the need for action was apparent even to those in opposition. Often, bills were passed with little floor debate and by overwhelming majorities. In some instances, where the margin for victory was small, the collaboration of Republicans could be the critical factor. It was forthcoming from such Republicans as Tom Kuchel of California, John Sherman Cooper of Kentucky, Clifford Case of New Jersey, Jacob Javits and Kenneth Keating of New York, Hugh Scott of Pennsylvania, George Aiken of Vermont, and J. Glenn Beall and Charles Mathias, both of Maryland.

The output of socially significant legislation of the Mansfield Senate was by far the greatest in volume since the New Deal, and it was something more than bulk. It was a critical factor in major turning points in the nation's history. The Civil Rights Act of 1964 cannot be regarded in any other light. Nor can ratification of the Nuclear Test Ban Treaty. These two measures, pivots in a redirection of the nation's orientation at home and abroad, were dependent on action in the Senate.

In the case of the Nuclear Test Ban Treaty, the Senate's action was a milestone in shaping the nation's course with regard to the rest of the world. Acceptance of the treaty depended on the Senate's unique constitutional power to consent to the ratification of treaties. The Senate vote was overwhelming for ratification, thus supporting President Kennedy's efforts to find common grounds on which to begin at last to establish rational control over nuclear weapons. Moreover, the action had an immediate and tangible benefit in that it curbed the environmental hazard of radioactive fallout that had until then accompanied nuclear testing. The acceptance of the treaty by the Senate was a symbolic act of great significance in the overall course of the nation's foreign policy. After the ratification, fear in other nations that the United States would use the lead it possessed in nuclear technology to impose by force or threat of force a *Pax Americana* diminished perceptibly. It was a formal acknowledgment that nuclear weapons were viewed in Washington not as simply an increment in battlefield capabilities but as doomsday weapons of a different order of magnitude. Thereafter, no matter how frustrating a situation, presidents would no longer muse even in passing, as had Truman during a low point in the Korean conflict, on the use of a nuclear first strike as a viable option. While the treaty, of course, guaranteed nothing in this respect, it did move the nation and the world away from what was an ever-present prospect of a sudden military collision of cosmic proportions. In particular, it marked the beginning of a series of agreements with the Soviet Union designed to mitigate progressively this threat to humankind.

Even though they were increasingly at odds over Vietnam, Johnson and Mansfield worked effectively in pursuing the legislative program. Weekly breakfast meetings at the White House helped focus their joint efforts. On those occasions, Mansfield usually surrounded himself with other Senate leaders as a way of constricting his unilateral role and underscoring the collective responsibility of the Senate.

Most significant in winning Senate passage of the Great Society legislation was the conduct of the committee chairmen. After the consideration of the civil rights bill in 1964, they were disposed to accommodate the president and to defer to Mansfield's practice of giving priority to measures sponsored by the White House. On the whole, chairmen were generally well informed on bills in their committees and were well equipped to handle them on the Senate floor, as Mansfield insisted they do. Even when personally opposed to measures, the chairmen rarely sought to introduce procedural blocks into the process. In short, the committee system functioned very well for fashioning and clearing legislation that was reflective of the collective will of the Senate.

To be sure, the system also revealed its other side. During the Mansfield period, as in other times, committees produced legislation that confused special interests with national interests. Individual senators used their positions on committees to write into federal law special favors for their states, certain industries or occupations, and privileged individuals. Thanks largely to the persistent advocacy of Senator Lawton Chiles, later governor of Florida, closed-door meetings of committees were generally frowned on, and formal committee work was done almost entirely in open sessions. How much of a corrective this provided to keeping the public's business public is hard to say. Venues other than committees have always been available for activities associated with the seedier side of the legislative process.

Campaign Finance Reform

The difficulty in controlling corrupting influences in the legislative process is illustrated by the efforts to regulate the role of money in federal elections. These efforts reached a peak during the latter part of the Mansfield period when the Federal Elections Act of 1971 was adopted by large majorities in both houses. The new law was a response to the experience of earlier years during which the then existing statutes had proved inadequate in revealing, much less regulating, the flow of money into elections.

During the post–World War II years, the cost of campaigning for federal office had grown rapidly, although by 1971 it still was not anywhere near its current astronomical levels. During the Mansfield years, it was possible in most instances for candidates for the Senate to raise the funds needed to mount a competitive campaign largely through in-state sources of funding, with perhaps a modest supplement from national party sources such as the Senate and House Campaign Committees of both major parties. Most campaigns for Congress remained essentially state focused in content and, often, heavily nonprofessional in conduct. By and large, contributions flowed in moderate amounts into campaign chests, often coming out of the candidate's own pocket or from friends, relatives, local political clubs and organizations, and, often, by simply passing the hat at social events and political rallies. Indeed, large contributions from a single source, whether a union or a business organization, especially one based outside the state, tended to be regarded by voters as tainted. Recipient candidates often sought to brush them under the rug or even shun them as counterproductive. Except in the larger states, an otherwise viable candidate with limited personal financial resources could reasonably expect not to go into heavy debt in order to contest a seat for the Senate. If elected, moreover, he or she did not have to begin immediately to solicit contributions to build up a fund adequate for the next election. There was still room for financing a campaign free of suspicion of serious special-interest claims on the integrity of the candidates.

In the post–World War II years, the number of businesses and other private interests setting up tents in and around Washington grew in an ever-widening circle. Trade unions, industrial, and "nonprofit" associations with Washington addresses also skyrocketed. So, too, did the demand for public relations services and legal and similar skills related to government activity. The ranks of practitioners were swollen by the addition of former congressmen and former government officials, who knew their way around or, at least, could give the appearance of knowing. Lobbying for various private interests trying to steer their way through the ins and outs of government became the growth industry of the nation's capital.

At the same time that these changes were taking place, the financial requirements for mounting an effective political campaign began to rise precipitously, primarily due to advertising and other costs associated with television electioneering. Candidates found themselves dipping deeper into their personal wealth or assiduously cultivating well-heeled contributors, corporate leaders, unions, and even potential sources of contributions from abroad. Obliging donors were not hard to find either for an incumbent or a challenger with good prospects of winning a seat in Congress, especially in the Senate. Generous financial aid to candidates promised to serve as a most useful tool to contributors in attempting to influence the content and flow of legislation coming from Capitol Hill. To be sure, it was rarely the crass expectation that contributions would buy specific votes on specific legislative questions. Instead, it was enough that contributions might facilitate a prompt and warm access to key sources of power.

In the circumstances, the Senate and House Campaign Committees of both parties, as well as the national committees, sponsored huge campaign dinners at which influence seekers were sold not only very expensive steaks but also an opportunity to rub shoulders with party leaders and members of Congress, with the proceeds going into the party coffers. Increasingly popular was the direct contribution to senators running for reelection or promising candidates challenging incumbents. These contributions came from all parts of the country, thus serving to erode the previous close connection between senator and voters in his or her state by building up another relationship, that of senator and major contributors wherever they might be. Moreover, such contributors were less and less concerned with party labels and more concerned with a recipient's potential for assignment to standing committees having jurisdiction over matters of particular concern to them.

And with sophisticated professional advice from skilled lobbyists, they were not averse to hedging their bets by contributing to both candidates in a given race!

The Baker scandal served to highlight these trends on Capitol Hill and hence probably acted as something of a brake on them during the Mansfield period. At that time, a display of lavish personal wealth or financial backing from special interests could still backfire against a candidate. The potential wrath of voters over "bought seats" by wealthy political dabblers or by tainted contributions remained something to be taken seriously by candidates. Financial excesses on the part of candidates in campaigns still rated at least as high as sexual peccadillos on the scale of negative public titillation. Either could ruin a candidate, and most aspirants for a Senate seat were at least as discreet about the one as the other.

Candidates did not feel compelled to be apologetic about how little but how much money they had raised for their campaigns. Restraint in finances remained the prevailing political wisdom. As little as possible was said about them unless a candidate's resources were minuscule compared with those of an opponent. His or her penury was then worn as a badge of integrity. In subsequent years, however, the public seemed to attach less and less onus to the lavish use of money in political campaigns. Except in situations of blatant influence peddling, voters became increasingly indifferent or, perhaps, inured to this factor in politics. Indeed, in recent years, the situation appears almost the reverse of what prevailed during the Mansfield period. Some candidates now go so far as to point to their personal wealth or ability to raise huge sums for campaigning as proof positive of their superior qualifications for public office!

The extremes to which the need for campaign money can distort an otherwise astute politician's judgment was illustrated by Senator Lloyd Benson of Texas, who was chairman of the Senate Finance Committee, a committee whose work is of immense dollars-and-cents significance to private corporations. At one point, Benson offered to brief businessmen in regard to congressional developments in an intimate breakfast club setting, provided, of course, that they were prepared to pay a substantial price in campaign contributions for membership privileges in the club! The scheme proved too much even for an already cynical press, and as the newsmen prepared to zero in on the arrangement, Benson hastily withdrew the offer. Later, as vice presidential candidate, he acknowledged that his scheme had been a mistake, but as he pointed out, it illustrated the extent to which access to money, personal wealth or otherwise, had become a sine qua non for a seat in the Senate.

If access to huge sums of money for campaigns is a prerequisite to candidacy, it may well lead to the serious loss of the Senate's contact with the complex needs of the nation's populace. At best it will very likely make for a less creative legislative body in its capability for meeting those needs. As Walter Lippmann, a distinguished journalist of the time, put it: "When all think alike, no one thinks very much." One must ask whether a Senate membership based preponderantly on candidates who are either rich themselves or skilled money raisers is likely to have the diversity of viewpoints that prevailed during the Mansfield period. Such diversity, like an adequate gene pool to a species, is a source of great strength and survivability for the nation. Can the George Aikens, for example, find a place in such a Senate? George Aiken—farmer, wildflower authority, and former governor of Vermont—before the addition of saturation coverage of television to U.S. political campaigning ran repeatedly and successfully for the Senate on a pittance usually provided out of his own pocket and that of a few friends. One of Aiken's successful campaigns involved expenditures of less than $100! Contrast that with $3.5 million, the median expenditure on Senate campaigns in the 1996 elections. As a senator, Aiken lived in a small apartment near the Capitol, walked to work, and had his breakfast at the Senate cafeteria and his dinner at another cafeteria in the Methodist building. Aiken's indifference to personal affluence was supplemented by a homespun wisdom that led him to coin such phrases in regard to the Vietnam morass as "declare victory and get out" and be "neither a hawk nor a dove but rather an owl." Such phrases produced an intuitive echo throughout the nation and helped bring the disaster of Vietnam to an end and tune legislation to national realities.

How many Hubert Humphreys will emerge in a Senate homogenized by the prerequisite of raising astronomical amounts of campaign money—Humphrey the drugstore errand boy, the teacher, the urban politician from Minneapolis with little in the way of personal financial resources but with enormous insight into such great issues as civil rights? Where will the Pat McNamaras of Michigan be found? McNamara proudly clung to his card in the Plumbers Union while bringing the empathetic insights of one who knew the plight of the poor from the inside into the consideration of legislation on behalf of the less fortunate. Or a Bill Proxmire of Wisconsin, who turned down large contributions to his campaigns from his fellow Wisconsinites even as he rejected all contributions from outside his state? Nevertheless, his view of the world was hardly a parochial one. While deeply concerned with the dollars and cents of government expenditures, he also found time to make U.S. adherence to the Genocide Convention, long-stalled, his personal cause and, after years of unremitting effort, finally succeeded in persuading the Senate to ratify it.

The reform minded in the Mansfield Senate sensed an encroaching corruption in the increasing interweave of money and elections, and they sought in the Federal Election Campaign Act of 1971 to erect a legislative block to its further development. After lengthy study of the problem, the Senate Rules Committee, with Howard Cannon of Nevada as chairman, produced what was widely hailed as a comprehensive solution to the problem. The proposed legislation required disclosures of sources and amounts of campaign contributions in presidential and congressional elections. Such disclosure was expected to bring into focus the connection between contributors and candidates. That, in turn, would discourage successful candidates from showing partiality to their contributors in their subsequent votes in Congress. In addition, however, the reform was aimed at curbing the excessive use of wealth, personal or otherwise, in campaigns, thus moderating glaring funding disparities between candidates. Finally, the law provided for a permanent bipartisan agency, the Federal Elections Commission, as a new and independent overseer of political campaign finances.

This basic reform was supplemented by another legislative measure sponsored by Senator Russell Long of Louisiana, that permitted an option of a small earmark on one's income tax to build up federal funds for use by candidates for the presidency, presumably in lieu of dependency on private sources of funding. A similar attempt at public financing of congressional elections was defeated in the Senate. Although it did little to curb private contributions in presidential elections, what was most significant about the measure was that it injected the principle of public financing into the federal electoral process for the first time.

Still another law that passed during this reform period gave private licensees of the nation's airways greater freedom from the Federal Communications Commission in deciding how to provide equitable access to airtime for candidates in federal elections. Under the then prevailing rule of the commission, if free time was given to one candidate, the private broadcaster was required to provide matching time to his or her opponents. The contention of the networks was that the existing rule led to frivolous claims for free time by candidates and minor parties. Hence, they argued, rather than risk legal challenges, the regulations compelled them to cut down on free time for all candidates. In short, instead of educating the public more fully and fairly, as intended, the television industry's representatives contended, the existing regulations were having the opposite effect. They offered effusive assurances that they could provide better, more extensive, and equitable coverage of election campaigns than that imposed by the Federal Communication Commission's blanket ruling on equal time. In short, they said, leave it to us. Congress agreed by legislation to do so, settling the issue with little debate. Thus, control of public-service time for elections passed from the federal government to private licensees.

Generally, changes affecting the electoral system were hailed as going a long way toward neutralizing the money factor in politics. It soon became obvious, however, that this expectation was highly inflated. In 1976, five years after its passage, the kingpin of the reforms, the Federal Campaign Contribution Act, was hobbled by an adverse Supreme Court decision in *Buckley v. Valeo*. One of the Court's findings was particularly devastating in that it equated expenditures on elections with free speech. Hence the Court threw out, on First Amendment grounds, the attempt by law to limit spending of personal funds by candidates, as well as expenditures by individuals on elections, provided that the expenditures were not routed to a candidate or clearly made on his or her behalf.

Moreover, the complex filing requirements established by the Federal Elections Commission under the law tended to work against its broader purpose of "leveling the playing field." These requirements increased the need for accountants, lawyers, and other professionals in the conduct of campaigns and tended to frighten away would-be candidates as well as small contributors and volunteers. Thus, the law not only failed to halt the growing power of money in elections but dramatically increased the costs of campaigning.

The political campaign reform movement suffered another setback in connection with the law giving private broadcasters themselves control over the allocation of free television time in elections. The statute had been passed with assurances that it would result in more equitable coverage among competing candidates. Instead, private control of free public television time that could be labeled even generously as public service in the sense of its nonpartisan educational value shrank steadily. Regrettably, this diminution took place even as television was becoming by far the most powerful medium for influencing elections and by far the most expensive item in campaigning for public office. In the circumstances, candidates with plenty of money to buy television advertising time gained a significant advantage in setting the tone and agenda for contesting elections, and it put enormous pressure on candidates to campaign for money even before seeking votes. In short, the loosening of federal control over private broadcasters not only failed to contribute to "leveling the playing field" in elections, it did little for enhanced public enlightenment on the issues. It appears to have contributed primarily to an increase in paid political advertising.

Mansfield supported the campaign reforms enacted during his leadership of the Senate, but he did not play an active role in bringing about their adoption. His disinclination to join in beating the drums for reform may have been due in part to his innate wariness, as well as a touch of skepticism growing out of long experience with political reforms. Nevertheless, he went along with the reformers, perhaps out of a reluctance to be dubbed antireform at a time when the nation was in one of its periodic reformist modes or perhaps out of residual idealism that this time the reformers would get it right and the public would buy it.

In any event, the glowing expectations engendered by the Federal Elections Campaign Act of 1971 seem to have receded with each successive federal election, even as expenditures were increasing, the total reaching an estimated $2 billion in the 1996 election. With the search for funds by candidates growing ever more frenetic, the American electorate gives the appearance of becoming increasingly acquiescent, seeming either to see nothing incongruous in the system or accepting corruption of the political process as the inevitable order of things. How else to explain the fact that the number of voters going to the polls has shrunk steadily to barely half of the eligible electorate in recent federal elections?

Other Significant Measures

Other measures hammered out by Congress under the label of the Great Society have fared better than election campaign reforms. These were the work of many members of the Mansfield Senate. To cite the contributions of some, Albert Gore Sr. has already been mentioned in connection with the Medicare legislation and Humphrey of Minnesota and Dirksen of Illinois for their work on civil rights. In addition, Alabama's Senator Lister Hill, as chairman of the Committee on Labor and Public Welfare, was critically important in extending the work of the National Institutes of Health into the whole range of human suffering. Legislation that Lister Hill sponsored also provided a federal stimulant in building hospital facilities throughout the nation, legislation of particular importance to rural and impoverished regions. His long-time colleague from Alabama, John Sparkman, the son of a southern sharecropper, was a key figure in promoting the concept of government responsibility for adequate shelter for all Americans. Under his chairmanship, the Committee on Banking, Housing and Urban Affairs fashioned legislation of great importance in promoting homeownership for a suburbanizing population and adequate housing for the less privileged in the urban areas. Phil Hart and Pat McNamara of Michigan, Vance Hartke of Indiana, and others designed laws to safeguard labor's welfare in a period of social and economic transition. Harrison "Pete" Williams of New Jersey took up the cause of migrant labor, leading the Senate and the nation to look closely at the exploitation of legal and illegal migrants who were forming another underclass in American life. A deepening of federal concern with environmental problems owes much to the initiatives of Senators Clinton Anderson of New Mexico and Edmund Muskie of Maine. Birch Bayh of Indiana designed and secured the passage of a constitutional amendment to provide for orderly succession in the event of vacancies in the presidency and vice presidency. The Bayh Amendment came in time to resolve two potential succession crises that arose as a result of the resignation of Spiro Agnew from the vice presidency and Richard Nixon from the presidency.

Mansfield's participation as majority leader, in working out the details of legislation, was by his own design minimal and very low key. He sought to avoid interference in the committees, shunned the role of advocate, and rarely, and always reluctantly, accepted that of broker in resolving disputes.

As majority leader, Mike Mansfield avoided personal identification with what he regarded as the work of others, but he was not averse to being associated with questions of foreign policy or what was of interest to his constituents in Montana. Throughout his years of service in Congress, whatever mattered to his state mattered to him, whether it was a veterans' hospital in Miles City or the conversion of a shutdown air force base at Glasgow or building a dam on a Montana River. Such questions invariably received priority treatment from Mansfield because he recognized the primacy of his responsibility to the people who had elected him. But he was not parochial, having long since recognized that just as states were not islands unto themselves, neither was the nation an isolated island in a sea of nations. His deep involvement with foreign relations throughout his Senate career reflected that conviction. Although his concern with international affairs was worldwide, he looked more toward the Pacific and the Far East than the Atlantic and Europe, seeing the former as the direction of the future. As for national issues, Mansfield was particularly pleased with his initiative in reducing the minimum voting age to eighteen. The idea of opening up the polling places to youths was not a new one, but it had lain dormant for years in the Congress. Vietnam brought the issue once again to the fore. As the casualties mounted into the tens of thousands, it became obvious that there was a blatant incongruity in drafting teenagers for military service while withholding the franchise from them on the grounds of their immaturity. In a nation that prided itself on the principle of "no taxation without representation," the concept of "old enough to fight, old enough to vote" became an ever more persuasive rationale for extending the franchise. Mansfield sensed the moment was ripe for resolving the issue, and he brought it to the forefront directly on the floor of the Senate. On what can perhaps be termed an "impulse," after a brief debate the Senate approved extending the vote to eighteen-year olds by an overwhelming margin.

Mansfield's most unusual vote was one cast in favor of a gun-control measure. The juxtaposition of "gun" and "control" was anathema to many voters in Montana, as in other western states. Since frontier days, the fetishism of the rifle has been shared by many westerners, along with the pursuit of largely unfettered hunting and fishing. A politician who voted contrary to those sentiments did so at prohibitive political risk, with the certain knowledge that the National Rifle Association would spare no effort or expense to end his career. Legislative attempts, however modest, to extend federal control over weapons of any kind, whether ancient dueling pistols or artillery pieces, was a clarion call to western congressmen to rise up and be counted in opposition.

For Mansfield to endorse a gun-control bill was an act of exceptional political courage. It was the only time he had voted for such a measure, and he stood conspicuously alone among his western colleagues in doing so. His vote astounded them and the press, not to speak of his Montana constituents. By way of explanation of his position, Mansfield made reference to an incident that had taken place some days before in the Georgetown section of the city of Washington. What had begun as a minor late-night altercation between several youths at a lunch-counter restaurant turned ugly when a handgun was introduced into the dispute and ended with a U.S. Marine being shot to death. The incident shocked the city and disturbed Mansfield particularly, since the murdered serviceman happened to be from Montana. As Mansfield told the Senate, the senseless death had prompted him to cast his vote as an expression of outrage.

From time to time, Mansfield did register a personal protest by a "conscience" vote of this kind. He voted several times, for example, against military appropriations bills that he regarded as inflated beyond all reason, often more by pressure from special interests in Congress than from the Pentagon. He opposed, too, log-rolling foreign aid bills and generally voted against them. Such votes were primarily significant as protest and were usually accepted with little criticism by his Montana constituents. In the case of gun control, however, he could do little to mollify the anger of a sizable block of Montana voters. His action generated adverse mail, including threats to his life; it was among the heaviest and most furious mail he had received in his long career. Such were the passions aroused that the governor of Montana felt it wise to assign state police to protect Mansfield when he campaigned for reelection in the state. The senator suffered a sharp drop in the overwhelming popularity that he had previously enjoyed among Montana voters. As Lee Metcalf, the other senator from Montana, had predicted: "Mike is the only man in the Senate from a western state who can run against the gun lobby and still get elected."

That a great deal of innovative legislation passed in the Senate during the years of Mansfield's leadership was due in large measure to a confluence of competence on the part of senators willing and anxious to deal with the social needs of the nation. This creative outpouring was released by the majority leader's unique style. Mansfield did "let a hundred flowers bloom," and the Senate responded mightily.

Except for the Civil Rights Act of 1964, the spadework for the legislative achievements was done largely in committee, with Mansfield moving bills through the Senate somewhat like a policeman directing a heavy flow of traffic. The rush to pass innovative social legislation began in the Johnson administration, and continued during the Nixon and Ford administrations, although slowing somewhat when it encountered a more active use of the presidential veto power. By that point, however, the legal underpinnings for refurbishing and extending the New Deal in the expectation of building a more equitable and humane society in the United States were largely in place. For the most part, the measures adopted in those years were designed to remove racial, sexual, and other blocks to equal treatment of all Americans; to meet more fully the special needs of the aged, the young, and the impoverished; and to curb the runaway wear and tear on the nation's great, but not inexhaustible, natural endowment.

Changes in the Senate Substructure

During the Mansfield years, the substructure of the Senate also underwent major adjustments designed to update its ability to maintain its role in the federal system. Perhaps the most significant changes grew out of the Congressional Budget Act of 1974. Sponsored in the Senate by Edmund Muskie of Maine, the legislation sought to introduce order into the system of congressional review, adjustment, and adoption of the annual budget as formulated by the president's Office of Management and Budget. Before the reform, the budgetary process that took place was more ritual than system, a ritual that opened with a round of polite sparring and sometimes angry confrontation between the president and opposing congressional leaders. The opening clash would often be followed by a standoff, this one between the Appropriations Committees of the two houses, with the Senate Appropriations Committee ignoring the House assertion that it was unconstitutional for the Senate to take any action on appropriations measures until the Representatives had completed their work. Along the way, flurries of rhetoric between the parties, and often directed at the president, could be counted on to come from both houses on "balancing the budget," "cutting the deficit," "tax cuts," and so on.

But the changes made in Congress, more often than not, had more to do with providing tax breaks for favored interests and restoring cuts contained in the president's budget or add-ons for federal programs or executive branch agencies. The changes also involved funding not contained at all in the president's budget to finance congressional log-rolling deals or to accommodate the state interests of powerfully placed senators.

There was broad agreement during the Mansfield period that existing congressional budgetary practices were inadequate to the needs of effective government. The problem was usually defined by the glib assertion that Congress finds it "too hard to say no to proposed tax cuts and too easy to say yes to expenditures." Certainly, that was a fact of political life then, as it is now, and is likely to continue to be. In a more fundamental sense, however, Congress at the time was unable to grasp the full dimensions of the annual budget or to make rational adjustments among its components. In short, Congress was not equipped to answer such basic questions as these: How much money needs to be raised overall? How shall its spending be earmarked to conform to priorities that best serve the national interest? Even assuming the readiness to do so, Congress simply lacked an adequate organizational substructure that would permit finding rational answers to such questions.

The Congressional Budget Act provided machinery that supplemented rather than replaced, the cumbersome rituals and the piecemeal committee approach to financial policy that existed at the time. The act put into place congressional research facilities and coordinating committees that allowed for an informed and integrated review of the president's annual budget, as well as an orderly and open system for making changes.

In the quarter century that the law has been in place, the Congressional Budget Office has proved to be something of a counterweight to the president's Office of Budget and Management. It does provide for an independent review and evaluation of the annual budget. It acts to highlight differences between the executive and legislative branches on priorities, and it permits rational compromises between the president and Congress. It may also serve to discourage back-door and last-minute congressional add-ons, although how effectively is an open question; an objective evaluation of its overall effectiveness has yet to be made. In the meantime, the price tag for whatever improvements there have been has been another layer of costly bureaucracy in the legislative branch as a counterbalance to the costly bureaucracy of the Office of Management and Budget in the executive branch.

Another major structural change in the Senate that occurred during the Mansfield years grew out of the first full-scale Senate investigation of the intelligence activities of the government. The investigation was conducted by a special committee headed by Senator Frank Church of Idaho and centered on the Central Intelligence Agency. The Church committee found that, for all practical purposes, the CIA had operated without supervision or control by Congress and with not a great deal from the president. To be sure, the agency was under the theoretical control of both but, as the U-2 incident during the Eisenhower administration had revealed, the reach of the White House or Congress into the doings of the agency, even when the highest priorities of national policy were involved, was tenuous at best. Moreover, in its zeal, the agency had not only freewheeled abroad, at times with little reference to resident U.S. ambassadors, it had also meandered into pursuit of espionage at home, with a highly questionable impact on the constitutional rights of Americans. The only restraints it had experienced there, ironically, were the scowls of J. Edgar Hoover, who regarded such activities as an FBI monopoly.

In short, the Church committee confirmed what, in retrospect, were serious abuses of power on the part of the CIA. Church did not react with the stylized "shocked disbelief" that any agency of the U.S. government would do what the press had long pointed out the CIA was doing. Instead, his committee's investigation focused on the underlying reasons for the unchallenged continuance of the abuses. It found the problem to be, in large measure, the failure of the Congress, especially the failure to provide effective oversight. Once having set up the CIA by law as the successor to the World War II Office of Strategic Service, Congress thereafter had acted almost as though the agency did not exist. To be sure, Congress appropriated huge sums, year after year, for the support of the CIA and its manifold activities without knowing with some precision the nature of these activities. Unlike other divisions of the executive branch, the CIA had enjoyed a virtual carte blanche in its disbursement of public funds. No committee of the Senate, for example, had ever been assigned substantive responsibility for the agency. In the Senate, both the Foreign Relations Committee and the Armed Services Committee shunned such responsibility. To be sure, both conferred in executive session from time to time with directors and others officials of the CIA, but usually at the agency's request. These encounters were stiff and formal and rarely of any eye-opening relevance. As Mansfield once commented, "You can get the same briefing by reading the *New York Times* and without having to remain silent about the source of what you learn."

In the Senate, responsibility for the CIA devolved by default on the Appropriations Committee. Funds for the agency were concealed in various appropriations measures and approved without accurate knowledge, not only on the part of the Senate as a whole but even of most members of the

Appropriations Committee! Such awareness as there was of the CIA's activities prior to the Church reform rested, for all practical purposes, with a small group of senior senators self-designated or sought out by the agency itself. This select group was reluctant to question the agency's activities closely, reflecting what was a general attitude in the Senate: "We don't want to know what they are doing," notwithstanding the billions of dollars of public funds expended over the years. Without any Congressional body prepared to say no, the door was wide open for abuses. As it had with the president, the head-in-the-sand attitude in the Senate had something to do with a reluctance to become involved in CIA pursuits. There was fear that if these activities were brought to light, and had they been informed of them, senators might be tarred with the onus. Throughout the investigation, the Church committee walked a delicate line between the critical needs of national security and the responsibility to know on the part of elected representatives. The result was a series of recommendations that altered the relationship of the CIA and Congress. The investigation cast aside the Senate's reluctance to become involved by setting up a permanent Select Committee on Intelligence. On the one hand, the arrangement erected a barrier to free-for-all Senate meddling in the agency's operations; on the other, it provided for continuous oversight of its operations by a bipartisan group of elected senators. The committee was charged with keeping itself fully informed on the intelligence activities of the government and on their cost. The arrangement has worked well, except when the committee has been lied to by executive branch officials, as in the case of the Iran-Contra scandal during the Reagan administration. A legislative body can offer little deterrence against that kind of irresponsibility on the part of appointed executive branch officials except through public disclosure or impeachment when it may serve as the people's last recourse against arbitrary behavior.

Mansfield took the lead in producing another major change in the Senate's practices. After breaking the filibuster of the Civil Rights Act of 1964 by mustering more than two-thirds of the Senate to shut off the prolonged debate, he led a successful attempt to tighten the Cloture Rule. The Senate reduced the required vote to cut off filibusters from two-thirds to three-fifths of the senators voting. The change enhanced the Senate's ability to discharge its responsibilities, although some believed it did not go far enough to sustain the constitutional requirement for a simple majority vote on most legislative matters. Over the years, moreover, it has become almost routine for opponents to force the Senate to assemble sixty procedural votes before action is taken on the substance of controversial legislative questions.

Mansfield's Senate leadership followed a period of significant change in social attitudes and practices in the nation. Even as the new legislation was removing blocks and otherwise enhancing the ability of the federal government to deal with these changes, the Senate's social mores clung to the past, seeming almost impervious to the new ways of thinking and doing that were spreading through the nation. The position of women in the Senate is a case in point. When Mansfield became leader, there were two women senators, one a Republican, Margaret Chase Smith of Maine, and the other, Democrat Maureen Neuberger of Oregon. They had been preceded by only one other elected woman, Hattie Caraway of Arkansas, who after being appointed to fill the unexpired term of her late husband was then elected in her own right to a seat from Arkansas. Neuberger had followed the same route of appointment and then election in Oregon.

Smith of Maine, however, was the first woman to begin a Senate career by election. She won the Maine seat in 1948 on her own after serving in the House, where she had won a special election in 1940 to fill her late husband's term. She was repeatedly reelected to the Senate in a career that lasted twenty-four years.

While there was no question of the equal constitutional status of women in the Senate, full acceptance in what had been a male citadel was another matter. Even as late as the Mansfield period a certain snideness was still discernible toward the two women senators. But, by that point, there was already acceptance of the fact that women were in the Senate to stay. Such vestiges of nonacceptance that remained were covered by an excess of deference to the "ladies" that fit in with the antiquated courtliness of other aspects of Senate behavior. The condescension did not mislead Margaret Chase Smith. While always gracious in responding, her sharp mind had no difficulty in discerning the difference between the shadow and substance of power. She went along with the former but insisted on and obtained a fair share of the latter. She made a place for herself on the otherwise male-oriented Armed Services Committee and was sometimes a thorn in the side of nonresponsive Defense Department witnesses. Smith threw her weight not only into the fight for equal treatment of women in the armed services but also into the range of political and social issues then current in the nation. Her firm denunciation of McCarthyism, for example, was among the first to be heard in the Senate and contributed to the eventual downfall of the senator from Wisconsin.

Both Smith and Neuberger departed before the Mansfield period ended. The temporary disappearance of women during Mansfield's tenure of the leadership was ironic, since he was a strong proponent of equal treatment of the sexes. He opened staff opportunities to women. His administrative assistants for Montana affairs and for majority-party affairs were both women, as was the chief clerk of the Majority Policy Committee, Elizabeth O. Shotwell.

Mansfield's wife, a schoolteacher, had been a powerful influence in his transition from soldier and mine-mucker to college professor and Montana political leader. When he was first elected to federal office, Maureen Hayes Mansfield worked without compensation in his office in the House of Representatives.

He was instrumental in adding a statue of Montana's Jeannette Rankin to Statuary Hall. Rankin was the first elected woman in the House of Representatives. When Montanans sought to honor Mansfield's contributions by establishing an educational foundation in his name at the University of Montana, Mansfield insisted that it be called the Maureen and Mike Mansfield Foundation.

Mansfield's personal attitude toward women acted to accelerate the full integration of women into the operation of the Senate. It was a time when the last rampart of male exclusivity, the Senate barbershop, slid into oblivion, and a restroom in the Capitol was provided for the exclusive use of women senators.

During the period, females were included for the first time in the Senate page corps. Well paid and high in prestige, Senate pages were analogous to cabin boys aboard the sailing vessels of an earlier time. Although hired and utilized by the Senate as a whole, the nomination of pages was a perquisite of individual senators, who usually chose them from their home states. The page corps remained an exclusive preserve for boys until Senator Jacob Javits, a liberal Republican from New York, recommended the appointment of a girl. His request caused considerable consternation among older senators, notably Carl Hayden of Arizona, the President Pro Tempore. It was as though Captain Ahab in his pursuit of Moby Dick had been asked to include a cabin girl in his crew. The matter was put on hold in the office of the sergeant-at-arms, who had responsibility for supervising the pages. It probably would have remained in abeyance indefinitely had Javits not threatened to go public with this "evidence" of Senate discrimination at a time when the popular winds were blowing in the opposite direction. Javits took his challenge to the chairman of the Rules Committee, B. Everett Jordan of North Carolina. Jordan, in turn, took the problem to the majority leader and then, with Mansfield's endorsement, cleared the Javits designee for appointment. Thus, the page corps was opened to females, with the proviso, however, that sponsoring senators agree to assume responsibility for their security, not to speak of their virtue, while in the employ of the Senate. It was never made clear just how this pledge was to be honored in the event of a breach. Nevertheless, for the first time, girls as well as boys, in blue pants and white shirts, were seated on the steps of the dais in the Senate chamber, poised to jump at the snap of senatorial fingers.

The breaking of the sex barrier in the page corps was part of the expansion of job opportunities for women in all parts of the Senate's staff support structure. From groundskeeping to waiting tables in the Senate restaurant, to the Capitol police, the sexual barriers came down. Apart from penetrating these formerly masculine strongholds, women with the requisite legal, administrative, and similar professional skills also appeared in increasing numbers in the higher-paid jobs of the Senate. They came out from behind the typewriters and file cabinets to serve as speechwriters, researchers, and in other professional categories. Women were routinely named staff directors for individual Senate offices and a scattering of committees. They appeared on the Senate floor next to senators as prompters and consultants during proceedings. In time, the two highest all-Senate offices, that of the secretary of the senate and sergeant-at-arms, were filled by women, duly chosen by majority caucuses and formally endorsed by the Senate.

Another major change in the Senate's internal practices during Mansfield's leadership was the establishment of a bipartisan Senate Committee on Standards and Conduct. At the time of its creation, the committee was seen as a way of finally getting rid of the stench left by the Bobby Baker affair. Nevertheless, the step represented a significant break with the past. While the Constitution authorizes the Senate to pass judgment on the qualifications of its members, Mansfield had reservations about giving wide reach to this provision. From time to time, the Senate had applied on an ad hoc basis the corrective of a vote of censure to an errant member, not so much on the basis of his qualifications but usually for an abuse of office so flagrant as to bring the institution itself into disrepute. The Joseph McCarthy and Thomas Dodd censures were cases in point. The idea of prying into the behavior of colleagues or judging their fitness for office, however, was repugnant not only to Mansfield but many of his colleagues. To be sure, this reluctance underwrote a broad leeway for each senator in the conduct of his or her affairs. It left senators free to behave as they saw fit, constrained only by their own moral codes, by the law, and by the need to face their constituencies in elections. The latter consideration was paramount in Mansfield's view because he believed that subjecting members to the judgment of other senators in addition to that of their constituencies would not only weaken the power of the ballot but also open the door to the play of politics in regard to who is, and who is not, fit to be seated, even after a choice has been made by the people. Finally, it raised the specter of arbitrary exclusion of the duly elected because they held viewpoints intolerable to the majority. For the Senate to place itself in a position to exclude a member for any of these reasons would be to contradict the concept of the supremacy of the popular ballot on which American democracy rests.

So strong were these concerns that, at first, it was difficult to persuade senators of either party to accept membership on the new Ethics Committee. In due course, Senator John Stennis of Mississippi, urged by the majority leader, accepted the chairmanship. One of the senior members of the Senate at the time and a leader among conservative Democrats, Stennis was given a free hand by Mansfield to set up and staff the committee as he saw fit.

As majority leader, Mansfield played a leading role in the protection and enhancement of the Capitol building as a symbolic continuum of the legislative history of the nation. To that end, he opposed the plans of one architect of the Capitol to turn the building primarily into a tourist attraction while moving Congress itself into "modern" quarters elsewhere. By the same token, he supported another architect in his plans to restore two historic rooms in the Senate wing of the Capitol, one the site of the first Supreme Court and the other the chamber of the Senate on the eve of the Civil War. With the full support of the Republican leader, Mansfield also acted to establish a Senate Commission on Arts and Antiquities after he was unable to interest the House Speaker in joining with the Senate in creating an all-congressional commission. Finally, he sponsored the setting up of a Senate Historical Office to promote a better understanding of the Senate's continuing role in the nation's history.

Postlude

"A Time to Go"

Mansfield did not relish dealing with a fourth administration after Nixon left the presidency. It was not that President Ford presented problems for the majority leader. The two men knew and respected each other from their years of service in the House. Ford was not a boat rocker. Instead, he was a long-time politician who delighted in describing himself as a "Ford not a Lincoln." Although an avid Republican, he believed in working in reasonable harmony with Democrats, and he was capable of recognizing a national need when he encountered one.

For Mansfield, beginning anew with the Ford administration promised to be something of a tedious anticlimax. His personal agenda in both foreign relations and domestic objectives as one member of the Senate had been largely cleared before Nixon's resignation. At the top of the "done" list was the enhanced role of Montana in national affairs. Attitudes in the state had shifted sharply from pre–World War II isolationism, as personified by Senator Burton K. Wheeler. Montana's discovery of the rest of the world was part of a nationwide awakening, but it also received a powerful boost from the work of Mike Mansfield in the Senate and his readiness to share his experiences in international affairs with his constituency. Thanks in part to Mansfield's stubborn efforts, U.S. military involvement had ended in Indochina before spreading completely out of control, and the U.S. armed forces had come home from Vietnam. The nation's relations with the western Pacific countries, notably China, were on a more stable and sustainable basis. Major ties with Japan had survived a difficult period of transition involving the return of Okinawa and a shift from Japanese dependency to an independent role on the world stage. During the transition, the Japanese economy was raised to a very high level of development, paving the way for what would become the most important trade relationship of the United States with any nation outside the Western Hemisphere. Although Mansfield's involvement in these situations had received national and worldwide recognition, other contributions would bear fruit only in the years after his departure from the Senate. One such contribution was his unremitting effort, as a member of the Appropriations Committee, to curb the enormous costs of maintaining huge U.S. military installations abroad, notably in Western Europe. He offered repeated Senate resolutions over the years designed to pressure the executive branch to cut the U.S. military deployment in Western Europe in line with an observation of General Dwight D. Eisenhower that the function of the American military presence in Europe was essentially that of a trip-wire. The size of the presence could be cut drastically and still serve the same purpose. Mansfield was defeated by successive administrations in this attempt, only to see the reductions come about for reasons of economy after he left the Senate. Similarly, Mansfield sought to restrain foreign aid, particularly military assistance, as the bureaucratized instrument of foreign policy that it had become. He voted repeatedly against foreign aid appropriations.

Mike Mansfield was not one to look back on his achievements. If he had been inclined to review what was done during his leadership, he would more likely fix, not on his successes, but on the places where he may have failed or taken a wrong turn. During the decade and a half in which he led the Senate, there was little for him to regret. At the outset, he had found a Senate with a split Democratic Party masquerading as a majority and the whole institution shot through with suspicion and mistrust. He had set as his initial goals, holding the Democratic majority together and restoring a reasonable degree of trust and comity in the Senate as a whole. He succeeded beyond his own expectations in doing both, an achievement he himself would attribute to "just luck." In pursuit of his goals, he did much to redirect the Senate closer to what he felt the Constitution meant the institution to be. The payoff was to be found in the extraordinary legislative record of the Senate during his tenure, notably in civil rights and social legislation, as well as the Senate's major role in ending the Vietnam disaster.

In 1976, Mansfield was confronting another general national election. By that point, he had been elected a senator from Montana for four consecutive terms. He had also served as Senate majority leader for sixteen years, longer than any other leader in history. Throughout his service in the leadership, the Democrats had retained their majority through both Democratic and Republican presidencies. The Senate had come to enjoy enhanced respect in other parts of the government and throughout the nation. With another election looming in November and the prospect of having to work with still another administration if he were to continue as majority leader, Mansfield began to consider whether it was time to close out his Senate career.

As much as anyone in the Senate, he could anticipate reelection both as a senator from Montana and as majority leader. The question he had to answer was whether he wanted one more go-round? Even more to the point was there that much to do in the Senate that he would be able to do? The more he pondered such questions, the more he was persuaded that the time had come to go. In the ensuing months, he turned over more and more of the routine of operating the Senate to his likely successor, Democratic whip Robert C. Byrd of West Virginia, and quietly made arrangements for withdrawal. On 4 March 1976, Mike Mansfield announced to the Senate that he would not run again.

In announcing his retirement from the Senate, Mike Mansfield chose a moment when the Senate Chamber was almost empty.

In his brief remarks, the Majority Leader pointed to his age of 73 years and noted that in his period of service in the Congress, 1942–1976, he had witnessed

- one-sixth of the nation's history since independence
- the administrations of seven presidents
- the assassination of a president and his brother
- able political leadership and seamy politics and chicanery
- the dawn of the nuclear age and men on the moon
- a great war and a prelude to two more wars
- a dim perception of world order and an uncertain hope for international peace

There was, as he observed, ". . . a time to stay and a time to go. Thirty four years is not a long time, but it is time enough."

Years before, in answering a reporter's question concerning what he would like to be remembered for when he left the Senate, Mansfield had replied: "I'd just like to be forgotten."

Mike Mansfield left the Senate in 1977, but he was not forgotten.

- In 1977, he was named by President Carter to head a mission to Hanoi concerning Americans Missing in Action during the Vietnam War

- From 1977 to 1989, he served as U.S. ambassador to Japan, a designation, first by President Carter and then by President Reagan, that added up to twelve years of continuous service—longer than that of any previous American ambassador to Japan
- In 1994 the U.S. Congress established the Mansfield Fellows Program for advanced study by American students in Japan
- in 1999, he celebrated his ninety-sixth birthday

Republican Minority Leader Hugh Scott said when learning that Mike Mansfield would leave the Senate:

> I have never known a man who is more distinguished by his complete fairness and his total integrity. He has in every instance put the interests of the country above any other consideration. He has never stooped to anything which would demean his conduct or lower the respect for the institutions of government.
>
> This is sad news for me and sad news for his colleagues and for the country. We believe that there is no such thing as an indispensable man. Nevertheless, we believe that there are some people whose services are so great that the very thought of the termination of those services is a recognition of a loss too vast to be smoothly or quickly measured.

And Ted Kennedy of Massachusetts concluded: "No one in this body personifies more nearly than Mike Mansfield the ideal of the Senate. Wisdom, integrity, compassion, fairness, humanity—these virtues are his daily life. He inspired all of us, Democrat and Republican, by his unequalled example. He could stretch this institution beyond its ordinary ability, as easily as he could shame it for failing to meet its responsibility."

Index